Comments on *Terrorism and Violence in Southeast Asia . . .*

"Terrorism and Violence in Southeast A ␣␣␣ ␣me
the leading authorities on politically ␣ in
one of the key theatres of the war ␣ of
contributors offer insightful analysis ␣ ␣ nd
historically nuanced accounts of the ␣␣␣␣␣␣␣␣ of
transnational terrorist groups in So ␣␣␣ ␣␣␣. ⌐aul J. Smith has
compiled an edited collection that will be essential reading both for students
as well as those with a more general interest in this important, yet too
often neglected region."

—**David Martin Jones**, University of Queensland

"This book offers us considerable insight and fact-based information on
the issues surrounding terrorism. . . . While the chapters in this volume
mainly focus on Southeast Asia, many of the themes apply to both organized
crime and terrorism more broadly. This book should be useful for both
academics and policy makers. I highly recommend this book to anyone
interested in these crucially important issues."

—**Margaret E. Beare**, Nathanson Centre for the
Study of Organized Crime and Corruption,
York University, Toronto

"This timely and informative study of terrorism and transnational security
threats in Southeast Asia is unique in examining the threats and
challenges from different national perceptions and in consideration of
complex political, social, and economic factors affecting policymaking.
Moreover, it highlights regional vulnerabilities to international violence and
Islamic militancy. . . . The incisive insights, research, and new policy
directions suggested by the authors of this illuminating volume warrant the
priority attention of government policy makers, including the United States."

—**Rear Admiral L.R. Vasey**, Usn Ret., Asia Pacific Strategist and
Founder, Pacific Forum CSIS

Terrorism and Violence in Southeast Asia

Transnational Challenges to States and Regional Stability

Paul J. Smith, editor

An East Gate Book

M.E.Sharpe
Armonk, New York
London, England

An East Gate Book

Library of Congress Cataloging-in-Publication Data

Terrorism and violence in Southeast Asia : transnational challenges to states and regional
stability / edited by Paul J. Smith
   p. cm.
"An East Gate book."
Includes bibliographical references and index.
ISBN 0-7656-1433-2 (hardcover: alk. paper) — 0-7656-1434-0 (pbk.: alk. paper)
  1. Terrorism—Asia, Southeastern. 2. Islam and terrorism—Asia, Southeastern. 3. Qaida
(Organization) 4. Transnational crime—Asia, Southeastern. I. Smith, Paul J., 1965–

HV6433.A785T47 2004
303.6'25'0959—dc22   2004007994

Contents

I. A Transnational Perspective of Terrorism in Southeast Asia

II. Regional Perspectives on Terrorism in Southeast Asia

III. Southeast Asia's Ideological and Physical Enabling Environment

List of Figures

Introduction

Paul J. Smith

Within hours after the September 11, 2001 terrorist attacks in the United States, law enforcement officials in the Philippines reported on their experiences with an earlier plot involving airplane bombing and suicide missions that was uncovered six years earlier. This plot, known as Operation Bojinka, appeared to have had similar elements as the 9/11 attacks. Police discovered the conspiracy when an accidental fire broke out in a Manila apartment building. Police later uncovered evidence that indicated plans to assassinate Pope John Paul II. However, authorities would later find a laptop computer that described the Bojinka plot in great detail. The essence of Bojinka was a plan to simultaneously bomb eleven U.S. airliners as they crossed the Pacific Ocean. A secondary plot involved hijacking an airplane in the United States and crashing it—in a suicide attack—into CIA headquarters or the Pentagon. Later, investigations would reveal that Khalid Sheikh Mohammed, a key tactical planner for al-Qaeda until his arrest, was linked to both Bojinka and the 9/11 attacks in the United States.[1] Moreover, Ramzi Yousef, a key operative in the Bojinka planning, was also linked to the first attempt to destroy the World Trade Center in 1993.

The Bojinka linkage to 9/11 demonstrated that Southeast Asia had played an important role in the attacks in the United States. But it would not be the only connection. A subsequent U.S. congressional investigation revealed that Malaysia had also played an unwitting although important role in the 9/11 attacks.[2] Two of the principal hijackers, Khalid al-Mihdhar and Nawaf al-Hazmi, had participated in a meeting in early January 2000 in Malaysia, which also involved another man, Khallad bin Atash, who was linked to the bombing of the USS *Cole* in October 2000. Later, al-Mihdhar and al-Hazmi would board an international flight from Bangkok, Thailand, to Los Angeles, where they entered the United States unhindered. On September 11, 2001, the two men would later board American Airlines Flight 77 and crash it into the Pentagon.

Within weeks of the 9/11 attacks, international media sources began to report that Washington had declared Southeast Asia to be the "second front" in the global war on terrorism, although U.S. officials have tended to resist such a characterization.[3] Nevertheless, the perception of Southeast Asia as a "second front" largely stemmed from the initial U.S. focus on the Philippines. In particular, the United States sought to counter the Abu Sayyaf Group, which had been waging a guerrilla war and conducting terrorist attacks—including kidnappings—against the government for years and was known for its extreme violence. In December 2001, attention turned to another group, previously unknown to most governments in the region. Known as Jemaah Islamiya, the organization was implicated in a plot to bomb Singapore government and Western targets in Singapore, including military targets connected with the United States. Singapore's Internal Security Department (ISD) arrested fifteen people in relation to the plot, thirteen of whom were alleged to be members of Jemaah Islamiya.[4]

Ironically, throughout this period (from late 2001 through 2002) many Southeast Asian leaders and prominent scholars urged caution regarding the war on terrorism. Some argued that the threat in the region was being overblown or that concerns about terrorism were excessively "alarmist."[5] Others argued that not only was the United States overreacting, it was also unjustifiably putting pressure on moderate Muslims in the region, pressure that might "stimulate moderate Muslims to develop a sense of solidarity with the radical groups."[6] Within ASEAN, although terrorism was generally acknowledged as a problem, the general attitude that prevailed could be summed up by the following assessment: "For many Association of Southeast Asian Nations [ASEAN] countries, terrorism is a continuing low-level threat that must be managed, but is not the defining (nor even the most significant) security issue."[7]

Many of these attitudes would change dramatically following the terrorist attacks conducted in Bali, Indonesia, on October 12, 2002. On that day, terrorists associated with the pan–Southeast Asian Jemaah Islamiya group bombed two nightclubs in the resort district of Kuta, an attack that killed approximately two hundred people—many of whom were Australian nationals—and injured roughly three hundred more. The bombing marked a new milestone in mass casualty terrorism in Indonesia, but it also reflected the rising power of Islamic militancy groups throughout the region. Apart from the large number of casualties, the bombing was not particularly unique. Indonesia had endured an array of terrorist attacks in previous years, although mostly small in scale. For instance, in 2000, Indonesia witnessed a bombing campaign spanning several months in which the Jakarta stock exchange and the Philippine ambassador's residence were bombed. Overall, more than seventeen people were killed in these attacks.[8] On Christmas Eve of that year, Jemaah Islamiya orchestrated simultaneous bombings of churches across the country, which resulted in more than fifteen deaths.[9]

Terrorism's shift to Southeast Asia can be attributed to a number of factors, many of which are related to deep social and economic trends that have been evolving for decades. Many Southeast Asian countries are religiously pluralistic and, despite ethnic or religious conflict being held in abeyance by authoritarian governance, economic prosperity, or simply an embedded tradition of cultural tolerance, such tensions have flared up during times of social or economic crisis. Moreover, some terrorist or insurgency organizations—such as the Abu Sayyaf or the Moro Islamic Liberation Front (MILF) in the Philippines—are the products of unresolved land, ethnic, and religious disputes that have festered for decades and even centuries.

Islamic militancy is partially the product of internal conflict and unsettled historic grievances, but there is also an international dimension to the phenomenon. For years Southeast Asia was viewed as cultivating a "softer and gentler" version of Islam—in other words, a moderate Islam that tolerated diversity and even compatibility with other religions. While this is still generally true, the mood has begun to change in recent years, especially as more radical religious ideologies from outside have penetrated the region. Many observers believe that this trend can be linked to the export of conservative and perhaps militant ideologies emanating from the Middle East.

One of these ideologies is Wahabbi Islam, named for its founder Mohammed ibn Abd al-Wahhab, who lived in Arabia during the 1700s and aided Mohammed ibn Saud in consolidating power over the various tribes of Arabia. The ideology of Wahhabism is relevant to Southeast Asia because it has been—and reportedly still is being—exported to the region via extensive funding from charities, with some of this funding allegedly being diverted to terrorism.[10] One of the charities linked to this effort and that has been active in Southeast Asia is the Al Haramain charitable foundation. Recently the U.S. government announced that it had joined with Saudi Arabia to freeze four branches of this organization, including a branch in Indonesia.[11] U.S. Presidential Executive Order 13224 specifically names this charity as being subject to U.S. sanctions.[12]

In addition to the importation of Middle Eastern Islamic ideologies, the hardening of Islamic attitudes in Southeast Asia is also linked to recent historical developments. Barry Desker attributes the trend to two major historic events: the Iranian Revolution of 1979, and Afghanistan's struggle against the former Soviet Union: "The psychological impact of the Iranian Revolution and the subsequent revolutionary experience of many Southeast Asian Muslims, who either volunteered in the Afghan jihad against the Soviet army or studied in Saudi and Pakistani *madrassas* imbibing the local culture of political violence and change, polarized the Islamic milieu in the region."[13]

The Afghanistan experience has had particular relevance to Southeast Asia. Law enforcement and intelligence officials in the region have determined that many of the terrorists in Southeast Asia were trained—ideologically as well as logistically—in Afghanistan. Thousands of so-called "Afghan alumni" have returned to Southeast Asia, imbued with a new sense of militant fervor. In late 2001 a report in the *Wall Street Journal* described the Afghan alumni in these terms: "In Southeast Asia, hundreds—perhaps thousands—of local Muslims have trained and fought in Afghanistan in the past 15 years and now have returned to Indonesia, Malaysia and the Philippines."[14] For Jemaah Islamiya, the Afghanistan experience was particularly critical. As a report from the International Crisis Group notes: "All of JI's [Jemaah Islamiya's] top leaders and many of the men involved in JI bombings trained in Afghanistan over a ten-year period, 1985–95. The jihad in Afghanistan had a huge influence in shaping their worldview, reinforcing their commitment to jihad, and providing them with lethal skills. Their experience there was also critical in terms of forging bonds among themselves and building an international network that included members of al-Qaeda."[15]

Thus, the common Afghanistan experience has allowed Jemaah Islamiya, al-Qaeda, and other groups to propagate a pan-Islamic ideology that has infiltrated many parts of Southeast Asia.

Additionally, Southeast Asia is vulnerable to international terrorism for another reason, its physical "enabling environment" that fosters the growth of transnational violence. The region features a nearly ideal climate for nonstate-actor terrorists seeking to train clandestinely and avoid authorities. Weak states and poor governance help create a fertile environment for secretive terrorist organizations, particularly where such weakness aids and abets preexisting transnational conflicts or internal conflicts, such as ethnic disputes.[16] Other aspects of the enabling environment in Southeast Asia include the abundance of transnational crime, a surfeit of small arms, porous borders, and a relatively sophisticated communications infrastructure. This physical enabling environment—as this book will later contend—makes Southeast Asia particularly vulnerable to terrorism.

Given the complexity of this subject, this book seeks to assess and analyze the current problem of terrorism and transnational violence in Southeast

Asia from a variety of angles. The book tackles the subject from three unique vantage points, which in turn constitute the book's three major sections. Section one examines the problem of terrorism from a transnational perspective—essentially a "birds-eye" perspective of large trends affecting the entire region. Section two takes a different approach by emphasizing the importance of country-specific perspectives. In this case, two countries—the Philippines and Indonesia—were chosen for in-depth analysis because it was determined that they face particularly acute risks. Section three examines the overall "enabling environment" within Southeast Asia—in particular the role of transnational crime, smuggling, illegal migration, and communication technology and their links to terrorism—that makes this region attractive to and supportive of nonstate terrorist organizations.

The book begins with an introductory chapter by Alan Dupont, who provides an overall analysis of transnational issues that establishes a foundation for much of the rest of the book. The author argues that transnational crime and terrorism represent "two prominent sources of nonstate violence and instability in the Asia-Pacific region." The chapter proceeds to describe how this concept fits into the larger paradigm of security studies. The author asserts that the definition of "security threat" must be expanded to include nontraditional issues such as terrorism, transnational crime, narcotics trafficking, human smuggling, and disease. "Transnational forces are recasting notions of power and sovereignty away from their traditional rootedness in the territorially bounded state," according to the author. The chapter emphasizes the interconnectedness of transnational issues—how these seemingly disparate issues foster and build upon themselves. According to the author: "Increasingly, terrorists and insurgents are making common cause with drug traffickers and criminals."

In chapter 2, Peter Chalk provides an overview of terrorism trends in Southeast Asia and details the extent of terrorist activity in three major countries: Malaysia, the Philippines, and Indonesia. Additionally, the chapter discusses transnational linkages between these groups, and exogenous groups from Central Asia and the Middle East (i.e., al-Qaeda). The chapter explores the historical basis of many groups in the region, such as the links between Jemaah Islamiya and the Darul Islam rebellions that took place in Indonesia in the 1950s. The chapter also explores regional responses to terrorism. Moreover, the author spends much time detailing the shortcomings of these responses, such as the lack of a truly integrated information-sharing arrangement: "Exchange of information is largely perfunctory, tending to focus on the most basic issues of mutual concern."

In chapter 3, Zachary Abuza specifically describes the entry of al-Qaeda into Southeast Asia and its links with indigenous groups, such as the Moro

Islamic Liberation Front (MILF) and Jemaah Islamiya. The chapter describes some of the ideological transformations occurring in the region that are permitting terrorism to flourish. Among other things, the author asserts that militant Islam is growing in the region because of "economic dispossession, the lack of political freedom, the spread of Wahhabism and Salafi Islam, the failure of secular education, and an increased number of religious students studying in Middle Eastern and South Asian *madrasah* [Islamic schools]." The chapter also explores the intricate relationship between al-Qaeda and Jemaah Islamiya and elucidates the extent of their mutual dependence.

In chapter 4, Rohan Gunaratna provides a very detailed operational view of terrorism in Southeast Asia, with a particular emphasis on the modus operandi of how terrorist organizations plan and finance their attacks. The chapter details the degree to which Jemaah Islamiya and al-Qaeda have established an operational partnership: "Al-Qaeda and its associate group JI have divided their responsibilities, personnel, infrastructure, and areas of operation into territorial organizations called *mantiqis*." The chapter makes an argument that al-Qaeda has encouraged mass casualty attacks and, consequently, the Bali attack is perhaps an indication that these lessons have been learned. Moreover, and perhaps most important, the chapter describes why, in light of al-Qaeda's loss of a training infrastructure in Afghanistan, Southeast Asia is viewed as a rich environment in which to create new operational bases.

Section two moves away from a transnational approach to terrorism to a more country-specific approach. In chapter 5, Carl Thayer makes the case that to properly understand terrorism, one must understand the specific context in which terrorism is occurring. He argues that there are three general approaches to analyzing terrorism: an international focus, a regional focus, and a country-specific focus. Many of today's prominent terrorism specialists tend to focus on the international or regional dimensions of terrorism. This chapter, however, argues for a country-specific approach. For example, the author states that "scholars who focus on individual countries are able to bring different skills to their analysis of terrorism in Southeast Asia" and thus, they are able to achieve a deeper understanding of terrorism within local contexts. The country-specific approach places a premium on knowledge of language, local politics, and culture. Analysts with such backgrounds can develop a rich and nuanced understanding of terrorism trends, which are invariably colored by unique local circumstances.

In chapter 6, Anthony Smith proceeds with the country-specific approach with an analysis of Indonesia in the context of recent terrorism trends. The chapter asserts that Indonesia's domestic weaknesses are impeding the capacity of Jakarta to confront its growing terrorist threat—which in many ways is rooted in political movements that were once suppressed under the

Suharto regime. The chapter also explores the growing Middle Eastern influences on Islam within Indonesia and the flow of money emanating from Saudi Arabia since the mid-1970s. The author does note, however, that Indonesia is far from becoming a radical theocracy: "Islamist parties simply do not have the political strength to bring about a constitutional change that would turn Indonesia into even a moderate version of an 'Islamic state.'" The author also explores reasons why the Megawati administration has been relatively slow to address terrorism.

In chapter 7, Paul Rodell examines terrorism in the Philippines and provides an historical and political context to current trends in that country. Many of Southeast Asia's terrorist incidents have occurred in the Philippines and, moreover, the Philippines hosts at least three groups that have a direct or indirect affiliation with al-Qaeda, including the Abu Sayyaf Group, the Moro Islamic Liberation Front, and Jemaah Islamiya. The chapter examines the linkages between terrorism and various separatist movements that have plagued the southern province of Mindanao for many decades. It also explores the political problems that have prevented Manila from effectively curtailing the growth of terrorism. The author argues that any long-term solution to terrorism in the Philippines will require the government to "negotiate a genuine peace treaty, curb military corruption, set aside divisive politics, and undertake a serious economic and social development program for Mindanao's Muslim population."

Section three addresses the larger "enabling environment" that is allowing terrorism to grow in the region. In chapter 8, Kumar Ramakrishna presents an exhaustive analysis of the group Jemaah Islamiya (JI). He presents both the ideological and physical enabling factors that are responsible for this group's rise and success. The author describes JI's "functional space," which he defines broadly as "the freedom to carry out the various activities necessary to support the terrorist agenda." Factors contributing to JI's functional space include weak regulatory capacities of regional governments, poor tracking of dubious money transfers, and the ready availability of weapons, among others. In addition, JI also flourishes because of its "political space" generated by sympathy that the organization generates from scattered Muslim communities.

Chapter 9 continues with the enabling environment theme by focusing on the linkage between transnational crime and terrorism in the region. In this chapter, Tamara Makarenko examines how transnational crime is fostering the growth of terrorism in Southeast Asia. The author argues that a convergence between terrorism and crime organizations is occurring (in varying degrees depending on the groups involved) in both the operational realm as well as in ideology. In some cases this convergence can be attributed to the decline of state support of terrorist organizations and the resultant loss of financial support: "In response to the virtual elimination of state support after the end of the Cold War, criminality was the most pragmatic avenue to secure finances for future terrorist operations." It is this convergence that allows substate (or nonstate) actors to exist and prosper. More alarmingly, it is this trend that allows terrorist groups to exist outside of the state realm—thus they are more difficult to track and control.

Chapter 10 focuses on the enabling environment from the perspective of small arms availability and proliferation within Southeast Asia. In this chapter, David Capie makes the important point that despite international concern about weapons of mass destruction (WMD), "the weapons most commonly employed by terrorist groups around the globe continue to be small arms and light weapons." In terms of sources of these weapons, the author asserts that "insufficient attention has been paid to the domestic sourcing of weapons by terrorists, in particular from corrupt security forces and poorly safeguarded state armories." The typical inventory of Southeast Asian armed groups includes sidearms, automatic rifles, light machine guns, and rocket-propelled grenades (RPGs). The author argues that these armed groups may gain access to these weapons via the regional or international black market, from "gray market" transfers from sympathetic states, from civilian stocks or illicit transfers from security forces, or from their own production capacity.

Chapter 11 examines the enabling environment from the perspective of Southeast Asia's porous borders, lax immigration procedures, and vibrant forged passport industry. Paul Smith—this writer—makes the point that border porosity is a major—although often underappreciated—security problem for Southeast Asia. Governments cannot easily regulate migration between the various countries in the region. Consequently, terrorists have taken advantage of this fact to establish bases throughout the region and particularly in the Philippines and Indonesia. Analysts in the Philippines blame lax immigration and visa policies for facilitating an influx of terrorists and criminals there; similar conditions exist elsewhere in the region. The author asserts that in an era of global terrorism, border security takes on a much greater significance, and it is doubtful—under current conditions and attitudes—that Southeast Asian countries will be able to effectively confront this challenge.

Chapter 12 presents a critical yet often overlooked enabling factor—the role of communication networks, the media, and new media technologies. Shyam Tekwani examines the linkage between the information revolution and terrorism in Southeast Asia. He argues that throughout history "terrorists have relied on various forms of media as a means of pursuing their particular political or military goals." The information revolution has transformed the way that terrorists communicate with each other and their broader audience (i.e., other terrorist groups, the general public). Our "construct" of terrorism—the way we view the phenomenon—is largely generated by media images. Moreover, the author argues, computers and the Internet have given terrorist groups a new avenue for instant and clandestine communication. This chapter examines this phenomenon first from a global perspective and then from the perspective of Southeast Asia.

Overall, this book provides a unique collection of perspectives on a complex and sensitive issue that will likely remain a long-term challenge to states and societies in Southeast Asia. Historically, transnational security issues have always, in varying degrees, existed in the region. The arrival of terrorism—and particularly mass casualty terrorism—suggests that a new and more disturbing era in transnational threats has finally arrived. Moreover, if states or regional organizations cannot, or choose not to, confront these challenges, these threats will ultimately undermine the long-term economic and social viability of the region.

To solve a problem first requires understanding it, including all of its complexities. With this objective in mind, the authors of this book seek to provide the critical knowledge necessary for effective policy responses. Terrorism and transnational security threats may never be completely eliminated, but they can be effectively managed and mitigated. However, to achieve that goal, states—and their general populations—must acknowledge and confront these challenges honestly.

Notes

1. Terry McDermott, "Early Scheme to Turn Jets into Weapons," *Los Angeles Times,* June 24, 2002, p. 1.

2. Report of the Joint Inquiry into the Terrorist Attacks of September 11, 2001—by the House Permanent Select Committee on Intelligence and the Senate Select Committee on Intelligence, July 24, 2003, available at http://news.findlaw.com/usatoday/docs/911rpt (accessed April 1, 2004).

3. "U.S. Steps into Asian Minefield," *Australian Financial Review,* October 12, 2001, p. 82; Maura Reynolds, "Bush Stops Off in Bali for Talks After Asia Summit," *Los Angeles Times,* October 22, 2003; see also Department of Defense news briefing with Deputy Secretary of Defense Paul Wolfowitz, May 31, 2003, reported in *M2 Presswire,* June 2, 2003.

4. Richard Evans, "Singapore Reports on Jemaah Islamiah," *Jane's Intelligence Review* (February 1, 2003).

5. Harold Crouch, "Qaida in Indonesia? The Evidence Doesn't Support Worries," *International Herald Tribune,* October 23, 2001, p. 8.

6. "Western Countries Overacting [*sic*], Says Indonesian Observer," *Malaysia General News* [Bernama: Malaysian National News Agency], October 22, 2002.

7. Jim Rolfe, "Security in Southeast Asia: It's Not About the War on Terrorism," *Asia-Pacific Security Studies* 1, no. 3 (June 2002): 2.

8. Ali Kotarumalos, "New Bomb Rocks Human Rights Group Office Ahead of Suharto Hearing," *Associated Press Worldstream,* September 27, 2000.

9. Zachary Abuza, *Militant Islam in Southeast Asia: Crucible of Terror* (Boulder, CO: Lynne Rienner, 2003), p. 153.

10. Jane Perlez, "Saudis Quietly Promote Strict Islam in Indonesia," *New York Times,* July 5, 2003, p. A3.

11. Edmund L. Andrews, "U.S. and Saudis Act to Freeze Charity's Assets," *New York Times,* January 23, 2004, p. A4.

12. http://www.ustreas.gov/offices/eotffc/ofac/sanctions/t11ter.pdf (accessed March 29, 2004).

13. Barry Desker, "The Jemaah Islamiyah (JI) Phenomenon in Singapore," *Contemporary Southeast Asia* 25, no. 3 (December 2003): 495.

14. Jay Solomon et al., "Bin Laden Alumni Are Cause for Fear Around the World," *Wall Street Journal (Europe),* December 14, 2001, p. 1.

15. *Jemaah Islamiyah in South East Asia: Damaged But Still Dangerous,* Jakarta/Brussels, International Crisis Group, report no. 63, p. 2.

16. Stephen M. Walt, "Beyond Bin Laden: Reshaping U.S. Foreign Policy," *International Security* 26, no. 3 (winter 2001–2): 62.

List of Abbreviations

ABIM	Angkata Belia Islam Malaysia
AFP	Armed Forces of the Philippines
APEC	Asia Pacific Economic Cooperation
ARF	ASEAN Regional Forum
ARMM	Autonomous Region of Muslim Mindanao
ASEAN	Association of Southeast Asian Nations
ASEANPOL	Southeast Asian Association of National Police
ASG	Abu Sayyaf Group
BIN	State Intelligence Agency
CBRN	chemical, biological, radiological, and nuclear
CSCAP	Council for Security Cooperation in the Asia Pacific
CTC	crime-terror continuum
DDII	Dewan Dakwah Islamiyah Indonesia
FTO	foreign terrorist organizations
GAM	Free Aceh Movement
GIA	Armed Islamic Group
GMIP	Cerakan Mujahideen Islami Patani
GSPC	Salafist Group for Call and Combat
HuJI	Harkat-ul-Jihad-al-Islami
ICMI	Ikatan Cendekiawan Muslim se-Indonesia
IDSS	Institute for Defense and Security Studies
IED	improvised explosive devices
IIRO	International Islamic Relief Organization
IMU	Islamic Movement of Uzbekistan
ISA	Internal Security Act
ISD	Internal Security Department
JI	Jemaah Islamiya
KMM	Kumpulan Mujahideen Malaysia
KPSI	Komite Pengerakan Syariat Islam

KWP	Korean Workers Party
LeT	Lashkar-e-Tayyiba
LJ	Laskar Jihad
LTTE	Liberation Tigers of Tamil Eelan
MaK	Maktab al-Khidmat lil-Mujahideen al-Arab
MILF	Moro Islamic Liberation Front
MIS	Islamic State of Mindanao
MMI	Majelis Mujahideen of Indonesia; Mujahideen Council of Indonesia
MNLF	Moro National Liberation Front
MPR	Upper House (Indonesia)
MUI	Majelis Ulema Indonesia (Council of Ulema)
NGO	nongovernmental organization
NICA	National Intelligence Coordinating Agency (Philippines)
NMCT	new media and communication technologies
NU	Nahdlatul Ulama
OIC	Organization of Islamic Conferences
PAN	National Mandate Party
PAS	Parti Islam Se-Malaysia
PBB	Moon and Star Party
PCTC	Philippine Center on Transnational Crime
PDI-P	Indonesia Democracy Party
PK	Justice Party (Indonesia)
PKB	National Awakening Party
PNP	Philippine National Police
PPP	United Development Party
PULO	Patani United Liberation Organization
RM	Rabitatul Mujahideen
RSO	Rohingya Solidarity Organization
SMS	short messaging service
SOG	special operations group
TCO	transnational criminal organization
UBS	underground banking system
UPM	unregulated population movement
UTM	Universiti Teknologi Malaysia
UWSA	United Wa State Army
WGTNC	Working Group on Transnational Crime
WKR	WAE KA Raeh
WML	World Muslim League

I

A Transnational Perspective of Terrorism in Southeast Asia

1

Transnational Violence in the Asia-Pacific

An Overview of Current Trends

Alan Dupont

Transnational Threats to Security

The devastating terrorist attack on the World Trade Center and the Pentagon in September 2001 underlines the growing power of nonstate actors to challenge the traditional monopoly over organized violence held by the state. Terrorism of this order belongs to a new class of threats that is stretching the boundaries of conventional thinking about security. Some of these threats are economic; others relate to the earth's physical environment; many are contemporary manifestations of age-old afflictions. They stem from demographic pressures, resource depletion, global warming, unregulated population movements (UPMs), transnational crime, virulent new strains of infectious diseases, and a host of other issues not previously associated with international security. Complex, interconnected, and multidimensional, these nonmilitary, transnational issues are moving from the periphery to the center of security concerns for both states and people. Collectively they represent a new security agenda that will increasingly demand the attention of policy makers and military planners everywhere. Asia and the Pacific are particularly at risk because of their large populations, ethnic and religious diversity, and history of sectarian conflicts. It is also a region overwhelmingly comprised of developing states, precisely the kind of state that is most vulnerable to transnational threats.

Many transnational causes of conflict are the result of forces outside the traditional framework of strategic analysis that have little to do with the exercise of coercive power by competing nation-states, but everything to do with the stability of states and human survival. Transnational phenomena are likely to become more prominent causes of conflict and insecurity in Asia and the Pacific as pressure on natural resources increases, people become more mobile, and nonstate actors compete with states for money, influence, and power. Environmental degradation is intensifying the problems of governance and development in poorer countries and precipitating transborder and internal migration. The very existence of some Pacific states may be threatened by sea levels rising as a result of human-induced climate change. Access to food, energy, and water is dependent on preserving and sustaining the earth's natural resource base. Drug trafficking distorts economic development and promotes the spread of AIDS, a disease that is destroying the social fabric of many communities and causing millions of preventable deaths. Terrorism is closely linked to the spread of radical ideologies that germinate and spread in impoverished and dislocated societies.

Transnational forces are recasting notions of power and sovereignty away from their traditional rootedness in the territorially bounded state.[1] It is this detachment from territory that distinguishes economic and political activity in the twenty-first century. To paraphrase Jessica Matthews, many resources and threats that matter—be they money, information, infectious diseases, or militant ideologies—circulate and shape lives and economies with little regard for political boundaries.[2] Moreover, war itself is being transformed—away from high-intensity conventional combat between states to asymmetric contests involving nonstate actors such as terrorists and criminal organizations that may command formidable human, organizational, and financial resources. Separatism, ethnic struggles, guerrilla insurgencies, terrorism, and armed criminal challenges to the state are today more frequent than interstate war, and the security consequences are just as severe.[3] On the other hand, major wars between states over territory and power are declining in frequency and magnitude. Of the 120-armed conflicts fought during the Cold War, most were between states, and eleven accounted for more than two hundred thousand casualties each. By contrast, the great bulk of those recorded since 1989 have been internal.[4]

This is not to argue that the old threats have gone away or that future conflicts will resemble Afghanistan. States and their military forces still matter—it is just that they matter less than they once did. In the world of the twenty-first century, states will be forced to cede a large measure of control over the totems of sovereignty, namely borders, capital, people, and territory. National power will increasingly be shared with nonstate actors and nongovernment organizations that have at their disposal resources and influence that may equal or even exceed those of many states. As P.J. Simmons observes, they are "changing societal norms, challenging national governments and . . . muscling their way into areas of high politics."[5] Unfortunately, not all are benign or eschew the use of force. As we have seen, some terrorist groups have demonstrated a penchant for high levels of violence and a capacity for military action rivaling that of national defense forces.[6] However, while transnational challenges to security are becoming more salient and numerous, they are relatively immune to traditional enforcement strategies, do not conform to national borders, and are usually beyond the jurisdiction of individual states.[7] They may also result from domestic institutional weakness or policy failure rather than the calculated actions of a rival state.

Transnational threats are often interconnected. Increasingly, terrorists and insurgents are making common cause with drug traffickers and criminals. Sometimes it is difficult to distinguish between them. Furthermore, many contemporary security problems do not have a distinct beginning, middle, and end. Their cause and effect are circular rather than linear. Ecological breakdown is a root cause of migration, but the large-scale unregulated movement of people contributes in turn to environmental degradation.[8] Both can cause conflict. Zero sum calculations in which security is measured according to the relative losses and gains by competing nation-states are of little use in helping to understand or assess the threat from terrorism, environmental degradation, people-smuggling, or violence perpetrated by transnational criminal organizations. Terrorism and transnational crime cannot be combated by military means alone, although armed force is an essential tool in the fight against both. More holistic, whole-of-government responses are required that target their sources of power and wealth. Money laundering is illustrative. Terrorists need money to finance their operations, and they must be able to move it quickly and anonymously. Halting or disrupting these clandestine flows would seriously weaken their capacity for action.

Transnational Crime and Terrorism

This paper focuses on two prominent sources of nonstate violence and instability in the Asia-Pacific region—transnational crime and terrorism.[9] The essential difference between them is that criminals are primarily driven by money while terrorists are politically motivated. However, there are many similarities in the way they operate, and each poses a major security threat to the region. During the Cold War, transnational crime and terrorism were located at the lower end of the national security continuum. Although more likely to occur than major interstate war, they represented a lesser threat to life, liberty, economic well being, and national sovereignty.

Since the end of the Cold War, however, criminal and terrorist activities—particularly those that are conducted on a large scale and involve significant international cooperation—have moved up the threat continuum toward the traditional concerns of the national security apparatus. At the same time, the threat probability curve has extended outward, mirroring these groups' accretion of political, economic, and military power.[10] In recent years the capacity and willingness of terrorist organizations to use lethal force has dramatically increased as the events of 11 September graphically demonstrate.

Transnational Crime and Security

At the end of the twentieth century, the financial and human resources at the disposal of the major transnational criminal organizations (TCOs) surpassed those of many states. It is this development perhaps more than any other that accounts for their newfound ability to threaten international security. Bill Gates, head of the Microsoft Corporation and reputedly the richest man in the world, accumulated a personal fortune of $100 billion before a U.S. government antitrust case in 1999 left him $40 billion poorer.[11] By comparison, organized crime turns over US$1.5 trillion a year, and the IMF estimates that half a trillion dollars, or 2–5 percent of global GDP is illegally "laundered" through banks and financial institutions, illustrating the formidable financial power and global reach that modern TCOs have acquired.[12]

The internationalization of crime and the criminalization of war have become key strategic issues for the Asia-Pacific region. As historian Martin van Creveld argues, there is a clear link between war and crime—soldiers may become criminals, criminals may become soldiers, war may become criminalized, and shadow states may exploit the resulting ambiguities.[13] Capitalizing on the opportunities provided by economies in transition and a thriving global market for their unlawful products and services, a new breed of Asian criminal entrepreneurs has acquired an unprecedented level of financial and political influence. Borders are no longer serious impediments to criminal transactions, and transnational criminal organizations are taking advantage of the jurisdictional limitations on national police forces and weak international law enforcement cooperation to maximize their illicit profits. Sovereignty-bound regional governments, on the other hand, have been hamstrung by their attachment to the paramount "noninterference" norm and their slowness to recognize that the expansion in major crime can only be combated by international cooperation.[14]

Figure 1.1 **The Cold War National Security Continuum**

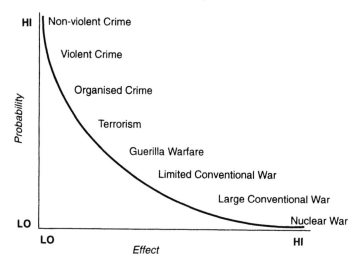

Source: John Cicarelli, ed., *Transnational Crime: A New Security Threat?* Australian Defence Studies Centre, Australian Defence Force Academy, University of New South Wales, Canberra, 1996, p. 10.

Figure 1.2 **The Post–Cold War National Security Continuum**

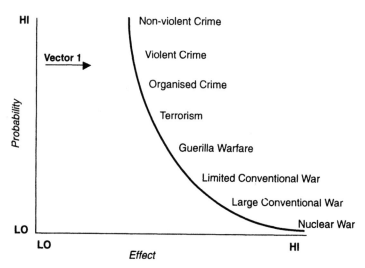

Source: John Cicarelli, ed., *Transnational Crime: A New Security Threat?* Australian Defence Studies Centre, Australian Defence Force Academy, University of New South Wales, Canberra, 1996, p. 10.

The factors responsible for the spread of crime internationally are manifest in Asia and the Pacific. Globalization, decades of strong economic growth, market liberalization, booming intraregional trade, the rise of the biggest middle class in history, and the development of regional growth triangles have facilitated illicit business as well as legitimate enterprise.[15] Rapid modernization has made governments in the region acutely vulnerable to criminal penetration and allowed TCOs unparalleled access to the indispensable tools of their trade—sophisticated information systems, high-speed data transfer links, electronic banking, and world-class transport and communication hubs. Asian use of the Internet is increasing by more than 50 percent a year, and there has been a comparable rise in criminal exploitation of the Web, which takes two principal forms. One is computer "hacking" for financial gain, and the other is the use of the Internet for more traditional criminal purposes such as drug trafficking and money laundering. In Thailand, for example, amphetamine dealers have been using the Internet to directly market their product to a region-wide market and to launder the proceeds.[16]

Furthermore, as the political scientist Robert Leiken notes, developing states are transitional, not traditional, and transition involves institutional and cultural contention that breeds corruption.[17] Developing states are more vulnerable to corruption because their political and bureaucratic elites are poorly paid, and the moral code that underpins traditional society often breaks down during the modernization process. The Asian economic crisis stripped away the thin veneer of financial accountability and revealed that insufficient priority had been accorded to the rule of law and sound prudential management. All these developments in conjunction with ineffective law enforcement and the widespread availability of small arms have weighted the scales firmly in favor of the criminals.

Unless contained, the spread and institutionalization of transnational crime will be not only a major obstacle to the development of vibrant civil societies in Asia and the Pacific's democratizing states, it will also erode the performance legitimacy of the region's authoritarian regimes. TCOs are supplanting the functions of government while criminal violence threatens the stability of regional states and the survival and well-being of millions of people. In countries like Burma (Myanmar) and North Korea, crime and politics are virtually indistinguishable from one another, either because the state has been coopted by criminals or the people who run the state are criminals. The economic and societal impact of transnational crime is no less severe. The "laundering" of vast sums of money by TCOs weakens national economies while people-smuggling and drug trafficking may be as injurious to life and social harmony as war itself.

Money Laundering

International money laundering is in the order of US$500–700 billion annually and may account for as much as 5 percent of world GDP.[18] While drug trafficking accounts for a substantial proportion of money laundering globally, as much as two-thirds of laundered money is from non–drug related criminal activity such as prostitution, illegal migration, arms dealing, smuggling, and terrorist activities. The larger TCOs are responsible for the bulk of capital transfers and investments, but individuals, small-scale criminal enterprises, and terrorists are increasingly important contributors, mirroring the diversity and complexity of financial transactions in the legal economy.[19]

Money laundering is best thought for as a process of concealing the existence, illegal source, or illegal application of income and of then disguising or converting that income to make it appear legitimate. Money laundering is carried out through a variety of means and instruments. Front companies, disguised foreign currency transfers, and bank deposits made under false names are representative ploys, while the proceeds of criminal and terrorist enterprises are often invested in the stock, bond, and futures markets, real estate, or other hard assets.

The speed with which large volumes of money can be moved around the globe anonymously at low cost has facilitated money laundering. As Alvin and Heidi Toffler note, "capital itself is undergoing a historic transformation . . . the world financial system and money itself [is] being radically restructured."[20] Money, always a highly fungible commodity, has become an even more flexible and critical medium of exchange since the arrival of electronic commerce and virtual banking. Changes in telecommunications, the widespread availability of encryption technology, and the blending of legal and illegal money has vastly complicated the task of law enforcement and security agencies and shifted the balance of forces in favor of the criminals and terrorists.[21] Without the ability to move "hot" money around with minimal risk of disclosure or prosecution, the power and reach of drug traffickers, narco-insurgents, and terrorist groups would be substantially reduced. Concealing the source and purpose of financial transactions is crucial to rogue and criminal states intent on breaching international sanctions or obtaining small arms and weapons of mass destruction. Iraq, for example, spent considerable money and resources to set up elaborate money laundering facilities to disguise its purchase of components and technology essential for the development of its nuclear, chemical, and biological weapons programs in the 1980s.[22]

In the mid-1990s, Osama bin Laden oversaw the development of a clandestine financial system to service the pecuniary needs of the various jihadist organizations that constitute an emerging "Islamist International" dedicated to the overthrow of conservative Arab regimes and the destruction of the United States. Relying initially on family connections and wealthy Arab patrons, bin Laden was able to effectively conceal the terrorist money trail and avoid international scrutiny. This has made it extremely difficult for Western intelligence to connect terrorists with sponsoring states and trace the source of funding for weapons, printing presses, communications systems, and safe houses.[23]

Asian terrorists and criminals also make extensive use of the traditional underground banking system (UBS) or *hawalla* as it is known in South Asia. The UBS is a highly personalized, family-based network of gold shops, trading companies, and money exchanges that maintains minimal records and relies on mutual trust between brokers for its efficiency and internal discipline. If trust is breached, communal ostracism or death may follow. Financial exchanges typically rely on coded messages, telephone calls, handwritten chits, or symbols, which guarantee a high degree of personal security and virtual anonymity.[24] Large sums of money can be moved expeditiously all over the world with very little chance of detection by the authorities. According to the U.S. Drug Enforcement Agency, heroin traffickers can transfer US$500,000 from Hong Kong or Bangkok within hours simply by visiting a gold shop.[25] Typically, the money is wired to Chiang Mai (in Thailand) for forwarding to the drug lords of the Golden Triangle. All of these features make the UBS an attractive medium for those seeking to discreetly deposit or transfer money earned from criminal enterprises or for terrorist purposes.[26]

In Asia and the Pacific, criminal prosecution for money laundering is a rare occurrence. The region's vulnerability to money laundering is partly a function of institutional weaknesses and the absence of effective regimes for countering transnational crime in general and money laundering in particular.[27] Criminals cannot be prosecuted for money laundering in the absence of legislation that criminalizes the offense. Even where legislation has been enacted, prosecution is difficult because of stringent evidentiary requirements. Not only do the region's developing states generally lack workable antimoney legislation, there is little if any cash transaction reporting, and their financial and banking sectors are characterized by a lack of transparency and weak regulatory frameworks. These institutional deficiencies are exacerbated by human susceptibilities—the low pay received by bureaucrats and regulators makes them vulnerable to bribery. Inadequate police resources and the low priority given by governments to fighting corruption and money laundering also help minimize the risk for those who wish to disguise the sources of their funds.[28]

Money laundering's potential for creating insecurity is especially evident in Southeast Asia, where financial accountability and sound prudential management are lacking and legal sanctions and other judicial deterrents to criminal activities are either weak or nonexistent. The United States has named Thailand as one of the foremost countries for money laundering in the world because of its well-developed financial structure and robust stock market, the presence of international institutions, its modern communications, and an active underground money remittance system.[29] Money laundering is also rampant in Cambodia, which lacks even a rudimentary regulatory system for its banking sector. A confidential report prepared for the Interior Ministry assessed that two-thirds of Phnom Penh's twenty-nine banks were fronts for cleaning illicitly obtained money.[30] Hong Kong, as one of the region's main communications, banking, and entrepôt hubs, has acquired a less-than-savory reputation as a major money laundering center.

People-Smuggling

People-smuggling by transnational criminal organizations has become a defining characteristic of illegal migration and a major political and security issue for the region.[31] Asian TCOs engaged in people-smuggling range from small-time, local "entrepreneurs" geared to making a quick dollar to sophisticated international crime syndicates such as the Japanese *yakuza* and Chinese triads. The triads and other ethnic Chinese criminal groups, colloquially known as "snakeheads," are responsible for much of the illicit global and regional trade in people. Thriving in the comparatively freewheeling political and economic milieu of modern China, criminal gangs regard people-smuggling as a core business and a lucrative complement to other forms of criminal enterprise. They have established elaborate global networks to facilitate the movement of illegal migrants, which are also used for smuggling drugs and other illicit contraband. Typically, ethnic Chinese are moved by sea or air to the United States from clearinghouses in Cambodia and Thailand via South and Central America. Even faraway Greenland and the tiny Pacific state of Vanuatu have been used as transit stops for Chinese illegals en route to the United States.[32]

The new prominence of people-smuggling in regional defense and foreign policy circles underscores how certain criminal activities have crossed over from law enforcement into the international security domain, blurring the distinction between them. No state has been able to immunize itself from the explosion in unregulated population movements (UPMs) that has taken place in recent decades, a trend that shows no sign of being reversed anytime soon. While migration has been an enduring feature of the region's political and social development, enriching Asia-Pacific societies as well as destroying them, today's UPMs are far more numerous, of a qualitatively different order, and the product of multiple and diverse drivers.

Ethnonationalist conflicts, identity struggles, and repression are the main catalysts of refugee flows and internally displaced persons in the region. However, demographic, environmental, and economic forces are playing an increasingly influential role and are largely responsible for the rise in undocumented labor migrants who are being moved and exploited by mainly Asian people-smugglers. The future level of undocumented labor migration from China is the wild card in the migration pack. China's middle class is leaving in record numbers, seeking economic opportunity in more affluent parts of the globe. As incomes increase, emigration will become more affordable and living overseas a viable and much sought-after option. Should Beijing prove unable or reluctant to stem the exodus, migration-induced tensions could increase further in East Asia as well as in Europe and North America.

Narcotics Trafficking, Terrorism, and Crime

Narcotics trafficking is blurring the boundaries between politics, crime, and terrorism in many parts of the region. There is clear evidence that both the Taliban and al-Qaeda used drugs to finance their operations in Afghanistan and internationally.[33] China's overtures toward the now-defunct Taliban regime were motivated by fear that a hostile Afghanistan, once the largest producer of opium in the world, could further encourage the spread of drugs and radical Islamic politics into China's Xinjiang Province, fueling ethnic separatism in the Uighur community.[34] Heroin from Pakistan and Afghanistan has found its way into Xinjiang, and arms and explosives used by the separatists have been traced to Afghanistan. Uighurs have long enjoyed close ties with the various Afghan groups, and some have trained and fought with the mujahideen since 1986. Many received training in Taliban religious schools, or *madrassas*. The nightmare scenario for China's leaders is that the Uighurs may use drug money and their Islamic connections to finance and strengthen their challenge to Beijing's rule in Xinjiang.[35]

During his tenure as president, the Philippines' Fidel Ramos was forced to crack down on criminal gangs in response to a rash of kidnappings of foreign businessmen and armed robberies that Ramos admitted threatened political stability.[36] However, the Philippines faces a more vexing challenge from the resurgent Abu Sayyaf Group, which purports to be fighting a war of liberation in the southern Philippines, but frequently resorts to the kind of anarchic criminal violence more often associated with Africa, Latin America, and Central Asia.[37] The criminalization of war and internal conflicts is a trend that is evident elsewhere in the region. The remnants of the pro-Jakarta militias, once united in their determination to keep East Timor a part of Indonesia, have degenerated into semiautonomous gangs pursuing their own narrow interests and using criminal violence against the U.N. peace-keeping forces and vulnerable East Timorese border communities. In Burma, many of the former ethnic insurgents who once opposed the central government are now free to pursue a range of criminal activities provided they do not directly challenge the writ of the military regime in Rangoon.

One of these groups, the United Wa State Army (UWSA), dominates the Asian heroin and amphetamine trade and has established a large settlement in the Mong Yawn Valley, adjacent to Thailand's northwestern border, that has all the hallmarks of an emerging criminal state.[38] The UWSA provides the military muscle and protection for the drug caravans that ply their trade in the triborder region of Burma, Thailand, and Laos. Its 15,000–20,000 troops are well armed and equipped with mortars, heavy machine guns, and Russian-made SA-7 surface-to-air missiles, which makes the UWSA, by any standard, a formidable military force and arguably the most potent narco-insurgency in East Asia. If the fragile cease-fire with Rangoon should fail, the Burmese government may find it virtually impossible to reassert its notional control over the UWSA or the fiefdom that the UWSA is carving out in the Shan Hills.

Thailand has been frustrated by neighboring Burma's inability or unwillingness to control the cross-border flow of drugs into Thailand's northern provinces. Key members of the Thai political and military establishment believe that Burma is deliberately flooding Thailand with heroin and amphetamines. In 1999, Thailand's National Security Council declared the narcotics trade the number one threat to national security and ordered the closure of several border crossing points in a pointed warning to Burma that Thai patience with cross-border drug trafficking was wearing thin.[39] In July of that year, a thousand-strong Thai force supported by armored cars and helicopter gunships attempted to seal off a fifty-kilometer stretch of its western border. Several firefights ensued with the UWSA. Thai troops were instructed to shoot first and ask questions later if the Wa ventured across the border, and elite ranger units were given the green light to aggressively locate and destroy drug laboratories inside Burma.[40]

While weak governments are commonly exploited for criminal purposes, some states are directly complicit in the spread of transnational crime. Persistent though fragmented reports of North Korean involvement in criminal transactions date back to the mid-1970s. The closed nature of North Korean society made it initially difficult to determine whether these were the actions of individuals or the results of a conscious policy decision by the regime.[41] Since the mid-1990s, however, there has been a marked escalation in the intensity and scope of drug trafficking by North Korean diplomats and officials as well as smuggling and counterfeiting. Given the tight control that the ruling Korean Workers Party exercises over all levels of North Korean society, it is extremely unlikely that this increase in criminal activity could have taken place without the explicit endorsement of the party leadership, including Kim Jong-Il himself.

Information gleaned from U.S., South Korean, and Japanese intelligence agencies and police investigative reports leaves little doubt that Pyongyang is deliberately using the instruments of state power for criminal purposes. In 1994 the KWP established a special office to coordinate attempts to obtain foreign currency, which also seems to be in charge of all "crime-for-profit" activity. Bureau No. 39, which is directly answerable to Kim Jong-Il, uses North Korean diplomatic missions, government offices overseas, and trading enterprises as fronts for a range of criminal enterprises. Much of the money obtained is channeled through the Kaesong Bank, and diplomatic pouches are routinely used for illicit purposes.[42] Pyongyang has also begun to use the services of the *yakuza* and other TCOs to gain access to their narcotics distribution networks and markets.[43] The money obtained is used to prop up North Korea's ailing economy, buy elite loyalty, support diplomatic missions, and finance intelligence operations.[44]

Conclusion

Three broad conclusions may be drawn from this analysis of the transnational challenge to security in Asia and the Pacific. First, the strategic "drivers" of the region's future security environment will be substantially different from those of the past. While competitive state behavior and ethnic disputes will remain important sources of instability, new problems are crowding onto the regional security agenda that transcend the borders of the territorial state and require cooperative, international solutions. They constitute a broader set of security considerations that affect people as well as states.

I argue that our notions of security must therefore extend outward to include those acts of organized violence by nonstate actors that demonstrably jeopardize human security, state sovereignty, and international order. The need for a broader conceptualization of security to take account of transnational threats has already won endorsement from influential epistemic communities in the region. In a highly significant but little-noted shift, the "second track" Council for Security Cooperation in the Asia Pacific (CSCAP) has explicitly rejected a balance of power as an appropriate organizing principle for the region, maintaining that the security of vital interests and core values extends "beyond the military sphere."[45] Instead, Asians have embraced the notion of comprehensive security, defined as "the pursuit of sustainable security in all fields (personal, political, economic, social, cultural, military, environmental) in both the domestic and external spheres, essentially through cooperative means."[46]

Second, an extended security praxis strengthens the hand of those who argue that modern military forces must be configured and employed for conflict prevention and constabulary tasks as well as for conventional war-fighting and hybrid forms of warfare.[47] This is not an argument for attenuating the core war-fighting tasks of the military, but rather for a sensible and modest reordering of defense priorities to include some capacity for combating nonmilitary threats and conducting military operations other than war. Transnational phenomena will inevitably force changes in national intelligence priorities and defense planning. Intelligence collection and assessment is already beginning to reflect the demand by governments for a more integrated analysis of security trends as well as for specific reporting on transnational developments.

Third, as the rise in terrorism and organized crime attests, transnational threats are primarily nonmilitary in nature and inextricably linked—to other transnational security issues as well as more traditional causes of conflict—in a complex web of interdependence that is altering the strategic calculus of many states. These threats are unlikely to be resolved by military force alone or traditional security approaches. The agencies responsible for formulating and implementing national security policy in Southeast Asia are often poorly equipped, intellectually and organizationally, for dealing with transnational issues, which tend to fall across bureaucratic jurisdictions rather than neatly fitting into them. Many of these issues are complex; most are beyond the authority and competence of defense and foreign ministries and require whole-of-government responses. A more comprehensive and inclusive approach to security planning at the national level is essential for dealing with the transnational security agenda.

Notes

1. David Held and Anthony McGrew, "Globalization and the Liberal Democratic State," in *Global Transformation: Challenges to the State System,* ed. Yoshikazu Sakamoto (Tokyo: United Nations University Press, 1994), p. 60.

2. Jessica T. Matthews, "Power Shift," *Foreign Affairs* 76, no. 1 (January–February 1997): 50.

3. See Michael E. Brown, ed., *The International Dimensions of Internal Conflict* (Cambridge, MA: MIT Press, 1996), p. 1. Many ethnic minority groups are effectively stateless, few states are ethnically homogeneous, and borders seldom correspond to natural ethnic, linguistic, or cultural boundaries. Of 161 states surveyed in one study, only 41 were found to be ethnically homogeneous (where one group comprises over 95 percent of the state's population). Few ethnic groups have their own state. Gunnar P. Nielsson, "States and 'Nation Groups': A Global Taxonomy," in *New*

Nationalisms of the Developed West, ed. Edward A. Tiryakian and Ronald Rogowski (Boston: Allen and Unwin, 1985), Table 2.1, pp. 30–31, 33.

4. Not only have interstate wars become relatively rare; internal conflicts have on the whole been much bloodier, featuring high levels of "collateral damage" to civilian populations caught up in the fighting or its immediate aftermath. Nearly 90 percent of war-related casualties during the 1990s were civilian. Indra de Soysa and Nils Petter Gleditsch, *To Cultivate Peace: Agriculture in a World of Conflict,* PRIO Report 1/99 (Oslo, Norway: International Peace Research Institute, 1999), pp. 7, 13–15.

5. P.J. Simmons, "Learning to Live with NGOs," *Foreign Policy,* no. 112 (fall 1998): 84.

6. Burma's narco-insurgents, for example, command significant military power as well as considerable wealth, patronage, and political influence.

7. Richard A. Matthew and George Shambaugh, "Sex, Drugs, and Heavy Metal: Transnational Threats and National Vulnerabilities," *Security Dialogue* 29, no. 2 (1998): 164.

8. Alexander Carius and Andreas Kraemer, "'Complexificacao' of Environmental Security," paper prepared for the Seminar on Global Security Beyond 2000: Global Population Growth, Environmental Degradation, Migration, and Transnational Crime, University of Pittsburgh, Pittsburgh, PA, November 2–3, 1995, p. 13.

9. For a more detailed discussion of these issues and the broader transnational security agenda, see Alan Dupont, *East Asia Imperilled: Transnational Challenges to Security,* (Cambridge and New York: Cambridge University Press, 2001).

10. This analysis draws on John Ciccarelli, "Crime as a Security Threat in the 21st Century," *Journal of the Australian Naval Institute* (November–December 1996): 43–44.

11. According to the July 3, 2000 edition of *Forbes* magazine. "Gates Still the World's Richest Man, says 'Forbes,'" *Jakarta Post,* June 17, 2000, p. 8.

12. Although these are only estimates, they probably err on the conservative side. See the United Nations International Drug Control Programme, *World Drug Report* (Oxford: Oxford University Press, 1997), p. 31; *U.N. Human Development Report 1999,* overview, http://www.undp.org./hdro; Matthews, "Power Shift," pp. 57–58; Nigel Morris-Cotterill, "Funking the Fight in War on Dirty Money," *The European,* April 25–May 1, 1996, pp. 6–7; and *The Military Balance, 1999–2000* (London: Oxford University Press for the International Institute for Strategic Studies, October 1999), pp. 183–209.

13. Martin van Creveld, quoted in Alice Hills, "Criminality and Policing in Stability and Support Operations," *Military Review* 79, no. 6 (November–December 1999): 18.

14. The principle of noninterference in the internal affairs of member states has long been enshrined in ASEAN's (Association of Southeast Asian Nations) declaratory policy.

15. On this theme, see Jim Rohwer, *Asia Rising: How History's Biggest Middle Class Will Change the World* (Singapore: Butterworth-Heinemann Asia, 1995).

16. Bruce Gilley and Shawn W. Crispin, "A New Game of Cops and Robbers," *Far Eastern Economic Review* (April 20, 2000): 50–52.

17. Robert S. Leiken, "Controlling the Global Corruption Epidemic," *Foreign Policy,* no. 105 (winter 1996–97): 60.

18. "Money Laundering," *International Enforcement Law Reporter* 11, no. 9 (September 1995): 378; Michel Camdessus, managing director IMF, "Money Laundering: The Importance of International Countermeasures," address to the Plenary Meeting of the Financial Action Task Force on Money Laundering, Paris, February 10, 1998.

19. On this point, see Ernesto U. Savona and Michael A. De Feo, "International Money Laundering Trends and Prevention/Control Policies," in *Responding to Money Laundering: International Perspectives,* ed. Ernesto U. Savona (Amsterdam: Harwood Academic Publishers, 1997), p. 10.

20. Alvin Toffler and Heidi Toffler, "The Discontinuous Future," review essay in *Foreign Affairs* 77, no. 2 (March–April 1998): 137.

21. Gary L. Dain, "Hacking through the Cyberspace Jungle," in *Global Organized Crime: The New Empire of Evil,* ed. Linnea P. Raine and Frank J. Cilluffo (Washington, DC: Center for Strategic and International Studies, 1994), p. 38.

22. Raymond Baker, "The Biggest Loophole in the Free-Market System," *Washington Quarterly* 22, no. 4 (autumn 1999): 38.

23. Yossef Bodansky, *Bin Laden: The Man Who Declared War on America* (Rocklin, CA: Forum, 2001), p. 43.

24. Mark Gaylord, "Money Laundering in Asia," in *Enterprise Crime: Asian and Global Perspectives,* ed. Ann Lodl and Zhang Longguan (Chicago: Office of International Criminal Justice with the Shanghai Bureau of Justice and the East China Institute of Politics and Law; University of Illinois, 1992), pp. 82–83.

25. Bertil Lintner, "Washing Up," *Far Eastern Economic Review* (November 6, 1997): 35.

26. For an illuminating insight into the UBS and its mode of operation, see "Money Laundering (UBS)," *Burma Debate* (February–March 1995): 30–32.

27. The absence of money laundering legislation in Indonesia moved one senior official of the state-owned PT Bank Negara Indonesia to declare that Indonesia had become a haven for money launderers. K. Basrie, "Containing Money Laundering," *Jakarta Post,* February 5, 1997, p. 4.

28. "Issue Brief: Money Laundering in Asia," *Assessment No. PR4/96,* Office of Strategic Crime Assessments, December 1996, Canberra, Australia, pp. 1–2.

29. *International Narcotics Control Strategy Report, 1997,* Bureau for International Narcotics and Law Enforcement Affairs, U.S. Department of State, Washington, DC, March 1998.

30. Nate Thayer, "Medellin on the Mekong," *Far Eastern Economic Review* (November 23, 1995): 25.

31. There is a clear legal distinction between people-smuggling and human trafficking, although in practical terms there is often little difference. For a comprehensive discussion of these definitions, see John Morrison, *The Trafficking and Smuggling of Refugees: The End Game in European Asylum Policy?* Prepublication edition, July 2000, originally commissioned by the United Nation's High Commissioner for Refugees, Policy Research Unit, Center for Documentation and Research, http://www.unhcr.ch/evaluate/reports/traffick.pdf.

32. Bertil Lintner, "World Wide Web: The Tangled Trail of Illicit Chinese Immigration," *Far Eastern Economic Review* (May 14, 1998): 34.

33. Bodansky, *Bin Laden,* p. 42.

34. Estimated at forty-four hundred tons in 1999. "The Fergana Valley: A Magnet for Conflict in Central Asia," *Strategic Comments* 6, issue 6 (July 2000).

35. Ahmad Rashid, "Taliban Temptation," *Far Eastern Economic Review* (March 11, 1999): 21, and "Heart of Darkness," *Far Eastern Economic Review* (August 5, 1999): 8–11.

36. "Philippine Govt Pledges to Curb Rising Crime," *Jakarta Post,* January 3, 1996, p. 11.

37. Abu Sayyaf, which has an estimated two hundred combatants, has specialized in high-profile kidnappings and extortion, including in one particular case, the abduction of twenty-one foreign tourists from the Malaysian resort island of Sipadan in April 2000. Anthony Davis, "Philippines Set for Wider Conflict," *Jane's Intelligence Review* (June 2000): 3, and "Separatist Rebellion in the Southern Philippines," *Strategic Comments* 6, issue 4 (May 2000).

38. Anthony Davis, "Thailand Tackles Border Security," *Jane's Intelligence Review* (March 2000): 31.

39. Shawn W. Crispin, Santi Suk, and Bertil Lintner, "Drug Tide Strains Ties," *Far Eastern Economic Review* (September 9, 1999): 26.

40. Julian Gearing and Ban Huai San, "Thailand's Battle for Its Soul," *Asiaweek,* August 10, 1999, http://www.pathfinder.com/asiaweek/current/issue/nat9.html.

41. There were also doubts about the reliability of some of the reports, particularly those sourced to South Korea's intelligence agencies, which have a vested interest in portraying the North as a criminal state.

42. Raphael Perl, *North Korean Drug Trafficking: Allegations and Issues for Congress,* CRS Report for Congress (U.S. Congress, Washington, DC, February 8, 1999), p. 5; Douglas Farah and Thomas W. Lippman, "The North Korean Connection," *Washington Post,* March 26, 1999, p. A21; and discussions with Japanese police officials and Western intelligence analysts.

43. "NK Selling to Drug Rings," *Chosun Ilbo,* April 11, 1999, http://www.nautilus.org/napsnet/dr/index.html citing a document published by South Korea's National Intelligence Service.

44. Perl, *North Korean Drug Trafficking,* p. 5.

45. "Concepts of Comprehensive and Cooperative Security," *Council for Security Cooperation in the Asia Pacific (CSCAP) Newsletter,* no. 6 (June 1997): 2. For an analysis of CSCAP and its record, see Desmond Ball, "The Council for Security Cooperation in the Asia Pacific: Its Record and Its Prospects," *Canberra Papers on Strategy and Defense No. 139* (Strategic and Defense Studies Centre, Australian National University, Canberra, October 2000).

46. "Concepts of Comprehensive and Cooperative Security," p. 2.

47. Paul Mann, "Fathoming a Strategic World of 'No Bear, But Many Snakes,'" *Aviation Week & Space Technology* (December 6, 1999): 61.

2

Militant Islamic Extremism in Southeast Asia

Peter Chalk

Introduction

Terrorism is not new to Southeast Asia. Indeed, for much of the Cold War, the activities of a variety of internal ethnonationalist and religious militant groups posed, arguably, one of the most significant threats to the polities of the region. During the 1990s, however, the residual threat posed by substate extremism rose—both in reaction to the modernization pursued so vigorously by many Southeast Asian states and as a result of the political influence of Islam (which has itself been further amplified by the contemporary force of South Asian, and more specifically, Afghan radicalism).

International attention on the threat of Southeast Asian Islamic extremism has also escalated markedly since al-Qaeda launched its devastating attacks against the United States on September 11.[1] Not only is this part of the heightened global awareness of terrorism in general, it also reflects the fact that groups and militants based in the region are known either to have passed through training camps formerly under the charge of the Taliban or to have established links with Osama bin Laden and his global terror network.

This chapter examines the principal Islamic entities of concern currently existing in Southeast Asia, focusing its analysis on the outside links of movements in the southern Philippines, Malaysia, and Indonesia. The emergence of a budding regional network in the guise of Jemaah Islamiya (JI) is also discussed, and a critique of the effectiveness of current counterterrorism contingencies is offered.

Militant Islamic Extremism in Southeast Asia

The most serious Islamic threats in Southeast Asia originate in three main countries: the Philippines (particularly Mindanao), Malaysia, and Indonesia.

The Southern Philippines

Two main Islamic groups are currently fighting in the southern Philippines: the Moro Islamic Liberation Front (MILF), and the Abu Sayyaf Group (ASG, literally the "Bearer of the Sword"); both organizations have been linked to al-Qaeda and bin Laden–instigated transnational Islamic extremism.

ASG

The ASG first emerged in 1989 under the leadership of Abdurajak Janjalani. The group is committed to the establishment of an exclusive, independent Islamic State of Mindanao (MIS) and is infused with a highly intolerant religious credo that calls for the deliberate and systematic targeting of all southern Filipino Christians. In pursuit of this objective, the ASG has explicitly defined its ideological and operational agenda as being intimately tied to an integrated effort aimed at asserting the global dominance of Islam through armed struggle.[2]

ASG links with outside Islamist extremists date back to the early 1990s, when it is believed that the ASG received financial and material support through front organizations originally created by Jamal al-Khalifa, the Saudi renegade's brother-in-law.[3] Prior to his arrest in San Francisco in December 1994, Khalifa doubled as president of the Philippine chapter of the International Islamic Relief Organization (IIRO) and director of the World Muslim League (WML).[4] Financial investigations conducted in the wake of the September 11 attacks in New York and Washington have identified both of these bodies as providing key logistical conduits that have been established (or at least abused) for the explicit use of international terrorist operations.

In addition, the ASG is known to have facilitated the creation of local logistics for international Islamic organizations wishing to operate out of the Philippines. Concrete evidence of these transnational ties first emerged in 1995, when Abu Sayyaf cells were linked to a multipronged plot—known as Operation Bojinka (after the Serbo-Croatian word for explosion)—to bomb Washington's embassies in Manila and Bangkok, assassinate President Clinton during the 1996 Asia Pacific Economic Cooperation (APEC) summit meeting in Subic Bay, and destroy eleven U.S. commercial airliners flying trans-Pacific routes from American West Coast cities.[5] The plan was developed by Ramzi Yousef—the convicted mastermind of the 1993 attack against the World Trade Center in New York—who had been dispatched to the Philippines as a personal emissary of bin Laden to establish a tactical working relationship with the ASG.[6]

The United States remains particularly concerned that the ASG continues to define its operational and ideological agenda as one intimately tied to an integrated effort aimed at asserting the regional dominance of Islam through jihad. Certainly this has been one of the main justifications given for the decision to initiate joint military exercises and training missions with Filipino special forces, which have been ongoing since 2002. Targeting ASG strongholds in Sulu and on Basilan Island, the so-called Balikatan exercises have been viewed as an integral component of President Bush's war against global terrorism and generally recognized as the first dedicated attempt to prevent the emergence of a second front of pan-Islamic extremism in Southeast Asia.[7] At the time of writing, the U.S.-supported operations had successfully reduced active ASG numbers to around 400, a significant reduction from the roughly 1,100 militants that had made up the group's membership in 1999.[8]

U.S. concerns notwithstanding, it is unclear what, if any, links the ASG retains with outside, panregional Islamists. The group's ties with bin Laden very definitely atrophied in the wake of the discovery of Bojinka, further diminishing three years later following the death of the organization's ultrafundamentalist leader, Abdurajak Janjalani. Indeed, for the past three years the ASG has been effectively devoid of any unified command structure, essentially operating as a loose collection of bandits and warlords motivated less by ideology and self-defined religious piousness than pure financial gain and greed.[9] Currently there is no conclusive evidence to support the U.S. assertion that the ASG is actively associated with either the JI or al-Qaeda, something that even representatives of the Philippine government have acknowledged.[10]

MILF

The MILF was founded in 1984, emerging from a 1977 rift within the larger Moro National Liberation Front (MNLF), which has traditionally served as the main vehicle for the insurgency in Mindanao.[11] The front's avowed objective is the creation of a sovereign Islamic state in all areas where Muslims have traditionally existed as a majority in the southern Philippines.[12] Despite the common emphasis on religion and independence, MILF is generally acknowledged to be infused with a more tolerant ideology than the ASG and certainly does not subscribe to the latter's wholesale rejection of religious cohabitation.

MILF's links with outside Islamist elements are difficult to discern. On the one hand, the group has stated its vehement opposition to transnational extremism, with the group's former leader, Hashim Salamat, explicitly renouncing terrorism just prior to his death in mid-2003.[13] The front has also stated a willingness to engage in peace talks with Manila and has repeatedly portrayed itself as a tolerant entity that is ready to coexist with members of other religious faiths.[14] Obviously any attachment to transnational terrorism would be totally counter to an open (and accommodating) political agenda of this sort.

On the other hand, the MILF is known to have established so-called special operations groups (SOG) for urban sabotage missions. This covert wing of the organization is alleged to have worked in conjunction with various regional and outside jihadists, both operationally as well as in terms of providing logistics and basing. According to certain commentators, these ties were forged following the 1998 U.S. embassy attacks in Kenya and Tanzania, when bin Laden made a specific request to access MILF training facilities in Mindanao to offset the increased international exposure then being directed at his operations in Afghanistan.[15]

Considerable circumstantial evidence also exists to connect the MILF with al-Qaeda and outside extremists. Philippine army sources have periodically reported the existence of "Arab-looking" individuals with turbans and heavy beards uncharacteristic of Filipinos in MILF camps they have overrun; on several occasions foreign documentation has also been recovered, including visas and passports from Pakistan, Saudi Arabia, and Indonesia.[16] The front has additionally been linked to bin Laden's terror network through the late Fathur Rohman al-Ghozi, a senior bomb-maker in the group and formerly a close associate of Riduan Isamuddin (a.k.a. Hambali, arrested in Thailand in August 2003)—al-Qaeda's suspected point man in Southeast Asia.

Prior to his being killed by Philippine security forces in October 2003, al-Ghozi was believed to be one of the joint leaders (as well as chief operations officer) for the al-Qaeda-affiliated JI. By his own admission he has confirmed that he was a key figure in JI's planned 2001 operation to bomb several high-profile Western targets in Singapore (see below). According to Philippine authorities, al-Ghozi traveled to the city-state in October 2001, where he worked in conjunction with Mohammed Mansour Jabarah, a Kuwaiti-born Canadian, to coordinate local surveillance over attack venues and assess explosive requirements for their destruction.[17] Although the death of al-Ghozi might suggest diminished linkages between the MILF cadres and JI, recent evidence suggests the opposite may be true. In November 2003, evidence emerged that JI was continuing to deploy militants to the Philippines to train in camps in Mindanao under the protection of the MILF.[18] The revelations reportedly stunned Philippine intelligence officials, some of whom acknowledged that they had ignored the serious threat that JI posed to their country.

A further point of al-Qaeda–MILF contact has been identified in the guise of Mohamad Sabri Selamah, a Palestinian teaching at a Saudi-funded Koran Recitation Center outside Cotabato City. Police and intelligence sources believe that Selamah—who was arrested in Manila in November 2001—had provided technical training to front members and had been recruiting from within the organization's ranks to fight in Afghanistan for several years.[19]

It remains unclear, however, whether MILF links to outside extremists are the product of sanctioned directives from the front's leadership or merely reflect individual contacts that have been made by renegade units as a token of jihadi solidarity. The territorially dispersed nature of the group is certainly such that it would be perfectly conceivable for semiautonomous local commanders to make operational decisions that do not necessarily reflect the thinking or wishes of the central command structure. As one Western diplomat has commented: "The MILF is a loose collection of commanders and warlords, political leaders, religious people and others. There are certainly personal connections with Indonesia, Malaysia and the Middle East, but to see Hashim Salamat and the central committee as part of a network of terror around the world—I think the record is far less clear there."[20]

Malaysia

The threat emanating from Malaysia is more diffuse and less easily discerned than that in the Philippines. Although no concerted radical insurgent Islamic groupings exist per se, the country is known to contain extremist elements that have formed the basis for a loose logistical network that has figured prominently in the activities of Muslim militants, both regionally and internationally.

Perhaps the clearest indication of these contacts at work is the example of the Pattani United Liberation Organization (PULO) and the smaller New PULO—two Islamic separatist groups that were active in southern Thailand for much of the 1990s.[21] Both organizations are known to have retained operational and logistical bases in the northern Malaysian state of Kelantan, allegedly supplied with the active sanction of the province's ruling hardline Parti Islam Se-Malaysia (PAS). This assistance is widely acknowledged as being one of the main factors that allowed the Pattani insurgency to continue for so long. The Thai government also believes it was critical to allowing for the perpetration of several high-profile civilian attacks, including a string of thirty-three bombings and assassinations in late 1997 that targeted state officials, law enforcement personnel, schoolteachers, and other perceived symbols of Buddhist repression.[22] Intelligence sources in Bangkok firmly believe that assaults such as these could not have taken place in the absence of sustained external Malaysian support.[23]

Malaysia has also been connected to the activities of Islamic militants in the Philippines and Indonesia. Manila has long alleged, for instance, that weapons and logistics bound for the ASG and MILF (and originating in South Asia) have been smuggled via the porous Sabah border and that indigenously based expatriates and militants have availed these movements.[24] Equally, various Indonesian intelligence sources have claimed Malaysian-based associates of bin Laden have worked in conjunction with Laskar Jihad (LJ) and JI, implicating these militants in several acts of terrorism that hit the archipelago between 2000 and 2003 as well as more generalized civil violence in the Moluccas (Malukus) and Sulawesi.[25]

More recently, the administration of former prime minister Mahathir has linked members of the Kumpulan Mujahideen Malaysia (KMM)—a radicalized local movement allegedly founded in the mid-1990s as a radical defense militia that could be activated in the event of a government crackdown against the Parti Islam Se-Malaysia (PAS)—to wider transnational imperatives.[26] Police and intelligence officials in Kuala Lumpur allege that the KMM was progressively drawn into the ideological and organizational ambit of the JI network during the 1990s and now fully accords with its fundamentalist vision of violent pan-Islamism. Government sources have also directly linked the KMM to the 2001 Singapore plot, portraying the group as a key logistical hub in JI's explosives procurement network (see below).[27] Authorities further attest that through linkmen such as Hambali, the KMM has been actively cultivated by bin Laden and used to facilitate planning and logistics meetings in the Malaysian heartland.[28]

U.S. officials have provided some tentative (though by no means conclusive) evidence to back these latter claims. The Central Intelligence Agency (CIA), for instance, has confirmed it possesses video evidence verifying that an al-Qaeda operatives meeting took place at a condominium in Kajang, Selangor, in January 2000 during which plans for several anti-American attacks were discussed. Moreover, it is now known that Khalid al-Mihdhar and Nawaf al-Hazmi, two of the terrorists involved in the September 11 strikes, attended this gathering and that Zacarias Moussaoui, the so-called "twentieth hijacker" currently standing trial in the United States, was also in the country later that year.[29]

It is reasonable to assume that at least some connection exists between the KMM, the JI, and/or al-Qaeda. The group does seem to have oriented itself around an ideological agenda that goes beyond simple Malaysian considerations—KMM statements since September 11 have increasingly come to emphasize the rhetoric of pan-Islamism and anti-Americanism—and certainly individual ties are apparent, many of which do appear to have been fostered for specific transnational imperatives.

However, as with the MILF, it is difficult to assess the true significance of these contacts, largely because the Malaysian government has conspicuously played the Islamic fundamentalist "card" to justify a crackdown on mainstream Muslim opposition parties. Indeed, of the several dozen KMM militants who have been detained under the provisions of the country's Internal Security Act (ISA), a sizable proportion are senior party functionaries or provincial religious leaders within PAS.[30] While residual institutional connections may exist between these individuals, Kuala Lumpur has yet to provide any conclusive evidence that this is the case. Indeed, the very use of the ISA precludes such a requirement as it effectively allows suspects to be held indefinitely without trial. The problem with this approach is that it inevitably casts doubt on the veracity of wider intelligence claims pertaining to what may very well be established links between local and transnational entities.

Indonesia

In Indonesia, Islamic extremism has emerged as an increasingly salient threat since the overthrow of President Suharto in 1998. Almost overnight the republic moved to shed the vestiges of nearly four decades of authoritarian rule in favor of an open political system based on democratic principles. Successfully achieving such a transition was always going to be fraught with difficulties; the increasingly critical state of the country's financial health, however, combined with a succession of poor leaders, have dramatically escalated the latent risks associated with this transformation.[31] Not only have poverty, inflation, and unemployment interacted with a more fluid domestic environment to produce major outbursts of civil protest and violence, general dissatisfaction with the administrative performance of Jakarta has galvanized a reawakening of atavistic Muslim identity that has further entrenched and radicalized popular sentiment across the archipelago.

Indonesia has been singled out as one of Southeast Asia's main areas of concern in terms of acting as a base for transnational Islamic extremism. Not only has the republic acted as JI's ostensible base since 1998 (see below), associated militants based in the country are now generally acknowledged to have played a central role in the October 2002 Bali bombings, which remains the worst act of international terrorism since 9/11.[32] Notable in this regard are Imam Samudra, Ali Ghufron, Ali Imron, and Amrozi bin Nurasyim, all of whom have since received the death penalty for their part in the attack. According to state prosecutors, the four individuals attended a secret planning meeting in Java in January 2002 where, under the alleged aegis of JI, they were given the "green light" to bomb soft targets of opportunity across Indonesia in pursuit of wider Islamic designs.[33]

In addition, some residual ties seem to have been forged between domestic Muslim rebel groups and outside forces. A sizable component of Laskar Jihad (now disbanded), which was behind much of the anti-Christian violence that broke out across Sulawesi in 2000,[34] is known to have been recruited from Central and South Asia, and the group itself is thought to have provided terrorist training facilities for JI militants near to the port city of Poso.[35] Equally Laskar Jundullah, a hard-line Islamic group committed to imposing Sharia law throughout Indonesia, has been linked to JI through its leader Agus Dwikarna. The outspoken radical was arrested in the Philippines in 2002 for illegally possessing explosives and remains a chief suspect in a series of bomb attacks that rocked Manila and Jakarta in December 2000.[36]

This being said, no decisive evidence has yet emerged to suggest that Islamists within Indonesia have been co-opted by outside extremists in the same manner that has occurred in Afghanistan, Pakistan, Algeria, and Egypt. Both LJ and Laskar Jundullah continue to couch their justifying rhetoric very much in local terms, and the vast bulk of their membership does not appear to attach any great salience to the concept of international jihad as espoused by bin Laden or his principal associates and deputies.[37]

Muddying the picture further is a lack of consensus in Jakarta over the degree of LJ's militant transnationalism. Certain sources, including senior officials in the State Intelligence Agency (BIN), are adamant in their conviction that the group has established concerted outside ties.[38] Other government and police personnel, however, tend to be far more circumspect in their interpretation, arguing that it is simply not known how broad LJ and Laskar Jundullah contacts with extraregional militants have been.[39]

More telling, questions exist over the evidence that has been presented in terms of directly tying Indonesia into a wider Islamist operational front. It is still not clear, for instance, whether the real masterminds behind the Bali attacks were renegade elements within the armed forces (rather than JI) seeking to institute a strategy of tension in order to bolster the military's declining grip on political power in Jakarta.[40] The veracity of the alleged JI terrorist training camp in Poso has also been challenged; not least by nongovernmental human rights groups that insist the facility was in fact a refugee holding area for Muslims fleeing the ethnoreligious violence in Sulawesi.[41]

Whatever the truth of the matter, Western sources have grown increasingly worried about the potential link between ex-LJ and Laskar Jundullah militants and transnational Islamic extremism. One of the main fears is that bin Laden and other al-Qaeda leaders are seeking to use actual or latent extremist structures in Indonesia to avail the logistical relocation of al-Qaeda forces post-Taliban and are moving to exploit the general permissive and chaotic climate in the country to further facilitate the "transmigration" of al-Qaeda's terror network.[42] Certainly this remains one of the key concerns of the Bush administration. As Deputy Defense Secretary Paul Wolfowitz has remarked: "You see the potential for Muslim extremists to link up with radicals in Indonesia and establish themselves in a soft corner of that country."[43]

The Regional Dimension

Compounding the overall perceived threat of Islamic extremism in Southeast Asia are signs that a transnational network in the guise of JI (literally "Islamic community") has begun to take root in the region. The movement's history dates back to the Darul Islam rebellions that took place in Indonesia during the 1950s. JI was originally founded by Abdullah Sungkar and Abu Bakar Bashir and based out of a religious boarding school located in central Java known as Pondok Ngruki. In 1985 an inner core of JI members fled to Malaysia—the so-called *Ngruki* network—to escape the anti-Islamist repression of the Suharto dictatorship.[44] It was here that the movement allegedly developed a specific regionwide ideological agenda aimed at creating a hardline caliphate comprising all of Indonesia, Malaysia, and Brunei in addition to the southernmost regions of the Philippines and Thailand (to be known as Darulah Islamiah Raya/Nusantara).[45]

Following the collapse of Suharto's government in 1998, Sungkar and Bashir returned to Indonesia, taking with them much of the *Ngruki* inner core that had originally fled to Malaysia in the 1980s. Sungkar died in 1999, after which Bashir established the Majelis Mujahideen Indonesia (MMI) in Yogyakarta, which various sources outside Indonesia have since claimed essentially serves as a political cover for JI's top ideological leadership.[46] Bashir was convicted in September 2003 for treason against the Indonesian state (his sentence has since been commuted from four to three years), but has yet to be tried as of this writing—with any offenses specifically relating to terrorism. He denies any association with JI or its agenda of violent militant Islamic extremism, and there was, at the time of writing, little indication of Jakarta moving to levy such charges against him.[47]

It is believed that JI commenced establishing militant cells across Southeast Asia as early as 1993. During the past two years, regional intelligence

sources have identified two figures as central to the group's overall recruitment and placement effort: Riduan "Hambali" Isamuddin, a veteran of the
anti-Soviet mujahideen campaign in Afghanistan, who was thought to be bin
Laden's main point of contact in Indonesia, and Abu Jibril (alias Mohammed
Iqbal Abdurrahman), a spiritual leader of the KMM and alleged to be "head
of training" for al-Qaeda in Southeast Asia (detained in Malaysia under the
Internal Security Act since January 2002).[48] Both men have been arrested
and are no longer actively engaged in terrorist activities. Abu Jibril, an Indonesian national who had been detained by Malaysia for two years, was finally handed over to Indonesian authorities in late 2003. As noted above,
Hambali was arrested in Thailand in August 2003 and, at the time of writing,
remained under U.S. custody at an undisclosed location.

JI is thought to work in much the same networked manner as al-Qaeda,
comprising: (1) a central command (*qiyadah maraziyah,* which is part of a
wider governing council, the *majelis qiyadah*); (2) a hard core of dedicated
jihadists (numbers of whom vary greatly by source); and (3) a wider associate
base drawn both from established insurgent militant organizations as well as
loosely based radical groups scattered across the region.[49] According to a 2003
Singapore government white paper, these cadres are organized into specific
territorial cells—known as *mantiqis*—that cover the following areas:

- M1—Singapore, Malaysia (except Sabah), and southern Thailand;
- M2—Indonesia (except Sulawesi and Kalimantan);
- M3—Sabah, Sulawesi, Kalimantan, and the southern Philippines;
- M4—Australia and Papua New Guinea.[50]

Fears associated with JI first arose in December 2001 when a major international terrorist plot was uncovered in Singapore that was allegedly to have
involved the combined bombings of U.S. warships docked at the Changi
Naval Base, the Ministry of Defence, a shuttle bus serving the Sembawang
Wharves and Yishun subway, the British and Australian high commissions,
the U.S. and Israeli embassies, and commercial complexes housing American firms.[51] The plan first came to light following the seizure of a videotape
and notes from an al-Qaeda leader's house in Afghanistan detailing reconnaissance of potential targets in Singapore.[52]

It is now known that the actual mechanics of the Singapore operation,
which intelligence authorities estimate took two years of planning, fell to the
late Fathur Rohman al-Ghozi and Mohammed Jabarah. Working under the
respective aliases of "Mike" and "Sammy," the two JI members coordinated
a local preestablished cell of militants, helping to select appropriate targets
and "fine tune" the logistics for the planned bombings.[53] The specific choice

of Singapore as the ultimate venue for the attacks appears to have been influenced by several factors, including the country's:

- Close defense and economic relationship with the United States;
- Standing as one of the most stable polities in Southeast Asia (meaning a successful attack would have had particularly unsettling effects);
- Multicultural and pluralist character (which is inimical to the group's emphasis on religious exclusivity and sectarianism); and
- Status as a capitalist and economic hub in Southeast Asia.[54]

While the Singapore plot never eventuated, several other acts of violence have been directly linked to JI since 2000. Prominent atrocities tied to the movement over the last three years have included a series of near simultaneous bombings that killed twenty-two people in the Philippine capital in December 2000; thirty-eight church explosions that struck Java the same month; a further string of attacks that hit Manila in 2002; the October 2002 Bali atrocity; and, most recently, a suicide attack on the U.S.-owned Marriott Hotel in Jakarta in August 2003 that killed thirteen people and left dozens injured.[55]

Although there is as yet no concrete proof verifying the existence of an entrenched Islamic network dedicated to the creation of a transnational Southeast Asian caliphate, intelligence sources, both internal and external to the region, view such a development as a distinct possibility. As Concepcion Clamor of Manila's National Intelligence Coordinating Agency (NICA) has explained in the context of the Philippines: "Asia is ripe for militant Islamism. . . . The possibility that . . . [extreme] groups could band together and challenge secular governments cannot be discounted. Islam serves as a strong rallying point for these organizations. It is [possible] . . . that the presence of foreign radical Islamist groups in the country [is] part of an effort to make the Southern Philippines part of a reported international terrorist plot to create an 'Islamic state' that will include Malaysia and Indonesia."[56]

Certainly Southeast Asia remains acutely vulnerable to the development of this type of militant Islamic network and general exploitation as a springboard for local and wider international terrorist attacks. Not only is the region characterized by highly porous land and sea borders well suited for smuggling arms and personnel, many governments also retain close links with the West—notably Singapore, Thailand, and the Philippines—which make them ideal as substitute targets for anti-American aggression. In addition, there exists a substantial Islamic demographic milieu that extremists can quickly disappear into (Indonesia, for example, currently boasts the world's largest Muslim population), while political corruption and general economic mismanagement both mitigate against effective internal security provisions and provide fertile ground for the fundamentalist rhetoric of outside demagogues. Finally, Southeast Asia's status as a global commercial and tourist hub has provided a highly developed transport and finance infrastructure that can be used as effectively for illicit as licit purposes, something that years of drug smuggling and money laundering bear ample testimony to.[57]

Southeast Asian Collaboration Against Terrorism

Governments throughout Southeast Asia have pledged their determination to cooperate against Islamic extremists and reiterate their willingness to enact joint police and intelligence measures under the Association of Southeast Asian Nations (ASEAN) and other multilateral arrangements. To be sure, a number of institutional mechanisms do exist for such coordination, including the Southeast Asian Association of National Police (ASEANPOL), the ASEAN Regional Forum (ARF), and the Philippine Center on Transnational Crime (PCTC) as well as nonofficial "track two" forums such as the Council for Security Cooperation in the Asia Pacific's (CSCAP) Working Group on Transnational Crime (WGTNC).

Despite these various regionwide groups, remarkably little integrated action has yet taken place. Exchange of information is largely perfunctory, tending to focus only on the most basic issues of mutual concern. Equally, most intergovernmental deliberations are held hostage to highly charged political and domestic ceilings that largely preclude the option of concerted collaboration. Indonesia, for instance, has strongly resisted pressure from Malaysia and Singapore to enact draconian internal security measures against alleged Islamic extremists and terrorists for fear of triggering a fundamentalist religious backlash and provoking widespread domestic instability. One of the most contentious issues has been Jakarta's consistent refusal to charge Bashir as the ideological force behind JI and the inspiration for acts of transnational terrorism carried out in its name.

To a certain extent, this state of affairs reflects the general mistrust and suspicion of a region that has been beset by numerous territorial conflicts over the last four decades. However, it is also very much indicative of the consensual and nonintrusive preference for decision-making that continues to underscore ASEAN—which is itself largely a product of the desire to avoid inadvertently inflaming cross-border sensitivities. Resolutions are generally not adopted unless they are unanimous and typically never allude or make reference to the internal policies and security of another member state. While such modalities may be conducive to furthering (the sham) of harmonious regional relations, they are hardly suited to the type of frank and honest discussion needed to effectively deal with terrorism, particularly in a region where internally based actors can so easily transcend and impact across national frontiers.[58]

Thus far, the most concerted action has been in the form of bilateral and trilateral agreements enacted between countries that have specifically identified an urgent need to enhance functional and procedural cooperation in the intelligence and communication areas. Foremost among these polities have been the Philippines, Malaysia, and Singapore. Several agreements and protocols have already been concluded within this so-called "coalition of the willing." If properly fostered, these could help to provide a more nuanced and defined approach to regional counterterrorism while, simultaneously, lending greater legitimacy to individual efforts conducted at the national level.

The key challenge will be to avoid "knee-jerk" actions that seek to impose heavy penalties on domestic groups simply on the basis of a pre-assumed connection to outside fanaticism. Inappropriately conflating and penalizing domestic groups on the basis of a pre-assumed connection to outside fanaticism will not only dangerously destabilize sensitive internal Islamic contexts and balances, it will also make it far harder to institute viable peace agreements on the ground (both of which are liable to provide fertile ground for the growth of the very fanaticism that Western and regional governments so fear).

Notes

The opinions and conclusions expressed in this paper are derived entirely from the author's own personal research into Southeast Asian terrorism and unconventional security over the past eight years. They should not be interpreted as representing those of RAND or the sponsors of any of the corporation's work.

1. The attacks launched against the United States were the largest and most lethal the world has seen. Altogether, four American internal flights were seized. Two planes were flown into the twin towers of the World Trade Center in New York, precipitating the collapse of both structures. The third jet smashed into the Pentagon in Virginia, while the fourth crashed into a field in Pennsylvania after passengers resisted the hijackers; the intended target of the plane is not known, although there is speculation it was bound either for Camp David in Maryland or the White House or Capitol Building in Washington, DC. The official death toll from the various attacks has been estimated at thirty-five hundred.

2. Mark Turner, "Terrorism and Secession in the Southern Philippines: The Rise of the Abu Sayyaf," *Contemporary Southeast Asia* 17, no. 1 (June 1995): 15; Concepcion Clamor, "Terrorism in the Philippines," paper presented before the Council for Security Cooperation in the Asia Pacific's (CSCAP) Working Group on Transnational Crime (WGTNC), Manila, May 1998, p. 5; "Validation of the Existence of the ASG," internal document prepared for the Philippine National Intelligence Coordinating Agency

(NICA), February 14, 1997; "Separatist Rebellion in the Southern Philippines," *IISS Strategic Comments* 6, no. 4 (May 2000): 2.

3. Philippine intelligence sources also believe that funds were channeled to the ASG via a Malaysian company that had been set up by Riduan "Hambali" Isamuddin—one of the coleaders of JI—ostensibly to export palm oil to Afghanistan. See "Asia's Own Osama," *Time,* April 1, 2002.

4. Author interview, Manila, June 1998. See also Peter Chalk, "The Abu Sayyaf Group and Bin Laden: An Unholy Alliance," *Jane's Intelligence Review Pointer* (December 1998); John Cooley, *Unholy Wars: Afghanistan, America, and International Terrorism* (London: Pluto Press, 2000), pp. 255–56; "Validation of the Existence of the ASG," p. 3; and "Master of Terror," *The Courier-Mail* (Australia), August 29, 1998. Khalifa was arrested for illegally trying to enter the United States. Extradited to Jordan to face terrorism charges, he was acquitted and has since remained in Saudi Arabia.

5. According to Rohan Gunaratna, had Operation Bojinka taken place, over four thousand civilians would have been killed. Comments made during the Globalising Terror, Political Violence in the New Millennium Conference, Hobart, Tasmania, May 8–10, 2002.

6. See, for instance, "Asia's Own Osama," *Time,* April 1, 2002; Anthony Spaeth, "Rumbles in the Jungle," *Time,* March 4, 2002; Turner, "Terrorism and Secession in the Southern Philippines," p. 8; "Disparate Pieces of Terrorist Puzzle Fit Together," *Washington Post,* September 23, 2001; "Muslim Militants Threaten Ramos Vision of Summit Glory," *The Australian,* January 13, 1996; and "The Man Who Wasn't There," *Time,* February 20, 1995.

7. "Back to the Jungle," *The Economist,* March 1, 2003; "Philippines Approves Counterterrorism Exercise with the US," *The Star,* February 18, 2003; "When Local Anger Joins Global Hate," *The Economist,* October 19, 2002; "Grumblings Surface During 'Balikatan,'" *Philippine Daily Inquirer,* February 3, 2002; "Are We Losing Our Sovereignty (2)?" *Philippine Daily Inquirer,* February 3, 2002; "Game Na?" *Philippine Daily Inquirer,* February 4, 2002.

8. Anthony Davis, "Resilient Abu Sayyaf Resists Military Pressure," *Jane's Intelligence Review* (September 2003): 17. Two main ASG factions currently exist: a Basilan group, which probably numbers no more than 80 operatives; and a more prominent Sulu group composed of between 200 and 300 cadres. Author interview, Manila, February 2002.

9. Over the past two years the bulk of ASG activities has taken the form of kidnappings, some of which have been highly profitable. A string of Western abductions carried out in the first half of 2000, for instance, are believed to have netted the perpetrating group an estimated US$20 million in ransom payments. See "A Hostage Crisis Confronts Estrada," *The Economist,* May 6, 2000; "Philippine Military Begins Assault on Muslim Rebels," *CNN Interactive World Wide News,* April 22, 2000; "Philippine Forces Hit Rebel Stronghold," *Washington Post,* April 24, 2000; "Gunmen Take Foreigners Hostage in Malaysia," *Washington Post,* April 25, 2000; and "Military Finds 2 Beheaded by Philippine Rebels," *Washington Post,* May 7, 2000.

10. Comments to this effect were made during informal discussions at the Institute for Defense and Security Studies (IDSS), Singapore, March 2002.

11. The split with the MNLF essentially resulted from the latter's willingness to negotiate for autonomy rather than full independence in the southern Philippines. The MNLF itself signed a peace agreement with Manila in 1996, which created a limited

Autonomous Region of Muslim Mindanao and provided for peace and development efforts in the south. For an overview of the accord, see Peter Chalk, "The Davao Consensus: A Panacea for the Muslim Insurgency in Mindanao?" in *Terrorism and Political Violence* 9, no. 2 (1997).

12. Thanks to vigorous transmigration programs, most of the southern Philippines is now Christian-dominated; indeed by 1983, it is estimated that as much as 80 percent of the Mindanao population was non-Muslim. It is for this reason that MILF places its demands in the context of areas where Islamists were traditionally (as opposed to currently) in the majority.

13. Tony Davis, "Attention Shifts to Moro Islamic Liberation Front," *Jane's Intelligence Review* (April 2000): 22; and Tony Davis, "Philippine Army Prevents MILF Reorganisation," *Jane's Intelligence Review* (March 2003). Salamat died of a heart ulcer in July 2003; Ali Haj Murad, who formerly acted as MILF's military chief, now leads the group.

14. See Peter Chalk, "Separatism in Southeast Asia: The Islamic Factor in Southern Thailand, Mindanao and Aceh," *Studies in Conflict and Terrorism* 24, no. 4 (2001): 247; Clamor, "Terrorism in the Philippines," p. 8; and Davis, "Philippine Army Prevents MILF Reorganisation," pp. 16–21. At the time of writing, the MILF had announced its intention to pursue comprehensive peace talks with the Manila government aimed at consolidating a final settlement to the conflict by the end of 2003. Essential to progress in this regard was Salamat's 2003 renunciation of terrorism.

15. Author interview, Singapore, March 2002. See also "Singapore Announces Arrest of 21 Militants," *Washington Post,* September 17, 2002. A similar request was allegedly made to the Armed Islamic Group (GIA) in Algeria.

16. Zachary Abuza, "Tentacles of Terror: Al Qaeda's Southeast Asian Linkages," paper presented before the Transnational Violence and Seams of Lawlessness in the Asia-Pacific: Linkages to Global Terrorism Conference, Hawaii, February 19–21, 2002, pp. 9–10.

17. Rohan Gunaratna, "The Singapore Connection," *Jane's Intelligence Review* (March 2002): 11; "US Holding Canadian in Embassy Plot," *Washington Post,* August 2, 2002; Davis, "Attention Shifts to Moro Islamic Liberation Front," p. 23. Jabarah was arrested in Oman in August 2002 and is currently being held at an undisclosed location in the United States.

18. Alan Sipress and Ellen Nakashima, "Al Qaeda Affiliate Training Indonesians on Philippine Island," *Washington Post,* November 17, 2003, p. A18.

19. Davis, "Attention Shifts to Moro Islamic Liberation Front," p. 23; Spaeth "Rumbles in the Jungle," pp. 16–17.

20. Cited in Spaeth, "Rumbles in the Jungle," p. 17. It should be noted that the MILF does not appear on the U.S. State Department's list of designated foreign terrorist organizations (FTOs).

21. Overviews of Malay Muslim separatism in southern Thailand can be found in Omar Farouk, "The Historical and Transnational Dimensions of Malay-Muslim Separatism in Southern Thailand," in *Armed Separatism in Southeast Asia,* ed. Lim Joo Jock and S. Vani (Singapore: ISEAS, 1984); Muthiah Alagappa, *The National Security of Developing States: Lessons from Thailand* (Dover, MA: Auburn House, 1987); R.J. May, "The Religious Factor in Three Minority Movements," *Contemporary Southeast Asia* 13, no. 4 (1992): 403–5; and David Brown, *State and Ethnic Politics in Southeast Asia* (London: Routledge, 1994), pp. 16–70.

22. The string of attacks, which were code-named "Falling Leaves" and carried

out by a group calling itself Bersatu (literally "Solidarity")—now known to have been a flag of convenience for a coordinated PULO/New PULO operation—resulted in nine deaths, several dozen injuries, and considerable economic damage. According to Tony Davis, Specialist Asia correspondent with *Jane's Intelligence Review,* this particular campaign marked the most serious upsurge of Muslim separatist violence in southern Thailand since the early 1980s. Author interview, Canberra, September 1998.

23. See, for instance, Chalk, "Separatism in Southeast Asia," pp. 244–45; "Minister: 'Southern Separatists Receive Foreign Training,'" *The Nation* (Thailand), January 6, 1995; "Malaysia Denies Thai Terrorist Claims," *The Australian,* January 6, 1998; and "Malaysia 'Not Training Ground for Thai Rebels,'" *Straits Times* (Singapore), January 5, 1998.

24. Author interviews, Canberra, November 1999. See also "Worse to Come," *Far Eastern Economic Review* (July 29, 1999); and "Malaysia Denies Supporting Separatists in Indonesia," *CNN Interactive World Wide News,* July 20, 1999.

25. "Osama bin Laden and Indonesia," *Laksamana Foundation,* accessed via http://www.laksamana.net/vnews.cfm?/news_id=175.

26. See, for instance, "KMM's Opposition Link," *New Straits Times* (Malaysia), October 12, 2001; "Eye of the Storm," *Time,* February 11, 2002, p. 26.

27. See International Institute for Strategic Studies, *Strategic Survey 2001/02* (London: IISS, May 2002), pp. 301–2.

28. Author interview, Singapore, March 2002. See also "Recruiting for Terrorism in Malaysia," *Globe and Mail,* November 12, 2002. Malaysian police claim that the KMM was complicit in establishing at least two terrorist training camps for transnational Islamist militants in remote villages around Kelantan.

29. "Suspected al-Qaeda Agent Held; Saudi Arrested," *Washington Post,* November 5, 2001; "Suspect Held in Al-Qaeda Terror Attacks," Associated Press, November 5, 2001; "Malaysian Mujahideen Group Has Links with Al Qaeda," Deutsche Presse-Agentur, January 5, 2002; "Militants Will Be Hunted Down, Says Mahathir," *Straits Times,* January 7, 2002.

30. As of November 2002, a total of 120 detainees was being held at the Kamunting Detention Center under the provisions of Kuala Lumpur's ISA. "War on Terror a Two-Edged Sword for Malaysia," *Asia Times On-Line,* November 23/24, 2002; "Malaysia Arrests 4 Men Suspected of Suicide Plot," *Washington Post,* November 27, 2002; "Mahathir's Drive Against Militants Wins Over West," *Daily Telegraph,* November 1, 2002; "The Elusive Enemy," *The Economist,* August 3, 2002; "Singapore Terror Group 'Aimed for Race Conflict,'" *Financial Times,* September 20, 2002.

31. For detailed overviews of Indonesia's recent internal problems, see Angel Rabasa and Peter Chalk, *Indonesia's Transformation and the Stability of Southeast Asia* (Santa Monica, CA: RAND, 2001); Paul Dibb, "Indonesia: The Key to South-East Asia's Security," *International Affairs* 77, no. 4 (2001); Donald Emerson, "Will Indonesia Survive?" *Foreign Affairs* 79, no. 3 (May–June 2000); Kerry Collison, "Indonesia: Disintegration of the Last Great Colonial Power?" *Defense and Foreign Affairs Strategic Policy* XXVIII, no. 10 (2000); and "Indonesia Is in Danger of Coming Apart," *The Australian,* August 12, 2000.

32. Two hundred and two people were killed in the Bali bombings, the vast bulk of who were Australian tourists.

33. See, for instance, "The Terrorist Talks," *Time,* October 5, 2003; Anthony Davis, "Thailand Faces Up to Southern Extremist Threat," *Jane's Intelligence Review* (October 2003): 14–15; "Bali Bombing Coordinator Sentenced to Death for Role," *Los*

Angeles Times, October 3, 2003; "Bali 'Mastermind' Sentenced to Die," *Financial Times,* September 11, 2003; "Islamic Militant Amrozi Sentenced to Death for Bali Bombing," *Bernama,* August 7, 2003; "Indonesian Militant Gets Life over Bali Blasts," Reuters, October 16, 2003.

34. LJ was originally created in response to what was seen as the deliberate persecution of Muslims in Maluku (the Moluccas). Thousands of activists were subsequently dispatched to the islands to support their coreligionists, with the year 2000 officially declared as the year of the jihad against *kafir harbi* (belligerent infidels). For further details see Greg Fealy, "Inside Laskar Jihad," *Inside Indonesia* (January–March 2001), available online at http://www.insideindonesia.org/edit65/fealy.htm; "Leader of the 'Jihad Army' in Indonesia to 'Al-Hayat': We Plan to Target American Interests," *Mideast Media Research Unit* 359 (March 2002); "Who Are the Laskar Jihad?" *BBC Interactive News,* June 20, 2000; "Java's Angry Young Muslims," *The Economist,* October 20, 2001; and "Holy War in the Spice Islands," *The Economist,* March 17, 2001.

35. Author interview, Jakarta, January 2002. See also International Institute for Strategic Studies, *Strategic Survey 2001/02,* p. 301; "The Links that Bind Terror Groups," *The Guardian,* October 15, 2002; "Asia's Own Osama," *Time,* April 1, 2002; "Qaeda Moving into Indonesia, Officials Fear," *New York Times,* January 22, 2002; "Indonesia Base for al-Qaeda," *Daily Telegraph,* January 12, 2002; "Spain Holds Key to Sept. 11 Plot," *Washington Post,* November 19, 2001; and "Al Qaeda Feared to Be Lurking in Indonesia," *Washington Post,* January 11, 2002. Most of the claims pertaining to Poso are based on the evidence of an Indonesian national, Parlindungan Siregar, who was arrested in Spain in early 2002. According to *El Pais,* Siregar claimed to be a key recruiter for JI and was in Europe to arrange the training for foreigners at the Sulawesi facility.

36. See "Jemaah Islamiyah in Southeast Asia: Damaged But Still Dangerous," *International Crisis Group Asia Report* 63 (August 2003): 19–23, 38; "Indonesian Arrested in Manila Had Ties to al-Qaeda," *Washington Post,* May 9, 2002; "Manila Mulls the Repatriation of Jailed Indonesian," Agence France-Presse, August 19, 2002.

37. Author interviews, Canberra and Sydney, March and July 2003.

38. RAND interview, Jakarta, January 2002. See also "Asia's Own Osama," *Time,* April 1, 2002; "Qaeda Moving into Indonesia, Officials Fear," *New York Times;* and "Indonesia Base for al-Qaeda," *Daily Telegraph.*

39. Author interviews, Hawaii and Jakarta, February–March 2002. Similar circumspect views were expressed by senior Indonesian academics and intelligence personnel in discussion sessions held during the New Dimensions of Terrorism Workshop, Singapore March 21–22, 2002.

40. Author interviews, Canberra and Sydney, March and July 2003.

41. A senior Indonesian official charged with investigating the alleged Poso facility verified that there was no definitive proof to support the claim that it was an international terrorist training center. He did concede, however, that testimonial and forensic evidence indicated that LJ had attempted to penetrate the camp and use it both for military training and indoctrination purposes. Author interview, Hawaii, February 2002.

42. Indonesia currently lacks any form of antisubversion or counterterrorism law that can be brought to bear against potential threats to the country's national security. In addition, the republic suffers from a lack of strong leadership under Megawati and remains chronically afflicted by severe corruption (according to the Hong Kong–based

Political and Economic Risk Consultancy [PERC], Indonesia remains Asia's most corrupt nation, with problems that transcend the governing, finance, and security sectors). Author interviews, Hawaii, Jakarta, and Singapore, February–March 2002. See also "Corruption: An Obstacle to Regional Security," *Jakarta Post,* March 20, 2002.

43. Paul Wolfowitz, cited in presentation given by James Cotton during the Globalising Terror, Political Violence in the New Millennium Conference, Hobart, Tasmania, May 8–10, 2002.

44. See generally, "Al-Qaeda in Southeast Asia: The Case of the 'Ngruki Network' in Indonesia," International Crisis Group (ICG) Asia Briefing (August 2002). This analysis is one of the more detailed and in-depth pieces of research on the historical evolution of JI.

45. Author interview, Jakarta, March 2002. See also "Asia's Own Osama," *Time,* April 1, 2002; and "The Wrong Target," *Far Eastern Economic Review* (April 18, 2001).

46. See, for instance, Abuza, "Tentacles of Terror," pp. 23–24. Indonesian intelligence claims there is no definitive evidence to link the MMI either to JI or acts of terrorism. The group itself continues to insist that it acts as a "legitimate" civil society, ostensibly committed to the peaceful implementation of Sharia law across the archipelago.

47. See "Jemaah Islamiyah in Southeast Asia," p. 37; "Indonesian Cleric Convicted," *Los Angeles Times,* September 3, 2003.

48. "Al-Qaeda in Southeast Asia: The Case of the 'Ngruki Network' in Indonesia," pp. 1–2; Abuza, "Tentacles of Terror," p. 20.

49. "Jemaah Islamiyah in Southeast Asia," p. 11.

50. *White Paper: The Jemaah Islamiyah Arrests and the Threat of Terrorism* (Singapore: Ministry of Home Affairs, January 2003), p. 10. See also Richard Evans, "Singapore Reports on Jemaah Islamiah," *Jane's Intelligence Review* (February 2003); and "Singapore Offers Grim View of Future Terror," *Sydney Morning Herald,* January 11–12, 2003.

51. Singaporean authorities have claimed that JI was planning further attacks in 2002 to foment a possible conflict between the city-state and neighboring Malaysia. Among the alleged targets were cross-border water supply lines, the disruption of which has long remained a potential spark for war between the two countries. According to the Singaporean Ministry of Home Affairs, JI's ultimate aim is "to create a situation in Malaysia conducive to overthrowing the . . . government and [transforming the country] into an Islamic state. The attacks on key Singaporean installations would be portrayed as acts of aggression by the Malaysian government, thereby generating animosity and distrust between [the two countries]." See "Singapore Terror Group 'Aimed for Race Conflict,'" *Financial Times,* September 20, 2002.

52. Gunaratna, "The Singapore Connection," pp. 10–11; "Singapore Announces Arrest of 21 Militants," *Washington Post,* September 17, 2002; "Singapore Terror Group Had Plan to Bomb US Warships," *South China Morning Post,* January 12, 2002; "A Tale with Many Beginnings," *Straits Times* (Singapore), January 11, 2002.

53. Author interview, Singapore, March 2002. See also Gunaratna, "The Singapore Connection," p. 11; and "US Holding Canadian in Embassy Bomb Plot," *Washington Post,* August 2, 2002.

54. RAND interview, Singapore, June 2002.

55. "Bomb Maker Gunned Down in Philippines," *Los Angeles Times,* October 13, 2003; "Philippine Police Comb Wreckage for Clues," *Washington Post,* December

31, 2000; "Holiday Bombings Tied to Afghanistan," *Washington Post,* January 7, 2001; "In the Wake of Terror," *Globe and Mail,* October 16, 2002; "When Local Anger Joins Global Hate," *The Economist,* October 19, 2002; "Thirteen Dead, Scores Injured in Bomb Blast at Jakarta Marriott Hotel," *Malaysian National News Agency/ Bernama,* August 5, 2003; "Jakarta Police Name Hotel Suicide Bomber," Reuters, August 8, 2003.

56. Clamor, "Terrorism in the Philippines," pp. 16–17.

57. See, for instance, "Thai Expert Warns of Terrorists Spreading in Southeast Asia," Xinhua General News Service, December 26, 2001.

58. See, for instance, "ASEAN Way Prevails in Tea Party's Polite Talk," *The Australian,* July 30, 1998; "Minutes of the Calamity Club," *The Economist,* July 29, 2000; "Ties That Bind," *Far Eastern Economic Review* (August 10, 2000); and "Putting Regionalism in Its Place," *South China Morning Post,* February 8, 2002.

3

Al-Qaeda Comes
to Southeast Asia

Zachary Abuza

The horrors of the September 11, 2001 terrorist attacks on the United States and the ensuing war on terrorism galvanized the global community to come to terms with the reality of international terrorism. While the focus of the war on terrorism has been on Afghanistan and Pakistan, one of the key arenas is now Southeast Asia. This has caught both states and individuals in that region by surprise. Though most states in Southeast Asia have a Muslim population, ranging from 5 percent in the Philippines to 85 percent in Indonesia, the fact is that the region has always been considered the Islamic periphery. Muslims in Southeast Asia have long been characterized as secular, tolerant, modernist, and development-oriented. Moreover, many people within and outside Southeast Asia had believed that violence and terrorism, a daily reality in the Middle East, was anathema to Southeast Asia.

The disclosure of the extent to which al-Qaeda cells were established and linkages between militant Muslim organizations in Southeast Asia to al-Qaeda were made has shocked Southeast Asian governments. Al-Qaeda had slowly penetrated the region for more than a decade beginning in 1991, co-opting individuals and groups, establishing independent cells, and finding common cause with local militants for four main reasons.

First, whereas there have long been militant Muslim groups fighting for their own homeland in the southern Philippines, in Aceh (northern Sumatra), and to a degree in southern Thailand and Myanmar, these groups were seen to have completely domestic agendas with little interest in linking up with international Muslim organizations. Al-Qaeda emerged in Southeast Asia at a time when state sponsorship of terrorism, notably by Libya, was waning. Moreover, al-Qaeda was able to build on its personal relationships with veterans of the mujahideen in Afghanistan. The leadership of almost every militant Islamic group in Southeast Asia, including the Kumpulan Mujahideen Malaysia, Jemaah Islamiya (JI), the Moro Islamic Liberation Front (MILF), and Laskar Jihad, had fought with the mujahideen. By linking their domestic struggles with an international network, the leaders of these groups were able to pool and share resources, conduct joint training, assist each other in weapons and explosives procurement, and engage in money laundering and financial transfers.

Second, although the majority of the populations in Southeast Asian societies are secular and tolerant, militant Islam is growing for a variety of reasons. These include economic dispossession, the lack of political freedom, the spread of Wahhabism and Salafi Islam, the failure of secular education, and an increased number of religious students studying in Middle Eastern and South Asian *madrassas* (Islamic schools). Although radical Islamists are a distinct minority in Southeast Asia, in many cases they have shaped the agenda, and secular nationalists have not always stood up to them.

Third, Southeast Asian states have been what might be termed "countries of convenience" for terrorists, with tourist-friendly policies and minimal visa requirements, generally lax financial oversights, well-established informal remittance systems for overseas workers, porous borders, often weak central government control, endemic government corruption, and a vast supply of illicit arms.

Finally, Southeast Asia's multiethnic, tolerant, and secular societies have actually attracted al-Qaeda to the region. As states focused on other threats, they had dropped their guard in relation to the potential terrorist risk. Although the Philippines raised the specter of international terrorists operating in the region in the mid-1990s, its cries fell on deaf ears. States saw terrorism as a problem, but not a problem they considered a direct threat to themselves.

One of the reasons analysts were oblivious to the emergence of Jemaah Islamiya and al-Qaeda's presence was that there were a myriad of groups. The goal of this chapter is to introduce the readers to the groups and the development of the network.

The Al-Qaeda Organization

The roots of al-Qaeda are found in the Maktab al-Khidmat lil-Mujahideen al-Arab (MaK), the Afghan Bureau, established between 1982 and 1984.

The MaK was responsible for coordinating the recruitment of "Arab volunteers" to the mujahideen; bin Laden became the organization's principal fundraiser. Bin Laden established al-Qaeda, literally "the base," in 1988 with help from the head of Saudi Arabian intelligence in order to organize Arab recruitment for the mujahideen. In this context, he has always been involved in "international" networking.

The central leadership of al-Qaeda has always been small, comprising only some thirty individuals; its strength is derived from its international network of about twenty-four constituent groups, with cells spread across some sixty countries. Al-Qaeda is thought to have between 5,000 and 12,000 members. As John Arquilla has noted, al-Qaeda was developed along "diverse, dispersed nodes who share a set of ideas and interests and who are arrayed to act in a fully internetted 'all-channel' manner."[1] Thus the "network as a whole (but not necessarily each node) has little to no hierarchy, and there may be multiple leaders. Decision-making and operations are decentralized, allowing for local initiative and autonomy. Thus, the design may appear acephalous (headless), and at other times polycephalous (hydra-headed)."[2]

In addition to establishing independent cells, al-Qaeda was brilliant in its co-optation of other groups, those that had a narrow domestic agenda, and in bringing them into al-Qaeda's structure. In short, bin Laden tried to "align with local militant groups with country-specific grievances to increase his reach and influence."[3] The groups are an amalgam of organizations: "They have not been subsumed into Al Qaeda," but "[t]hey work with Al Qaeda," giving the organization "a degree of rootedness in their countries."[4] Associates, who pledge *bayat,* a form of allegiance to bin Laden, share intelligence, money, equipment, and recruitment. Although, independently the cells are too small to make an impact, their strength lies in the network itself. Al-Qaeda is able to graft itself onto radical groups in a region like Southeast Asia or establish new cells from scratch; and increasingly, these cells are using the overall network to coordinate their activities.

The MILF's Afghan Connection

The MILF is currently the leading Muslim rebel movement fighting the Philippine government. The MILF fields between 12,000 and 15,000 combatants. The Philippine government continues to enter into negotiations with the movement. Nonetheless, whereas the MILF may have legitimate national liberation aspirations, it has forged linkages with international terrorist groups, notably al-Qaeda, for financial support, especially after funding from Libya waned substantially in the mid-1990s following the Lockerbie attack.

The roots of MILF contact with al-Qaeda date back to the period of the Soviet invasion of Afghanistan, when the MILF sent an estimated 700 Filipino Muslims to undergo military training and join the mujahideen. According to a classified Philippine intelligence report, the MILF dispatched the trainees in three waves. Of the first group of 600, only 360 underwent the yearlong military training; 180 of these actually joined the mujahideen.[5] The MILF saw the training in Afghanistan as very important in the development of the movement. A Philippine intelligence report notes that: "Usually those selected were on field commander status, with leadership potential, with armed followers and had money to finance the trip."[6]

Closer ties to al-Qaeda were forged by Osama bin Laden's brother-in-law, Mohammed Jamal Khalifa, a senior member of the Muslim Brotherhood who moved to the Philippines in 1991 and established corporate and charitable fronts, including a branch of the International Islamic Relief Organization (IIRO). Established in the Philippines, Khalifa began to provide covert assistance to the MILF in two ways—financially and through training. In addition, he provided overt assistance by funding development projects in zones under MILF control or in areas that constituted core constituencies of MILF supporters. In a 1998 interview, Al Haj Murad, the MILF vice chairman for military affairs, admitted that bin Laden and Khalifa provided "help and assistance" to MILF cadres who volunteered in the 1980s to help the Taliban struggle against the Soviet-backed Afghan regime.[7] On February 7, 1999, Hashim Salamat admitted in a BBC interview to receiving aid from bin Laden, although again stating that it was humanitarian aid for mosque construction and social welfare. This new source of assistance was imperative to the MILF, as its traditional supporter, Libya, was reducing military assistance to both the MILF and the MNLF as it was trying to broker a peace agreement with the Philippine government. Libya, hoping to get sanctions lifted that were imposed after the Lockerbie bombing (where its involvement had been proven), used its leverage to get the MNLF to sign an autonomy accord with the government.

The second type of assistance that the MILF has received from al-Qaeda has been in the form of training, both in Mindanao and abroad. For example, Al Haj Murad admitted to receiving "substantial help and assistance from bin Laden, including the training of his fighters in bin Laden's camps in Afghanistan."[8] More common, however, has been the infiltration of Middle Eastern trainers into MILF camps. Beginning in the mid-1990s, a steady flow of trainers began to arrive in the Philippines to train MILF and Abu Sayyaf guerrillas—and later, members of Jemaah Islamiya. These included Mughiri al-Gaza'iri, commander of an al-Qaeda camp in Afghanistan and a very close associate of Abu Zubaydah, Omar al-Faruq, and Fathur Rohman al-Ghozi.

One of the most visible manifestations of this relationship came in 1999–2000, when al-Qaeda operatives helped the MILF, hitherto a guerrilla force, develop their own terrorist arm, the Special Operations Group. Though the MILF denies it, they frequently engage in terrorism when confronted with losses on the battlefield.

The Abu Sayyaf: Degenerating into Thugs

Of greater public interest than the MILF is the small but very violent Abu Sayyaf. The origins of the Abu Sayyaf can be traced to Afghanistan, where one of the hundreds of Moro fundamentalists, Ustadz Abdurajak Janjalani, emerged as a leader and befriended Osama bin Laden. Janjalani and his younger brother Khadafi Janjalani received training in the late 1980s and into the 1990s at a training camp near Khost, Afghanistan. Janjalani was committed to waging a jihad back in his native Philippines to create a pure Islamic state in the Moro islands based on Salafi Wahhabism. When Osama bin Laden wanted to expand his al-Qaeda network, he turned to Janjalani to establish a cell in Southeast Asia. At the same time, Ramzi Yousef, the mastermind of the 1993 World Trade Center bombing, was teaching at the Khost camp and encouraged the formation of the Abu Sayyaf. Yousef traveled with Janjalani to the Philippines and stayed from December 1991 to May 1992 at bin Laden's request, where he trained Abu Sayyaf members in bomb making in their camp on Basilan Island. Very quickly the ASG made its mark. It began its terrorist attacks in the Philippines in 1991. Between 1991 and 1996 Abu Sayyaf was responsible for sixty-seven terrorist attacks, more than half of which were indiscriminate bombings. These led to the deaths of 58 people, with another 398 injured.

Although Abu Sayyaf's scope primarily focused on their domestic grievances, they had linkages to the broader al-Qaeda network. Using the Philippines as his base of operations, Ramzi Yousef planned a series of spectacular terrorist plots. The Bojinka plots included attempts to bomb eleven U.S. airliners and to assassinate the pope, who visited the Philippines in early 1995. Known as Operation Bojinka, the plot was foiled only when the volatile explosives prematurely caught fire in a Manila apartment complex. Yousef's network included both Abu Sayyaf guerrillas as well as operatives, such as Khalid Sheikh Mohammed, centered around Mohammed Jamal Khalifa's network of charities.

Although Operation Bojinka was foiled and Ramzi Yousef and two lieutenants were arrested, authorities treated the plot as an isolated incident and not part of a broader network; there were no other arrests. Khalifa was forced from the Philippines, and at the time, al-Qaeda's efforts at developing a Southeast Asian network refocused on Malaysia.

Origins of Jemaah Islamiya

The origins of the Jemaah Islamiya network are found in Indonesia, dating back to the 1960s when two radical clerics, Abdullah Sungkar and Abu Bakar Bashir, began demanding the imposition of Sharia, which got them into trouble with the Suharto regime. The two considered themselves the ideological heirs of Sekarmadji Maridjan Kartosuwiryo—the founder of Darul Islam.[9] In 1972 they established an Islamic boarding school in Solo, Al Mukmin, which taught a hard-line Wahhabism. One of the masters, Abdul Qadir Baraja, was arrested for writing the *Jihad Guide Book* for his students that urged jihad against all opponents of Sharia law. The school's alumni reads like a who's who of Southeast Asian terrorism, and includes Fathur Rohman al-Ghozi, Ali Imron, and others.

On November 19, 1978, Bashir and Sungkar were arrested and sentenced to nine years for violating a 1963 subversion law. In 1985, while on appeal, they fled to Malaysia, where they lived and preached openly for several decades and built up a large following of radical Indonesian exiles. They served as a way station for Indonesians and Malaysians who were on their way to Afghanistan and Pakistan to study and fight the Soviets or train in one of the forty al-Qaeda camps established in the late 1990s.[10] Sungkar met bin Laden and other senior al-Qaeda members around 1994 and pledged *bayat,* effectively absorbing his movement into al-Qaeda. Sungkar espoused violent jihad to create a pan-Islamic state in Southeast Asia. And he instructed two lieutenants, both veterans of the jihad in Afghanistan and members of al-Qaeda, Riduan Isamuddin (Hambali) and Mohammed Iqbal Abdurrahman (Abu Jibril), to develop a regional network of cells. All four of the individuals were itinerant preachers unaffiliated with any mosque that preached jihad and recruited in private settings before groups of hard-core followers whom they slowly cultivated across Malaysia and also in Singapore. They began to espouse the doctrine of Nusantara Raya, the establishment of a pan-Islamic republic incorporating Malaysia, Indonesia, southern Thailand, and the southern Philippines.[11]

One point that deserves particular attention is that, although Jemaah Islamiya was founded in 1993–94, it did not conduct its first terrorist acts until 2000. The leaders spent those first six or seven years patiently building up their network, recruiting, training, and gaining technical proficiency. In the 1990s, JI was at al-Qaeda's disposal, establishing front companies and accounts for al-Qaeda and recruiting. For example, the first time Hambali appeared on any intelligence service's radar screen was when his name appeared on the board of directors of a firm established to facilitate the Operation Bojinka plot.[12] They also set up a network of *madrassas* in Indonesia,

Malaysia, and southern Thailand as the center of their recruiting efforts. They established a network of cells in each country in the region, each with a particular responsibility or role in the pursuance of the organization's overall mission: the creation of a pan-Islamic state in Southeast Asia.[13] The capabilities of JI were limited. Through 2000, JI members were simply helping al-Qaeda operatives execute attacks in the region. For example, in mid-2000, JI members assisted a six-man Yemeni team plan the truck bombing of the U.S. embassy in Jakarta, though the attack was thwarted.[14] Clearly by 2000, al-Qaeda's leadership was looking to expand its theaters of operation to keep the United States off balance. To do so, they increasingly turned to Jemaah Islamiya, whose network had grown considerably.

Organizational Structure

Jemaah Islamiya has a formal structure, with Abdullah Sungkar and Abu Bakar Bashir serving as the group's amirs, or spiritual leaders. Hambali became the chairman of the five-member *shura*—"regional advisory council." Other members included Mohammed Iqbal Abdurrahman (Abu Jibril), Agus Dwikarna, Abu Hanifah, and Faiz bin Abu Bakar Bafana. Bafana, a Malaysian businessman and former Singaporean, was a key aid to Hambali and served as the JI's treasurer.[15] Beneath the *shura* were the secretaries and different committees, including Missionary Work, Military Committee, Security Committee, Financial Committee; and the heads of the four regional commands, or *mantiqis*.

> *Mantiqi 1* covered the peninsula of Malaysia, Singapore, and southern Thailand.
>
> *Mantiqi 2* covered Java and Sumatra Indonesia.
>
> *Mantiqi 3* covered the Philippines, Brunei, eastern Malaysia, Kalimantan, and Sulawesi Indonesia.
>
> *Mantiqi 4* was being developed to establish cells in Australia and Papua (formerly Irian Jaya), though not Papua New Guinea.

Each *mantiqi* in turn had several subcells, or *fiah*. The JI has between 500 and 1,000 members, though the former is a more likely estimate, spread throughout the region.[16]

Mantiqi 1, with an estimated 200 members, is perhaps one of the two largest JI cells. It was led by Abu Hanifah and Faiz bin Abu Bakar Bafana and recruited actively among both Indonesian exiles and educated Malays—especially technical students. At least five senior JI members and recruiters were lecturers in the Universiti Teknologi Malaysia (UTM).[17]

Mantiqi 1 had four discernable functions. First, it worked very closely with the KMM in Malaysia, with whom there is some overlap in membership and goals. Second, it was the primary conduit between the JI and Osama bin Laden and al-Qaeda in Afghanistan. The Malaysian cell was the logistical hub for up to 100 JI operatives who were sent to Afghanistan for training in al-Qaeda camps, and also ran its own camp in southern Malaysia.[18] Third, it was responsible for recruiting and education. Much of the recruiting was done through two *madrassas,* Tarbiyah Luqmanul Hakiem school, in Johor Baru, and the Sekolah Menengah Arab Darul Anuar, in Kota Baru. Fourth, *Mantiqi 1* was responsible for establishing dozens of front companies that could be used to channel al-Qaeda funds and procure weapons and bomb-making matériel. These included Green Laboratory Medicine, which was responsible for procuring twenty-one tons of ammonium nitrate, and Infocus Technology, an Internet firm that was used to get Zaccarias Moussaoui into the United States.[19] Front companies were not the only businesses established by al-Qaeda. There were also many cases in which JI members established businesses, received contracts and businesses from JI supporters, and then plowed the proceeds back into the organization. According to the Singapore government's white paper, "All JI-run businesses had to contribute 10 percent of their total earnings to the group. This money was to be channeled into the JI's special fund called Infaq Fisbilillah (contributions for the Islamic cause or jihad fund)."[20]

Mantiqi 2 provided the bulk of the membership. In the mid-1990s there appears to have been very little JI activity in the authoritarian state. Yet, following the fall of Suharto in May 1998, there was a surge in JI activity as hundreds of radical Indonesians returned to the archipelago. The Indonesian cell would provide the bulk of the membership, and it was in Indonesia that the JI developed its two paramilitary arms: the Laskar Mujahideen and the Laskar Jundullah in 1999 to 2000. The Indonesia cell is thoroughly connected to Abu Bakar Bashir's overt political organization, the Mujahideen Council of Indonesia (MMI), a large umbrella grouping for approximately a hundred small radical and militant groups from across the archipelago. In addition to recruitment and running a network of radical *madrassas,* the Indonesian cell was responsible for running a network of training camps, including some seven in Sulawesi and one in Kalimantan. The Indonesian cell was also very important in liaising with al-Qaeda–linked Islamic charities, especially Al Haramain, and became a very important conduit for foreign funding.

Mantiqi 3 was important as a major logistics cell for the network responsible for acquiring explosives, guns, and other equipment as well as liaising with the MILF and supporting al-Qaeda operatives and trainers in the region. They included senior al-Qaeda trainers Omar al-Faruq, Mughiri al-Gaza'iri, and Omar al-Hadrani.[21] These trainers also played an important role in establishing the MILF's own terrorist arm, the Special Operations Group, in 1999.[22] In addition to obtaining explosives, al-Ghozi was responsible for the purchase of light arms and assault rifles used by the JI's two paramilitary arms engaged in sectarian conflict in Indonesia starting in 1999. These were shipped to Poso, for Agus Dwikarna's Laskar Jundullah and for Abu Jibril's Laskar Mujahideen in Ambon.[23] The cell leader was an Indonesian, Fathur Rohman al-Ghozi, an Indonesian who had studied at Al Mukmin from 1984 to 1990 before going on to study in a Pakistani *madrassa*, where he was recruited into Jemaah Islamiya.

Mantiqi 4 was the smallest and least developed of the JI cells. It included northern Australia, which the JI leaders frequented to recruit and fund-raise from among the large population of Indonesian exiles there.[24]

The Fall of Suharto and the Jihad in the Malukus

The fall of Indonesian president Suharto in May 1998 created a radically changed political environment in the archipelago. The strongman's resignation left a weak democracy in which there was intense political competition between the new president and a Parliament that had a newfound and intense sense of empowerment. Strong central government control also broke down as the provinces clamored to redress the historical legacy of overcentralization and demanded more autonomy and revenue sharing. Suharto's fall had another important impact: hundreds of radical Muslim exiles, including Abdullah Sungkar and Abu Bakar Bashir, returned to Indonesia and demanded political space. They were encouraged by statements of political leaders that it was no longer tenable that the position and aspirations of all people and interests could be ignored. In mid-2000, Bashir established the Majelis Mujahideen of Indonesia (MMI). The group is ostensibly a civil society organization that tries to implement Sharia peacefully and through the democratic process.[25] Yet there is substantial evidence that the MMI is also a front for Abu Bakar Bashir's militant and terrorist activities as many MMI leaders are also JI members. For example, the MMI's board included Mohammed Iqbal Abdurrahman (Abu Jibril) and Agus Dwikarna; both headed JI's two paramilitary arms and both were members of the JI *shura*. The head of the fatwa council is Abdul Qadir Baraja. The MMI's director of daily operations is Irfan Suryahardy Awwas, the younger brother of Abu Jibril.

The MMI also serves as an important financial conduit, especially in getting foreign money to the very small radical groups which otherwise would be unable to network abroad. Much of al-Qaeda's funding is thought to come from charities, either unwittingly or intentionally siphoned off.

This is possible as al-Qaeda inserted top operatives in Southeast Asia into leadership positions in several charities.[26] Indonesian intelligence officials estimate that 15 to 20 percent of Islamic charity funds are diverted to politically motivated groups and terrorists. JI and al-Qaeda leaders assumed leadership positions, often becoming regional branch chiefs, or formed alliances with several important Saudi-backed charities, including MERC, the IIRO, and Al Haramain as well as an Indonesian charity that served as their counterpart or executing agency, KOMPAK.[27] The leadership of these charities in Indonesia is overlapping. For example, Agus Dwikarna, the fourth in command of the MMI, was the local representative of the Saudi charity Al Haramain in Makassar in south Sulawesi, which, one al-Qaeda official admitted, was the largest single source of al-Qaeda funds into Indonesia, and he was also a branch officer of KOMPAK.[28]

The turning point in JI's operations came in 1999 with the outbreak of sectarian conflict in the Malukus. In the late 1990s, Hambali and Abu Jibril were fund-raising furiously and focusing their efforts into putting together the JI's paramilitary arms, the Laskar Mujahideen and the Laskar Jundullah. It was through the membership in these organizations that JI would recruit many of its members. It cannot be emphasized enough what an important event the jihad in the Malukus and Poso was to the JI. Although there were local causes, the influx of some jihadis escalated the conflict to a new level. More important, the jihads in the Malukus and Poso were a formative experience for the participants. They were every bit as important as the jihad against the Soviets was in the 1980s, albeit to a smaller number of people. The Maluku conflict gave the members of the Laskar Jundullah, Laskar Mujahideen, and the much larger Laskar Jihad their taste of jihad. It whetted their appetites for more. Thousands of people were members of these groups and have now returned home, much the way the members of the G272 returned to Indonesia from Afghanistan in the late 1980s to early 1990s, ready to lead their own jihads to implement Sharia. Second, the conflict was manipulated and used by al-Qaeda to a much greater degree than anyone imagined at the time.

The Laskar Mujahideen was established in 1999 by Abu Jibril, who recruited among Indonesian exiles living in Malaysia who were inspired to return home to fight a holy war. Jibril first traveled to the Malukus in January 2000, leading several hundred jihadis, and introduced a centralized command structure and led attacks on Christian communities by high-speed boats. Though there were only some 500 Laskar Mujahideen fighters in the Malukus, they were far better armed and disciplined than the largest group of the Laskar Jihad, which fielded some 3,000 poorly armed and radical students, until they raided a police armory. Jibril's forces also liaised closely with al-Qaeda operatives who were funding and filming the Malukus crisis for propaganda and recruiting purposes.

The second JI paramilitary group, the Laskar Jundullah, a small militant organization that conducted "sweeps" of foreigners in Solo and was at the forefront of sectarian conflict in Poso, Sulawesi, was founded by Agus Dwikarna in October 2000.[29] It was the armed wing of Dwikarna's civil society organization, the Committee for Upholding Islamic Law in South Sulawesi, that was committed to implementing Sharia. Laskar Jundullah was funded by al-Qaeda through Omar al-Faruq and funds skimmed from the Saudi Al Haramain foundation, which Dwikarna headed. It also received funding from the charity KOMPAK, a branch office of which Dwikarna also headed.

These holy wars gave JI the network it needed, a core of members and supporters. It gave them a taste of jihad and served as a catalyst for radicalizing JI's behavior. The fact that the government did not curtail their activities only emboldened them. The role of al-Qaeda in the conflicts in the Malukus and Sulawesi was significant. For one thing, al-Qaeda provided significant funding for the paramilitaries. According to Darul Islam's Al Chaidar, Indonesian militant radicals "maintain contact with the international Mujahideen network, including Osama bin Laden's group."[30] "Wherever a jihad is in force, this network provides money and weapons and all [the] tools needed for the jihad, and they mobilize fighters to go to the jihad area," Mr. Chaidar said. "This is exactly what is happening in the Malukus. Osama bin Laden is one of those who have sent money and weapons to jihad fighters in the Malukus."[31] Second, the Maluku conflict served to attract radical Islamists from around the Muslim world. For example, seven Afghans arrived in Ambon on July 7, 2000, and were spirited away by Laskar Mujahideen forces. They joined some two hundred other Afghans, Pakistanis, and Malays.[32] Abu Abdul Aziz and one other bin Laden lieutenant were dispatched to Ambon at the height of the crisis, and Mohammed Atef visited the Malukus in June 2000. The Maluku crisis convinced al-Qaeda's leaders that the emphasis of their jihad in Southeast Asia should be shifted to Indonesia. To that end there was a flow of top al-Qaeda operatives to the region between 1999 and 2001.[33] They trained, funded, and armed JI militants, and established the financial infrastructure to make these groups self-sustaining.

The Back Office

Al-Qaeda saw the region first and foremost as a back office for their activities (especially to set up front companies, fund-raise, recruit, forge documents, and purchase weapons). Indeed, some of the aspects that made Southeast Asia so appealing to the al-Qaeda leadership in the first place was its network of Islamic charities, the spread of poorly regulated Islamic banks, business-friendly environments, and economies that already had records of extensive money laundering. It is my contention that al-Qaeda regarded Southeast Asia as a secondary theater for its activities, and the region became a theater of operations in its own right only later as its affiliate organization in Southeast Asia, the Jemaah Islamiya, developed its own capabilities.

Most alarming was the fact that, starting on January 5, 2000, there was a major meeting of key bin Laden lieutenants who for four days planned both the attack on the USS *Cole* in October 2000 and the September 11 hijacking as well as reviewed the failed millennium bombing attacks. Attendees at the meeting included two of the September 11 hijackers, Khalid al-Mihdhar and Nawaf al-Hazmi;[34] Tawfiq bin Atash (Khallad), who the FBI described as "the intermediary between bin Laden himself and the [USS *Cole*] attack planners" and "a key operative in Osama bin Laden's terrorist network"; Khalid Sheikh Mohammed; Ramzi bin al-Shibh, a close associate of September 11 leader Mohammed Atta and named as the missing twentieth hijacker;[35] Fahad al-Quso, responsible for the U.S. embassy attacks in East Africa; Ahmad Hikmat Shakir, an Iraqi al-Qaeda operative; and Riduan Isamuddin, a senior al-Qaeda leader in Southeast Asia and the operational chief of Jemaah Islamiya. By virtue of Malaysia being a predominantly Muslim country, it is easier for radicals and terrorists to fit in there. The FBI described—though later retracted for diplomatic reasons—Malaysia in January 2002 as a key springboard state for al-Qaeda operations, including the September 11 attack on the United States.

Evolving into a Terrorist Organization: The JI from 2000 to 2001

Such equivocation by the Indonesian government emboldened both the JI and al-Qaeda, who by 2000 had decided to escalate their operations to a new level. Although the JI was founded in 1993–94, it did not commit any known terrorist acts until 2000. Years of planning, training, and the confidence they gained in the Malukus and Poso emboldened them, and in 2000 they began to engage in terrorist attacks around the region. At that time the JI carried out operations according to their limited capabilities against soft targets with limited loss of human life.

Beginning in 2000 there was a spate of terrorist attacks around the region, though neither regional security services nor journalists nor academics ever linked the attacks at the time. The first attack was in July 2000, when a Jakarta mall was bombed by a Malaysian man. In August 2000, the Philippine ambassador to Indonesia was the target of a bombing. In December

2000, bombs were planted in thirty Indonesian churches in order to "spark a religious civil war in Indonesia."[36] The JI and the MILF engaged in joint operations, also in December 2000, when the light rail in Metro Manila was bombed. In April 2000, in Yala, Thailand, a train station and hotel were bombed by JI-linked militants.

For the most part these attacks were not overly successful. For example, in the case of the church bombings in Indonesia, JI operatives set thirty bombs, though only eighteen went off, killing fifteen people.[37] This was a far cry from their intended goal of killing thousands. These bombs were small and directed against soft targets. The fact that they tried to launch simultaneous bombings, an al-Qaeda hallmark, indicates a degree of sophistication. But these bombings gave JI members confidence, and as more JI operatives were recruited and trained in al-Qaeda camps in Afghanistan and the southern Philippines, and as their technical proficiency increased and the network became more developed, al-Qaeda and JI plotted larger-scale operations against harder targets. The JI, like its parent organization al-Qaeda, always placed a very high premium on education and training. JI operatives were very important support personnel in al-Qaeda operations in Southeast Asia. The first case was in mid-2000, when JI members helped a six-man Yemeni team plan the truck bombing of the U.S. embassy in Jakarta, though the attack was thwarted (see note 14).

Following the September 11, 2001, attacks on the United States, al-Qaeda was planning a series of spectacular attacks against U.S. interests across the region.[38] In August 2001, a young Canadian-Kuwaiti al-Qaeda recruit, Mohammed Mansour Jabarah, was dispatched to the Philippines to prepare an attack on the U.S. embassy in Manila, which was called off as the embassy was sufficiently far from the road that a truck bomb would not damage it. He was then sent to identify targets in Singapore. Video footage was taken and reviewed by Hambali in Kuala Lumpur and then later found in the wreckage of Mohammed Atef's house in Kabul, Afghanistan. In all, seven targets within Singapore were chosen: the U.S. Embassy, the British High Commission, the Israeli embassy, and several office towers owned or occupied by U.S. firms.[39]

Malaysian and Singaporean security officials were able to arrest many suspects in late 2001, including several members of the JI *shura*. While officials in Singapore and Malaysia were confident that they had eradicated much of the senior Jemaah Islamiya leadership in their own countries, both expressed tremendous frustration about the lack of cooperation that they received from Indonesian authorities. Most JI fugitives were known to have left for Indonesia, but little assistance was provided. Although Abu Bakar Bashir was named by both Malaysia and Singapore as a prime suspect and a leader of the Jemaah Islamiya network, he continued to live and preach openly until October 2002, following the Bali attacks. Although Bashir was brought in for questioning on January 24, 2002, he was released the next day. He acknowledged teaching thirteen of those detained in Malaysia, Singapore, and the Philippines. Bashir denied being a member of al-Qaeda: "I am not a member of al Qaeda, but I really respect the struggle of Osama bin Laden, who has bravely represented the world's Muslims in their fight against the arrogant United States of America and their allies." Following the arrest of a senior al-Qaeda operative in Indonesia, Omar al-Faruq, in the summer of 2002, there was further evidence linking Bashir to terrorist operations.[40] The Indonesian government, under pressure from the Americans and its neighbors, announced that it would "carry out an investigation" of Bashir, but went on to say that it would "not arrest Abu Bakar just because foreign governments have their suspicions of him."[41] The Indonesians distrusted the CIA report and resented American pressure, and there was considerable popular and political pressure to stand up to the United States.

Leading operatives met in Bangkok in January 2002, where they received orders to attack soft targets: tourist venues that would target Westerners.[42] The result of the meeting was played out in October 2002 with the simultaneous bombings of two nightclubs in the tourist district of Bali.[43] It was al-Qaeda's second-most-deadly attack after the 9/11 attacks on the United States. Two hundred and two people were killed, nearly half of them Australian holidaymakers, provoking an immediate and firm response from the Australian government, which dispatched a large team of Australian Federal Police investigators. In addition, investigators from Japan, the United Kingdom, Germany, France, and the U.S. Federal Bureau of Investigation provided much-needed technical assistance and put intense pressure on the Indonesians.

The Bali attack finally galvanized the Indonesian leadership to begin the war on terror. It was only after the October 12 Bali attack that the Indonesian government had the conviction to arrest Bashir. Although he was linked to the church bombings in 2000, to date he has not been officially linked to the Bali attack and tried under a post-9/11 antiterrorism bill.[44]

The Rabitatul Mujahideen

The senior-most al-Qaeda leader in Southeast Asia, Omar al-Faruq, has admitted in interrogation that Jemaah Islamiya had tried to establish links with Muslim militants in Thailand and Myanmar.[45] In 1999, Abu Bakar Bashir established a coordinating body, known as the Rabitatul Mujahideen (RM). RM was erroneously first described by CNN as the armed wing of the Jemaah Islamiya, but in reality, it was simply a group of JI/MMI officials meeting with other regional militants.

There have never been strong ties between the Muslim insurgency in southern Thailand and international terrorist groups. Though militants in southern Thailand have long been a fact of life, for the most part they have given up their campaign to create an independent homeland. In late April 2004, clashes between Thai security forces and armed groups in southern Thailand resulted in more than one hundred deaths; this prompted speculation that local Muslim unrest was potentially linked to regional or transnational jihadi groups. However, as of this writing, such linkage has not been clearly established. Nevertheless, it is clear that some militants in southern Thailand have worked as logistics operatives for Acehnese rebels and the MILF, serving as an important financial and arms conduit. It is clear that al-Qaeda operatives have used Thailand as a base of operations for nearly a decade. Ramzi Yousef and many other al-Qaeda operatives have passed through Thailand. After the September 11 attacks, Thai supreme commander General Surayud Chulanond admitted that its military intelligence was monitoring a "small number" of bin Laden operatives in Thailand and that the government was cognizant of "countries in the Middle East provid[ing] training, education and financial support for fundamentalist groups in the south [of Thailand]."[46]

There are two very small Thai groups, the Wae Ka Raeh (WKR) and the Guragan Mujahideen Islam Pattani, that are thought to have some ties with Jemaah Islamiya and al-Qaeda; and the head of the WKR fought with the Mujahideen in Afghanistan. For the most part, however, they are criminal gangs. The WKR is thought to earn 10 million baht (Bt) a year in contract killings and "enforcement."[47] It is evident from the confessions of Omar al-Faruq that the JI was rapidly trying to expand its contacts with the Guragan Mujahideen. Yet, the Guragan Mujahideen remains a small and poorly funded organization with only about a hundred members. Another Thai-Muslim militant group, the Pattani United Liberation Organization (PULO), is suspected of having ties with the Abu Sayyaf.

There is little information about the al-Qaeda network in Myanmar, but its nationals have been identified as al-Qaeda terrorists. Indeed, the largest al-Qaeda cell in Southeast Asia is said to be in Myanmar, although Myanmar's links are much closer to al-Qaeda networks in South Asia. Myanmar does not offer terrorists the infrastructure they need, especially the ability to set up front companies and nongovernmental organizations (NGOs), nor is it a travel hub. Even if that is an overestimation, there are a few disturbing signs. Al-Qaeda has long been established in neighboring Bangladesh, where thousands of Muslims from Myanmar have taken refuge from the Myanmar military government's systematic repression of its Muslim ethnic minorities, the Bengalis, Rohingas, and Kachins. Muslims account for roughly 4 percent of Myanmar's population. Currently, there are three Muslim-based guerrilla movements in Myanmar: the Ommat Liberation Front, the Kawthoolei Muslim Liberation Front, and the Muslim Liberation Organization of Burma. The government has waged a harsh counterinsurgency campaign against these groups and has at times tacitly supported local militias to engage in communal violence against local Muslims.

Finally, we need to raise an issue that is truly demanding of further study, the JI's relationship to al-Qaeda cells in Bangladesh. In Bangladesh, the radical Harkat-ul-Jihad-al-Islami (HuJI), founded in 1992, is led by an associate of Osama bin Laden, Fazlul Rahman. The organization is closely tied to one of the al-Qaeda–linked groups in Pakistan/Kashmir. Fazlul Rahman signed Osama bin Laden's February 23, 1998, declaration of holy war against the United States. Harkat has recruited from Bangladesh's 60,000 *madrassas* and is now believed to have over fifteen thousand followers. HuJI was implicated in scores of bombings, including two attempted assassinations of then–prime minister Sheikh Hasina in July 2000. HuJI has also been increasingly involved in politics in Bangladesh. Its slogan, "We will all be Taliban and Bangladesh will be Afghanistan," belies its political agenda. Though it is not a political party, many of its members are part of Islamic Oikya Jote, which was one of two Islamic parties (the other being Jamaat-e-Islami) that joined into a coalition government with Prime Minister Begum Khaleda Zia's Bangladesh Nationalist Party (BNP) in October 2001. Both Islamic parties have a history of links to terrorist organizations and openly supported the Taliban and al-Qaeda.[48]

Fazlul Rahman's HuJI also actively recruited Burmese Rohingas and sent them to fight in Kashmir, Afghanistan, and Chechnya.[49] There are some two hundred thousand Rohingas in Bangladesh. The largest Rohingi organization in Bangladesh is the Rohingya Solidarity Organization (RSO), established in the early 1980s, which has a large training camp in Ukhia, southeast of Cox's Bazaar. This militant group has actively recruited from among the destitute community and in the 1980s sent volunteers to Afghanistan to fight the Soviets. Bertil Lintner found that the RSO had maintained close links and received material support from other South Asian militant organizations including the Hizb-e-Islami in Afghanistan, the Hizb-ul-Mujahideen in Kashmir, and the Jamaat-e-Islami in Bangladesh.[50] Over a hundred RSO fighters trained with the Hizb-e-Islami in Afghanistan, and Afghan trainers have come to RSO camps, which in the 1990s were taken over by Fazlul Rahman's HuJI.

On December 21, 2001, a ship, the MV *Mecca,* off-loaded some 150 Taliban and al-Qaeda fighters at the Bangladeshi port of Chittagong. "Portworkers that night said they saw five motor launches ferry in large groups of men from the boat wearing black turbans, long beards and traditional Islamic *salwar kameez.* Their towering height suggested these travelers were foreigners, and the boxes of ammunition and the AK-47s slung across their shoulders helped sketch a sinister picture."[51] HuJI officials later confirmed that the men were al-Qaeda fighters. On October 7, 2002, the Indian government arrested a Burmese-born HuJI operative, Fazle Karim (Abu Fuzi) as he arrived in Calcutta by train from Kashmir. The government arrested four Yemenis, an Algerian, a Libyan, and a Sudanese who were implicated in militant arms training at a *madrassa* in the capital run by the Saudi charity Al Haramain, which was also raided by intelligence forces. They were all later released, and the government stated that no incriminating evidence was found at the Al Haramain office, but concern remains that Bangladesh is becoming increasingly important to al-Qaeda. Bangladesh's military intelligence service maintains very close ties with its counterparts in Pakistan's Inter-Services Intelligence and has a history of providing operational support for Kashmiri rebels. Indeed, the port workers who saw the *Mecca* arrive claim that the man who greeted the militants was a major in the military intelligence service.

The JI's attempt to form alliances with other radical groups in the region, the Rabitatul Mujahideen, included the Rohinga Solidarity Organization. Moreover, there is a growing body of evidence that JI members, including Hambali, have sought refuge in Bangladesh, whose government has done little to crack down on the militants.

A Shared Worldview

In addition to al-Qaeda–linked organizations are many others that share the same worldview. Laskar Jihad is one of the best examples of al-Qaeda's influence and its ability to find common cause. Although there is considerable suspicion that the Laskar Jihad is linked to al-Qaeda, there is nothing more than circumstantial evidence to support it. Laskar Jihad was founded in January 2000 at a Yogyakarta football stadium. Jafar Umar Thalib was able to mobilize a small army to wage a jihad in the Maluku Islands. Arguing that there was an international campaign to create a Christian republic in the heart of Indonesia, by May he sent several hundred fighters to the Malukus armed with machetes and crude weapons "so that they could feel safe in their own country."[52] Not by coincidence, Osama bin Laden had mentioned East Timor in his 1998 fatwa, and there was a shared sense that never could the radical Muslims allow an Islamic state to be broken up. This explains the ferocity of the fighting in the Malukus. The influx of the Laskar Jihad paramilitary tipped the balance in favor of the Muslims,[53] and shortly thereafter Christians were ethnically cleansed from Ternate, the North Maluku capital. In all some nine thousand people died in the Maluku strife.

As noted earlier, the Maluku conflict attracted Islamists from around the Muslim world. When seven Afghans arrived in Ambon on July 7, 2000, they were welcomed and spirited away by Laskar Mujahideen forces. They joined a contingent of other Afghanis, Pakistanis, and Malays. But it is not just individuals, but financial support. According to Darul Islam's Al Chaidar, "They maintain contact with the international Mujahideen network, including Osama bin Laden's group."[54] "Wherever a *jihad* is in force, this network provides money and weapons and all tools needed for the *jihad,* and they mobilize fighters to go to the *jihad* area," Mr. Chaidar said. "This is exactly what is happening in the Malukus. Osama bin Laden is one of those who have sent money and weapons to *jihad* fighters in the Malukus."[55] Abu Abdul Aziz and one other bin Laden lieutenant were dispatched to Ambon at the height of the Laskar Jihad's jihad.

Bin Laden, who met Thalib in 1987, offered funding for Laskar Jihad but Thalib turned it down, though the Ambonese Laskar Mujahideen did not.[56] Thalib explains that he turned it down because he questioned bin Laden's piety. Indeed, there is evidence that much of the Laskar Jihad's funding came from within the Indonesian army (TNI).

Laskar Jihad, however, is unclear about its funding. The author has witnessed fund-raising members shaking people down in the streets of central and eastern Java. Yet Laskar Jihad's Web page provides details about an account at the Bank of Central Asia, Indonesia's largest bank, to which wire transfers can be made from anywhere in the world. One Laskar Jihad fundraiser stated in an interview that the average donation is about RP70,000 ($6.60), about half the cost of sending a fighter to the Malukus.

While there is sufficient evidence that much of the original funding for the Laskar Jihad forces came from rogue elements of the TNI, increasingly there is evidence that Thalib's assertion that the Laskar Jihad is a homegrown, locally funded movement is a sheer lie, and that his organization exists because of covert aid from Islamists outside of Indonesia and the al-Qaeda network.

In the immediate aftermath of the September 11 attacks, the Indonesian government put an inordinate amount of pressure on the country's most visible Islamic extremist group, the Laskar Jihad, to not take advantage of the attacks and mobilize its supporters for a jihad against the Americans. The military increased its presence in the Maluku Islands, where Laskar Jihad supported sectarian violence that killed some nine thousand people. And the Laskar Jihad leader, Jafar Umar Thalib, went to great pains to distance himself from bin Laden and the al-Qaeda network, though he had never previously done so. "Laskar Jihad does not have ties with al-Qaeda or any other organizations that are associated with Osama bin Laden or any form or part of his network. Lasker Jihad distances itself from Osama bin Laden and his followers."[57] And Thalib has suddenly gone out of his way to distance himself from bin Laden, now asserting that bin Laden is "very empty about the knowledge of religion."[58]

Yet Thalib has acknowledged that he maintains links with Malaysia's Kumpulan Mujahideen (KMM), and Thalib has coordinated his operations in Indonesia with Abu Bakar Bashir. Indeed, the Laskar Jihad attends and is a member of Bashir's umbrella organization, the Mujahideen Council of Indonesia. There is evidence that Laskar Jihad forces were involved in street fights with JI's paramilitary groups, the Laskar Jundullah and Laskar Mujahideen.

On October 16, 2002, days after the terrorist bomb attack in Bali, the Laskar Jihad announced that it was disbanding. This announcement should be met with considerable suspicion and seen as a PR tactic. The Laskar Jihad knows when to lay low. Following 9/11, they were one of the most reticent Islamic groups in the country. Now they understand the political liability of being "Islamic fundamentalists." They made a show of withdrawing some three hundred troops from Ambon, though this was just a fraction of the total number there. Even if they disband their paramilitary, the parent organization, the Forum Komunikasi wal Sunnah wal Jamaah, will not be disbanded. They have offices in seventy cities around the country. They operate several large *madrassas* and other organizations that espouse an intolerant brand of Salafi and Wahhabi Islam. Indeed, Thalib announced that he wanted to focus on his students.[59] The Forum Komunikasi owns businesses, fund-raises, and publishes a weekly newspaper. They are not going to relinquish this critical infrastructure even if they disband some of their paramilitary. They will lay low, rename themselves, and reemerge, bringing jihad, intolerance, and sectarian violence.

The fact is, the Laskar Jihad and al-Qaeda share a similar worldview: a sense of persecution against Muslims and a commitment to jihad. The Laskar Jihad may not be a constituent of al-Qaeda, but that does not mean that its members do not have a shared ideology or are not susceptible to al-Qaeda's calls for action and propaganda.

Conclusion

One of the things that al-Qaeda has managed to do so successfully in Southeast Asia has been to graft onto or co-opt preexisting radicals, radical movements, and groups. This raises two large and disturbing issues. The first is, at what point do parochial radicals, who had otherwise been concerned with a localized political grievance, become internationalists? At what point did they take their struggle to the next, higher, level? And how did that process occur? One thing is clear, the radicals across Southeast Asia seek to link their jihad to the global jihad against the Americans. They seek to bring Southeast Asia from the "Islamic periphery" into the Islamic core, and to that end are taking advantage of the growing piousness and Islamic manifestations and identifications in the region.

The second issue is, in what way did being linked to an organization such as al-Qaeda affect a movement such as the MILF, which otherwise enjoys considerable popular support and has a high degree of political legitimacy? Does it move away from a national liberation group when it crosses the line and engages in, or supports, international terrorism? At what point are their own goals subjugated to the patron's goals?

Notes

A paper that covers such a range of complex issues in so many countries is only the result of the time, assistance, and knowledge of many people. Most of the government officials whom I interviewed and spoke with requested anonymity. They hail from the United States, Australia, Canada, Singapore, Malaysia, Indonesia, the Philippines, Brunei, Thailand, Switzerland, and Germany. They know who they are and how grateful I am for their assistance. I would also like to thank members of the MILF, the MMI, Jemaah Islamiya, and their supporters for their insights. For a more comprehensive analysis, please see *Militant Islam in Southeast Asia: Crucible of Terror,* by Zachary Abuza. Copyright © 2003 by Lynne Rienner Publishers.

1. John Arquilla, David Ronfeldt, and Michele Zanini, "Networks, Netwar, and Information-Age Terrorism," in *Countering the New Terrorism,* ed. Ian O. Lesser et al. (Washington, DC: RAND Corporation, 1999), p. 49.

2. Ibid.

3. Richard Engel, "Inside Al-Qaeda: A Window into the World of Militant Islam and the Afghani Alumni," *Jane's Online,* September 28, 2001.

4. Peter Ford, "Al Qaeda's Veil Begins to Lift," *Christian Science Monitor,* December 20, 2001.

5. Interview with a colonel in the PNP-PSG, Makati, Philippines, January 15, 2002; Department of the Interior and Local Government, "Country Report of the Republic of the Philippines" (paper presented at the International Conference on Counterterrorism, Baguio City, Philippines, February 18–21, 1996), p. 5.

6. Department of the Interior and Local Government, "Country Report of the Republic of the Philippines," p. 6.

7. Christine Herrera, "Bin Laden Funds Abu Sayyaf Through Muslim Relief Group," *Philippine Daily Inquirer,* August 9, 2000.

8. Ibid.

9. Darul Islam was a Muslim-based guerrilla force that fought both the Dutch and the secular-nationalist forces of Sukarno, arguing that Sukarno's guerrillas were as much an enemy as the Dutch: "By rejecting Islam as the sole foundation of the state, [the government] had made itself as evil an enemy as the Dutch." This period became known as the "triangular war," after Kartosuwiryo established a secessionist Islamic state in West Java on August 7, 1949. Support spread to central Java, Aceh, and south

Sulawesi. The Darul Islam rebellion lasted until 1962, when its leader was captured and executed and the movement was driven underground. The Darul Islam organization exists to this day, and in many ways it operates much the way the Muslim Brotherhood operates in Anwar Sadat's Egypt. Though it is still an illegal organization, it is more or less tolerated, and members run for political office on the tickets of other parties. For more, see Adam Schwartz, *A Nation in Waiting: Indonesia in the 1990s* (Boulder, CO: Westview, 1994), p. 169.

10. Edy Budiyarso, "Indonesia's Afghan-Trained Mujiheddin," *Tempo,* October 2–8, 2001.

11. "Suharto's Detect, Defect, and Destroy Policy Towards the Islamic Movement," interview with Abdullah Sungkar, *Nida'ul Islam,* February–March 1997.

12. Mark Freeman, and Richard C. Paddock, "Response to Terror: Indonesia Cleric Tied to '95 Anti-US Plot," *Los Angeles Times,* February 7, 2002. This was confirmed in a CIA response to Philippine queries and can be found as an addendum to Philippine National Police, *After Intelligence Operations Report,* Camp Crame, Quezon City, Philippines, February 27, 1995.

13. Indictment of Abu Bakar Bashir, Office of the Attorney General, Republic of Indonesia, April 2003.

14. The United States came across diagrams and blueprints detailing the U.S. embassy and its security regimen from a terrorist suspect in the Middle East. When U.S. intelligence discovered that the six-member team was being dispatched to Surabaya, U.S. ambassador Robert S. Gelbard went to the Indonesian intelligence services to arrest the six Yemenis. Indonesian military intelligence, however, brought in local police to do the arrest, because it was a law enforcement issue. Although the United States had already flown in two CIA officials to assist in the arrest and a plane to take the Yemenis to America, they were tipped off and fled the country. Interview with a retired U.S. State Department official, October 27, 2002.

15. Classified interrogation report of Faiz bin Abu Bakar Bafana, Singapore 2002. Also see transcripts of Bafana's video testimony in the trial of Abu Bakar Bashir, June 26, 2003; Indictment of Abu Bakar Bashir, Office of the Attorney General, Republic of Indonesia, April 2003.

16. Indictment of Abu Bakar Bashir, Office of the Attorney General, Republic of Indonesia, April 2003.

17. AP, "KL Arrest Prime Terror Suspect," September 27, 2002.

18. Ministry of Home Affairs, *White Paper: The Jemaah Islamiyah Arrests and the Threat of Terrorism* (Singapore, 2003), p. 6.

19. "Indictment Chronicles 'Overt Acts' That It Said Led to Sept. 11 Attacks," *New York Times,* December 12, 2001, p. B6.

20. Ministry of Home Affairs, *White Paper: The Jemaah Islamiyah Arrests,* p. 6.

21. Romesh Ratnesar, "Confessions of an Al Qaeda Terrorist," Time, September 16, 2002; BIN Interrogation Report of Omar al-Faruq (June 2002).

22. Republic of the Philippines, National Intelligence Coordinating Agency, "An Update on the Recent Bombings in Mindanao and Metro Manila" (Quezon City, November 25, 2002).

23. Fathur Rohman al-Ghozi, written deposition, July 2002.

24. For new revelations on the extent of JI's penetration of Australia, see Sally Neighbour, "The Australian Connections," Australian Broadcast Corporation, aired on June 9, 2003.

25. "The MMI is an institution where a lot of people from a lot of Muslim groups

including the NU and Muhammadiyah gather at one table to discuss how to get our vision of Sharia implemented into national laws. . . . The long-term strategy is to get Indonesia 100 percent based on Sharia. As long as Muslims are the majority, the country should be ruled by Sharia." Interview with Abu Bakar Bashir, Ngruki, Solo, June 11, 2002.

26. Baden Intellijen Negara, "Interrogation Report of Omar al-Faruq" (Jakarta, June 2002).

27. KOMPAK officials, while acknowledging that they operate in regions struck by sectarian conflict (Aceh, Poso, the Malukus, and Bangunan Beton, Sumatra), assert they are there to alleviate the crises and provide necessary relief. They denied any links to "jihad activities." Interview with Dr. H. Asep R. Jayanegara, Secretary, Komite Penanggulangan Krisis, Dewan Dakwah Islam Indonesia, Jakarta, January 8, 2003.

28. BIN Interrogation Report of Omar al-Faruq (June 2002). The office was in Makassar, Sulawesi. Also see Romesh Ratnesar, "Confessions of an Al Qaeda Terrorist," *Time*, September 23, 2003, pp. 34–41.

29. Six foreigners (two Afghans, two Pakistanis, and two Arabs) were detained. The six were thought to be al-Qaeda operatives who conducted training of Laskar Jundullah and other al-Qaeda members in the camp in Poso. The police initially refuted the report, calling the six men "tourists." A.M. Hendropriyono, head of the State Intelligence Service, acknowledged that it was not just a Laskar Jihad or Laskar Jundullah base: "The training site was not used by Indonesians, but by foreigners . . . while those who are involved in the conflict in Poso are Indonesians against fellow Indonesians, Muslims against Christians." Hendropriyono stated unequivocally that "Poso has been used by international terrorist groups to support activities they plan from outside the country." An Indonesian National Intelligence Body (BIN) report, *Al Qaeda Infrastructure in Indonesia,* stated clearly that: "The training camp led by Omar Bandon consisted of 8–10 small villages located side by side on the beach, equipped with light weapons, explosives, and firing range. Participants of the training are not only from local people but also from overseas. The instructor of physical training in the camp is Parlindungan Siregar, a member of al-Qaeda's network in Spain." For more see Marianne Kearney, "Security Forces to Disarm Sulawesi Fighters," *Straits Times,* December 6, 2001; Fabiola Desy Unidjaja, "International Training Camp in Poso 'Empty,'" *Jakarta Post (JP)* December 14, 2001; Fabiola Desy Unidjaja, "Government Ready to Impose a State of Emergency in Poso Town," *JP,* December 5, 2001; Fabiola Desy Unidjaja, "State of Emergency in Poso on Hold: Police," *JP,* December 8, 2001; Baden Intellijen Negara, *Al Qaeda's Infrastructure in Indonesia,* Jakarta, February 2002.

30. Lindsay Murdoch, "Bin Laden 'Funded Christian Haters,'" *Sydney Morning Herald (SMH),* September 28, 2001.

31. Ibid.

32. Interview with a BIN official, Jakarta, January 17, 2003.

33. Baden Intellijen Negara, *Al Qaeda's Infrastructure in Indonesia,* Jakarta, February 2002.

34. After the meeting, Malaysian intelligence followed al-Mihdhar and al-Hazmi, and searched the hard drives of computers they had used, but did not have any evidence to arrest them. After the meeting, al-Mihdhar and al-Hazmi left Malaysia and flew to Los Angeles via Bangkok, Thailand, and Hong Kong respectively on January 15, 2000. They lived openly and enrolled in a San Diego–area flight school, using their real names. The Malaysian intelligence service obviously shared the surveil-

lance videotape and photos with the CIA. Although the CIA knew that al-Mihdhar had a multiple-entry visa to the United States, they did not put him on a terrorist watch list or inform the INS or State Department. Indeed, al-Mihdhar was able to leave the country for Frankfurt, Germany, on June 10, where he played a role in the October 12 attack on the USS *Cole*, while al-Hazmi applied to extend his visa on July 7, 2001. Following the attack on the USS *Cole*, Khallad was under intense investigation, and on January 4 he was named as a key planner of the attacks. In July 2001 a CIA officer assigned to the FBI rediscovered a CIA cable that detailed Khallad's presence at the Kuala Lumpur meeting and sent an e-mail to the CIA's counterterrorism center: "This is a major league killer, who orchestrated the Cole attack and possibly the [1998 East] Africa bombings." The FBI discovered that al-Mihdhar had reentered the country on July 4, 2001. The CIA put al-Mihdhar and al-Hazmi on its "terrorist watch list," but only on August 21, eighteen months after the Kuala Lumpur meeting, causing a huge scandal in the United States. According to recent congressional testimony, the CIA learned that the two were in the United States in March 2000 but did not inform the FBI. According to Eleanor Hill, a staff director of the Joint Congressional Inquiry, who testified on September 19, 2002, "Unfortunately, none of these things happened. The failure to watchlist al-Mihdhar and al-Hazmi or, at a minimum, to advise the FBI of their travel to the United States, is perhaps even more puzzling because it occurred shortly after the peak of the intelligence community alertness to possible millennium-related terrorist attacks." When the INS was eventually informed, it was too late—the two were already in the United States. The FBI began looking for the two immediately, but were unable to find them. A New York–based FBI agent requested his superiors on August 29, 2001, to allow "full criminal investigative resources" to find al-Mihdhar. The request was denied as al-Mihdhar was not under criminal investigation. The frustrated agent replied: "Someday someone will die—and wall or not—the public will not understand why we were not more effective and throwing every resource we had at certain 'problems.'" After the World Trade Center was struck, when the FBI agent reviewed the passenger manifests from the four hijacked planes, he told the Joint Congressional Inquiry that he yelled angrily: "This is the same al Mihdhar we've been talking about for three months!" His supervisor, replied: "We did everything by the book."

35. Ramzi bin al-Shibh, a Yemeni who was named as the "missing twentieth hijacker," had tried to enter the United States four times but was denied a visa. Like his roommate Mohammed Atta, bin al-Shibh attended Al Quds Mosque in Hamburg, Germany, where they were recruited by a Syrian-German, Mohammed Haydar Zammar, and then put in touch with Khalid Sheikh Mohammed, who came to Hamburg in early 1999 and sent them to Afghanistan for training that same year. Bin al-Shibh was related by marriage to one of the hijackers, Khalid al-Mihdhar, the pilot of the hijacked plane that crashed in Pennsylvania, and another 9/11 hijacker, Ziad al-Jarrah, tried to enroll bin al-Shibh into the Florida Flight Training Center in Venice, Florida. Between August and September 2000, bin al-Shibh was in his native Yemen, which investigators believe also links him to the October 2000 attack on the USS *Cole*. Unable to enter the United States, bin al-Shibh remained an important planner and financial backer of Atta. The two attended a meeting in Spain in July 2001 with a senior al-Qaeda official to go over the last details of the September 11 attack before Atta left for the United States. Bin al-Shibh wired $6,200 to Marwan al-Shehhi and $14,000 to Zaccarias Moussaoui, the French Moroccan who was thought to be the twentieth hijacker, to pay for his flight training. Bin al-Shibh fled Germany on Sep-

tember 5, traveling via Spain to Pakistan. He was one of the most wanted terrorists, as he had attended both the Kuala Lumpur and Madrid meetings, and was captured in a shootout in Karachi, Pakistan, on September 11, 2002.

36. Ratnesar, "Confessions of an Al Qaeda Terrorist," pp. 34–41; also see the transcripts of Bafana's video testimony in the trial of Abu Bakar Bashir, June 26, 2003.

37. Indictment of Abu Bakar Bashir, Office of the Attorney General, Republic of Indonesia, April 2003.

38. Canadian Secret Intelligence Service, "Interrogation Report of Mohammed Mansour Jabarah," (2002); Baden Intellijen Negara, "Interrogation Report of Omar al-Faruq" (Jakarta, June 2002).

39. Ministry of Home Affairs, *White Paper: The Jemaah Islamiyah Arrests*, p. 27.

40. Central Intelligence Agency, "Terrorist Connections of Abubakar Basyir; and Further Details, Connections, and Activities of Umar Faruq" (September 2002).

41. "Government to Investigate Abu Bakar Bashir's Alleged Involvement in Terrorist Network," *Tempo*, September 18, 2002.

42. Canadian Secret Intelligence Service, "Interrogation Report of Mohammed Mansour Jabarah" (2002).

43. Indictment of Abu Bakar Bashir, Office of the Attorney General, Republic of Indonesia, April 2003; indictment of Ali Ghufron, alias Mukhlas, Denpassar Office of the Counsel of the Prosecution of Justice, Republic of Indonesia, June 2, 2003; indictment of Abdul Aziz, alias Imam Samudra, Denpassar Office of the Counsel of the Prosecution of Justice, Republic of Indonesia, May 20, 2003.

44. Indictment of Abu Bakar Bashir, Office of the Attorney General, Republic of Indonesia, April 2003.

45. Ratnesar, "Confessions of an Al Qaeda Terrorist"; BIN Interrogation Report of Omar al-Faruq (June 2002).

46. John McBeth, "The Danger Within," *Far Eastern Economic Review* (September 27, 2001): 21.

47. "Muslim Group Linked to Attacks in Thailand," *Straits Times*, March 25, 2002.

48. Alex Perry, "Deadly Cargo," Time Asia, October 21, 2002.

49. Bertil Lintner, "A Recipe for Trouble," *Far Eastern Economic Review (FEER)* (April 4, 2002): 17; and Lintner, "A Cocoon of Terror," *FEER* (April 4, 2002): 14–17.

50. Bertil Lintner "Championing Islamist Extremism," *South Asia Intelligence Review* 1, no. 9 (September 16, 2002).

51. Perry, "Deadly Cargo."

52. Dan Murphy, "Indonesia's Far-Flung 'Holy War,'" *Christian Science Monitor*, August 23, 2000.

53. "Indonesia: Overcoming Murder and Chaos in Maluku," ICG Asia Report No. 10 (December 2000).

54. "Waiting for Osama's Blessing," *Tempo*, September 18–24, 2001.

55. Ibid.

56. Ibid.

57. http://www.laskarjihad.org.

58. Warren Caragata, "Radical Blasts: Megawati wants to reassure the U.S. of her support, but growing Islamic opposition at home puts her in a bind," *Asiaweek*, October 5, 2001.

59. Interview with Jafar Umar Thalib, Jakarta, January 10, 2002.

4

Understanding al-Qaeda and Its Network in Southeast Asia

Rohan Gunaratna

Al-Qaeda al-Sulbah—now renamed al-Qaeda al-Jihad—is the first multi-national terrorist group of the twenty-first century. While past and present terrorist groups recruited from one single nationality and limited their campaigns to recover one single territory,[1] al-Qaeda is waging a global jihad with the United States of America and its allies and friends as its primary enemy.[2] Through its umbrella organization—the World Islamic Front for Jihad Against the Jews and the Crusaders, al-Qaeda is waging multiple campaigns both against the West and Muslim regimes friendly to the West. Prior to the U.S. intervention in Afghanistan in October 2001, al-Qaeda enjoyed a core force of 3,000–4,000 members[3] and linkages with two dozen Islamist groups worldwide such as the Moro Islamic Liberation Front (MILF) in Southeast Asia, the Islamic Movement of Uzbekistan (IMU) in Central Asia, and the Salafist Group for Call and Combat (GSPC) in North Africa.[4]

While based in Pakistan (1988–91), Sudan (1991–96), and Afghanistan (1996–2001), al-Qaeda was able to build a state-of-the-art global network for moving funds, goods, and personnel in order to attack its targets. Driven by the ideal of a universal jihad, al-Qaeda has been able to radicalize and mobilize adherents all over the world. As a group with a global reach, having a multidimensional character and possessing a multinational composition, al-Qaeda presents a new kind of threat hitherto unimagined by counter-terrorism practitioners and security and intelligence professionals alike. For instance, al-Qaeda's operational code forbade subscription to a universal code. Code words, generally established by the individual cells, were periodically changed. For example, some code words used in Asia were: Market = Malaysia; Soup = Singapore; Terminal = Indonesia; Hotel = Philippines; Book = Passport; and White Meat = American.[5]

Al-Qaeda tactics and targeting reflect its sophistication as a terrorist group. After the East Africa bombing—a land suicide attack on a U.S. diplomatic target—the U.S. security community strengthened the security of all U.S. missions overseas. However, instead of another land suicide operation, al-Qaeda mounted a seaborne suicide operation. After al-Qaeda attacked the USS *Cole* in October 2000, the U.S. security community invested in preventing another land or maritime attack by strengthening its perimeter security. However, al-Qaeda evaded security measures and struck one of America's most outstanding landmarks on 9/11. Thereafter, al-Qaeda planned to strike the United States once more with a radiological dispersal device and the organization allegedly turned to Jose Padilla, an American Muslim, to accomplish the task. The operation was disrupted at the reconnaissance stage in mid-2002.

In the world of terrorism, al-Qaeda has set new standards. With al-Qaeda increasing the threshold for attacks from hundreds to thousands, some existing and emerging groups will seek to match it or even exceed it by conducting mass casualty attacks using both conventional and unconventional means. As an Islamist group, the responsibility of the members is only to Allah, and as such the group engages in long-term planning and preparation and regard human and material losses as temporary setbacks. In keeping with al-Qaeda's "losing and learning" doctrine, if it succeeds in rebuilding its capability, and the target it failed to acquire is once again vulnerable, the group is likely to attack the target again.[6] As al-Qaeda has also effectively demonstrated, current and future terrorist groups are likely to use civilian infrastructure—from airplanes to commercially available fertilizer or chemicals—to attack infrastructure and human targets.

When the Palestinian-Jordanian sheikh Dr. Abdullah Azzam and his Saudi protégé, Deputy Osama bin Laden, founded the Maktab al-Khidmat lil-Mujahideen al-Arab (MaK; Afghan Service Bureau) in 1984 and al-Qaeda in 1988,[7] they set these organizations very lofty goals. While MaK aimed to defeat both the Soviet military, the largest land army in the world, and communism as an ideology, al-Qaeda sought to destroy the United States and defeat capitalism as an ideology. In its founding charter, al-Qaeda was designated to play the role of a "pioneering vanguard" or be the "spearhead" of Islamist movements.[8] Because of its obligation to inspire, instigate, and show the way to other groups and the community, al-Qaeda's preference is to attack strategic targets by usually resorting to suicide attacks (martyrdom operations). In addition, to strengthen Islamist movements worldwide, al-Qaeda, together with its former host—the Islamic Movement of Taliban, the de facto government of the Islamic Emirate of Afghanistan—trained several tens of thousands of Muslims all over the world until the U.S. intervention in Afghanistan in October 2001.

Decentralization

Al-Qaeda's training infrastructure has gravely suffered as a result of the U.S. campaign in Afghanistan. Except for the first three months of the confrontation, there have not been signs of mass desertions from the Taliban or al-Qaeda, indicating the persistent state of morale within the rank and file. Like the dispersal of bees when a hive is attacked, al-Qaeda operatives, financiers, organizers of attacks, and other experts are moving from the center of Pakistan and Afghanistan to the periphery. The groups that al-Qaeda and the Taliban once trained and financed in Asia, the Horn of Africa, the Middle East, and the Caucasus are now using these very places for sanctuary and protection. Al-Qaeda's relations with its associate groups that were active in local and regional conflicts intensified after the formation of the World Islamic Front for Jihad Against the Jews and the Crusaders in 1998. By decentralizing the organization and also opening new facilities for training recruits in many of the regional theaters, such as in Mindanao in the Philippines, the Pankishi Valley in Georgia, in Algeria, and other lands of jihad that provided the opportunity, al-Qaeda has successfully networked with disparate groups and in some cases co-opted their leaders. This was particularly the case in Southeast Asia.

Immediately after al-Qaeda attacked U.S. diplomatic targets in East Africa in August 1998, and when Pakistan started to arrest al-Qaeda recruits and operatives in transit to and from Afghanistan, al-Qaeda once again began to establish regional training facilities. Al-Qaeda recruits from Southeast Asia were trained in MILF camps in Hodeibia, Palestine, and in Vietnam, all in the Abu Bakar complex. With the removal of Camp Abu Bakar by Philippine forces, the training facility shifted to Poso, Sulawesi, in Indonesia, where another al-Qaeda associate group—Lashkar Jundullah—established another training facility.

The loss of Afghanistan was a massive blow for al-Qaeda's guerrilla and terrorist capability. However, both the support it enjoys in the tribal areas as well as its pre-9/11 decentralization is likely to ensure the survival of the group. Although al-Qaeda has lost some of its key leaders, such as its military commander Mohammed Atef, alias Abu Hafs, and its head of the military committee, Khalid Sheikh Mohammed, al-Qaeda's core and penultimate leadership that provides the strategic and tactical direction is still intact.[9] As long as Osama bin Laden and Ayman al-Zawahiri survive, the group itself will survive. Furthermore, the Islamist milieu both in Muslim territorial (Asia, Middle East, Caucasus) and migrant communities (Europe, North America, Australia) continues to provide the bulk of the recruits as well as financing and other forms of support. As the focus of the coalition is largely military, the robust Islamist ideology of al-Qaeda—that has gone unchallenged—is ensuring the survival of the group. Al-Qaeda is trying to replenish its human losses (killed, captured, and arrested) and material wastage (in weapons and other supplies) both inside and outside Afghanistan. As a result, al-Qaeda's global network—with members drawn from forty-six countries and activities in ninety-eight countries—is still functional, including its operatives in Europe.[10] Although al-Qaeda operational cells planning and preparing for attacks have been disrupted in France, the Netherlands, Belgium, Germany, Italy, Spain, the United Kingdom, and Scandinavia, al-Qaeda support cells disseminating propaganda, raising funds, recruiting, procuring supplies, and mounting surveillance on intended targets are still active. Its collaborators, supporters, and sympathizers are filling the leadership vacuum created by the first wave of arrests of al-Qaeda leaders in Europe immediately after 9/11. The post–9/11 al-Qaeda cells are more clandestine, compact, and self-contained, and thus harder to detect and disrupt. As such, Western societies and their governments will face a low-level, long-term continuous threat from al-Qaeda.

Current Threat

Post 9/11, al-Qaeda attempted but failed to destroy U.S., U.K., Australian, and Israeli diplomatic missions. They also failed in striking a U.S. warship off Singapore as well as U.S. and British warships in the Strait of Gibraltar. In addition to Richard Reid, the shoe-bomber, who attempted to destroy a commercial aircraft over the Atlantic, al-Qaeda also attempted to bomb the U.S. embassy and American cultural center in Paris and attack the U.S. base in Sarajevo. It even attempted to poison the water supply to the U.S. embassy in Rome. A Sudanese al-Qaeda member fired a surface-to-air missile at a U.S. warplane taking off from the Prince Sultan Air Base in Saudi Arabia in 2001, and a similar attempt was made against an Israeli commercial airliner in Mombasa a year later. Al-Qaeda suicide bombers also attacked a French oil tanker off Yemen and U.S. troops in Kuwait in October 2002. To instigate Islamists to strike worldwide Jewish targets, Nizar Seif Eddin al-Tunisi (Sword of the Faith, or The Tunisian) alias Nizar Nouar, a Tunisian al-Qaeda suicide bomber, rammed a liquid petroleum gas vehicle into the Ghriba Synagogue,

Africa's oldest Jewish synagogue, in Djerba, Tunisia, killing fourteen German tourists, including one child, and five Tunisians on April 11, 2002. An al-Qaeda front, the Islamic Army for the Liberation of the Holy Sites, claimed responsibility for the attack, and subsequently an interview by Abdul Azeem al-Muhajir, an al-Qaeda military commander, confirmed it as an al-Qaeda operation.

Due to the difficulty of operating in the post-9/11 environment, al-Qaeda has delegated and devolved many of its responsibilities to other Islamist movements (parties and groups) that operate under the al-Qaeda umbrella. In a number of theaters, al-Qaeda is operating directly and through a number of groups with which it hitherto shared training, financial, and operational infrastructure in Afghanistan. This phenomenon is most visible in Pakistan, where two dozen attacks by al-Qaeda and its associated groups have occurred since 9/11. Beginning with the massacre of the Christians in Bahawalpur in the Punjab District in October 2001, al-Qaeda has launched a number of terrorist operations, including the kidnapping and murder of *Wall Street Journal* journalist Daniel Pearl and a church bombing in Islamabad, killing a U.S. diplomat's wife and daughter. A suicide bomber of Harkat-ul-Mujahideen-al-Aalami, an al-Qaeda associate group, killed eleven Frenchmen and twelve Pakistanis in Karachi on May 8, 2002. The well-planned attack was conducted after mounting surveillance on the Sheraton hotel and the bus route used by French naval engineers and technicians working on the submarine project in Karachi. The suicide vehicle-bomb attack by an al-Qaeda associate group against the U.S. consulate in Karachi on June 14, 2002, injured a U.S. marine and killed eleven Pakistanis. Using the same vehicle, they also targeted Pakistani president Pervez Musharraf on April 26, 2002, but the remote control failed to detonate the explosives-laden vehicle.

While the Taliban is a guerrilla force, al-Qaeda remains a terrorist group. The Taliban operates somewhat openly and al-Qaeda operates clandestinely. The Taliban–al-Qaeda combined strategy is to install a regime in Pakistan that is at the very least a regime neutral to the Islamists. Its leaders believe that the future survival of al-Qaeda and the Taliban along the Afghanistan-Pakistan border will depend on their ability to generate sustained support from Pakistan. As such, they are likely to target President Musharraf repeatedly until he is killed or removed from office. Despite the capture or death of nearly five hundred al-Qaeda and Taliban members, al-Qaeda has realized that Pakistan is more important than Afghanistan for its survival. Al-Qaeda has also mounted at least two clandestine operations to assassinate Afghani president Hamid Karzai and other cabinet ministers there. After a traffic accident, both an Afghan and a foreigner in an explosive (Semtex)-laden Toyota were arrested in the center of Kabul on July 29, 2002. In September 2002, al-

Qaeda mounted a second assassination operation that was disrupted by Karzai's U.S. bodyguards. In addition, an unknown group positioned a claymore mine on a route usually taken by the presidential motorcade in Kabul. Al-Qaeda has since established attack cells to topple Karzai in Afghanistan and Musharraf in Pakistan.[11]

In an effort to make a comeback, the Taliban and al-Qaeda have attempted to replace losses in their rank and file by promoting middle-level and junior leaders as well as engaging in fresh recruitment. For example, to compensate for the loss of Pakistani state support for the Taliban, Mullah Omar has established Lashkar-e-Omar—a covert network of support organizations in Pakistan—to sustain a low-intensity campaign in Afghanistan and in the area. By instigating its associate groups in Kashmir, such as Harakat-ul Mujahideen and Jayash-e-Mohammed, to intensify violence there, the Taliban has also forced Pakistan to redeploy its troops from the Afghan border to the 2,414-kilometer-long India-Pakistan border. By exploiting the porosity of the Pakistan-Afghanistan border, the Taliban and al-Qaeda are trying to reestablish their lines of communication, supplies, and recruits. The Taliban, al-Qaeda, and other associate groups are all harnessing the Islamist milieu in Pakistan and overseas (both territorial and migrant) to ensure a revival in support (encouragement, funds, and supplies) necessary for survival and sustenance. Nonetheless, the response has been weak.

With the loss of Khalid Sheikh Mohammed, the surviving al-Qaeda leadership will now have to reestablish communications with its associate groups and its various scattered cells. For example, to revive support, al-Qaeda will have to reestablish linkages with its affiliate NGOs and other charities overseas. Most of these NGOs and charities have been targeted by the United States and other governments actively working with the United States to fight terrorist-infiltrated organizations. With the failure of al-Qaeda to strike tactical U.S., allied, and coalition targets worldwide after 9/11, the group is considering reverting to both tactical and strategic targets. Although suicide terrorism coupled with conventional attacks have proved to be the most effective, the group is also considering revisiting the maritime and the chemical, biological, radiological, and nuclear (CBRN) scenarios,[12] options al-Qaeda considered prior to 9/11.

Al-Qaeda has suffered setbacks and lacks the capability to launch large attacks. Still, its members still desire to be the "elite" of the terrorist groups and always attempt to operate on the cutting edge of "terrorist" technology. Despite severe losses, al-Qaeda continues to inspire and instigate a wide constituency of groups and individuals to take on the fight for Allah. As seen in a number of small and sporadic attacks in Europe, the Middle East, and Asia, Islamist groups are engaging in a range of options—arsons, shootings, throwing grenades, and exploding improvised explosive devices (IEDs) against Jewish, Christian, and Hindu targets. The Islamists continue to inspire and instigate violence against "the enemies of Islam," "the infidels," and the "unbelievers" both by word of mouth and in over a thousand sites on the Internet. The Islamists are operating across a wide spectrum, from the low-tech to the high-tech, stretching government resources and weakening security countermeasures. This demonstrates the success of al-Qaeda in educating a much wider constituency to challenge the West and Muslim regimes friendly to the West.

Primary Target

As the protector of "false Muslim leaders" and "corrupt Muslim regimes" in the Middle East, the United States of America has been identified as the "head of the poisonous snake" and therefore remains the principal target of al-Qaeda. Al-Qaeda's preference was reflected when Osama bin Laden announced, "The battle has moved to inside America. We will continue this battle, God permitting, until victory or until we meet God."[13] Until U.S. intelligence agencies infiltrate terrorist groups, a task that cannot be accomplished in the short term (one or two years), it is reasonable to assume that the United States is as vulnerable as it was before 9/11. The governments that assist the United States in its campaign in Afghanistan as well as the governments that have disrupted al-Qaeda cells on their soil have earned the wrath of al-Qaeda. After, for example, the Singaporean government disrupted cells of Jemaah Islamiya (al-Qaeda's Southeast Asian arm operating in Singapore), the leadership relocated in Indonesia and attempted to crash a plane onto the Changi International Airport in Singapore. Similarly, in retaliation for Pakistan's support for the United States, several Islamist groups in Pakistan have attacked soft targets there nationwide. For instance, Islamist terrorists killed four Pakistanis at a Christian school for children of foreign aid workers in Murree Hills on August 5 and three others in the church of a Christian hospital in Taxila on August 9, 2002.

The threat picture clearly shows that al-Qaeda is constrained from launching another large-scale attack akin to 9/11, but is still able to conduct small- and medium-scale attacks on the scale of Bali and Mombasa. With unprecedented security, intelligence, and law enforcement cooperation and heightened public alertness, al-Qaeda is finding it difficult to engage in extensive reconnaissance/surveillance and rehearsals, prerequisites for conducting coordinated simultaneous attacks. Being aware of the virtues of patience, al-Qaeda is likely to mark time, tasking its associate groups. Nonetheless, if the security situation deteriorates, al-Qaeda is likely to identify the gaping holes in the post-9/11 security architecture and task its supercells to plan, prepare, and execute multiple mass casualty attacks. For the time being, due to the limitations of mounting large-scale operations against population centers, economic targets, and transportation infrastructure, al-Qaeda's supercells will likely be hibernating. As the group wishes to select its targets wisely, it is unlikely to expend resources on opportunity targets unless absolutely necessary, such as to make its presence felt. Of the dozen medium- and small-scale attacks conducted by al-Qaeda and its associate groups against U.S., allied, and coalition targets worldwide, only a fraction have been successful. Al-Qaeda has acknowledged that it has failed due to tighter international security measures. Nevertheless, al-Qaeda, like a wounded animal, is determined to strike back. As a result of effective security measures, al-Qaeda is shifting tactics, stretching the threat spectrum to include a wider range of targets. Al-Qaeda's change in its modus operandi includes: marking time; operating through associate groups; providing them trainers and funds; and directly and indirectly influencing their strategic and tactical direction. As long as the threat to al-Qaeda remains, the network is likely to invest and operate through its associated groups.

Especially since the arrest of its operational commander Khalid Sheikh Mohammed on March 1, 2003, al-Qaeda has lost tactical control of its operational cells. Nevertheless, until the command and communication network between the surviving leadership and the cells are rebuilt, al-Qaeda will compensate for the lack of direction by issuing audio recordings and public statements. For instance, through its Web site alneda.com, al-Qaeda has dispensed advice to the Iraqi people and the few hundred foreign mujahideen groups inside Iraq and in neighboring countries to be patient and to prepare slowly but steadfastly for guerrilla warfare. In its initial reaction to the fall of Baghdad on April 11, 2003, al-Qaeda posted an article on the Internet entitled "The Crusaders' War in Iraq," in which guerrilla warfare was suggested as:

> The Most Powerful Weapon Muslims Have, and It Is the Best Method to Continue the Conflict with the [Superior Force of a] Crusader Enemy. . . . With guerrilla warfare, the Americans were defeated in Vietnam and the Soviets were defeated in Afghanistan. This is the method that expelled the direct Crusader colonialism from most of the Muslim lands, with Algeria the most well known. We still see how this method stopped Jewish immigration to Palestine, and caused reverse immigration of Jews from Palestine. The successful attempts of dealing defeat to invaders using guerrilla warfare are many, and we will not expound on them. However, these attempts have proven that the most effective method for the materially weak against the strong is guerrilla warfare.[14]

Al-Qaeda's post-9/11 pronouncements—including its spokesperson Sulayman Abu Gaith's recorded message—reveals that neither its intention nor its will to attack Western, especially U.S., targets has diminished. With the erosion of its capability to strike, al-Qaeda is likely to invest more in propaganda and other forms of information warfare. Conflicts of international neglect where Muslims are suffering—Palestine, Kashmir, Chechnya, Maluku, Mindanao, Algeria, and now Iraq—will continue to be featured prominently on the al-Qaeda propaganda agenda.

The Southeast Asian Network

Most academics find it difficult to understand al-Qaeda because the group functions both in the operational and ideological domain. Apart from dispatching its operatives to target countries (such as the 9/11 team led by Mohammed Atta), it also provides the experts, training, and resources to other Islamist political and military organizations so as to advance a common goal. As it has done in the case of existing Islamist networks worldwide, in Southeast Asia al-Qaeda has penetrated Jemaah Islamiya (JI), a regional organization with overt and underground networks extending from Southern Thailand to Australia. Among the parties and groups it has established, infiltrated, and influenced are Jamaah Salafiyah in southern Thailand, Kumpulan Mujahideen Malaysia in Malaysia, Lashkar Jundullah in Indonesia, and the Moro Islamic Liberation Front in the southern Philippines.

Al-Qaeda and its associate group JI have divided their responsibilities, personnel, infrastructure, and areas of operation into territorial organizations called *mantiqis. Mantiqi 1* or *M1* is based in Malaysia and covers Malaysia, Singapore, and southern Thailand. *Mantiqi 2* or *M2* is based in Solo, Central Java, and covers the whole of Indonesia except for Sulawesi and Kalimantan. *Mantiqi 3* or *M3* is based in Camp Abu Bakar, Mindanao, Philippines, and covers Borneo, including Brunei, the east Malaysian states of Sarawak and Sabah as well as Kalimantan and Sulawesi in Indonesia and the southern Philippines. *Mantiqi 4* or *M4* covers Irian Jaya and Australia. By maintaining a low numerical strength, operating in the religious milieu, refraining from acquiring weapons until immediately before targeting, and strictly conforming to operational security, JI terrorist cells operated below the intelligence radar screen of Southeast Asian governments and the public for nearly a decade until their detection in Singapore in December 2001.

Through physical and intellectual contact, al-Qaeda ideologues, trainers, and operatives physically and ideologically strengthened a dozen Islamist terrorist groups, political parties, charities, and individuals in Southeast Asia. In addition to emphasizing the importance of participating in a global jihad, it created a mission and a vision for the Islamists to build a caliphate, or Darulah Islamiah Raya, comprising Malaysia, Singapore, Brunei, Indonesia, Cambodia, and Mindanao.

Al-Qaeda—and JI—have been credited with many atrocities in Southeast Asia. In addition to its plans to assassinate Pope John Paul II and President Bill Clinton in Manila as well as attempting to explode eleven airliners over the Asia-Pacific in early 1995, al-Qaeda detonated a bomb on a Tokyo-bound Philippine Airlines flight in December 1994, injuring eleven and killing one Japanese passenger. JI was responsible for bombing the residence of the Philippine ambassador in Jakarta, and the simultaneous bombing of thirty churches that killed twenty-two and wounded ninety-six people in Jakarta, West Java, North Sumatra, Riau, Bandung, East Java, and Nusatenggara on Christmas Eve 2000.[15]

JI has also played a pivotal role in the violence in Maluku that has killed over five thousand people during the past five years. Further, al-Qaeda's Malaysian cell also hosted the USS *Cole* planners and provided the critical cover and finances (and nearly the flight training) to Zaccarias Moussaoui, the alleged "twentieth" suicide hijacker. Moussaoui was originally sent to the Malaysian Flying Academy in Malacca for training. However, as the multiengine planes he wished to learn to fly were not available, he left for the United States. Indonesian national Riduan Isamuddin, alias Hambali, who holds both al-Qaeda and JI membership and was featured in all these activities, has been arrested and is being held by U.S. authorities in an undisclosed location. Recent recoveries from Afghanistan include documents with extensive references to al-Qaeda's spiritual leader in Southeast Asia, Abu Bakar Bashir, Hambali, and other directing figures of the al-Qaeda network in the region.

With the dismantling of its training infrastructure in Afghanistan, al-Qaeda is increasingly looking toward the periphery, including Southeast Asia. Although al-Qaeda has neither physically nor ideologically abandoned Afghanistan, it is seeking to compensate for the loss of a state-of-the-art training infrastructure by developing regional operational bases elsewhere, including in Southeast Asia. As such, under the instruction of core leaders in al-Qaeda, JI has established regional training camps for both ideological and physical training and makeshift familiarization camps, particularly in Malaysia and Australia. Islamists have been trained in facilities in Malaysia (Negri Sembilan), Indonesia (Poso, Sulawesi), the Philippines (Mindanao), and Australia (the Blue Mountains) since 1993. The regional leader, Hambali, resident of Malaysia from 1985–87 and who fought in the anti-Soviet campaign in Afghanistan, was, as noted earlier, arrested in Thailand in August 2003.

There are indications that JI Indonesia is clearly the distinct node of the al-Qaeda network in the region. As a result of official Spanish investigations into al-Qaeda, the Indonesian government has reluctantly admitted that al-Qaeda operated a training camp in Poso. According to a 2002 report by the Indonesian state intelligence agency, BIN, "The training camp led by Omar Bandon consisted of 8–10 small villages located side by side on the beach, equipped with light weapons, explosives and a firing range. Participants of the training are not only from the local people but also from overseas. The instructor of the physical training in the camp is Parlindugan Siregar, a member of the al-Qaeda network in Spain."[16]

Recently several videotapes of the training have also been recovered.[17] Apart from the ten "millennium bombers," the Indonesian government has yet to arrest and prosecute both the Poso trainees and the trainers. While it would be tempting to blame Indonesia, it is more pressing for governments within and outside the region to work steadfastly with President Megawati or her successor. Failure to do so will mean Islamism moving from the periphery to the center, threatening both Indonesia and its neighbors.

By continuing to work together with the local groups in Southeast Asia, al-Qaeda has access to a wide range of targets. As much as the local groups have depended on al-Qaeda in the past, the parent network has depended on local groups to advance its agenda. Immediately after al-Qaeda conducted the first World Trade Center bombing in February 1993, the network looked eastward in a quest to bomb eleven U.S. airliners. Similarly, after al-Qaeda targeted U.S. icons on 9/11, it planned to target U.S. and other diplomatic targets in Southeast Asia. When al-Qaeda failed to conduct a significant attack in the world after 9/11, its most senior representative in Southeast Asia, Hambali, masterminded the Bali attack on October 12, 2002, and on Jakarta's JW Marriott on August 5, 2003.

Despite partial government successes and failures against terrorist networks, al-Qaeda remains a threat to Southeast Asian governments and societies. Largely due to the tireless efforts of the intelligence community, especially of the Singaporean service, the region is aware of the existence of a resilient terrorist network. Only about a fourth of the operatives have suffered arrest or death. To be sure, parts of the network have suffered extensive damage, such as its Singaporean, Malaysian, and Filipino (only Luzon) components. Nevertheless, the organization's leadership, support (propaganda, recruitment, fund-raising, procurement, transportation, safe houses), and operational (surveillance, attack) organs remain fully functional. Only through a regional approach involving all the countries can the group be successfully hunted down. For example, even with the success of apprehending many of the Bali bombing perpetrators, JI is still a threat in Indonesia as only the JI cells responsible for the Bali bombing have been targeted, and JI as an organization is still functional in Indonesia.

The Road to Bali

Immediately before al-Qaeda launched Operation Holy Tuesday, its mastermind Khalid Sheikh Mohammed dispatched a twenty-one-year-old Canadian operative of Kuwaiti origin, Mohammed Mansour Jabarah, alias Sammy, to Southeast Asia to conduct attacks against U.S. and allied targets. After spending two weeks in Karachi, Pakistan, with Khalid Sheikh Mohammed and Hambali, Jabarah traveled to Malaysia through Hong Kong to meet with the JI cell planning to strike U.S. and Israeli embassies in the Philippines. Jabarah contacted Zulkifli Marzuki, alias Azzam, the secretary of JI, and met with Faiz Bafana, alias Mahmoud.[18] In order to meet with Fathur Rohman al-Ghozi, alias Saad, an Indonesian JI member working with the MILF, Jabarah left for the Philippines with an al-Qaeda suicide bomber, Ahmed Sahagi. After Jabarah and Ahmed reached Manila, they checked into the Horizon Hotel in Makati. Saad e-mailed Jabarah and provided a telephone number in Manila.[19] The al-Qaeda–trained explosives expert, Saad,[20] who spoke fluent Arabic, arrived in the hotel two days after and said that he had only three hundred kilograms of TNT and needed additional time and money to procure four tons of explosives. After taking Jabarah to the U.S. embassy and the office building housing the Israeli embassy, Saad added that the U.S. embassy in Manila was not a good target since it was set back too far from the main road. Meanwhile, the Israeli embassy was staffed by too few Israelis. After ten days in Manila, Jabarah, Ahmed, and separately, Saad, returned to Malaysia in October 2001. Following a JI meeting in Kuala Lumpur, it was decided to strike targets in Singapore. As a prelude to mounting a suicide strike, Jabarah and Saad left for Singapore to work with a JI Singapore cell to videotape U.S., Israeli, British, and Australian targets. After Saad returned to the Philippines to obtain the TNT in November 2001, Hambali arrived in Malaysia from Pakistan and advised Jabarah to cancel the Singapore operation and revert to the diplomatic targets in the Philippines.[21] Hambali believed that operations in the Philippines could be accomplished sooner since the explosives would not have to be shipped to Singapore. He stated that if the targets in the Philippines were unacceptable, they should find better targets in the Philippines. With the arrests of the JI members in Singapore, Jabarah and Hambali left for Thailand in mid-January 2002. As Jabarah provided nearly US$70,000 of al-Qaeda funds to JI, Hambali said he would "conduct small bombings in bars, cafes or nightclubs frequented by westerners in Thailand, Malaysia, Singapore, Philippines and Indonesia."[22]

Jabarah and Ahmed Sahagi were arrested in Oman in March 2002. Jabarah was in Oman to assist al-Qaeda operatives traveling through Oman to Yemen. Jabarah believes that Ahmed was deported to Yemen. When FBI interrogators asked about the potential targets in Asia, Jabarah noted that the planned attack in Singapore would not have been difficult. He said: "The U.S. embassy is very close to the street and did not have many barriers to prevent the attack. An attack on the U.S. Embassy in Manila would have been much more difficult, requiring at least two operations."[23] Jabarah added that this would most likely not have been successful, adding that a plane would have been needed to attack this building because security was very tight.[24]

Al-Qaeda dispatched four Afghan-trained Arab suicide bombers to Southeast Asia to destroy the U.S., British, Australian, and Israeli diplomatic targets in Singapore. Moreover, regional groups had also started to commit their own suicide missions. The bomber that struck Paddy's Bar in Bali was discovered to be a suicide bomber, and the police recovered his last will together with the last will of three other suicide terrorists.[25] As Bali was the first mass casualty attack in Southeast Asia, this clearly demonstrates how successfuly al-Qaeda has ideologically indoctrinated local and regional groups. Although the numbers of attacks will be small and infrequent, Southeast Asia is likely to witness further suicide attacks with time. Former JI chief in Singapore, Mas Selamat Kastari, who was arrested in Tanjung Pinang, Bintan, Indonesia, on February 3, 2003, was planning to crash an Aeroflot plane onto Changi International Airport both to "destroy" the airport and also to send a message to Russia for its "treatment of the Chechens." This action demonstrated how al-Qaeda has transferred its tactic of suicide and, more important, its ideology of a global jihad to local and regional groups.

Conclusion

In many ways, Islamism of the al-Qaeda brand will survive because al-Qaeda has been successful in decentralizing. With the targeting of the Afghan-Pakistan border, where both al-Qaeda and the Taliban (the Mullah Omar faction) are concentrated, the group will depend on its regional networks to continue the fight. Events in the region clearly demonstrate that JI, the most important partner of al-Qaeda's Southeast Asian network, has taken on the role of its mother group. Al-Qaeda's disrupted Singapore operation clearly demonstrates the group's intentions and capabilities. The threshold for terrorism—both the rapidly increasing scale of support for conducting attacks and the attacks and attempted attacks themselves—has clearly increased in Southeast Asia.

Recent experience suggests that the fight against terrorist networks has proven to be difficult. The groups in Southeast Asia present no exception. Islamist terrorist groups have suffered gravely, particularly in Afghanistan, but their core leaderships are alive and their ideology remains intact. The periodic attacks and fresh propaganda indicate that the leadership and membership will continue the fight.[26] Amid security countermeasures, the groups have demonstrated their capacity to replicate, regenerate, and reorganize. Despite the reverses and damage suffered at all levels, the threat posed by the global terrorist organization has not diminished. The group's highly experienced and committed "experts" are planning and preparing for the next operation. Al-Qaeda cells are probing the gaping holes to strike in the post-9/11 security architecture. Wherever there are resources available and the opportunity, al-Qaeda supercells will strike. Today, no single country can protect itself from a multinational terrorist organization. For instance, Malaysia and Singapore cannot protect themselves as long as the al-Qaeda–JI network has a robust presence in Thailand and Indonesia. The first step toward reducing the immediate threat to Southeast Asia is to develop and implement a multipronged, multidimensional, multiagency approach by ASEAN countries to target al-Qaeda's support and operational infrastructure at home and in the immediate neighborhood. In parallel, the region must contribute to the international effort to fight the global network. For example, both human intelligence and technical intelligence generated by Southeast Asian and Australian agencies have played an important role in the global fight against terrorism. Indeed, the war on terror in Southeast Asia will be a long and arduous one. Governments in this region must work together if they are to have any chance of eliminating the terror threat.

Notes

I wish to thank Dr. Andrew Tan for his valuable comments, and Yeo Wei Meng for his research assistance. This chapter first appeared in the book edited by Kumar Ramakrishna and See Seng Tan, *After Bali: The Threat of Terrorism in Southeast Asia* (Singapore: World Scientific Publishing and the Institute of Defence and Strategic Studies, 2003).

1. For example: the Kurdish Workers Party, northeastern Turkey; the Liberation Tigers of Tamil Eelam, northeastern Sri Lanka; the Palestine Liberation Organization, Palestinian Hamas, and the Palestinian Islamic Jihad, the Occupied Territories; the Armed Islamic Group and Salafist Group for Call and Combat, Algeria; the Moro Islamic Liberation Front and Abu Sayyaf Group, southern Philippines; the Revolutionary Armed Forces of Colombia, Colombia; the Irish Republican Army, Northern Ireland; the Communist Party of Nepal (Maoists), Nepal.

2. Osama bin Laden, untitled audiotape, Al Jazeera, Arab Satellite Television Network, November 12, 2002. In addition to the United States and Israel, Osama identified Britain, France, Germany, Italy, Canada, and Australia as its enemies.

3. The numerical strength of al-Qaeda is based on debriefings of al-Qaeda members in U.S. custody. Most informed members estimate the strength at between 3,000–4,000 members at the time of the U.S. intervention in Afghanistan in October 2001.

4. Rohan Gunaratna, *Inside al-Qaeda: Global Network of Terror* (New York: Columbia University Press, 2002).

5. Mohommad Mansour Jabarah, debriefing, Federal Bureau of Investigation (FBI), U.S. Department of Justice, August 6, 2002.

6. As al-Qaeda is a learning organization, it studies all operations where it has suffered losses and improves the next time. This "losing and learning" doctrine is typical of sophisticated groups.

7. Al-Qaeda's original funding name was Al Qaeda al-Sulbah, or "The Solid Base."

8. Abdullah Azzam, "Al Qaidah al Sulbah," *Al Jihad* 41 (April 1998): 46.

9. Gunaratna, *Inside al-Qaeda,* pp. 288–89.

10. Estimate by U.S. operational agencies working with counterpart agencies elsewhere.

11. Interview with chief of police of Afghanistan, General Din Mohammed Jurat, and other officials, Asia Counterterrorism Conference, Tokyo, March 19, 2003.

12. For instance, al-Qaeda paid US$1.5 million to a Sudanese military officer in 1993 to purchase a uranium canister from South Africa. However, the group was duped, as it was sold an externally radiated canister.

13. Interview, al-Jazeera's Kabul correspondent, Tayseer Allouni, October 21, 2001.

14. http://www.alneda.com, April 11, 2003. Link now defunct.

15. For more details, see Gunaratna, *Inside al Qaeda,* chapter on al-Qaeda in Asia.

16. Al-Qaeda infrastructure in Indonesia, BIN, Jakarta, 2002.

17. While the first tape was recovered in an Egyptian bazaar, a second tape was recovered in the residence of an al-Qaeda supporter in Leicester, U.K. Another tape was recovered in Afghanistan by CNN journalist Nic Robertson.

18. Jabarah, FBI debriefing, August 6, 2002.

19. Jabarah, FBI debriefing.

20. In Afghanistan, Saad trained under Abu Kebab, al-Qaeda's Egyptian bomb-making expert, in 1995.

21. Jabarah, FBI debriefing.

22. Ibid.

23. Ibid.

24. Ibid.

25. Personal communication, General I.M. Pastika, Chief Investigator, Bali bombings, February 2003.

26. To nurture existing and rekindle new Muslim migrant and territorial support, on September 10, 2002, al-Qaeda issued a one-hundred-page document seeking to justify why they struck America's most outstanding landmarks on September 11, 2001.

II

Regional Perspectives
on Terrorism
in Southeast Asia

5

Al-Qaeda and Political Terrorism in Southeast Asia

Carlyle A. Thayer

Introduction

Southeast Asia has long experienced domestic political violence in the form of communist insurgencies, regional separatism, and ethnoreligious strife. Generally, each group operated in isolation from the other. Perhaps the major exceptions were communist movements during the period when the Communist International (1919–43) was in business. This added the element of external state sponsorship to internationally linked movements seeking to overthrow the colonial state. But even in the case of communist insurgencies, such as in British Malaya and Burma, French Indochina, and the Philippines in the 1940s, there was little evidence of effective regional coordination. The threat that each of these groups posed to the state was easily contained. For example, with the exceptions of Indochina and East Timor, no other insurgency or ethnic separatist group has been successful.

In 2001, Singaporean and Malaysian security officials arrested a number of individuals engaged in planning acts of terrorism against Western embassies and other targets. In October 2002, terrorists executed a mass casualty attack on tourist haunts on the island of Bali. These events revealed the emergence of a new phenomenon in Southeast Asia—an internationally and regionally networked group of terrorists capable of executing coordinated mass casualty attacks. The discovery of this terrorist network followed the dramatic terrorist attacks on the World Trade Center and Pentagon on September 11, 2001, and President George Bush's declaration of a global war on terrorism.

In order to understand the appearance of this new phenomenon in Southeast Asia, the media turned to international terrorism experts for an explanation. These commentators quickly identified al-Qaeda as the prime suspect. Regional security specialists who had heretofore focused on traditional forms of political violence were caught off guard by the emergence of internationally networked terrorism in Southeast Asia. They too quickly adopted the al-Qaeda–centric paradigm as their framework for analysis. Country specialists were initially skeptical that there were any linkages between al-Qaeda and local groups.[1] These views mirrored that of senior politicians in Malaysia, Indonesia, Thailand, and the Philippines who initially outright denied that internationally linked terrorist groups existed in their countries. Another key factor contributing to initial skepticism by country specialists was the suggested linkage between international terrorism and Islam.

This chapter discusses the emergence of internationally networked political terrorism in Southeast Asia in four parts. Part 1 discusses the problems of defining terrorism. Part 2 critically analyzes three main approaches to the study of terrorism. Part 3 reviews Southeast Asia's proscribed terrorist groups. The chapter concludes with a net assessment of political terrorism in Southeast Asia.

Defining Terrorism

Quite simply there is no internationally agreed definition of terrorism. In 1937 the League of Nations considered and then rejected a draft convention that defined terrorism as "all criminal acts directed against a State and intended or calculated to create a state of terror in the minds of particular persons or groups of persons or the general public."[2] The United Nations General Assembly has had a draft resolution defining terrorism on its books since 1999 but has not been able to reach a consensus.

Surprisingly, the United States government, the leader in the global war on terrorism, does not have a single comprehensive definition of what constitutes terrorism. A legal definition of terrorism may be found in the U.S. Code of Federal Regulations, but the State Department, Defense Department, and Federal Bureau of Investigation all use their own separate definitions. President George Bush added yet another when he issued an executive order on terrorist financing in the wake of September 11.

Finally, to conclude this point, the Organization of the Islamic Conference (OIC) also has been unable to reach agreement on a definition of terrorism. At the OIC summit held in Kuala Lumpur in April 2002, Malaysia's Prime Minister Mahathir proposed that any deliberate attack on civilians, including those by Palestinian suicide bombers, should be classified as acts of terror. Delegates disagreed. In the final OIC Kuala Lumpur Declaration, they stated inter alia: "We reiterate the principled position under international law and the Charter of the United Nations of the legitimacy of resistance to foreign aggression and the struggle of peoples under colonial or alien domination and foreign occupation for national liberation and self-determination. In this context, *we underline the urgency for an internationally agreed definition of terrorism, which differentiates such legitimate struggles from acts of terrorism*" [emphasis added].[3]

The OIC conundrum may be summed up with the cliché that "one person's terrorist is another person's freedom fighter." The OIC threw the hot potato of defining terrorism to the United Nations for consideration. The General Assembly's Sixth Committee is presently considering a draft Comprehensive Convention on International Terrorism that would include a definition of terrorism, if adopted. The failure of the international community to define terrorism poses a difficult methodological problem for scholars who specialize in terrorism studies.

The analysis presented in this chapter attempts to sidestep this definitional problem by defining a terrorist group as any organization proscribed by the United Nations. Under the terms of Resolution 1267 (1999), the Security Council Committee maintains a consolidated list of individuals and entities belonging to or associated with the Taliban, Osama bin Laden, and the al-Qaeda organization. In Resolutions 1267 (1999), 1333 (2000), 1390 (2002), and 1455 (2003), the Security Council requires all states to freeze the assets of individuals and entities included on the consolidated list, prevent their entry into or transit through their territories, and prevent the direct or indirect supply, sale, and transfer of arms and military equipment to them. This list currently includes ninety-eight entities and several hundred individuals. Three organizations operating in Southeast Asia are classified as terrorist groups: al-Qaeda, the Abu Sayyaf Group (ASG), and Jemaah Islamiyah (JI). It should be noted that the U.N. list is not comprehensive.[4]

Approaches to the Study of Political Terrorism

There are three distinct approaches to the study of terrorism: international, regional, and country specific. At the outset it must be acknowledged that the three approaches do not constitute formal schools as such. Further, there is some overlap between the approaches, particularly between the international and regional levels. Individual experts differ in their assessments of the roles of particular groups and individuals in sponsoring political terrorism.[5]

The first approach to the study of political terrorism is that adopted by international terrorism experts.[6] Rohan Gunaratna is the most prominent representative of this group. He argues that al-Qaeda (and its leader Osama bin Laden) is the key factor to our understanding of the emergence of political terrorism in Southeast Asia.[7] According to Gunaratna, Osama bin Laden was able to convert Islamic resistance to the Soviet occupation of Afghanistan into a global jihad against the United States and its allies and supporters. According to Gunaratna and other specialists, bin Laden was able to forge personal ties with the top leaders of the ASG, JI, and Moro Islamic Liberation Front (MILF). Through these personal ties, al-Qaeda was able to develop a regionally linked network of terrorists comprised of Southeast Asian graduates of religious schools in Pakistan and paramilitary training camps in Afghanistan. In addition, key al-Qaeda operatives were sent to Southeast Asia to provide financing and training in the terrorist tradecraft. According to international terrorism experts, after the fall of the Taliban regime, al-Qaeda operatives were dispersed globally. Many reportedly fled to Southeast Asia, which then became the second front in the global war on terrorism.[8]

International terrorism experts argue that al-Qaeda has deliberately targeted political organizations in Southeast Asia to win them over to the global jihadist cause. At the same time, Southeast Asian regional leaders have willingly permitted their organizations to become co-opted by al-Qaeda. Several have even sworn an oath of loyalty (*bayat*) to bin Laden. Based on these personal links, al-Qaeda operatives have been able to penetrate Southeast Asia to stoke the fires of international jihad by building up the capacity of local groups by offering financial support and training in terrorist operations.

Hundreds of Southeast Asians were recruited from Indonesia, the Philippines, Malaysia, and Singapore to attend terrorist training camps in Afghanistan. After completion of their training, they formed the hard core of local militant groups. Terrorist training camps were established near Poso on the Indonesian island of Sulawesi and on Mindanao in the southern Philippines. In sum, the framework adopted by international terrorism experts portrays Osama bin Laden as a chief executive officer presiding over a global terrorist organization composed of al-Qaeda franchises and associates.

The second approach to the study of international terrorism is that adopted by regional security analysts.[9] By and large this group has adopted the al-Qaeda–centric paradigm used by international terrorism experts as their framework to analyze Southeast Asia's militant organizations. In their view, key al-Qaeda figures, such as Hambali,[10] are the central actors fostering regional linkages between the Abu Sayaaf Group, JI, and the MILF.

But regional security specialists have extended their analysis to embrace virtually every militant Islamic group operating in Southeast Asia generally and in Indonesia in particular. Regional specialists have produced organizational charts to illustrate the pattern of subordination to al-Qaeda's leadership and direction.[11] Regional security specialists routinely treat such groups as the Mujahideen Council of Indonesia, Laskar Jihad, Laskar Jundullah, Laskar Mujahideen, the Islamic Defenders Front, Gerakan al-Maunah, Kumpulan Mujahideen Malaysia (KMM),[12] Pattani United Liberation Organization (both PULO and New PULO), and a host of other organizations, as terrorist affiliates of al-Qaeda. For example, Peter Chalk has asserted "the most visible threat in terms of global Islamic extremism and links to al-Qaeda exists in the guise of Laskar Jihad."[13] But a detailed study of Laskar Jihad[14] reveals that it was formed under the protective wing of Muslim officers in the Indonesian army (TNI) as a counter to the policies of the Indonesian president who encouraged religious accommodation. When sectarian strife broke out in the Maluku Islands, the TNI was responsible for training, arming, and transporting Laskar Jihad fighters to do battle with local Christian militia groups and alleged separatists. After the Bali bombings, Laskar Jihad ostensibly disbanded. Subsequently, Laskar Jihad veterans reportedly have been employed to oppose regional separatists in Papua and Aceh. In other words, far from serving the end of "global Islamic extremism," Laskar Jihad has served to support the unity of the Indonesian secular state. According to Michael Davis, the emergence of Laskar Jihad "reveals the low level of support for their brand of political Islam among Indonesian Muslims."[15]

The third approach to the study of political terrorism is that adopted by country studies specialists.[16] Scholars who focus on individual countries are able to bring different skills to their analysis of terrorism in Southeast Asia. Through their knowledge of regional languages they are able to provide deeper insights into the history, politics, culture, religious values, and societies they are studying. This has led to three very important contributions to our understanding of political terrorism in Southeast Asia.

First, the country studies approach provides a multidisciplinary framework in which to analyze the emergence and development of militant and terrorist groups. Second the country studies approach critically questions whether a demonstrated linkage between a local militant group and al-Qaeda is a sufficient basis for describing that group as an al-Qaeda affiliate or franchise. Country studies experts do not deny that local terrorist and militant groups and their leaders have linkages to al-Qaeda. Neither do they deny the existence of a transregional network of terrorists. Significantly, country studies specialists have alerted us to the question of agency. Agency refers to the ability of local groups and their leaders to leverage their connections with Osama bin Laden and al-Qaeda in order to pursue their own agenda and objectives.

Third, country specialists are able to bring a deeper understanding of the role of Islam in state-society relations into their analysis of militant organizations and terrorist groups. International terrorism and regional experts are prone to present a less nuanced view. Country studies specialists are able to place national religious trends within the larger context of intellectual currents in the Muslim world, thus adding texture to their analysis of Islam in a particular country.[17]

In summary, both the international and regional approaches have made important contributions to our understanding of political terrorism in Southeast Asia. International terrorism experts have drawn attention to the international linkages between terrorist and militant groups in Southeast Asia and the network of religious schools and terrorist training camps in Pakistan and Afghanistan, respectively. Regional security analysts, for their part, have correctly drawn attention to the emergence of a regional terrorist network centered on JI in Indonesia, Malaysia, the Philippines, and Singapore and the collaboration among terrorist groups in the provision of training and services. The objective of this regional network was to create an archipelagic Islamic state (*Darulah Islamiah Nusantara*) by uniting the Muslim peoples of Southeast Asia. The main contribution of the country studies approach is to provide a framework for the analysis of agency in studying the relationship between al-Qaeda and terrorist and militant groups in Southeast Asia. The question of agency enables us to distinguish between al-Qaeda affiliates and autonomous local groups and avoid lumping terrorist groups and militant Islamic organizations together in the same analytical basket.

Southeast Asia's Proscribed Terrorist Groups

This section examines three organizations in Southeast Asia that have been proscribed by the United Nations—al-Qaeda, the Abu Sayyaf Group, and Jemaah Islamiya.

Al-Qaeda

The Soviet invasion of Afghanistan in 1979 sparked a movement throughout the Islamic world in support of the Afghan resistance movement, or mujahideen. An estimated 1,000 Southeast Asians volunteered, with approximately 700 from the Philippines, the largest number. The first batch arrived in January 1980. Only 360 Filipinos actually completed basic training and only half that number actually engaged in combat. They were reportedly grouped together in a Moro military unit. The remainder of Southeast Asia's jihadis came primarily from Indonesia and Malaysia. Southeast Asia's militant Muslims acquired religious indoctrination, military training, and in some cases combat experience.

During the period of the Soviet occupation of Afghanistan (December 1979–February 1989) and during the early 1990s, Southeast Asian militants forged personal relationships with key Afghan resistance leaders including Osama bin Laden. Prominent among the Southeast Asians were Abdurajak Abubakar Janjalani, founder of the Abu Sayyaf Group, Abdullah Sungkar, the first spiritual leader of the Jemaah Islamiyah, and Salamat Hashim, leader of the Moro Islamic Liberation Front (until his death in July 2003). It was sometime during 1988–89 that al-Qaeda was founded at the initiative of Osama bin Laden.[18] The purpose of al-Qaeda was to maintain contact with the worldwide alumni network of Afghan veterans and to support the struggle of Muslims against oppression.

In February 1989 the Soviets withdrew from Afghanistan and a civil war erupted among various mujahideen factions. During 1990, bin Laden was preoccupied with events in the Persian Gulf following Iraq's invasion of Kuwait, and he returned home to Saudi Arabia. Bin Laden became increasingly critical of the Saudi regime for allowing U.S. military forces into the country. In 1991 he went into exile in Sudan. It was not until 1994 that the Taliban emerged as a military force and began its drive to power. It was only in May 1996 that bin Laden left Sudan and returned to Afghanistan, where he assisted the Taliban forces in their armed struggle with the Northern Alliance. The Taliban seized control of Kabul in September 1996 and established their regime. Under the Taliban's protective wing, bin Laden set up a network of paramilitary and terrorist training camps.

In February 1998, bin Laden announced the formation of the World Islamic Front for Jihad Against the Jews and the Crusaders. Bin Laden's major priority was to create an international network to fund operations designed to overthrow conservative Islamic governments and drive the United States out of the Holy Land. Al-Qaeda terrorists struck in August 1998 with simultaneous car bombings outside U.S. embassies in Kenya and Tanzania, in October 2000 with an attack on the USS *Cole*, and on September 11.

In retaliation, during the final quarter of 2001, the United States led an international coalition that intervened in Afghanistan, overthrew the Taliban regime, and closed down all the main al-Qaeda terrorist training camps. Al-Qaeda members were forced to seek refuge in remote areas of eastern Afghanistan and in Pakistan's North-West Frontier. Other al-Qaeda members dispersed overseas, including to Yemen, Chechnya, Iran, and Southeast Asia.[19]

These events coupled with counterterrorist operations on a global scale resulted in the death or capture of key operatives and the degradation and destruction of much of al-Qaeda's command and control structures.

International and regional terrorism experts, in their discussion of al-Qaeda's rise, portray al-Qaeda as the dominant group among the foreign mujahideen community in Afghanistan. This presents a misleading and ahistorical account. For example, during the seven years that bin Laden was in Saudi Arabia and Sudan, his involvement in and influence over the running of terrorist camps in Afghanistan and Pakistan "was negligible," according to Jason Burke.[20] Burke offers the assessment that one key misconception "was the idea that bin Laden led a cohesive and structured terrorist organization called 'al-Qaeda.'" Burke argues that "the nearest thing to 'al-Qaeda,' as popularly understood, existed for a short period, between 1996 and 2001. Its base has been Afghanistan. . . ."[21]

In discussing the international terrorist linkages between Southeast Asia and Afghanistan, international terrorism experts tend to emphasize the importance of bin Laden and al-Qaeda to the exclusion of other actors, including "freelance" terrorists. The discussion below will underscore these points.

Abu Sayyaf Group

International terrorism experts argue that al-Qaeda first penetrated Southeast Asia as early as 1988 when Mohammed Jamal Khalifa, Osama bin Laden's brother-in-law, first visited the Philippines to make contact with Muslim militants on Basilan Island in the south. Khalifa was ostensibly under orders to make contact with and provide funds to local Islamic militant groups through the International Islamic Relief Organization (IIRO), a Muslim charity. The standard accounts of al-Qaeda's penetration of the Philippines stress the importance of the personal contacts between bin Laden and Abdurajak Abubakar Janjalani noted above. Much is made of the arrival of Ramzi Yousef in 1993, who provided explosives training to the ASG at one of its base camps.

Country specialists point out that the ASG emerged in the mid-1980s as a breakaway militant group from the Moro National Liberation Front (MNLF). After the Soviet withdrawal from Afghanistan, Janjalani sought support for the Moro struggle in the southern Philippines. Filipinos who were recruited for training in Pakistan and who later saw service in southern Afghanistan came under the influence of Abdul Rasul Sayyaf, leader of one of the mujihadeen's several factions, and not bin Laden. In 1991–92, Janjalani renamed his organization the Abu Sayyaf Group in recognition of his benefactor.

The roles of Mohammed Jamal Khalifa and Ramzi Yousef as key al-Qaeda operatives may also be questioned. Khalifa's charities were primarily concerned with providing aid to oppressed Muslims around the world. Khalifa donated money for the construction of orphanages, hospitals, and mosques in the southern Philippines. Khalifa returned in October 1991 and began to expand his network of charitable and commercial interests including contacts with the Abu Sayyaf Group. Jason Burke argues that bin Laden did not provide direct funding to Janjalani at this time. Burke argues, "There is nothing to indicate that those monies [provided by the IIRO] included funds from bin Laden himself. There would have been no need for Khalifa to be in touch with bin Laden. His own connections were broad-ranging."[22]

The much-vaunted kin relationship between Khalifa and bin Laden has also been overvalued. Bin Laden had nearly fifty siblings and, according to a senior Saudi diplomat, "a brother in law . . . in Saudi Arabia [is] not even considered part of the family."[23] After Khalifa fled the Philippines he went to the United States where he was arrested and deported to Saudi Arabia to stand trial. After his acquittal, he denounced bin Laden's terror tactics and cut off family ties.[24] During the second half of the 1990s, Filipinos began to replace Arabs in the running of Islamic charities and nongovernmental organizations that had been set up with funds donated primarily from Saudi Arabia.

In 1991, Khalifa was joined by Ramzi Yousef, his nephew, and Wali Khan Amin Shah. Yousef accompanied the ASG leader Janjalani on a tour of the Philippines sometime during the period from late 1991 to May 1992. The following year Yousef reportedly provided training in bomb-making techniques to twenty ASG personnel at a camp on Basilan Island.

International and regional terrorism experts invariably portray Ramzi Yousef as an al-Qaeda official. Yet a detailed biographical study, which does confirm intermittent links to al-Qaeda, concludes that Yousef was largely a "freelance terrorist" who pursued his own agenda.[25] For example, in 1994, Yousef, Wali Khan Amin Shah, and another associate, Abdul Hakim Murad, began planning a series of high-profile terrorist actions that took the code name Operation Bojinka. In December 1994, Yousef planted a bomb on a Philippines Airlines plane to test the feasibility of his master plan. Significantly, the ASG was kept out of the loop during the planning stages. According to Zachary Abuza, "Yousef really did not trust the ASG or think it capable enough to carry out serious terrorist acts."[26] In January 1995 a mishap resulted in the exposure of Yousef's terrorist cell and the eventual arrest of the three main plotters.[27]

In sum, the ASG's early ties to al-Qaeda were tenuous at best. The key to the ASG's external linkages was through the personal connections Janjalani had established with Yousef and Khalifa. According to a recent assessment, "by the mid to late 1990s these external ties had atrophied as the ASG veered into criminality and MILF training facilities in south-central Mindanao proved far more attractive for al-Qaeda and its regional allies."[28] Between 1991 and 1997, for example, the ASG conducted sixty-seven terrorist attacks across the Philippines. The ASG targeted foreign missionaries and a Catholic bishop, but at least half of all its attacks were viewed as indiscriminate.

The character of the ASG changed with the death of Janjalani in December 1998. As a result of ASG's growing notoriety, it attracted the support of a number of criminal gangs active in the Sulu archipelago. In April 2000 the ASG kidnapped foreign tourists from a resort on the Malaysian island of Sipadan and the following year kidnapped a number of foreign tourists in Palawan. The unity of the ASG has degenerated into a number of semiautonomous factions whose stock in trade consisted of bombings, assassinations, extortion, and kidnapping for ransom.[29] Ransom and extortion are sure signs that the ASG is not receiving significant external funding from al-Qaeda.[30]

A country specialist perspective on the ASG indicates that, far from being an al-Qaeda affiliate, the ASG is a homegrown criminal gang that employs terror tactics as its modus operandi. The ASG has given only occasional lip service to its pretension of establishing an independent Islamic state in western Mindanao and the Sulu archipelago. The ASG has been able to persist mainly due to clan loyalties in its area of operations and because the local Muslim population does not trust the Armed Forces of the Philippines, an organization that is viewed as Christian oppressors.

Jemaah Islamiya

In the wake of the 2002 Bali bombings, JI emerged as the premier terrorist group in Southeast Asia. It was quickly proscribed by the United Nations and the U.S. government. As a result, JI is routinely identified by the media and international and regional terrorist experts as an al-Qaeda affiliate. Yet, according to one of Australia's leading counterterrorism experts, "[t]here is, as far as I'm aware, no evidence of al-Qaeda involvement [in the Bali bombings]."[31] Until security sweeps were conducted by Malaysia and Singaporean authorities in late 2001, JI was virtually unknown. Reportedly even the Singapore government was reluctant at first to identify JI by name in its white paper.

Jemaah Islamiya is in part the modern-day successor to the Darul Islam movement of the 1940s and 1950s.[32] Members of Darul Islam sought to create an Islamic state based on Sharia law in Indonesia. They fought first against the Dutch and then the Republic of Indonesia. The Darul Islam movement was crushed, but remnants survived and carried its spirit into the 1980s and 1990s. In 1992 a rift occurred between its two senior leaders that "resulted directly in JI's creation as an organization separate and distinct from Darul Islam."[33]

Prior to 1992, Jemaah Islamiya referred to a broad-based Islamic community bound together by common aspirations rather than to a de facto organization.[34] Abdullah Sungkar and Abu Bakar Bashir, two Muslim clerics, played a prominent role in the emergence of Jemaah Islamiya. During the 1960s they set up a pirate radio station to propagate the introduction of Sharia law in Indonesia. In 1972 they founded the Pesantren Al Mukmin school in Ngruki village in central Java and promoted the radical Salafi-Wahhabi school of Islamic thought.[35] Alumni from this school later formed the hard core of JI, which became known as a terrorist organization.

JI became caught up in a Machiavellian plan hatched by military intelligence chief Ali Moertopo designed to smoke out Islamic extremists in Indonesia. In 1978, Sungkar and Bashir were jailed, released in 1982 after an appeal, and then resentenced to jail by the Supreme Court. In 1985, Sungkar and Bashir fled to Malaysia to escape further persecution. There they reestablished themselves and began preaching among the exiled Indonesian community. Eventually Sungkar established a boarding school in Johor that taught a radical Islamic curriculum. Several Ngruki alumni gravitated to Malaysia to join their mentors. They soon attracted supporters from Malaysia and Singapore.

The Jemaah Islamiya movement established by Sungkar and Bashir actively recruited volunteers to study in Pakistan and undertake paramilitary training in Afghanistan. Figures based on CIA estimates suggest that the number of Indonesians who trained in Afghanistan during the civil war ranged between 210–450 (low estimate) to 450–600 (high estimate).[36] It is significant to note that all senior members of JI's future central command underwent training at an Afghan camp run by Adbul Rasul Sayyaf, head of the Islamic Union for the Liberation of Afghanistan, one of several mujahideen factions. The first class of future JI leaders commenced training in 1985, and the last class completed its three-year course in 1994. A few Indonesians attended short training courses between 1993–95.[37]

In 1992, when Darul Islam split, Sungkar went to Afghanistan and called on Indonesians who were training at Sayyaf's camp to join JI. The vast majority did so. Due to infighting among the Afghan mujahideen, JI set up a camp at Torkham in eastern Afghanistan with the assistance of Sayyaf. It was at this time that JI instructors began to train members of the MILF.

Further instability in Afghanistan prompted JI to move again. In 1996, JI relocated to Camp Abu Bakar in Mindanao under an agreement reached with the MILF. Hundreds of militants were trained mainly by Indonesian Afghan veterans. The MILF's camp was overrun by the Filipino military in mid-2000. Current intelligence has revealed that the MILF quickly set up a new camp where Indonesian instructors began offering eighteen-month training courses for groups of from fifteen to thirty of their countrymen.[38] After completion of their course, they returned to Indonesia. There is little evidence that bin Laden or his al-Qaeda were ever directly involved in JI's training program in any significant way.

After the fall of Suharto in 1998, Sungkar and Bashir returned to central Java and resumed teaching at their school in Ngruki. Whatever personal bonds linked Sungkar to bin Laden, they were terminated with the former's death in 1999. Bashir reportedly replaced Sungkar as emir or spiritual leader of JI. Bashir has no reported direct links with al-Qaeda or bin Laden. However, he has played a signal role in encouraging the growth of Islamic militancy, if not Islamic extremism, in Indonesia. In 2002, Bashir was instrumental in forming the Mujahideen Council of Indonesia (Majelis Mujahideen Indonesia, or MMI) that brought together groups that advocated introducing Sharia law in Indonesia, preferably through the creation of an Islamic state. When sectarian strife broke out in the Mulukus and Sulawesi, extremist groups such as Laskar Jihad and Laskar Jundullah joined the fray, supported by their brethren from Malaysia and the Philippines.

During the period when Sungkar and Bashir were in exile in Malaysia, a hard core of militant activists formed Jemaah Islamiya. JI consists of a close-knit group of individuals bound together by religious indoctrination, experience in Afghan training camps, and marriage. This group forged regional linkages with militants in Indonesia, Malaysia, Singapore, and the Philippines. JI Singapore, for example, was probably founded in 1993 after its leader, a Singaporean religious teacher named Ibrahim Maidin, returned from a short military training course in Afghanistan. Maidin's relations with Bashir date to the late 1980s.

JI Malaysia was established around 1994–95 by Hambali and Abu Jibril[39] acting on instructions from Sungkar and Bashir. Hambali and Jibril concentrated their recruitment efforts among Indonesian migrants and university lecturers and students at the Universiti Teknologi Malaysia. They also sought out promising recruits from among students at Islamic schools. One school in Johor Baru stood out in particular. Ali Ghufron (alias Mukhlas), the school's master, and Imam Samudra, a student, were both later involved in the Bali bombings. Young militants recruited in Malaysia and Singapore were then sent to religious schools in Pakistan for ideological indoctrination. An estimated fifty Malaysians and Singaporeans were sent to training camps in Afghanistan during this period. Others were dispatched to MILF camps in Mindanao.

In the 1990s, members of JI became more proactive in seeking out contacts in Afghanistan and across the Southeast Asian region. JI's organizational development reached its high point in 1999–2001 primarily as a result of local initiatives set against the backdrop of personal connections between regional leaders and mujahideen officials in Afghanistan. JI is unique in that it developed a full-blown hierarchical administrative structure on the Malaysian peninsula as well as regionally.

Ordinary JI members who were recruited in Malaysia and Singapore took their direction from senior veterans of the Afghanistan war. Hambali personally recruited a militant hard core that formed a faction within JI. In 1999, Hambali ordered his recruits to form operational cells. They were later ordered to begin planning for a series of high-profile terrorist attacks against selected Western embassies in Singapore, U.S. military personnel in transit on shore leave, a U.S. warship in the Straits of Malacca, Changi airport, Singaporean defense facilities, and other targets. Al-Qaeda was apprised of these plans but took no action. It was only in 2000 that JI undertook its first terrorist actions. In August, JI members, possibly acting in coordination with MILF elements, attempted to assassinate the Philippine ambassador to Indonesia in a car bomb attack. In December, JI terrorists conducted a series of bombings of Christian churches in Indonesia as well as a bomb attack on the Manila light rail transport system.

In late 2001, when Malaysian and Singaporean security authorities broke up the JI-KMM network (see below), Hambali was reportedly so angry at the disruption of his plans that he decided to turn to softer targets such as nightclubs frequented by Western tourists. This led to the tragic terrorist bombings at Kuta Beach in Bali in October 2002. Hambali's actions provoked dissension in JI's ranks, including opposition to his tactics by Bashir himself. Australian intelligence reports "show a clear split between some JI cells strongly pushing for a return to political agitation and propaganda and others that advocate nothing less than increased militancy."[40] A senior member of Australia's counterterrorism effort notes that "JI has become a bit fractured from within," with a disparate collection of cells working at cross-purposes due to deep divisions over strategy and the lack of a clear leader.[41]

Terrorist activities by the JI network on peninsular Malaysia and in Singapore came to an abrupt end in 2001 when Malaysian police and Singapore's Internal Security Department (ISD) separately carried out arrests of a number of suspects charged with planning terrorist attacks.[42] In August 2002 the ISD arrested another 21 suspects, of whom 19 were identified as members of JI. As a result of these roundups, it is believed that most members of JI in Malaysia and Singapore have fled abroad while others went underground. There have been no further reports of JI activities in Malaysia and Singapore subsequently.

In a detailed and exhaustive investigation of JI and its external links to jihadists in Afghanistan, the International Crisis Group (ICG) concluded, "The information emerging from the interrogation of JI suspects indicates that this is a bigger organization than previously thought, with a depth of leadership that gives it a regenerative capacity. It has communication with and has received funding from al-Qaeda, but it is very much independent and takes most, if not all operational decisions locally."[43]

This observation is supported by an emerging consensus among Western and Asian government analysts who now view JI as "a stand-alone regional operation, with its own camps, recruiting, financing and agenda: the establishment of an Islamic state across the arc of Southeast Asia."[44] In other words, the historical record to date does not convincingly demonstrate that JI is an al-Qaeda affiliate or franchise. The ICG and other reports demonstrate that JI leaders in Indonesia have been able to set their own agenda and conduct independent external relations. In other words, they have agency.

International terrorism experts and regional security analysts include all manner of militant Islamic groups in their analysis of political terrorism in Southeast Asia. This approach is methodologically unsound because, in the absence of an agreed definition of terrorism, the basis of classification of a group as a terrorist organization cannot be established.

The question of what constitutes a militant Islamic group is equally problematic. The security literature that discusses terrorism and Islam in Southeast Asia employs a number of descriptors such as: fundamentalist, deviationist, radical, militant, and extremist.[45] Often these terms are used interchangeably. Militancy is routinely equated with terrorism.

Merely establishing links between al-Qaeda officials and regional terrorists tells us very little about the substance of this relationship. For example, international and regional terrorism experts routinely identify the MILF as an al-Qaeda–affiliated terrorist group. Yet the MILF has not been designated by the United Nations, the United States, or the Republic of the Philippines government as a terrorist organization. As one of the leading specialists on Islamic movements in Southeast Asia has recently concluded, "[t]here is no evidence to suggest, however, that the MILF is itself a terrorist organization."[46] International and regional terrorism experts include groups such as the MILF in their discussion of terrorist organizations because it is a militant Islamic group with some form of historical connection to al-Qaeda.

The analysis presented in this chapter strongly supports the findings of country specialists that the al-Qaeda–centric paradigm adopted by international terrorism experts and regional security analysts is flawed. Such an approach overvalues the role and influence of Osama bin Laden and al-Qaeda. According to Michael Pillsbury, a terrorism consultant to the Pentagon, regionally focused terrorist groups have their own agenda, they cooperate with al-Qaeda to learn its operational techniques or to benefit from their contacts, but they are not subordinate to al-Qaeda.[47] Or as Robert Hefner has observed, "[n]otwithstanding its ability to foster proxy violence, so far al-Qaeda's ambition of linking Southeast Asian struggles to its own internationalism has little to show for the effort."[48]

While international and regional linkages do exist, the historical record indicates that Southeast Asia's politically violent groups have agency. They largely set their own objectives and act independently to achieve them. As noted by Jason Burke in his seminal study of al-Qaeda: "But the temptation to see these groups, 'the network of networks,' as 'bin Laden-linked' or part of al-Qaeda must be resisted. 'Al-Qaeda,' or even bin Laden, may perform a specific function for many of them at specific times but Algerian, Chechen and Indonesian groups are rooted in specific local contingencies and causes. Islamic militancy is a broad-based, multivalent, diverse movement. It goes far beyond the deeds or words of one man or one small organization."[49]

Political Terrorism in Southeast Asia: A Net Assessment

What sort of net assessment can be made about political terrorism in Southeast Asia at the end of 2003? First, the overthrow of the Taliban regime and the destruction of al-Qaeda's camp system in Afghanistan has broken up and severely disrupted al-Qaeda's international network. According to Cofer Black, the U.S. State Department's coordinator for counterterrorism, "More than two-thirds of the al-Qaeda leadership of the 9/11 period have either been arrested or detained or no longer represent a threat . . . and more than 3,000 al-Qaeda [members] and their supporters have been arrested and detained."[50] Second, the international community has been mobilized to cut sources of funding to al-Qaeda and prevent money laundering by terrorist groups. According to Black, over 172 countries have issued directions to freeze terrorist assets totaling US$136 million. Eighty-four countries have established financial intelligence units; and 685 accounts identified with terrorist groups around the world have been blocked.[51]

Third, as a result of cooperation by Western and Southeast Asian intelligence and law enforcement agencies, over two hundred top JI leaders have been arrested. This has knocked the wind out of the sails of the regional JI network. Several long-planned operations have been disrupted. Fourth, counterterrorism action by security authorities has eliminated JI cells in Singapore and Malaysia and left stillborn JI's efforts to forge links with militant groups in southern Thailand, Burma, Cambodia, and Brunei. Fifth, Indonesian police have been reasonably efficient in rounding up and putting on trial members of JI who were involved in the Bali and Marriott Hotel bombings. Sixth, military cooperation between the Philippines and the United States has been effective in rooting out the presence of the ASG on Basilan Island. Joint cooperation continues to be focused on rooting out the ASG in the southern Philippines.

Despite this generally upbeat assessment, political terrorism in Southeast Asia remains a potent threat. The U.S. government estimates that five hundred JI members are still active throughout the region. Australia's defense minister has offered this assessment:

> There are senior Malaysian and Indonesian operatives still at large who provide JI continuity of leadership and direction. And there are many other well-trained JI operatives who gained specialized bomb-making and military expertise at al-Qaeda mujahideen camps in Afghanistan, and who could serve as field commanders for operations. We have no indications that the ongoing arrests of JI members across the region have seriously damaged JI's command and control. JI has been able to continue planning and executing terrorist attacks despite the arrest of over 200 members, including some of its most senior operatives, since 2001.

A study by the International Crisis Group has revealed the existence in Indonesia of heretofore unknown local terrorist groups and signs of increasing cooperation between JI members and criminal syndicates. Australia's defense minister has also confirmed "a growing nexus of personal ties between JI and domestic extremist groups."[52] JI still retains its regional reach as the continued existence of JI training camps in the Philippines illustrates. And efforts to disrupt the terrorists' financial network in Southeast Asia are still at a nascent stage.[53] In sum, JI still maintains the capacity to conduct further terrorist attacks either against Western targets or aimed at destabilizing local governments, Indonesia's in particular.

Notes

The views expressed in this paper are the author's personal views and do not reflect the policy or position of the Australian government or any of its departments or agencies.

1. Greg Fealy, "Is Indonesia a Terrorist Base? The Gulf Between Rhetoric and Evidence Is Wide," *Inside Indonesia* (July–September 2002).

2. United Nations, Office on Drugs and Crime, "Definitions of Terrorism," http://www.unodc.org/unodc/terrorism_definitions.html.

3. "Kuala Lumpur Declaration on International Terrorism," adopted at the Extraordinary Session of the Islamic Conference of Foreign Ministers on Terrorism, April 1–3, 2002. http://www.oic-oci.org/english/fm/11_extraordinary/declaration.htm.

4. Michael Chandler, a U.N. specialist on international terrorism, has compiled an additional list of 104 terrorist individuals and entities from public sources that are

not included on the U.N. consolidated list; see Cable News Network, United Nations, December 18, 2002.

5. Jason Burke, *Al-Qaeda: Casting a Shadow of Terror* (London: I.B. Tarus, 2003), presents a rigorous challenge to the al-Qaeda–centric paradigm from an international perspective.

6. The following are representative: Rohan Gunaratna, *Inside al-Qaeda: Global Network of Terror* (New York: Columbia University Press, 2002); Peter L. Bergen, *Holy War, Inc.: Inside the Secret World of Osama bin Laden* (New York: Simon & Schuster, 2001); and Jane Corbin, *The Base: Al-Qaeda and the Changing Face of Global Terror* (London: Pocket Books, 2002).

7. See Gunaratna's post-Bali edition, *Inside al-Qaeda: Global Network of Terror* (New York: Berkeley Books, 2002).

8. Corbin, *The Base,* p. 313.

9. The following are representative: Zachary Abuza, "Tentacles of Terror: Al Qaeda's Southeast Asian Network," *Contemporary Southeast Asia* 24, no. 3 (December 2002): 427–65; Maria A. Ressa, *Seeds of Terror: An Eyewitness Account of Al-Qaeda's Newest Center of Operations in Southeast Asia* (New York: Free Press, 2003); and Peter Chalk, "Al Qaeda and Its Links to Terrorist Groups in Asia," in *The New Terrorism: Anatomy, Trends, and Counter-Strategies,* ed. Andrew Tan and Kumar Ramakrishna (Singapore: Eastern Universities Press, 2002), pp. 107–28;

10. Hambali (Riduan Isamuddin) was a graduate of the Pesantren al-Mukmin (see below), and a veteran of the Afghan conflict.

11. See Angel M. Rabasa, *Political Islam in Southeast Asia: Moderates, Radicals, and Terrorists,* Adelphi Paper 358 (London: Oxford University Press, 2003), p. 62.

12. KMM was first identified by the Malaysian government as Kumpulan Mujahideen Malaysia; this was later changed without explanation to Kumpulan Militan Malaysia. This shift in title from holy warriors to militants conforms to the official view that Malaysia's terrorists are mainly homegrown. Some country specialists believe the term KMM was coined by the Malaysia government as a means of highlighting Islamic militancy as a threat to the state. For a discussion, see James Cotton, "Southeast Asia after 11 September," *Terrorism and Political Violence* 15, no. 1 (spring 2003): 154–56.

13. Chalk, "Al-Qaeda and Its Links to Terrorist Groups in Asia," p. 115.

14. Michael Davis, "Laskar Jihad and the Political Position of Conservative Islam in Indonesia," *Contemporary Southeast Asia* 24, no. 1 (April 2002): 12–32.

15. Ibid., p. 28.

16. Representatives of this group include: John Funston (Malaysia); and Robert Hefner, Sidney Jones, Greg Fealy, Greg Barton, and Martin van Bruinessen (Indonesia).

17. Martin van Bruinessen, "Genealogies of Islamic Radicalism in post-Suharto Indonesia," *South East Asia Research* 10, no. 2 (2002): 117–24; Robert W. Hefner, *Civil Islam: Muslims and Democratization in Indonesia* (Princeton, NJ: Princeton University Press, 2000); and Greg Barton, "Indonesia at the Crossroads: Islam, Islamism, and the Fraught Transition to Democracy," paper presented to the conference Islam and the West: The Impact of September 11, cosponsored by Monash University and the University of Western Australia, Melbourne, August 15–16, 2003.

18. Bergen, *Holy War, Inc.,* p. 62.

19. Jessica Stern, "The Protean Enemy," *Foreign Affairs* 82, no. 4 (July–August 2003): 27–40.

20. Burke, *Al-Qaeda*, p. 80.

21. Ibid., pp. 4–5.

22. Ibid., p. 101.

23. Quoted in ibid., p. 263, n. 27.

24. Ibid., p. 101; and Bergen, *Holy War, Inc.*, p. 222.

25. Simon Reeve, *The New Jackals: Ramzi Yousef, Osama bin Laden, and the Future of Terrorism* (Boston: Northeastern University Press, 1999).

26. Abuza, "Tentacles of Terror," p. 443.

27. Abdul Hakim Murad was arrested almost immediately in the Philippines. Ramzi Yousef was apprehended in February 1995 in Islamabad and deported to the United States. Wali Khan Amin Shah, who was arrested, escaped, and rearrested, was deported to the United States in December 1995.

28. Anthony Davis, "Resilient Abu Sayyaf Resists Military Pressure," *Jane's Intelligence Review*, September 1, 2003, Internet edition.

29. U.S. Department of State, Office of the Coordinator for Counterterrorism, *Patterns of Global Terrorism, 2002,* appendix B.

30. For example, in a detailed account of Islamic separatism in the southern Philippines, al-Qaeda's provision of finance and training in explosives to the ASG rates only a brief mention. See Andrew Tan, *Armed Rebellion in the ASEAN States: Persistence & Implications.* Canberra Papers on Strategy and Defence no. 135 (Canberra: Strategic and Defence Studies Centre, Australian National University, 2000), pp. 24, 28.

31. Clive Williams, "Keeping Tabs on the War Against Terrorism," *Canberra Times,* May 14, 2003, p. 15.

32. The discussion in this section relies in part on: *Indonesia Backgrounder: How the Jemaah Islamiyah Terrorist Network Operates,* ICG Asia Report no. 43, Jakarta and Brussels, International Crisis Group, December 11, 2002; Republic of Singapore, Ministry of Home Affairs, *White Paper: The Jemaah Islamiya Arrests and the Threat of Terrorism,* January 7, 2003; and *Jemaah Islamiya in South East Asia: Damaged But Still Dangerous,* ICG Asia Report no. 63, Jakarta and Brussels, International Crisis Group, August 26, 2003.

33. *Jemaah Islamiya in South East Asia,* p. 6.

34. Note the distinction made recently by the Australian defense minister: "It should go without saying that in referring to 'Jemaah Islamiya' I am talking about the terrorist organization that has been listed by the United Nations, not about the peaceful 'community of Islam' that the term traditionally denotes." See Senator Robert Hill, Minister for Defence, "Regional Terrorism, Global Security, and the Defence of Australia," speech given to the RUSI Triennial International Seminar, Canberra, October 9, 2003, p. 2.

35. *Al-Qaida in Southeast Asia: The Case of the 'Ngruki Network' in Indonesia,* Indonesia Briefing, Brussels and Jakarta, International Crisis Group, August 8, 2002.

36. Chris Wilson, *Indonesia and Transnational Terrorism,* Current Issues Brief no. 6, Canberra, Parliament of Australia, Department of the Parliamentary Library, October 11, 2001, p. 4.

37. *Jemaah Islamiya in South East Asia,* p. 2.

38. Alan Sipress and Ellen Nakashima, "Al Qaeda Affiliate Training Indonesians on Philippine Island," *Washington Post,* November 17, 2003, p. A18.

39. He was arrested by Malaysian police in June 2003.

40. Quoted in Martin Chulov and Patrick Walters, "JI Deeply Divided on Use of Violence," *The Australian,* August 14, 2003.

41. Ibid.

42. Abu Jibril was apprehended in June 2001 by Malaysian police.

43. *Jemaah Islamiya in Southeast Asia,* p. i.

44. Raymond Bonner, "Officials Fear New Attacks by Militants in Southeast Asia," *New York Times,* November 22, 2003.

45. Mohamed Jawhar Hassan, "Terrorism: Southeast Asia's Response," Pacific Forum CSIS PacNet 1, January 4, 2002. For the challenge that militant Islam poses to ASEAN, see David Martin Jones and Mike Lawrence Smith, "From *Konfrontasi* to *Disintegrasi:* ASEAN and the Rise of Islamism in Southeast Asia," *Studies in Conflict & Terrorism* 25 (2002): 343–56; Robert W. Hefner, "Islam and Asian Security," in *Strategic Asia, 2002–03: Asian Aftershocks,* ed. Richard J. Ellings and Aaron L. Friedberg (Seattle, WA: National Bureau of Asian Research, 2002), pp. 351–61, 373–402.

46. Robert W. Hefner, "Political Islam in Southeast Asia: Assessing the Trends," keynote address to the conference on Political Islam in Southeast Asia, organized by the Southeast Asia Studies Program, Paul H. Nitze School of Advanced International Studies, Johns Hopkins University, Washington, DC, March 25, 2003, p. 7.

47. Quoted in Douglas Farah and Peter Finn, "Terrorism Inc.," *Washington Post,* November 21, 2003, p. A33.

48. Hefner, "Political Islam in Southeast Asia," p. 7.

49. Burke, *Al-Qaeda,* p. 235.

50. David Denny, Washington File (at www.usinfo.state.gov) staff writer, transcript of interview with Ambassador Cofer Black, "Counterterrorism Indicators 'All Very Positive,' Cofer Black Says," September 11, 2003, p. 3.

51. Ibid., p. 6.

52. Hill, "Regional Terrorism, Global Security, and the Defence of Australia," p. 2.

53. Zachary Abuza, "Funding Terrorism in Southeast Asia: The Financial Network of Al Qaeda and Jemaah Islamiya," *Contemporary Southeast Asia* 25, no. 2 (August 2003): 169–99.

6

Terrorism and the Political Landscape in Indonesia

The Fragile Post-Bali Consensus

Anthony L. Smith

Introduction

A year after the Bali blast (October 12, 2002) killed 202 people, Indonesia's president, Megawati Sukarnoputri, declined to attend the anniversary commemorations. Megawati claimed that she had a conflicting state engagement (a visit to Algeria), and that a memorial—an extension of mourning—was not consistent with the island's Hindu values (despite Bali's gubernatorial authorities involvement in commemorations). Indonesia's Coordinating Minister of Security, Susilo Bambang Yudhoyono, attended in place of his chief executive. While Indonesia has produced real results against Jemaah Islamiya (JI) in the wake of the Bali blast, with nearly one hundred jihadis imprisoned, the fact that Megawati could miss a memorial for the largest single terrorist incident on Indonesian soil—apparently with little or no domestic controversy—indicates that fighting "international terrorism" may not be regarded as Indonesia's top challenge by both the political elite and the masses. Although it ignored the problem prior to the Bali blast, the Indonesian government has freely acknowledged the terrorist threat since. But while a consensus has emerged among mainstream Muslim leaders about the need to check violent radical ideologies, a large section of the Indonesian public remains skeptical about the threat posed by Jemaah Islamiya—or indeed, whether such an organization even exists. The Indonesian population, as this chapter will argue, is not a prime recruiting ground for radical Islamist ideologies. Only moderate Islamist parties currently have achieved any political representation, and even they are far too weak to implement their agenda. The vast majority of Indonesia's population has been schooled to view political Islam as a direct contradiction to the Republic of Indonesia's survival as a multiethnic and multireligious state. However, Indonesia's "enabling environment" for Jemaah Islamiya has been a widespread public disbelief about the threat posed. Many still view the whole war against terrorism as a plan to weaken Islam.

Indonesia's Political Landscape and Islam

Indonesia is the world's largest Muslim nation, yet the role of Islam in political life has been constrained for most of Indonesia's postindependence history. Broadly speaking, there are two major reasons for this. First of all, Indonesia's constitutional framers, including founding President Sukarno, believed that a pluralistic and secular[1] state was the best way to create nationhood among the diverse peoples of the former Dutch East Indies. Generations of Indonesians were socialized to accept that any role for Islam in the public sphere would threaten the very cohesion of the multiethnic and multireligious republic. Second, while almost 90 percent of Indonesia's 220 million people state that they belong to the Islamic faith, Islamic practice varies markedly. Islam probably arrived in Southeast Asia around the thirteenth century, being established first in Aceh and then reaching the rest of maritime Southeast Asia in successive waves over several hundred years. The differences in Islamic practice generally reflect a division between interior and coastal peoples, as seaborne traders from Islamic countries established Islam during different time periods and with differing intensity. However, in recent years a growing Islamic revival coupled with religious education has given greater numbers access to a more orthodox understanding of Islam. Historically, much of Java has been described as Abangan, that is, a syncretic variation of Islam, Hinduism, and old Javanese animist traditions.

It is evident that in the last few decades there has been an emerging orthodoxy in Islamic practice. Many commentators have noted the "Arabization" of Indonesian Islam in recent decades, although the term is somewhat clumsy given that Islam as a faith has Arabic origins and is firmly grounded in the Arabic language. Arabic influences on Indonesian Muslims have old origins, and Muslim clerics across the religious and political spectrum look to scholars and institutions in the Middle East as sources of learning—a number of such scholars continue to defend a pluralistic and democratic Indonesia. Minor inroads have been made by Salafi teachers in a handful of Islamic boarding schools *(pesantren)* with the assistance of Saudi funding sources. Within this movement, some Salafist teachers have gone beyond the purist version of Islamic practice to adopt a radical political agenda—Robert Hefner, an authority on Islam in Southeast Asia, terms this a "neo-Salafi" movement.[2]

Beginning in the mid-1970s, funding from Saudi sources began arriving in Indonesia to fund organizations and religious schools. Rabita al-Alam al-Islami, a private Saudi charity, funded about 180 Indonesian institutions but the money was required by the Suharto government to be channeled through the Ministry of Religious Affairs.[3] While the money, public and private, has gone to an array of recipients, some of the money has landed in the hands of hard-line organizations and individuals.[4] For example, Jafar Umar Thalib, the infamous leader of Laskar Jihad, received his education and funding from Saudi authorities—although it should be noted that this was prior to Thalib's more radical phase. Nonetheless, Thalib retains a deep regard for the Saudi state, which remains his "model" and sets him apart from Jemaah Islamiya and its al-Qaeda allies.

The impact of this growing orthodoxy, perhaps contrary to the expectations of many outside commentators, has not been to undermine in any meaningful way the secular constitution or the democratic process—although a small minority that identifies with more orthodox Islam is opposed to secular democracy. But while democratization is far from complete in Indonesia, "Islamic forces" have not derailed it. In fact, many Muslim leaders in Indonesia have actively campaigned to bring authoritarianism to an end. In 1998, during the *reformasi* period, prominent Islamic leaders led the campaign to oust Suharto and restore democracy. Indonesia's two most well-known leaders, Amien Rais and Abdurrahman Wahid, emerged as the most prominent advocates of democracy at the time (despite the fact that both have spotty historical records with regard to prior support for the Suharto regime), while Nurcholish Madjid emerged as the most prominent of Indonesia's intellectuals to defend the idea of democracy—Madjid also happens to be Indonesia's most highly regarded neomodernist Islamic scholar.

While political Islam emerged into the open with the end of Suharto's authoritarianism, Suharto cultivated a more Islamic image during his last decade in office. Prior to the 1990s the Suharto administration had rigidly controlled fringe Islamic groups, even to the extent of allowing the army to brutally repress radicals from time to time. Many hard-liners left Indonesia, including the leadership of what was to become Jemaah Islamiya. But by the early 1990s, Suharto had become strongly involved in Islamic identity politics, which most interpret as his means of balancing the power of the military. The Suharto regime facilitated the creation of Ikatan Cendekiawan Muslim se-Indonesia (ICMI) under Suharto's protégé, B.J. Habibie, to bring together Islamic scholars. The Council of Ulema (Majelis Ulema Indonesia, or MUI) was also co-opted as a body for Islamic scholars, while Suharto ensured that its leaders were loyal to his rule. Suharto also made political capital out of his haj to Mecca, the adoption of a Muslim name ("Muhammad"), and the revoking of a ban on veils for women in public schools. As Suharto's reign drew to an end, it took a decidedly anti-American and anti-Jewish turn. Hardline Muhammadiyah cleric and Suharto loyalist Din Syamsuddin and others peddled the message that the 1997 financial crisis was the result of a Zionist plot. Suharto himself articulated these ideas: "Although once an ally of the United States, in his last years Suharto and his family members provided extensive support to groups promoting this fiercely anti-American, anti-Christian, and anti-Semitic message. In a rare interview with Japanese journalists almost a year after his resignation, Suharto again blamed Jews for his ouster.[5]

The "greening" of Suharto's regime was also accompanied by the president's earlier alignment with the Islamic right wing. Elements of the military ceased to regard radical Islamic groups as enemies of the state. Hefner notes that during the 1990s, Thalib and other radicals reconciled themselves to the Suharto regime.[6] However, other radicals, notably JI leader Abu Bakar Bashir, could return to Indonesia only once Suharto had stepped down. This indicates a clear division between those who made an accommodation with the state and those who did not. This gives a clearer indication of why elements of the armed forces gave substantial help to Thalib's Laskar Jihad during the Ambon and Poso conflicts without this being viewed as detrimental to national security.

Suharto's resignation from office in May 1998 ushered in a period of democratization in Indonesia that resulted in an election in 1999—the first relatively free election in Indonesia since 1955. The changing political landscape saw Indonesians returning in large part to the voting patterns that had existed in 1955. It could be said that Indonesians returned to more parochial interests, determined by habitual religious, ideological, or institutional affiliations, usually known as *aliran* (cultural streams) in Indonesia. Political parties failed to differentiate themselves on policy, instead opting to promote the personalities of their leaders. Megawati Sukarnoputri sought the "secular-nationalist" vote on the basis of being the daughter of the ever-popular founding president. However, while Megawati probably took the vast majority of the non-Muslim vote in Indonesia, well over half of all her votes were cast by Muslims, and Megawati herself is a Muslim by background. Those who belonged to Muslim organizations, however, largely cast their votes to parties that sought to capture an Islamic constituency. Indonesia's two largest Muslim organizations (also the world's largest) are Nahdlatul Ulama (NU) and Muhammadiyah, with followers numbering (in rough estimates) 35 million and 28 million respectively. NU and Muhammadiyah represent two obvious *aliran*—NU votes tended to remain behind their own leader, Abdurrahman Wahid, while Muhammadiyah votes were scattered between various Islamic political parties.

The current political configuration of Indonesia's legislature is revealing of the prevailing political culture. In the 1999 elections (regarded as largely free and fair), two secular parties won the lion's share of the vote: Megawati's PDI-P (Indonesia Democracy Party, or Struggle) gained 34 percent of the vote and Golkar, Suharto's old party, gained 23 percent. Wahid's party, PKB (National Awakening Party), based on the NU organization, gained 13 percent and has consistently promoted a secular state. PAN (National Mandate Party), with 7 percent of the vote, largely drawing from Muhammadiyah for support but actively recruiting non-Muslims as candidates, has also rejected the Islamization of the state. There is a tendency to refer to the various political parties in Parliament that have a Muslim constituency as "Muslim parties" or "political Islam." In the case of PKB and PAN, only their constituency was "Muslim" while their philosophy during the election remained behind a secular and democratic state. (A hard-line group within PAN has since advocated a more Islamist position.)

Some of the other Muslim parties together with PAN constitute a voting bloc known as the Poros Tengah (Central Alliance). The smaller Muslim parties have been more partisan in religious terms but are still far from promoting radical visions of a theocratic state, not least of all because they accept the supremacy of the ballot box and do not promote violence as a means to power. PPP (United Development Party, of the vice president, Hamzah Haz), PBB (Moon and Star Party), and PK (Justice Party) are minor parties that have urged an alteration to the Constitution—that states that Sharia law should apply to all Muslims in Indonesia—known as the Jakarta Charter. Given that Sharia already applies in theory to Muslims in terms of family and inheritance law, the change being proposed here is largely symbolic, but it is more than just cosmetic. Symbols are important to statehood, and such a change would alienate non-Muslims (as well as many moderate Muslims) as it would establish Islam as the state religion. To put this in context, these smaller Islamist parties are advocating a change that would bring Indonesia in line with Malaysia—which does formally list Islam as the official state faith. In any event, the percentage of the Indonesian electorate who voted for candidates advocating the Jakarta Charter hovered somewhere between 10–16 percent.[7]

Megawati, as leader of Indonesia's largest political party, has had a sometimes torrid relationship with the other parties in Parliament, and much of the debate has taken a religious identification tone. Megawati has proved quite vulnerable to criticism from the Islamic "right wing"—an issue that proved an important stumbling block after September 11 as the U.S. sought Indonesian assistance in the war against terrorism. The Indonesian president was undermined during 1999 when there was considerable discussion within the Muslim community about whether a woman could be president of Indonesia.[8] Subsequent events seemed to suggest that partisanship had triumphed over principle in this case, when it became no longer convenient to block a woman from Indonesia's top job. The smaller Islamic parties, who had earlier stated that a woman could not be president, changed their minds when they voted to oust Wahid and install Megawati in June 2001. Some leaders of these parties were rewarded with cabinet positions, as Megawati established her Gotong Royong (Mutual Assistance) multiparty cabinet. Indonesia's coalition cabinet barely conceals the fact that Indonesia's political parties are locked in serious competition. The line between government and opposition is blurred, with some of Megawati's main opponents sitting at her own cabinet table.

Megawati's political opposition has sought to use Megawati's weak Muslim credentials against her. The president's gender is grounds enough for the attack, but she is also regarded as "nominal." Megawati and her PDI-P Party have had to take great care to not provoke domestic criticism that they are somehow antithetical to the interests of the Islamic faith. This helps explain Megawati's apparent weakness in dealing with radicalized groups—particularly prior to the Bali blast. It also places constraints on the support that Indonesia can give to the United States and the rest of the international community.

However, it is important to note that this does not in any way mean that Indonesia is on the verge of having to decide between secular and theocratic forces. Islamist parties simply do not have the political strength to bring about a constitutional change that would turn Indonesia into even a moderate version of an "Islamic state." That support for an Islamic state in Indonesia is a redundancy was most evident at the Upper House (MPR) Annual Session in 2002. A number of amendments were introduced to strengthen the Indonesian political system and make it a more orthodox presidential system. Notable principally by its failure was an attempt to include the Jakarta Charter in the Constitution. The amendment did not even come close to gaining a third of MPR members in support—the minimum necessary to place an amendment on the floor. In an embarrassing setback for hard-line Islamist legislators, the issue is revealed as a nonstarter, even among the majority of Muslim lawmakers.[9]

What these political trends demonstrate is that there is very little support for a marriage of mosque and state, while violent Islamic movements have no representation in Parliament at all. That Indonesia is a "moderate" Muslim country is received wisdom inside Indonesia itself. However, this assessment, which is largely correct, may have caused the Indonesian political elite to underestimate the emergence of radical groups inside Indonesia.

September 11 and the Domestic Implications for Indonesia

The terrorist attacks of September 11 on the U.S. mainland had a noticeable impact on the domestic political situation in Indonesia. In the immediate aftermath of the attacks, Megawati traveled to the United States and issued a statement of condemnation of the attacks and moral support for the United States. One of Megawati's chief rivals, her own vice president, Hamzah Haz, attempted to undermine the Megawati government's reaction to September 11. Hamzah Haz, both second-guessing the motives of the terrorists and failing to offer sympathy to the United States, blamed America's "sins" as a cause for the attacks.[10] He subsequently explained that he was referring to U.S. foreign policy. Haz later backtracked a little by lauding U.S. President Bush for distinguishing between "Muslims" and "terrorists." Haz's remarks on U.S. foreign policy did reflect a mood in Indonesia, however. Most Indonesians appear to have been opposed to the U.S. counterattack on Afghanistan. Protests mounted on the streets of Jakarta, principally against the U.S. and British embassies.

Indonesia gained a US$400 million trade-and-aid deal from the United States during Megawati's visit, but there were strong indications that elements of the U.S. government were not happy that Megawati subsequently opposed the U.S. campaign in Afghanistan. However, given public opposition to an invasion of Afghanistan, whipped up by opposition parties, there was no possibility of the Megawati administration being able to countenance this type of U.S. military action. At first Megawati refused to support the U.S. attacks, and then subsequently asked the U.S. to limit its air strikes. Hard-line groups in Indonesia demanded that Indonesia cut ties, but the Indonesian political elite largely resisted this. Most leaders explained this to the domestic audience in terms of Indonesia needing good relations with the United States for trade and aid rather than portraying this as support for the United States in the global war against terrorism.

The U.S. war in Iraq, partly justified by the Bush administration as a war against terrorism, drew near-universal condemnation across the Indonesian political spectrum. On March 20, 2003, Megawati released a statement plainly stating that Indonesia "strongly deplores unilateral action against Iraq."[11] (Equally, Indonesia has long been an opponent of sanctions against Iraq, imposed after the 1990–91 Gulf War.) Even the moderate Nurcholish Madjid, one of Indonesia's most respected Islamic scholars and a democracy activist, labeled the U.S. action in Iraq as an act of "aggression."

Much of the discourse in Indonesia after September 11, from important political and civil society leaders, revolved around America's hasty reaction to the terrorist strike. Objections to the U.S. war on terrorism after September 11 focused on the United States producing real courtroom evidence of al-Qaeda's complicity in the terrorist attacks on the U.S. mainland and concentrated on addressing America's "crimes" in the Middle East (such as Palestine, a decade of sanctions against Iraq, and so on). Hasyim Muzadi, a leader of Nahdlatul Ulama, has questioned the conclusiveness of evidence against Osama bin Laden: "Proving the evidence is important to distinguishing which is Islam and which is terrorism. After it can be proven, attack the terrorists. Without the evidence . . . [retaliation] cannot be justified. If it does happen, the case for an attack will fade and be replaced by a war between Islam and Christianity."[12]

While it is a highly questionable assertion that al-Qaeda's attacks on the United States were inspired by U.S. foreign policy alone, it is the case that many in Indonesia have interpreted it through this prism. Achmad Sumargono, leader of the Indonesian Muslim Brotherhood, offered the following solution for the United States in a media interview: "[T]here must also be a correction made by . . . [the United States]. Firstly, their intelligence was very weak. And secondly, their policies regarding Palestine and their full backup for Israel must be corrected."[13] Well-known Indonesian academic and former presidential foreign policy adviser Dewi Fortuna Anwar has also suggested that September 11 was linked to U.S. policies toward Israel—remarks that the U.S. ambassador to Indonesia at the time, Robert Gelbard, described (perhaps harshly) as "anti-Semitic." These sentiments from prominent Indonesians reflect widespread beliefs about the cause of the problem, namely U.S. foreign policy, and partially explains why it has been so difficult to mobilize domestic opinion against the terrorists themselves.

In the aftermath of September 11, a number of small, hard-line groups in Indonesia, espousing a purist Islamic identity, upped the ante by suggesting more radical action against the United States. Some of these groups grabbed world headlines, particularly the Council of Ulema (MUI). MUI issued a statement even before the U.S. counterattack in Afghanistan, declaring a Jihad against the United States, causing great alarm.[14] Although this term has come to mean "holy war" in the West, in Islam it simply means "struggle" and covers a wide array of activities from Koranic study to personal salvation to political protest to "defense" in times of war. The Council of Ulema later clarified this statement to say that they were not referring to a violent jihad, but failed to retract the words or apologize. The Council of Ulema was plainly aware of the angst the word jihad would cause the U.S. and British diplomatic missions in Jakarta. The council also stated, "We condemn the attack of the U.S. in Afghanistan as a manifestation of arrogance and the true evil which challenges human rights and justice and truth."

Although in theory this is the highest body of Muslim scholars and clerics in Indonesia, it is the creation of President Suharto and widely regarded throughout Indonesia as a partisan body. Its influence is far less than the two largest mass Muslim organizations—NU and Muhammadiyah. It is notable that MUI continues to enjoy close personal links with the Golkar Party, Indonesia's second-largest political party and therefore the major rival of Megawati's PDI-P. MUI leader Din Syamsuddin has links to Laskar Jihad (which he supported in Ambon) and was instrumental is drumming up opposition to oust former President Wahid. Din Syamsuddin has a history of links to Suharto-era forces. MUI's statement highlighted the partisan nature of this debate in the aftermath of September 11. This shows how opponents of President Megawati were able to use the wider international backdrop. Megawati subsequently felt constrained in her actions, especially against the emergence of domestic terrorist cells.

A further political complication has been the use of fringe Islamic groups, and Islamic bodies created by the New Order state, which were a feature of Suharto's rule during the 1990s. It has even been claimed in a number of media sources that the terrorist group Jemaah Islamiya was established by military intelligence during this time[15]—although JI may well have taken an independent departure from its military creators in the *reformasi* era. One *Sydney Morning Herald* journalist, in the aftermath of the Bali bombing, noted that intelligence chief Ali Moertopo had, during Suharto's reign, co-opted extremist Islamic elements in order "to justify political crackdowns."[16] The point of this article was that elements of the military may not be clean on this issue—a theory that has some popularity in Indonesia itself. There is a great deal of evidence of military linkages with Islamic fringe groups and political parties, even in recent times.

Well prior to America's "war on terrorism," it has been evident for some time that some highly radicalized and violent groups have emerged in Indonesia—although the nature of possible links to al-Qaeda did not become clear until after the arrests of JI activists in Singapore and Malaysia in late 2001. While on current evidence it appears that of all such groups only Jemaah Islamiya is linked ideologically and financially to Osama bin Laden, Indonesia's failure to deal with other extremist groups demonstrates why the Megawati government failed to take adequate steps to stem a nascent threat.

Both the Islamic Defenders Front (FPI, or Front Pembela Islam) and Laskar Jihad have been the most high-profile of the radical groups in Indonesia prepared to use violence. FPI and Laskar Jihad are run by leaders who have ties of blood or friendship to the Middle East. Laskar Jihad's leader, Jafar Umar Thalib, is also a veteran of the mujahideen in Afghanistan during the Soviet occupation. Thalib claims to have met Osama bin Laden during this time, but has in a number of interviews (including interviews with the *BBC* and *The Economist*) dismissed him as having an unsound background in Islamic scholarship. Western intelligence sources claim that Laskar Jihad does gain funds, weapons, and personnel from the Middle East and Central Asia, allowing it to wade into the Ambon conflict with several thousand fighters. There is little evidence that al-Qaeda has made any sort of significant inroads into Indonesia through groups like Laskar Jihad or FPI, despite reports of past contact with al-Qaeda operatives.

However, even if these groups are not linked to Osama bin Laden, as they claim, they do represent an irritant to the cohesion of Indonesia. They threaten the notion of a pluralist society. Lack of police and military action has seen these groups act, until relatively recently, with disregard for the law. Both Laskar Jihad and FPI have caused internal trouble within Indonesia, but their threat is largely domestically confined, and their targets for violent action have also been domestic. The previous U.S. ambassador to Indonesia, Robert Gelbard, accused Indonesian security forces of being inactive and not taking terrorist threats seriously. Threats to U.S. citizens had occurred in the city of Solo since November 2000, when members of the FPI raided hotels for guest lists. The police interviewed FPI leaders at the time and expressed their disgust but failed to arrest any suspects. In that same month, the U.S. embassy briefly shut down due to security concerns. With the events of September 11, threats to the U.S. embassy were renewed. The Indonesian police claimed that they were powerless to intervene as no one had been injured. The disturbing trend here is that Indonesian law enforcement seemed unwilling to oppose such groups and may have contributed to Indonesia's reputation as a soft touch for terrorist cells.

Why was it that the Megawati administration was so slow to investigate the problem of terrorism? First of all, the Indonesian elite resisted strongly any notion of being seen to be giving in to foreign demands—especially after criticisms from its near neighbors. Second, politicians in Jakarta have been cautious in acting against Islamic groups, including Megawati herself, whose syncretistic Muslim background has been something her opponents have used against her (as mentioned earlier). Third, many in Indonesia have denied that Islamist extremists represent much of a threat, compounded by the fact that leaders like Bashir are sometimes seen as victims of Suharto-era repression. A fourth factor given by the Indonesia government for the failure to arrest Islamist radicals was the abolition of Suharto's antisubversion law that allowed for arbitrary arrest. But lack of will to investigate and prosecute in many cases—due to the first three reasons listed—seems a more convincing explanation, given that Laskar Jihad has broken the law on numerous occasions with near impunity.

The Indonesian military, "once a fierce opponent of radical Islam,"[17] according to Hefner, no longer treats jihadi groups as a principal threat to Indonesia's cohesion. Suharto's courting of conservative political Islamic groups spread to elements of the army that were loyal to the president himself. Furthermore, the Indonesian military is obsessed by the threat of separatism—particularly in the aftermath of East Timor's independence— and this is *the* primary threat. While the military has cut deals with groups like Laskar Jihad in Ambon, no such quarter is afforded to the Free Aceh Movement (Gerakan Aceh Merdeka, or GAM). In fact Laskar Jihad itself exhibits hypernationalist tendencies and has tried to set up operations in both Aceh and Papua to counter independence movements. GAM, often inaccurately described as an "Islamic insurgency" group, has distanced itself from both al-Qaeda and JI, stressing that it remains a nationalist grouping. After September 11, GAM members even issued a statement in support of the United States. While the United States and other members of the international community refuse to label GAM a terrorist link, the Indonesian government insists that GAM remains the most serious "terrorist" threat to Indonesia. Indonesian officials have accused Western officials of hypocrisy in attaching the terrorist label only to groups that target Western interests.

The United States has, in Indonesia's case, been quite careful about use of the terrorist label—Laskar Jihad and FPI are not listed as such. (Not that there is any pressure from Jakarta to do so.) In an interview, U.S. Assistant Secretary of Defense Paul Wolfowitz was asked if Laskar Jihad was a terrorist organization. He answered:

> I think the simple answer to "is it a terrorist organization?" is no. It is an organization that has engaged in some disruptive activity? I think the answer to that is yes. I know there are some Indonesians who very much don't like that sort of activity, who nevertheless feel they [Laskar Jihad] act more out of ignorance and more out of reaction to the difficult economic and social conditions in the country than out of a deep-seated sort of malice. . . . I know Indonesians whose opinions I respect a lot who think these people could be educated and persuaded to a different course of action. That's the reason why it's very difficult for people operating from the distance . . . to step into the middle of a country and make those kinds of judgments.[18]

Laskar Jihad's operations in Ambon and Poso are more than just "disruptive," as Wolfowitz euphemistically describes it. They are guilty of abuses against noncombatants—as is GAM in Aceh. However, the point is that the United States has taken great care in the case of Indonesia to reserve the "terrorist" label for al-Qaeda–linked individuals and groups in order to avoid being seen as supporting unpopular government actions (in the case of the military's human rights abuses in Aceh) or simply adding sundry Islamic groups to the list of terrorist groups. The differences between insurgent and terrorist groups are important. Noted Southeast Asian scholar Carl Thayer cautions against the application of a "homogenizing framework" in which groups responding to "long-standing local issues and grievances"—like separatist groups in the Southern Philippines—and groups that are linked to al-Qaeda are lumped together.[19] It should be noted that JI has established links with some members of the Moro Islamic Liberation Front (MILF), in which presumably JI gains training sites and provides the MILF with resources in return. There is no such evidence of cooperation between JI and members of GAM.

The Threat from Jemaah Islamiya

After the events of September 11, 2001, however, there was a more alarming development within Southeast Asia itself. A group more shadowy than the bellicose FPI and Laskar Jihad was uncovered by Singaporean and Malaysian authorities—a group that does have links to Osama bin Laden. Just several months after the attacks on the U.S. mainland, Singapore and Malaysia made the first of a series of arrests of activists associated with a group called Jemaah Islamiya (JI), which stood accused of threatening to blow up various targets in Singapore, including the U.S. Embassy. Both Singapore and Malaysia pointed to the existence of the network in Indonesia, in particular its operations leader, Riduan Isamuddin (usually known as "Hambali"), and its spiritual head, Abu Bakar Bashir. Indonesian authorities not only resisted regional pressure to arrest these suspects, but actively scotched the idea that there was a terrorist problem in Indonesia. Statements from Singapore, in particular, caused some angst in Jakarta.[20]

While emotional reactions to "foreign pressure" ran high through the early part of 2002, by June 2002 it was evident that the Megawati administration would cooperate to some extent with the United States on facing the terrorist problem in Indonesia itself. In early August, U.S. Secretary of State Colin Powell visited Indonesia and announced aid of US$50 million over three years to assist Indonesia in counterterrorist operations, with 50 percent of the funds tagged for the police. However, the money was not given without reservations. The U.S. ambassador to Jakarta, Ralph Boyce, stated at the time that this aid "does not represent a clean bill of health for past TNI [Indonesian military] actions which continue to be of concern to us."[21] Boyce's statement reflects the concern that the United States has over ongoing human rights abuses and a general lack of professionalism within the Indonesian military.

Even prior to the Bali bombings the Megawati government had proposed the introduction of a new, more robust antiterrorism law—although Indonesian legislators have consistently rejected the establishment of something akin to Singapore's Internal Security Act (ISA), which allows for the arbitrary detention of terrorist suspects. However, the lack of an ISA law does not explain why police have failed to act against radical groups that have openly broken Indonesia's civil code. For a number of years prior to the Bali blast, Indonesia's two most infamous radical Islamist groups, FPI and Laskar Jihad, openly broke the law many times. It was only after the Bali blast that leaders of both groups were arrested for violations of the law, including Laskar Jihad leader Jafar Umar Thalib, who incited a riotous crowd to attack a church. (Laskar Jihad announced its dissolution immediately after the Bali blast.)

A major breakthrough for security forces in undermining terrorist operations in Indonesia was the arrest in June 2002 of a senior al-Qaeda operative, Omar al-Faruq, who was residing in Bogor. Omar al-Faruq's revelations included: involvement in the 2000 Christmas Eve bombings in which churches were targeted in ten cities across Indonesia; an assassination attempt on Megawati; and plans for large-scale terrorist attacks against "U.S. interests" in Cambodia, Indonesia, Malaysia, the Philippines, Singapore, Taiwan, Thailand, and Vietnam.[22] The goal of these plans, to be carried out by JI, was to create an Islamic state in maritime Southeast Asia. Omar al-Faruq's evidence also led to the closing of the U.S. embassy in Jakarta on the eve of September 11, 2002. Hamzah Haz criticized the United States for closing its embassy, saying it unnecessarily damaged Indonesia's reputation.

Vice President Hamzah Haz, as a politician with his ear firmly to the ground of his political support, publicly embarrassed Megawati by openly associating with Bashir and Jafar Umar Thalib (the latter he visited in his jail cell). Haz also openly questioned evidence of radical Islamic groups and expressed contempt for both U.S. policy and the reliability of reports from the U.S. government. Denial was not confined to those courting the Islamic right wing. Even a well-regarded cabinet professional, foreign affairs minister, and career diplomat, Hassan Wirayuda, told reporters in February 2002 that the Indonesian cabinet laughed at suggestions from other countries that there may be a threat within Indonesia from radical Islamist groups.[23] It is also well known that many Indonesians regard warnings of terrorist cells within Indonesia as an American fabrication. One prominent articulator of this view is the president's own sister, Rachmawati Sukarnoputri, who has dismissed reports of radicalism within Indonesia as CIA "rumors" designed to undermine Islam and place Indonesia further under U.S. control.[24] A leader of the moderate Nahdlatul Ulama, Salahuddin Wahid (brother of the former president of Indonesia), accused Washington of engaging in "propaganda tricks."[25]

Before the Bali bombing there had been some guarded official recognition that there may be a problem. On the first anniversary of the September 11 attacks, Indonesia's National Police chief, General Da'i Bachtiar, said that although local terrorist groups existed in Indonesia, Bashir's alleged involvement in terrorism had not been proven.[26] He did, however, hedge a guess that when Hambali was arrested, there would be evidence pointing to Bashir. The national intelligence chief, Hendropriyono, had also publicly warned of a domestic terrorist threat and even spoken of an al-Qaeda terrorist camp in Central Sulawesi. In late September 2002, Indonesian military officials also acknowledged that there were terrorist groups in Indonesia. Army chief of staff Lieutenant General Ryamizard Ryacudu confirmed the existence of such groups at a press conference, but denied that they were linked to al-Qaeda.[27]

The Political Ramifications of Bali

The terrorist attack in Bali perpetrated by Jemaah Islamiya on October 12, 2002, had the immediate impact of forcing Indonesia to confront the home-grown problem of terrorism that the political elite had on the whole failed to take seriously. The governments of Malaysia, the Philippines, and Singapore had been warning for more than a year of the dangers of international terrorism in the region. Megawati's cabinet sang a different tune. Indonesia's minister of defense has announced that the Bali attack was the work of al-Qaeda—although in doing so he may have added to an impression that Bali was the work of foreigners. Mainstream Islamic groups in Indonesia also condemned the attack.

The Indonesian government had little choice but to respond. A warrant was issued for Bashir's arrest immediately after the bombing, as evidence was found to detain him (a detention that was initially delayed due to a health complaint). Bashir continues to deny that he is an al-Qaeda–linked terrorist leader, yet his protestations are highly suspicious when they are qualified by sympathy for Osama bin Laden. He told *Time:* "I don't have any link whatsoever with al-Qaeda, . . . but if al-Qaeda's struggle is for the best interest of Islam, I support it."[28] The Megawati administration then tried to speed up new antiterrorism laws. But, as noted earlier, groups like FPI and Laskar Jihad could have been prosecuted under existing laws for their blatant crimes some years ago—but for a long time there was no will to counter such groups. Hamzah Haz, a newfound (albeit temporary) convert to the war against terrorism, stated that the attacks were designed to break up Indonesia and ruin its economic recovery.[29] In what was seen as a reference to Haz, the coordinating security minister, Susilo Bambang Yudhoyono, stated that "[t]he government urges that statements that are not objective, that there are no terrorists in Indonesia, should not be repeated again."[30] Bambang most likely delivered this rebuke on behalf of the cabinet. With Indonesia's support, the United States added JI to its list of international terrorist groups.

Gone are the days when terrorist groups would crow about their actions. JI has committed acts of violence against chosen targets without articulating the purpose. Past acts of violence have occurred without JI declaring its existence. Much like the al-Qaeda attacks of September 11, the culprits have allowed the subtext of the violence to speak for itself. JI is now thought to be responsible for a bomb blast at the Istiqlal Mosque in Jakarta in 1999, the August 2000 bombing of the Philippine embassy, and the Christmas Eve 2000 church bombings, which involved more than thirty bombs in eleven cities, all wired to go off at around the same time. The attack on the Philippine ambassador, in which he was seriously injured, was in all likelihood out of solidarity for separatism in the southern Philippines. Bombing a mosque and a number of churches on the other hand was probably designed to sow the seeds of discord between Muslim and Christian communities—at the time of the Christmas Eve bombings, Christian and Muslim organizations held joint prayer sessions in order to thwart the bombers' suspected intentions. The bombings of churches may also have been a revenge attack on Christians for the violence in Ambon and Poso.[31]

The Bali blast, however, represented a shift of JI's operations. While the ultimate goal of JI is the creation of a regionwide Islamic state,[32] the Bali blast represented more direct solidarity with al-Qaeda's cause. The deliberate targets for this operation were Western civilians. Amrozi, one of the convicted bombers, stated that he hated Americans and expressed remorse that he got Australians instead. Other suspects have, however, confirmed that Australia was the target. A threat by Osama bin Laden to Australia in late 2001,[33] due to Australia's involvement in East Timor, adds strongly to the picture that al-Qaeda and JI have found common ground. The Marriott bombing in August 2003, in which eleven died, represents another "target." This blast was most likely aimed at the Indonesian political and commercial elite, who largely frequent the Marriott Hotel—all but one of the victims was Indonesian. (That said, some commentators have assumed that it was an attack on a Western establishment or investment.)

Not only has JI not owned up to its acts of violence, but key JI members have attempted to confuse the public about the nature of the organization. Abu Bakar Bashir denies that JI exists, and that he is the spiritual leader of the group. Abu Jibril, a close associate of JI founders Abu Bakar Bashir and the late Abdullah Sungkar—all three Indonesian nationals who fled to Malaysia—has stated from his prison cell in Malaysia that JI is an American "lie."[34] Abu Jibril denies that JI exists, denies that Omar al-Faruq is a terrorist, and claims that September 11 was a plot to destroy Mullah Omar in Afghanistan—and now, according to the cleric, Southeast Asia. He portrays himself and his fellow exiles as victims of Suharto's authoritarianism, which he virtually equates with Christianity: "Others came to escape the repressive government of Suharto, which was dominated by Christians in high positions. They were powerful in repressing our *Ulama* (religious teachers) and Islamic youths."[35] Agus Dwikarna, a leading JI operative arrested in the Philippines, denies he knows about JI. Agus also denied knowing the late Fathur Rohman al-Ghozi and al-Faruq despite the fact that their phone numbers were programmed into his phone, and years ago he once arranged for al-Faruq's release from jail. The pattern here is to confuse the public about JI or to state whether it even exists.

Like the statements of Osama bin Laden, responsibility is only claimed indirectly—as evidenced by the statements of leaders sympathetic to JI. Irfan S. Awwas, chairman of the MMI (Majelis Mujahideen Indonesia or Indonesian Mujahiddeen Council)—to which a number of JI leaders are linked—has stated: "Abdul Aziz alias Imam Samudra, Amrozi[36] or even Osama bin Laden, [are] accused of carrying out violence . . .—if the charges are proven—are results of *ijtihad*[37]—individual interpretation and judgement. We have no right to judge their *ijtihad* with negative accusations."[38] Awwas then makes his own judgment by noting the examples of Abraham, Moses, and Mohammed: "Are they radical because they fought tyrannical power with violence?" The article makes it clear that tyranny is any kind of "infidel" power. It may be worth noting that such a strategy of indirect support, without claiming responsibility, is also a tactic employed by al-Qaeda.

JI leaders are linked to the MMI and MMI's paramilitary wing Laskar Mujahideen. MMI contains some figures from the old Darul Islam movement of the 1950s that fought for an Islamic state. Military distrust of Darul Islam is probably one factor in the cool relations between MMI and the military (in contrast to Laskar Jihad for example). The core of JI met and formed links with bin Laden's network during the war against the Soviets in Afghanistan. Developments in Ambon and Poso, whereby communal violence between Christian and Muslim communities emerged, provided further battlegrounds for Afghan alumni to coalesce. MMI members came together in their desire to support Muslim communities in Ambon and Poso. Laskar

Mujahideen totaled roughly five hundred men by early 2000—much smaller than Laskar Jihad, with which a strong rivalry developed.[39] The late leader of Laskar Mujahideen, Haris Fadillah (alias Abu Dzar) is both a former Darul Islam figure and the father-in-law of Omar al-Faruq. The main tactic used by Laskar Mujahideen was hit and run raids against Christian leaders and structures while Laskar Jihad was involved in the more "conventional" objective of taking and holding territory.

The founding father of JI was the late Abdullah Sungkar, who, with Bashir, founded Pondok Ngruki *pesantren* in Solo, central Java. There are roughly fourteen thousand *pesantren* schools, and only a handful are thought to be involved with JI in some way.[40] Abdullah Sungkar advocated, through his teachings and writings, a situation whereby JI would remain latent until conditions were ripe for an Islamic state. Like Marx, he provided an intellectual framework for a revolutionary idea, but refrained from organizing the revolution. Just as Lenin was to Marx, younger radicals, notably Hambali, wanted to bring the conditions on and formed a cadre of jihadi to bring about the conditions for their political agenda. The JI network, grounded in schooling networks, is also secured through a number of marriages and family linkages. Links have also been made with *preman* (gangster) elements. Both Amrozi, a Bali bomber, and Haris Fadillah, the leader of Laskar Mujahideen, had *preman* backgrounds.

JI remains a serious problem in Indonesia despite the dent that the Indonesian police have made in the organization. Of the nearly 200 JI operatives arrested in Southeast Asia, almost 100 are in jail in Indonesia. Hambali was arrested in Thailand in August 2003 (where he was planning to bomb the APEC Summit) and is now is U.S. custody. There was an international outcry when Bashir received only a four-year sentence—later reduced to three years on appeal. Many media sources noted that this was a return to the reluctance of the Megawati administration to prosecute terrorists—without noting that this was an independent court decision. But it does highlight the problem that Indonesian prosecutors have had in convicting JI's spiritual leader, who cannot be charged with a tangible crime.

What the Bali and Marriott Attacks Mean for Indonesia's Future

In the aftermath of the Bali blast, the Indonesian government and important groups within civil society were forced to confront the terrorist problem. Although a number of Indonesian commentators have noted a surprising reluctance, even now, to accept the problem of radical Islamist groups, some important steps have been taken. For example, the Indonesia government has condemned JI and actively attempted to dismantle the organization.

NU and Muhammadiyah have both spoken out plainly against the more radical versions of political Islam in contrast to the previous hesitation. These two groups, theological and political rivals, even issued a joint condemnation of terrorism after both the Bali and Marriott blasts. Lily Zakiyah Munir, a highly regarded scholar and influential women's leader within NU, has written to defend the moderate nature of the *pesantren*, but nonetheless is highly critical of Bashir's school—an example of the emerging mainstream backlash against the radical fringe: "In *pesantren* like Ngruki [the school of Bashir], dialog with 'the other' [people with different interpretations of Islam or those who are non-Muslim] is not possible. These people are regarded as *kafir* [infidels] and thus, there is no point in communicating with them. Their blood is even considered *halal*, meaning that it is allowable to shed their blood."[41] She notes that these radical *pesantren* differ from the mainstream practices of stressing both legal aspects (*fikih*) and spirituality (sufism)—as derived from the nine original *wali* (saints) of Java. She sounds a warning to moderate *pesantren* to be on guard. This type of commentary from Islam's mainstream community leaders has emerged since the Bali blast and has gone some way to convince a skeptical public that there is a problem in their midst.

Peer pressure from Indonesia's Southeast Asian neighbors has also been brought to bear. Indonesia's reputation has been seriously tarnished, and warnings from ASEAN members can no longer be written off as "interference." The Bali blast in particular tarnished Megawati's image. Her failure to show leadership after this attack puzzled many. Although she visited Bali twice in the aftermath, she issued no public statements on the terrorist attack. (It is inconceivable that the American president, George Bush, would have nothing to say after September 11, or even a lesser type of terrorist attack.) Her muted and unemotional reaction to the Bali incident even had her own party members questioning her ability to lead Indonesia in such a time of crisis. It also surprised the international community.

The International Crisis Group (ICG), after the Bali blast, suggested that disillusionment might undermine the *reformasi* process itself and play into the hands of the military.[42] The continuing threat of terrorism could become a useful tool to justify an increased military role in internal security. What may militate against this is a widespread suspicion about the role of the military in Indonesia's pockets of regional instability (as ICG says of the military, it "leaks information and weapons like a sieve"), and suspicion lingers that an element of the military, through active support or sale of matériel, was involved in the Bali blast. (The blast was caused by C4 explosives, and the most ready supply of it in Indonesia is from military sources.)

A debate emerged in Indonesia in the aftermath of the Marriott explosion about restoration of the old Suharto era antisubversion law in order to target terrorist groups. Such a law, used in the past by Suharto to imprison political activists and radical Muslim leaders, is still quite unpopular with the public and raises the ghost of authoritarianism. Yet key Indonesian officials have drawn a strict dichotomy between freedom and stability. Susilo Bambang Yudhoyono, coordinating minister of security, has spoken generally of the possible need to put human rights on the back burner in the interests of community safety. The national intelligence chief, Hendropriyono, has advocated that powers of arrest be given to the intelligence services. The defense minister, Matori Abdul Djalil, has stated: "Several times Indonesia has been attacked by an act of terrorism which causes a loss of life. Therefore it's an emergency. That's why I am brave to say this nation actually needs an Internal Security Act which provides authority to the security apparatus to take preventative measures before terrorist attacks take place."[43] The message of this discussion is obvious—the public may have to choose between democracy and security.

A crucial question that emerges is whether or not the Indonesian government can sustain antiterrorism measures currently being enacted or under consideration. Megawati faces a number of competitive pressures on how to respond to this threat. First of all, there is a sizable element within the Indonesian public that is doubtful about the nature of the threat and may interpret the trial of Bashir as an anti-Muslim act. Media reports suggest that many Indonesians believe that U.S. agents were behind the Bali attacks.[44] A Detikcom survey showed that there were many who blamed the CIA or other foreign agents.[45] Second, for those within the elite who accept the gravity of the problem, including leaders of her own party, Megawati has failed to demonstrate the leadership necessary to carry the public with her on this issue and instill confidence during this time of national crisis. Third, international expectations have to be met, and Megawati will find herself under considerable pressure, both public and private, both regional and extraregional, to take this problem seriously. The Megawati administration, including the hitherto skeptical vice president, has indicated, rhetorically at least, that there is a threat from international terrorism and has taken steps to tackle the problem. However, serious doubts loom over the capacity of the Indonesian state to alter the conditions that have allowed terrorist cells to operate within Indonesia in the first place.

Conclusion

Whether all Indonesians acknowledge it or not, the Bali blast has changed Indonesia forever. Terrorism is now recognized by ASEAN as the gravest crisis to confront the region in recent times. The Indonesian government, perhaps lulled into a false sense of security due to the pluralist nature of its Muslim majority, has now faced up to a very real problem in the shape of local terrorist cells. Indonesia's Muslims do not, by and large, constitute a fertile landscape for even mild versions of Islamist governance, let alone violent theocratic movements like Jemaah Islamiya. But equally undeniable is the threat that JI poses to the peace and stability of Indonesia. The ignominious failure of the police to enforce the law against FPI and Laskar Jihad—a combination of poor policing and lack of political will—does not bode well for surveillance and enforcement against terrorist groups that shun the light of publicity but remain a real threat. Indonesia's lack of institutional capacity—a run-down bureaucracy, a horribly corrupt military, and a poorly trained police force—compounds the problem of controlling jihadi groups.

It is often alleged that Muslim-majority countries are not fertile ground for democracy. Yet it would be misleading to conclude that the emergence of political parties that represent either Muslim constituencies or advocate Islamic policies are a threat to Indonesia's fragile democratization process. Indonesia's largest Muslim organizations see no compatibility problems between democracy and Islamic practice, while smaller, more Islamist, parties in the Indonesian Parliament are content to work through the ballot process. The Jakarta Charter is unable to gain traction in Parliament. More radical Islamic groups outside Parliament enjoy no mass support at all, and groups like JI or MMI are not represented in the body politic. Support for religious pluralism is still the dominant view among Indonesian Muslims, and this intersects with Indonesian nationalism. It is received wisdom that attempts to create an Islamic state in Indonesia could spark secessionism in non-Muslim regions of the republic. While the vast majority of the population does not subscribe to radical visions of an Islamic "superstate" in Southeast Asia, there is still a real reluctance to see groups like Jemaah Islamiya as a real threat to national unity. The Indonesian government needs to convince its public that terrorism is a major threat to Indonesia's stability, its economic vibrancy, and its cohesion—as groups like JI have made deliberate attempts to polarize Indonesian society. Ambon writ large.

Events on the outside, particularly the actions of the United States, play a role in public perceptions of the war on terrorism. While it would be inaccurate to speak of a "clash of civilizations" with regard to Indonesia, there are clear coreligionist concerns. Anger was observed in Indonesia over the U.S. invasions of Afghanistan and Iraq, while events in Palestine often occupy the front-page news. The war in Iraq in particular saw a wide array of political and religious leaders condemn the actions of the United States. At core is an assumption that U.S. foreign policy is inherently unfair and biased against

Muslims worldwide. (Sometimes East Timor is offered as an example of U.S./Western meddling to cleave off a Christian territory from a Muslim country.) A settlement of the Palestinian issue would take a great deal of heat out of the debate over the United States in the Muslim world. While it may or may not be in Washington's power to achieve peace in Palestine and restrain Israel, the reality is that Indonesian opinion leaders continue to conflate the actions of Israel with the United States.

Direct comparisons to left-wing terrorist groups in Western Europe in the 1960s and 1970s, and past instances of insurgency, are bound to fall down. But in one sense there is a similarity. In order to defeat JI (as well as Laskar Jihad and FPI), the surrounding population must be on board. While active sympathizers of JI probably number only in the thousands, the wider Islamic community will take some convincing that "America's war on terrorism" is not somehow an attempt to extend Western influence and/or weaken Islam. Many Indonesians remain suspicious or even personally offended when foreign leaders and commentators draw implicit, or even explicit, links between Islamic piety and terrorism. Given the levels of public distrust—still evident after Bali and the Marriott Hotel bombings—and the tendency to accept wild conspiracy theories, the due process of law becomes critical. The head of the police inquiry into the Bali blast, General I. Made Pastika, said that the results of the Bali investigation "should put to rest widespread doubts about whether JI exists in Indonesia,"[46] yet he may have spoken too soon. There is now a greater awareness, but the battle for public opinion is far from over, even after the Bali blast. Indonesia's immediate neighbors have held up a Singapore- or Malaysia-style Internal Security Act—whereby suspects can be arrested without a proper trial—as a model for Indonesia. After the Marriott blast, members of the Megawati administration publicly admitted they had sympathy for casting aside certain liberal democratic rights in the name of public security. While one is sensitive to the ever-present threat posed by terrorism, arbitrary arrests without evidence will not win the battle for public opinion. The type of evidence collected by Indonesian police in the aftermath of Bali is vastly superior to the poor policing methods after the Christmas Eve bombings—which included forced confessions. There is a need for clear and irrefutable evidence, not only to convict guilty JI members but to bury JI itself. Clearly the link between public recognition of JI as a security threat and political action is strong. It is also the case that counterterrorism actions need not contradict democracy. The Bank of Indonesia has now—at last—frozen the accounts of arrested terrorists. Indonesia could go further and declare "hate organizations" illegal. Thus, leaders like Bashir could be convicted for spreading hate and advocating violence. Such leaders are unlikely to ever be caught with their fingers on the trigger.

Notes

The views expressed in this article are those of the author and do not reflect the official policy or position of the Asia-Pacific Center for Security Studies, U.S. Pacific Command, the U.S. Department of Defense, or the U.S. government.

1. Indonesia's state philosophy, the *pancasila* (or the "five pillars"), contains a stipulation that all Indonesians must believe in God. Some Indonesian scholars have argued that this technically means that Indonesia is somewhere between a secular and a religious state. However, in practice Indonesia has maintained secular governance to the extent that Islam is afforded no special role nor is it mentioned in any constitutional documents (in contrast to neighboring Malaysia).

2. Robert W. Hefner, "Islam in Indonesia's Political Future," *Project Asia,* CNA Corporation, September 2002, p. 20. Hefner prefers the spelling "Salafy."

3. Angel M. Rabasa, "Political Islam in Southeast Asia: Moderates, Radicals, and Terrorists," Adelphi Paper No. 358, International Institute for Strategic Studies (New York: Oxford University Press, 2003), p. 16.

4. See Hefner, "Islam in Indonesia's Political Future."

5. Ibid., p. 13.

6. Ibid., p. 8.

7. It is difficult to say with any precision. A splinter group within PAN has advocated the adoption of the Jakarta Charter while a splinter group within PPP (known as PPP-Reformasi) explicitly rejects it.

8. NU and Muhammadiyah declared that this was allowable. But this did not stop Wahid from publicly prevaricating on the issue in order to secure the presidency for himself. For an analysis of this debate, see Bernhard Platzdasch, "Islamic Reaction to a Female President," in *Indonesia in Transition: Social Aspects of Reformasi and Crisis,* ed. Chris Manning and Peter van Diermen (Singapore: Institute of Southeast Asian Studies, 2000), pp. 336–49.

9. The prospect of Islamic law in Indonesia seems to cause alarm in the outside world. By way of an anecdotal example, despite the fact that implementing Sharia law never came up for consideration in front of the Indonesian Parliament, it was the focus of the *New York Times* feature on constitutional changes ("Jakarta Rejects Muslim Law and Alters Presidential Voting," August 11, 2002). By contrast an article in the *Jakarta Post,* summarizing the same constitutional amendments adopted by the Upper House (MPR), ran the headline "MPR Forces Military Out, Allows People to Elect President" (August 13, 2002) and made no mention of attempts to include Sharia law.

10. "Megawati Off to US Amid Controversy over Deputy's Remarks," Associated Press, September 17, 2001. Haz's full statement to *Kompas* was: "Hopefully, this tragedy will cleanse the sins of the United States. . . . We are also concerned and regret deeply and condemn the act of terrorism toward the United States. But we also ask America not to make Islam a scapegoat."

11. "Indonesia Strongly Deplores Unilateral Action Against Iraq," Megawati Sukarnoputri, March 20, 2003. Accessed from Department of Foreign Affairs, Republic of Indonesia, www.deplu.go.id.

The Indonesian government did little to talk up human rights abuses in Iraq. The Indonesian ambassador to Baghdad, Dachlan Abdul Hamied, in an interview praised Saddam's intellectual ability and added that: "Saddam Hussein is a benevolent person.

That's what makes Iraqis so willing to die for Saddam. His policies are seen to be pro-people." "Dachlan Abdul Hamied, 'Saddam is an intelligent manager,'" *Tempo,* April 7, 2003, p. 33.

12. Heri Retnowati, "Interview: Indonesian Muslim Chief Warns U.S. of Back-lash," Reuters, September 27, 2001.

13. Vaudine England, "America Under Attack," *South China Morning Post,* September 14, 2001.

14. The English translation of the appropriate paragraph is: "According to the call for jihad, the MUI urges the entire Islamic world, especially the Islamic people in Indonesia, to unite and make a real effort to put pressure on all U.S. interests, another way to stop the evil of the U.S. and also to make humanitarian action to help [the] Afghanistan people."

15. See, for example, Slobodan Lekic, "Indonesian Intelligence Set Up Group in 1970s Now Accused of Terrorism, Report Says," Associated Press, August 12, 2002.

16. Hamish McDonald, "Jakarta Has Played with Fire of Islamic Extremism," *Sydney Morning Herald,* October 17, 2002.

17. Hefner, "Islam in Indonesia's Political Future," p. 7.

18. Interview with Paul Wolfowitz in "Active Engagement: U.S.-Indonesia Relations," *Brown Journal of World Affairs* 9, issue 1 (spring 2002): 5–6.

19. Carl Thayer, "Political Terrorism and Militant Islam in Southeast Asia," paper to Forum on Regional Security and Political Developments, Institute of Southeast Asian Studies, Singapore, July 24, 2003.

20. "Indonesia Says Rift with Singapore Due to Differing Perceptions," *Jakarta Post,* February 25, 2002. Lee Kuan Yew created a stir in Indonesia when he delivered a speech in which he lamented the growing piety of Islamic observance in Southeast Asia. Many Indonesians saw this as an implicit linkage between the Islamic faith and terrorism:

> Over the last three decades, as part of a world-wide trend, Muslims in the region, including Singapore, are becoming stricter in their dress, diet, religious observances, and even social interaction, especially with non-Muslims. Increasingly Muslim women will not shake hands with males. The generation of convivial and easy-to-get-along-with Muslim leaders in the region has given way to successors who observe a stricter Islamic code of conduct.

See "The East Asian Strategic Balance After 9/11," address by Senior Minister Lee Kuan Yew at the First International Institute for Strategic Studies Asia Security Conference, Friday, May 31, 2002. http://app.internet.gov.sg/scripts/mfa/sections/press/report_press.asp?1415.

21. "US Ambassador: Aid to Indonesia Military to Support Reform," Associated Press, August 7, 2002.

22. Taken from CIA documents seen by *Time.* See "Confessions of an al-Qaeda Terrorist," *Time,* September 15, 2002.

23. *Mark Steyn,* "They Want to Kill Us All," *The Spectator,* October 19, 2002.

24. "Rachmawati: 'Rumors Disseminated by CIA Are Like Rumors Disseminated Prior to G30S/PKI,'" *Tempo Interactive,* September 20, 2002. It should be noted that Rachmawati is a political opponent of Megawati, even to the extent of publicly condemning her sister's ascension to the presidency in 2001.

25. Raymond Bonner, "Indonesians Distrust Report by C.I.A. on Qaeda Suspect," *New York Times,* September 24, 2002.

26. "No Evidence of Baasyir's Involvement in Terrorism: Police Chief," *Jakarta Post,* September 11, 2002.

27. "No Al-Qaeda Network Found in Indonesia, Says Army Chief," *Jakarta Post,* September 27, 2002.

28. "Confessions of an al-Qaeda Terrorist," *Time,* September 15, 2002.

29. "Attacks Aimed to Break Up Indonesia, Says Hamzah," *Straits Times,* October 24, 2002.

30. Ibid.

31. For one articulation of this theory, see *Indonesia Backgrounder: How the* Jemaah Islamiya *Terrorist Network Operates,* International Crisis Group, Report No. 43, December 11, 2002, p. i.

32. See "The Jemaah Islamiyah Arrests and the Threat of Terrorism," *White Paper,* Ministry of Home Affairs, Singapore, January 7, 2003.

33. "Bin Laden Threatened Australia in Videotape: Report," Agence France-Presse, October 26, 2002.

34. "Abu Jibril: Jamaah Islamiyah Is an American Lie," *Tempo,* January 7, 2003.

35. Ibid.

36. Imam Samudra and Amrozi are both convicted Bali bombers.

37. *Ijtihad* is a word related to *jihad* but is not the same. An *ijtihad* is usually a formalistic judgment based on consideration of the Koran and other accepted scriptural texts.

38. Irfan S. Awwas, "Radical Islam in the Eyes of Secularists," *Tempo,* January 7, 2003, p. 80.

39. *How the* Jemaah Islamiyah *Terrorist Network Operates,* p. 22.

40. *Jemaah Islamiyah in South East Asia: Damaged But Still Dangerous,* International Crisis Group, Report No. 63, August 26, 2003, p. i.

41. Lily Zakiyah Munir, "Radicalism Atypical of Indonesian 'Pesantren,'" *Jakarta Post,* September 6, 2003.

42. "Impact of the Bali Bombings," International Crisis Group, October 24, 2002.

43. Matthew Moore, "Human Rights the Next Casualty?" *The Age,* August 16, 2003.

44. See "Who Are the Terrorists in Indonesia? Conspiracy Theories over Bali Bombing are Rife in Indonesia," *The Observer,* October 27, 2002.

45. See Greg Fealy, "Conspiracism, Republika, and the Bali Bombings," *Inside Indonesia,* forthcoming.

46. "Jamaah Islamiyah Operating in Indonesia: Police," *Jakarta Post,* November 30, 2002, cited in *How the* Jemaah Islamiyah *Terrorist Network Operates,* p. 4.

7

The Philippines and the Challenge of International Terrorism

Paul A. Rodell

It was raining heavily at 7:15 P.M. on Sunday, October 12, 2003, in Pigcawayan, North Cotabato Province, where an elite unit of the Philippine National Police (PNP) and soldiers from the Philippine army's 6th Infantry Division had set up a roadblock. According to the military account, the soldiers were responding to information from three independent informants that Fathur Rohman al-Ghozi of the Jemaah Islamiya would pass there on his way to General Santos City, South Cotabato. A motorcycle cab with a driver and passenger came into view and the officers attempted to flag it down. The motorcycle cab ignored the order and the passenger began firing a .45-caliber automatic pistol at the soldiers who returned fire. At the end of a brief shootout, the driver fled and the thirty-one-year-old Indonesian terrorist lay dying with five bullet wounds—two in the chest, one in each arm, and another in his side. Al-Ghozi was taken to the Midsayap Diagnostic Center in nearby Midsayap town, where he was pronounced dead, and fingerprints were taken for a definitive identification. The body was then driven the ninety miles to General Santos City, where forensics experts conducted a further examination.[1]

Al-Ghozi's dramatic death ending his extraordinary life was greeted with enthusiastic relief by the Philippine government. Earlier, on July 10, al-Ghozi along with Abdulmukim Ong Edris and Omar Opik Lasal, both members of the Abu Sayyaf bandit group, had escaped from their maximum security cells in Camp Crame, the PNP's headquarters in Quezon City. Al-Ghozi was serving a seventeen-year sentence for possession of explosives and was due to be arraigned the next day for his role in a series of bombings in Metro Manila on December 30, 2000. Their easy escape was an egregious embarrassment to the government of President Gloria Macapagal-Arroyo and sparked a massive manhunt that involved sixty-seven PNP tracker teams. With the announcement of al-Ghozi's killing, the president and Defense Secretary Eduardo Ermita immediately flew south to General Santos City to view the remains as national television covered the event.[2]

Despite his ignoble end, al-Ghozi's career illustrates how radical Islamic terrorism and the desire of many Philippine Muslims for political and cultural autonomy have intersected and collaborated for their mutual benefit. This modus vivendi has existed within a fluid context of religion, local aspirations, and grievances, numerous divisions and alliances within Philippine Muslim groups, and the wider anti-Western international agenda of Islamic terrorists. That al-Ghozi and other Jemaah Islamiya and al-Qaeda operatives have been able to operate with near impunity further illustrates the difficulty the government faces in its efforts to contain and eliminate radical Islamic movements as it struggles to play its part in the U.S.-led "war on terrorism." And finally, the absurdly easy escape that al-Ghozi and his companions made and the politically tinged controversy surrounding it as well as his final shootout raise critical questions about the capability of the Philippines' political system and military to meet national threats.

Before examining the life and death of Fathur Rohman al-Ghozi in more detail, this paper will first examine the context of Philippine Muslim separatism that has created the enabling environment in which Jemaah Islamiya agents operate. This review will begin with a look at the historic relationship between the Muslim southern islands and the dominant Christian government in Manila. Of critical importance are the fundamental changes since national independence in 1946 that saw the creation of a separate "Moro" identity by the late 1960s and the rise of the Moro National Liberation Front (MNLF) in 1972. The appearance of fundamentalist Islam began with an MNLF leadership schism in 1977 that eventually led to the founding of the Moro Islamic Liberation Front (MILF), while the creation of the radical Abu Sayyaf had clear ties to Osama bin Laden's al-Qaeda movement. As well, it is imperative to assess whether Philippine military corruption has contributed to the insurgency environment that has afforded Jemaah Islamiya agents security and relative freedom. Once this review is completed, we can return to al-Ghozi's story to see how these themes played themselves out in his case and what must be done if domestic and international terrorism is to be eliminated.

Historical Background to Philippine Islamic Militancy

During its lengthy colonial rule, Spain never really controlled the Muslim areas of the south. Until the advent of steam-powered patrol boats in the mid-nineteenth century, fast Muslim *vintas* could easily outdistance heavier Spanish sailing ships. The colonial government built Fort Pilar in the port of Zamboanga as early as 1635 and mounted occasional military raids against suspected Muslim strongholds, but these efforts did little to restrict the independent Muslims. Instead, for most of the Philippines' colonial history, the central Visayan Islands and even parts of Luzon were at the mercy of Muslim raiding parties looking for captives to sell in the lucrative slave trade.[3] The legacy of this imbalanced relationship between dominant Muslim warriors and terrorized Christian Filipinos can still be seen today in many of the islands' colonial-era churches built in coastal areas, which often included a bell tower constructed for additional use as a lookout for Muslim raiding ships. Missionary priests often organized complex signaling systems to relay warnings of approaching *vintas* so local residents and people in neighboring towns would have time to flee into the mountains.

As the tide of battle began to turn during the second half of the nineteenth century, Spanish policy shifted to more active military intervention. Assaults were made on Basilan Island in 1845, Jolo in early 1876, and against the Maranao people of Mindanao's Lake Lanao region in 1888–89 and 1895. These military campaigns were supplemented by political intervention in succession disputes in both the Sulu and Maguindanao sultanates. As a result of these sustained military/political pressures, traditional centers of Muslim power declined and a number of new minor sultanates arose that did not offer the same level of resistance to the colonial government. Still, Muslim resistance continued until the end of Spain's suzerainty so that the Iberian rulers could never truly claim to have conquered the region.[4]

With the collapse of Spanish rule in 1898, garrisons throughout the Muslim Philippines were harassed and took heavy losses. When the United States entered, Brigadier General John C. Bates attempted a political approach and signed a treaty with Sultan Jamalul Kiram II of Sulu on August 20, 1899. The so-called Bates Treaty was never ratified by the U.S. Congress and became a source of contention over the inclusion of the word "sovereignty" in reference to the United States in the English version that did not appear in the translated copy. By the end of October the Military District of Mindanao, Jolo, and Palawan was created and Muslim territories were successfully occupied, despite some armed opposition by the Maranao, and administered by military rule until June 1903, when the civilian Moro Province was created.[5]

Immediately after the creation of the American province, fighters in Sulu mounted a short-term resistance to American rule followed by engagements over a three-year period by guerrilla forces loyal to Datu Uto of Cotabato. In March 1904, Theodore Roosevelt unilaterally abrogated the Bates Treaty, further intensifying Muslim bitterness. Despite outward appearances of calm, resistance mounted and led to tragedy when, on March 5–8, 1906, over 600 men, women, and children were killed at Bud Dajo, an extinct volcano on the island of Sulu, where they were slaughtered by American troops who rained shells down upon them. The carnage at Bud Dajo did not curb Muslim resistance, and numerous small-scale encounters took place every year. Finally, on June 11–15, 1913, in a sickening massacre reminiscent of that at Bud Dajo, at least 500 Muslims were killed in the one-sided battle of Bud Bagsak that saw only 14 American attackers losing their lives.[6]

As large-scale resistance to the American occupation ended, the Muslim population was faced with a new three-part pacification campaign that proved to be a much graver threat than military conquest. After the 1912 presidential election of Woodrow Wilson, American colonial policy shifted to "Filipinization," wherein Filipino participation in the government was rapidly accelerated. This policy facilitated Christian Filipino involvement in all aspects of the national colonial government, including those that directly impacted Muslim areas. Concurrently, a program to populate Mindanao with Christian settlers began with a settlement of 100 families from Cebu Province who were brought to Cotabato. This program continued, albeit slowly, throughout the pre–World War II period. And finally, the government began a policy of attraction to co-opt Muslim leaders with official offers of protected status under the American regime and occasional appointments to the colonial government.[7] Under this initiative, a handful of prominent Muslim leaders gained national attention, but their numbers were never enough to offset the overwhelming influence of Christian Filipinos in either the national bureaucracy or the colonial legislature. Meanwhile, Muslim ancestral lands were steadily being lost to non-Muslims. By 1939, 97,000 hectares of Cotabato's lush Koronadal Valley was in the hands of Christian settlers while U.S. corporations such as B.F. Goodrich and the Del Monte Company held many thousands more hectares in Basilan, Cotabato, and Bukidnon.[8]

By 1948, Mindanao's 933,101 Muslims constituted only 32 percent of that island's population even though they had made up 76 percent in the first U.S. census of 1903. As disheartening as these statistics were, the Muslim position in their own territory deteriorated even more rapidly in the 1950s and 1960s. Large-scale resettlement programs in the 1950s brought thousands of Christian Filipino families to Mindanao, and President Ramon Magsaysay used the region as a resettlement area for surrendered members of the postwar Hukbalahap (or Huk) insurgency. By 1970 the island's 1,669,708 Muslims made up only 21 percent of Mindanao's population.[9] Beyond these depressing population figures, it should also be noted that much of the best land was taken by the settlers and the owners of corporate agriculture, and most development investments and government services went disproportionately to the Christian population. As a result, today the provinces with the highest percentage of Muslim population consistently rank among the poorest and most backward in the country.[10]

The Jabidah Massacre, Martial Law, and the MNLF

Even though the Muslims were slipping far behind the rest of the nation, the flash point that coalesced long-standing grievances came about not because of land tenure disputes or government neglect, but due to a chilling massacre in March 1968 of young Tausugs from Sulu who were recruited into an ultrasecret paramilitary unit that began in 1967 under the code name Operation Merdeka. Earlier, in 1962, President Diosdado Macapagal renewed the Philippines' 1922 claim to the territory of Sabah that was then being incorporated into the new state of Malaysia. The alleged goal of Operation Merdeka was to begin a rebellion in Sabah that would provide the Philippine military with an excuse to intervene. Major Eduardo "Abdul Latif" Martelino, a convert to Islam, was in charge of the operation, but the alleged masterminds included leading generals in the Armed Forces of the Philippines (AFP), Defense Undersecretary Manuel Syquio, and President Ferdinand Marcos. In December 1967 the recruits were transferred from their training camp in Simunul, Sulu, to a remote section of Corregidor Island at the mouth of Manila Bay, where they were instructed in jungle warfare and guerrilla operations. Once on the island, the operation's code name was changed to Jabidah.

On Corregidor the training program began to fall apart as the Tausug recruits complained about the nondelivery of their salaries and numerous other grievances, such as the quality of their food and living conditions. The officers' fears of a potential mutiny began to look possible in late February when over 60 out of the 180 trainees wrote a petition addressed to Marcos. The trainee complaints never reached the president, but wound up in Major Martelino's hands. The petitioners were all disarmed and some were sent back home. Meanwhile, other trainees were transferred to regular military camps on Luzon. Then, on March 18 two batches of twelve men each were told to prepare their belongings for a return flight home. What happened next is unclear because of Major Martelino's destruction of the documentary record, but all but one of these two batches of soldiers, plus training officer Lieutenant Eduardo Nepomuceno, were murdered. Jibin Arulas, the lone trainee survivor, was wounded, ran, and escaped to the sea. He swam in the direction of Cavite Province and was rescued by fishermen who brought the young Muslim to the provincial governor. News of the massacre rocked the nation and sparked an embarrassing congressional investigation and a strong condemnation from Malaysian Prime Minister Tunku Abdul Rahman.[11]

Quite beyond the national uproar and the contentious international controversy, the massacre's greater consequence was its impact on Filipino Muslims. More than any other atrocity before or since, Jabidah alienated Philippine Muslims and thoroughly discredited government programs intended to promote accommodation to Manila's rule. Instead, Muslims now saw themselves as fundamentally and irrevocably alien to the country's Christians such that integration and accommodation were impossible. A new Islamic mind-set began to emerge that would soon create a new "imagined community" of an independent Bangsamoro (Muslim nation) people.[12] It was this critical psychological turn that provided the basic rationale for all subsequent separatist movements.

Events began to move quickly after Jabidah. On May 1, Governor Datu Udtog Matalam of Cotabato proclaimed the formation of the Muslim Independence Movement, which issued a manifesto calling for the establishment of an Islamic state comprised of the Mindanao, Sulu, and Palawan regions. Meanwhile, Congressman Rashid Lucman sent ninety-two young Muslims to train in guerrilla warfare with the Royal Malaysian Special Forces. Upon returning, they organized training camps in Mindanao and Sulu, and by 1971 an estimated thirty thousand Muslims had received basic training in weapons and guerrilla tactics. A second batch was sent to Malaysia and still others went to Libya. In response to Moro militancy, armed Christian groups called Ilaga (Rats) perpetrated a number of massacres of Muslim civilians and were supported by Christian politicians.[13] In response, Muslim fighters staged counterattacks, and soon the country's armed forces became embroiled in the spreading conflict. When President Marcos declared martial law on September 21, 1972, he cited the mounting Muslim rebellion as one of his justifications.

With the declaration of martial law, Nur Misuari, a young professor at the Asian Center, University of the Philippines, rose to prominence. Much earlier, Misuari had been attracted to Marxism and was a founding member of the Kabataang Makabayan (nationalist youth), the youth organization of the Communist Party of the Philippines (CPP). Despite this early leftist flirtation, Misuari had difficulty rectifying the Left's hostility to religion and his own Islamic roots and beliefs. By 1967 he was one of the founders of the

Philippine Muslim Nationalist League. After the shock of the Jabidah massacre, Misuari became associated with both Lucman and Matalam and was a member of the first batch of recruits to receive training in Malaysia. With his fellow overseas trainees, Misuari went on to form the Moro National Liberation Front (MNLF) independent of his Muslim politician patrons. After the declaration of martial law, some eight hundred of Misuari's fellow Tausugs became the core of the MNLF, and by October their fierce fight for Jolo led to the destruction of that city.[14] Despite the initial mauling that the MNLF received in Jolo, their armed movement grew dramatically and spread throughout the Muslim region. By 1975, most of the Philippine military, some sixty battalions, were deployed in Mindanao at a cost that was seriously debilitating the national economy.[15]

The Tripoli Agreement and the MILF

Because of the large influx of government troops, fighting in the south reached a strategic stalemate by late 1975, forcing Misuari to recognize that an independent Muslim republic was unattainable. The consequence of this new realization was profound. Misuari was forced to change not only his own thinking, but he had to convince the rest of the MNLF leadership to lower their expectations to a more attainable goal of autonomy within the Republic of the Philippines. Meanwhile, Ferdinand Marcos was eager to reach a political accommodation with the MNLF. Negotiations were conducted under the auspices of the Organization of the Islamic Conference (OIC) and hosted by Libyan president Muammar al-Khadafi, and resulted in an agreement for full Muslim autonomy that was signed in Tripoli on December 23, 1976. Initially the agreement creating an autonomous regional government for Mindanao's thirteen Muslim provinces seemed to be what Misuari wanted, but he soon realized that Marcos was insincere. On March 3, 1977, Misuari accused Marcos of duplicity, and on the twenty-fifth, Marcos signed martial law Proclamation No. 1628 declaring the establishment of autonomous regions for central and western Mindanao to which he appointed all of its officials.[16]

Misuari lost a great deal of credibility in the eyes of his fellow Muslim leaders. Under Misuari's leadership the MNLF had been a united Moro organization transcending ethnic loyalties and supplanting traditional Muslim political leaders. It was also a secular political movement rather than a religious vehicle. With the Marcos betrayal of the Tripoli Agreement, Misuari's rivals took advantage of his blunder. These rivals included Sultan Rashid Lucman of the Bangsamoro Liberation Organization and former senator Salipada Pendatun of the Muslim Association of the Philippines, who supported a December 26, 1977, attempt by Islamic scholar and former Misuari ally Hashim Salamat to take over the MNLF. Principal among Salamat's complaints was that the MNLF was being led from its Islamic origins and turned into a Marxist-Maoist organization. Misuari survived the internal revolt, but the withdrawal of Salamat and a significant number of other leaders severely weakened the organization. Numerous attempts over a number of years were made by officials of the OIC, the Muslim World League, and even exiled former senator Benigno Aquino to heal the rift, but all efforts ended in failure. Additionally, in March 1982, Vice-Chairman Dimas Pundato broke from Misuari and formed another organization, the MNLF-Reformist Group.[17]

After years of heading up his separate MNLF faction, Salamat formally declared the founding of the Moro Islamic Liberation Front in March 1984. Immediately, the new organization stood in contradistinction to the still dominant MNLF. The very name denoted its emphasis on religious values, especially the upholding of Sharia law. Salamat was genuine about this shift and was an *ustadz* (Islamic teacher) with a degree from the Institute of Islamic Research, Al-Azhar University, Cairo. Under his guidance the MILF took on a profoundly religious character as imam (community religious leaders) and alim (Islamic scholars) began to play prominent roles.[18]

More basic than differences over political issues such as sovereignty versus autonomy or matters of religious adherence were those of ethnic identification, and these were represented in the fissures. So, for example, the MILF became identified with Salamat's ethnic Maguindanao Muslims of central and western Mindanao while Pundato's reformist group had the support of the Maranaos of the Lanao area. Meanwhile, Misuari is a Tausug from Sulu, and the majority of the remaining loyal MNLF cadres were of the same ethnicity. Later, Abu Sayyaf also became identified with the Tausugs since its founder, Abdurajak Janjalani, like Misuari, was from Sulu.[19]

In addition to these ethnic divisions, each organization has been plagued with internal divisions as leaders frequently quarreled and took their followers with them or remained in the organization, but in name only, and operated quite independently. This pattern became clear even before Salamat's break from Misuari, as the MNLF was plagued early on by "lost commands" that broke from the organization, usually to begin a life of banditry. Available information about Abu Sayyaf indicates that this small organization has as many as five different rival factions. Even the MILF has similar problems, as was seen during al-Ghozi's unsuccessful flight for freedom. After arriving in Mindanao, al-Ghozi was given refuge by a local MILF commander, Salip Aloy Alsree, at Camp Salam Alfarise in Sultan Naga Dimaporo, Lanao del Norte. This protection was extended despite orders from the MILF's top leaders, who were anxious to demonstrate to the government that they were not harboring terrorists for fear of jeopardizing future peace talks.[20] This lack of control over its troops and field officers has become worse as the MILF has grown, and the consequences have sometimes been considerable. In June 2003 the MILF admitted that its troops were responsible for a massacre in Siocon, Zamboanga del Norte, that the organization did not order and strongly condemned.[21]

From its founding until the mid-1990s, the MILF remained in the shadow of Misuari's MNLF, which was seen as the primary Moro independence movement. In this secondary role, the MILF portrayed itself as the more moderate of the two organizations and tried to convince the OIC to recognize it rather than the MNLF. At the same time, however, Salamat did not neglect his armed force, and by 1999 the MILF army had reached an estimated 8,000 to 15,000, fighters, with commanders who had been trained in Libya and Palestine or who had combat experience in Afghanistan. Important to the MILF's growing military strength was the Philippine navy's weak monitoring capability, and corruption within the AFP generally that allowed the accumulation of considerable firepower.[22] There have been numerous allegations over time that Muslim insurgents have been able to buy weapons and ammunition from AFP supplies. The most recent charges have come from two very different and unlikely sources. In her memoir about her year-long kidnapping by the Abu Sayyaf, Gracia Burnham related that on more than one occasion the terrorists would call a certain "Ma'am Blanco" to order munitions that came from the military's stockpile. Meanwhile, the young officers who led an inept one-day coup against the government in July 2003 made specific and highly credible allegations about the selling of misappropriated arms by senior officers.[23]

Between Tripoli and the 1996 Agreement

After the 1976 Tripoli Agreement, the level of fighting lessened significantly, with only occasional "pocket wars" and skirmishes. At the same time, Marcos attempted to undercut Misuari politically by entering into peace negotiations with Salamat's MNLF faction and diplomatically by trying to weaken Misuari's position with the OIC and other Islamic organizations. Marcos also attempted to link the MNLF to the growing insurgency of the leftist New People's Army in the non-Muslim areas of Mindanao.[24] None of his efforts succeeded, however, and by 1986 the situation in Mindanao had reached a point of virtual stagnation.

Both Misuari and Salamat welcomed the 1986 People Power Revolution that overthrew Marcos and brought Corazon Aquino to power, and they agreed to put aside their differences and negotiate jointly with the new government. In early September, however, Aquino chose to visit Misuari in Sulu, thereby shattering any possible reconciliation between the two Muslim leaders. The president's choice of Muslim leaders with whom to negotiate also boosted Misuari's claim to be the legitimate voice of the Philippine Moro population. In January 1987 the MILF began a three-day tactical offensive, effectively ending belated government attempts to counteract the diplomatic damage that Aquino's trip to Sulu had caused.[25] The eventual talks with the MNLF did not prosper, however, because the government insisted that it would implement the autonomy provisions of its newly approved constitution without negotiating terms with the Muslims. On August 1, 1989, the Philippine Congress passed legislation creating the Autonomous Region of Muslim Mindanao (ARMM), and in a November plebiscite, only four provinces voted to join the new body. Despite strong objections from both Misuari and Salamat, elections were held for positions in the new body that was officially inaugurated in November 1990.

Further negotiations did not take place until Fidel Ramos was elected president in May 1992. Meetings were held in Tripoli with the MNLF and in the Philippines with the MILF. Over the next four and a half years numerous other meetings were held, an amnesty commission was formed, and a ceasefire declared. Critical to the negotiation process was the fear of Mindanao's Christians that the final agreement might place them under Muslim control. A number of senators responded to this exaggerated fear by modifying and delaying the final peace agreement. Then, after the agreement was signed in September 1996, President Ramos issued an executive order that further modified the agreement on a number of important points.[26]

Misuari was again put in a weak position after signing yet another agreement that gave him much less than anticipated. The new ARMM was as limited as its predecessor, and the resources that the government allocated were never enough. Quite beyond these problems, Misuari never became a good administrator, and the political reality that members of certain families had to be given appointments created a bloated bureaucracy. All the while, peace-and-order conditions were poor, and the pursuit of personal gain rather than the delivery of social services became the ARMM's principal characteristic. Even the integration of MNLF troops into the AFP did not go smoothly, and only a fraction were ever incorporated, which further increased dissatisfaction.[27] Many disgruntled MNLF members joined the MILF, which further enlarged the rival organization's ranks.

The MILF, Abu Sayyaf, and Al-Qaeda/Jemaah Islamiya

The highly flawed 1996 agreement and the administrative failure of the ARMM had more profound consequences than simply Nur Misuari's political eclipse. First, the agreement's betrayal seriously compromised any remaining hope that the MNLF would improve the lives of the Muslim peoples or that the Christian government might honor a treaty. As well, the MILF emerged as the new champion of the vast majority of Philippine Muslims. Not only was Salamat a respected Islamic scholar with a good personal reputation, but his inner circle was composed of honest, competent, and dedicated men. Under Salamat's leadership the MILF's emphasis on religious values impressed many people and his fighting force was formidable. Meanwhile in Sulu, the Abu Sayyaf, instead of remaining an obscure bandit gang that had radical Islamic pretensions, emerged on the world scene thanks to its participation in a bloody raid on Ipil, Zamboanga del Sur, in 1995, and its spectacular kidnap-for-ransom raids in 2000 and 2002.[28] And finally, the increased role of religious fundamentalism within the Philippine context became an enabling factor that facilitated the entry into the country of non-Filipino groups such as al-Qaeda and the Indonesian group, Jemaah Islamiya.

From his enhanced position, Salamat engaged the AFP in a series of "pocket wars" in 1996–97, such as the vicious combat at Rajah Muda, North Cotabato, even while conducting peace negotiations. In the short term this strategy appeared to work because in July 1997 the government agreed to a general cessation of hostilities and recognized forty-four MILF camps as "zones of peace and development" where the AFP would not interfere.[29] Despite this appearance of success, the negotiation process never got beyond this general agreement, and when Joseph Estrada came into office, the peace process became problematic. In October 1999, Estrada set December as the deadline for both sides to finalize an agreement.[30]

New developments were also reshaping the situation in Sulu, where disappointment with Misuari and the MNLF ran so deep, even before the 1996 agreement, that some of his fellow Tausugs had already given up on him. One young radical, Abdurajak Janjalani, quit the MNLF in 1987, went to Libya to study Islam, and then traveled to Afghanistan where he fought with the mujahideen. While in Libya, Janjalani became an adherent of ultraconservative Wahhabism, and upon returning to the Philippines in 1990 he founded a radical Muslim group that became the core of the Abu Sayyaf. At first Janjalani's small group conducted relatively minor terrorist attacks and remained little known. It was the Abu Sayyaf's participation in the April 4, 1995, murderous Ipil raid that caught the attention of the nation. Though the raid was planned and mounted by Misuari's MNLF rivals headed by Melham Alam, the small kidnap gang profited from their association with the larger group, especially when they were singled out for blame by the military.[31] The end for Janjalani came on December 18, 1998, when he and two other Abu Sayyaf members died in a gun battle with police in Lamitan, Basilan. After his death, his younger brother Khadafi and Aldam Tilao, a.k.a. Abu

Sabaya, succeeded Janjalani. With Abdurajak's passing, Abu Sayyaf lost any claim that it was an Islamic religious group, and its leaders shifted entirely to criminality for personal profit.

The increased prominence of fundamentalist Islam in both the MILF and the pre-1998 Abu Sayyaf facilitated the linkage of both of these organizations with radical currents in the Muslim world. Al-Qaeda's entry into the Philippines in 1988 was through Osama bin Laden's brother-in-law Mohammed Jamal al-Khalifa, who married a Philippine woman and used an import-export business in rattan as a cover for his activities. Khalifa used al-Qaeda money to establish Islamic charities that funded religious schools, and he recruited volunteers for Afghanistan and made a number of important contacts, including Abdurajak Janjalani. When the war in Afghanistan ended, Khalifa left the Philippines, but returned often until early 1994. During his time in Afghanistan, Janjalani had met another important al-Qaeda agent, Ramzi Ahmed Yousef, whom he hosted in the Philippines in 1991–92 along with Abdul Hakim Murad and Wali Khan Amin Shah. The three men proved valuable to the Abu Sayyaf because they schooled the Filipino group in the use of explosives for terrorism.[32]

Later, in the fall of 1994, Yousef came back to Manila with his uncle Khalid Sheikh Mohammed and the two companions from his earlier trip. This small al-Qaeda cell began making ambitious terrorist plans under the code name Operation Bojinka (a Bosnian word for explosion) that at one time or another included the assassinations of Pope John Paul II, U.S. president Bill Clinton, and Philippine president Fidel Ramos; the bombing of the U.S. embassy, the International School, Catholic churches, and government installations; and an elaborate simultaneous aerial bombing of eleven airliners over the Pacific. Of these plans only two actions were carried out: a test bomb was exploded in a near-empty theater in Manila, and a Philippine Airlines flight to Japan was bombed, resulting in the death of a Japanese passenger. Their conspiracy was cut short thanks to a fire in their apartment that broke out while bomb material was being mixed. Khalid and Yousef escaped from the Philippines, although both were later arrested. In the meantime, the hard drive of their computer in the abandoned apartment revealed information to intelligence agents about their plans, including one that proposed crashing captured airliners into a number of important buildings in the United States.[33] Although chilling, the Yousef cell in Manila was an isolated group with few Philippine ties other than the distant Abu Sayyaf. Later, however, al-Qaeda made important links with the MILF in the mid-1990s, using companies Khalifa originally created and through international phone calls between al-Qaeda's Abu Zubaydah and key MILF officials.[34] An important additional relationship linked Jemaah Islamiya with MILF leader Hashim

Salamat, who was a friend of Abdullah Sungkar, the cofounder with Abu
Bakar Bashir, of, first, the radical Islamic school, the Pesantren al-Mukmin,
and then of Jemaah Islamiya.

Al-Ghozi's Terrorist Career and Conflict in Mindanao

Fathur Rohman al-Ghozi mastered a number of Southeast Asian languages
and operated with as many as five passports and three aliases. He was born
and raised in the city of Madiun, East Java, and his religious and ideological
beliefs were undoubtedly influenced by his father Zaenuri, who had been
imprisoned for his involvement with an earlier radical Islamic group, the
Komando Jihad. In 1989, al-Ghozi graduated from the radical Islamic school,
the Pesantren al-Mukmin, also known as the Pondok Ngruki, after which he
went to Afghanistan for two years of military and terrorist training. While
there he spent at least some time in al-Qaeda's camp at Torkham, which also
hosted MILF fighters. By 1996, al-Ghozi was ready to play a role in attaining the Jemaah Islamiya's dream of creating a single Islamic state for island
Southeast Asia that would encompass Malaysia, Brunei, and Indonesia as
well as parts of Thailand and the Philippines. He was assigned to the Philippines to work with the MILF.[35]

In the mid-1990s, as the domestic situation in Afghanistan deteriorated,
Jemaah Islamiya founder Abdullah Sungkar explored the possibility of sending young Indonesians to nearby and less expensive Mindanao for training.
Sungkar used his friendship with Hashim Salamat to make the arrangements,
and by 1995 construction had begun on what became known as Camp
Hudaibiyah, a facility set aside for exclusive Jemaah Islamiya use. The Indonesian training site occupied a remote corner of the MILF's Abu Bakar complex near the province of Lanao del Sur. Although other Jemaah Islamiya
agents preceded him, al-Ghozi's family background, education, and training
plus his natural abilities soon made him one of the camp's most valuable
instructors. Training began in earnest in 1997 with a three-year program for
future instructors and a six-month program for regular "cadets." Meanwhile,
non–Jemaah Islamiya trainees could take a variety of short courses of four
months to one year. From its beginning until midyear 2000, hundreds of
Indonesians passed through Camp Hudaibiyah under the watchful eyes of al-
Ghozi and the other camp instructors, who were all Afghanistan veterans. In
early 2000, however, President Joseph Estrada ordered military action against
the MILF, and by July the Philippine army's gains included Camp Abu Bakar.
Jemaah Islamiya then shifted some of its training to Poso in central Sulawesi,
Indonesia, but still continued training in Mindanao in areas not affected by the
Philippine military's advance.[36] More immediately, al-Ghozi returned briefly

to Indonesia, where he detonated a car bomb that seriously wounded the Philippine ambassador and killed two others in retaliation for the Philippine army's capture of Camp Abu Bakar.[37]

Al-Ghozi then returned to the Philippines, where he played a central role in a series of bombings on December 30, 2000. The masterminds and financiers of the bombings were two of Jemaah Islamiya's most important operatives, Riduan Isamuddin, alias Hambali, and Faiz Abu bin Bakar Bafana.[38] Al-Ghozi picked up Hambali at the airport on the first of the month and served as his Philippines contact, setting up bank accounts to funnel thousands of dollars and coordinating with members of the MILF's special operations group. An especially important member of this latter group was Saifullah Yunos, who knew Hambali from their time together in Afghanistan in 1987–89. He was allegedly sent to work with al-Ghozi and Hambali on the direct order of Hashim Salamat. Joining Yunos were five other MILF members including Cusian L. Ramos, who helped purchase explosives in Cebu. On the thirtieth, a bomb destroyed a Metro Manila light rail transit car, killing 22 passengers and wounding almost 100 others. At almost the same time, four additional bombs went off at various points in the city, killing another 10 people and wounding at least 88 more victims.[39] Philippine authorities knew of al-Ghozi's role in the bombings and began hunting for him. The elusive Jemaah Islamiya operative was eventually picked up in January 2002 as he attempted to board a flight to Thailand. After his capture, he led authorities to some twenty-one tons of explosives that, he claimed, were to be used in suicide attacks on Western embassies and other targets in Singapore.

Al-Ghozi's July 2003 escape was especially galling for the Philippine government because of President Macapagal-Arroyo's strong support for the American-led war on terror, which she had joined while on a White House visit in November 2001. In exchange, the Philippines received a substantial U.S. military and economic aid package, and in 2002, U.S. troops played a key supportive role in tracking down Abu Sayyaf bandits holding American hostages Martin and Gracia Burnham.[40] As well, Macapagal-Arroyo had a number of other successes against Islamic separatists, including the subtle support of alternative MNLF leaders who finally ousted Misuari from holding any positions of power. She also improved relations with Malaysian prime minister Mahathir bin Mohamad, who then shifted his Islamic country from supporting Islamic dissidents to helping the Christian government in Manila.[41] As well, under Macapagal-Arroyo the Philippines is on track to gain observer status at OIC meetings, which bodes well for future conflict resolution and peace negotiations with the MILF.[42]

On the other hand, when diplomacy has faltered, President Macapagal-Arroyo has not been reticent to use military options. In early 2003 she ordered an offensive into MILF areas for the ostensive purpose of chasing members of the notorious Pentagon kidnapping gang, who were supposedly being granted asylum by the Muslim insurgents. The February 2003 offensive shattered an existing cease-fire agreement and resulted in the fall of the MILF's Buliok Complex in North Cotabato and Maguindanao. The MILF responded with a series of bombings in February and March that struck Mindanao's power lines and Davao City's airport and public wharf, killing 21 innocent people and wounding over 130 others. These cruel acts were followed by deliberate attacks on civilians in the towns of Maigo, Lanao del Norte, on April 26, and Siocon, Zamboanga del Norte, on May 4. These terrorist counterattacks gave the government a strategic upper hand, as both the OIC and Malaysia were greatly upset with the MILF's behavior.[43]

Standing in sharp contrast to her progress against domestic Islamic separatists, al-Ghozi's effortless escape understandably upset the president and again called into question her military's ability to conduct basic and sustained antiterrorist and policing operations. Were this not bad enough, the escape became immediate grist for the Philippines' hyperactive political mill. Even as the jailbreak was first being reported, Ramon Magsaysay, Jr., chair of the Senate Committee on National Defense and Security, called for the resignation of PNP director general Hermogenes Ebdane, Jr. For his part, Ebdane accepted responsibility for the escape, but suggested that "politics" within the PNP may have played a role in the affair. This political wrangling intensified despite the sacking of those officers immediately responsible for the prisoners' security and expanded to include AFP interagency rivalry. Only a few weeks later, Director Eduardo Matillano of the PNP's Criminal Investigation and Detection Group caught two navy officers spying on him. He alleged that the officers were a part of a destabilization plot being conducted by certain elements within the armed forces acting in concert with opposition political leaders such as Juan Ponce Enrile, a former senator and defense secretary under Ferdinand Marcos. At the same time, suspicion was beginning to fall upon two dismissed officers of the PNP Intelligence Group for possibly aiding the terrorists' escape, perhaps for a handsome bribe.[44] In a move that undercut the counterproductive political wrangling and faultfinding, the president appointed an independent three-member fact-finding commission headed by former justice secretary Sedfrey Ordoñez. On August 27 the commission recommended the prosecution of seven PNP officers for negligence and the filing of charges against three inmates for their roles in assisting the escape.[45]

On August 7, as political squabbles still raged in Manila, the Abu Sayyaf escapee Abdulmukim Edris was captured by Philippine army troops at a roadside checkpoint in Sultan Naga Dimaporo, Lanao del Norte. Unfortunately,

Edris was shot when he attempted to grab the firearm of one of his captors.[46] With that potential lead lost, the search for al-Ghozi and Lasal dragged on through the rest of August and September. During this interregnum, there were a number of false sightings and a case of mistaken identity, and the MILF was accused of sheltering the fugitive. As well, rumors began to circulate that the military had already captured al-Ghozi and was holding him incommunicado, although why it was supposedly doing so was never made clear.

A break in the case came on October 8 when Lasal was captured in Dinas, Zamboanga del Sur. Lasal's description of their 2 A.M. escape confirmed suspicions of gross incompetence, as the padlock could be easily opened without a key. The guards were either asleep or too busy writing reports to notice them and the trio simply walked out of the PNP compound, occasionally nodding to passing soldiers who mistook them for fellow soldiers. Once outside, they took a taxi to a bus station, where they boarded a bus bound for Sorsogon Province in the Bicol region, from which they got an interisland boat to Surigao in Mindanao. They then went by bus to Butuan City in Agusan del Norte Province. While en route, Edris contacted Abu Sayyaf leaders by cell phone, and al-Ghozi called MILF friends in Cagayan de Oro City and Davao City. In Cagayan de Oro, al-Ghozi was hosted by the MILF's Akkidin Abdusalam, alias Commander Kiddie, who had been reported killed in an encounter with the military two years earlier. Al-Ghozi then joined the Zamboanga Peninsula–based MILF leader Salip Aloy Alsree, who brought him to a training camp in Lanao del Norte.[47] Since nothing can be learned for certain about al-Ghozi's activities beyond this point, it might be assumed that he enjoyed the protection of independent-minded MILF commanders who ignored the movement's official policies.

Epilogue and Conclusion

On October 2, ten days before al-Ghozi met his end, another high-ranking Jemaah Islamiya member was taken into AFP custody in Cotabato City. Taufik Refke, alias Abu Obaidah, was the JI's number two man in the Philippines, and his arrest has reportedly proven to be a bonanza for intelligence officers. His revelations led authorities to a JI safe house and confirmed that the group continued its training program in two camps, Jabal Quba and Hudaibiyah, after the government's 2000 offensive. Refke's capture also induced a flight back to Indonesia of some JI members, although as many as thirty or so of the extremists may remain in Mindanao.[48] The al-Ghozi affair and Refke's arrest have also confirmed to the president and her immediate advisers that the threat of international Islamic terrorism to the Philippines continues to be real.

Philippine civilian and military officials have renewed calls for the MILF to reject foreign terrorists, but many MILF officials seem to believe they need links with foreign Muslim groups and Middle Eastern governments for the help they offer. Significantly, current MILF leaders remain focused on the practical needs of their people and are not interested in starting an international war against the West. An unnamed MILF "political chief" recently acknowledged having links with unspecified foreign groups, but also said, "That doesn't mean we are interested in . . . fighting their fights."[49] Still, the rebel movement has become highly fractious since the death of Salamat in mid-July 2003, and Philippine government leaders describe a power struggle occurring between pronegotiation MILF pragmatist leaders and hard-liners who would continue armed resistance.

Ultimately, if the enabling environment for international terrorism in the Philippines is to be broken, the government must negotiate a genuine peace treaty, curb military corruption, set aside divisive politics, and undertake a serious economic and social development program for Mindanao's Muslim population. Military offensives have done their work. Peace negotiations are currently scheduled to begin in early 2004, but another flawed treaty such as either the 1976 Tripoli Agreement or the more recent 1996 effort will not bring peace or stem international terrorism. As welcome as American offers of assistance might be, the important thing is for Manila to show political courage and good faith if there is to be a long-term and just peace.

Notes

1. Background information on al-Ghozi and details of his killing were compiled from online newspaper accounts of the *Philippine Daily Inquirer* (http://www.inq7.net). Agence France-Presse with Christine O. Avendano, "Al-Ghozi Is a Key Figure in Regional Terror Network," July 15, 2003; and Julie S. Alipala, Edwin O. Fernandez, and Christian V. Esguerra, "Killing of Al-Ghozi: Shootout or Rubout?" October 14, 2003. See also Fel V. Maragay, Lolit Rivera-Acosta, Roy Pelovello, and Joel M. Sy Egco, "Grenade Bolsters Shootout Angle on al-Ghozi," *Manila Standard,* October 15, 2003; and Richard C. Paddock and Al Jacinto, "Bomb Maker Gunned Down in Philippines," *Los Angeles Times,* October 13, 2003.

2. See these *Philippine Daily Inquirer* stories in their online versions: "Al-Ghozi, Two Abu Prisoners Escape," July 14, 2003; Christian V. Esguerra and Juliet L. Javellana, "Manhunt Ordered for Escaped Bomber; Four Policemen Axed," July 15, 2003; and "Al-Ghozi Slay Big Victory in War on Terror: President," October 14, 2003.

3. James F. Warren, *The Sulu Zone, 1768–1898: The Dynamics of External Trade, Slavery, and Ethnicity in the Transformation of a Southeast Asian Maritime State* (Singapore: Singapore University Press, 1981); and Cesar Adib Majul, *Muslims in the Philippines* (Diliman, Quezon City: University of the Philippines Press, 1999), see especially chapters 4–8, pp. 121–375.

4. Salah Jubair, *Bangsamoro: A Nation Under Endless Tyranny,* 3d ed. (Kuala Lumpur: IQ Marin SDN BHD, 1999), pp. 48–50, 52–54.

5. Ibid., pp. 59–66.

6. Ibid., pp. 72–74; see also Norodin Alonto Lucman, *Moro Archives: A History of Armed Conflicts in Mindanao and East Asia* (Quezon City: FLC Press, 2000), pp. 276–83; and W.K. Che Man, *Muslim Separatism: The Moros of Southern Philippines and the Malays of Southern Thailand* (Quezon City: Ateneo de Manila University Press, 1990), pp. 49, 51.

7. Jubair, *Bangsamoro,* pp. 75, 77–78, 89–90, 96–97 and Lucman, *Moro Archives,* pp. 284–87.

8. Jamail A. Kamlian, *Bangsamoro Society and Culture: A Book of Readings on Peace and Development in Southern Philippines* (Iligan: Iligan Center for Peace Education and Research, 1999), p. 16.

9. Jubair, *Bangsamoro,* pp. 119–20; and Che Man, *Muslim Separatism,* p. 25.

10. Macapado Abaton Muslim, *The Moro Armed Struggle in the Philippines: The Nonviolent Autonomy Alternative* (Marawi City: Mindanao State University, 1994), pp. 33–72.

11. The most recent and authoritative review of the massacre is found in Marites D. Vitug and Glenda M. Gloria, *Under the Crescent Moon: Rebellion in Mindanao* (Quezon City: Ateneo Center for Social Policy and Public Affairs and the Institute for Popular Democracy, 2000), pp. 2–23. See also Jubair, *Bangsamoro,* pp. 131–33; Lucman, *Moro Archives,* pp. 301–3; and al-Rashid I. Cayongcat, *Bangsa Moro People in Search of Peace* (Manila: Foundation for the Advancement of Islam in the Philippines, 1986), pp. 70–73.

12. Benedict Anderson, *Imagined Communities: Reflections on the Origin and Spread of Nationalism,* rev. ed. (London: Verso, 1991). See Muslim, *The Moro Armed Struggle in the Philippines,* pp. 93–94 for the political awakening of young Muslims, while a broader discussion of the grassroots development of a separate Muslim mentality is found in Thomas M. McKenna, *Muslim Rulers and Rebels: Everyday Politics and Armed Separatism in the Southern Philippines* (Berkeley: University of California Press, 1998), pp. 3–4, 5–7, plus chapters 5, 6, and 11.

13. Lucman, *Moro Archives,* pp. 304–6; Jubair, *Bangsamoro,* pp. 134–43; and Muslim, *The Moro Armed Struggle in the Philippines,* pp. 94–104.

14. Cayongcat, *Bangsa Moro People in Search of Peace,* pp. 78–85.

15. Muslim, *The Moro Armed Struggle in the Philippines,* pp. 114–15; and testimony of Senator Benigno Aquino, Jr., U.S. Congressional hearing, Washington, DC, June 23, 1983, cited in Lucman, *Moro Archives,* p. 310. The AFP's story is told by Fortunato U. Abat, *The Day We Nearly Lost Mindanao: The CEMCOM Story,* 3d ed. (Quezon City: self-published, 1999).

16. Cayongcat, *Bangsa Moro People in Search of Peace,* pp. 91–95; and Lucman, *Moro Archives,* pp. 311–12.

17. Jubair, *Bangsamoro,* pp. 153–57; Lucman, *Moro Archives,* pp. 312–14; and Che Man, *Muslim Separatism,* pp. 84–88.

18. Patricio N. Abinales, "The Recluse," *Newsbreak* 3, no. 17 (September 1, 2003): 33; and Aquiles Z. Zonio, "Good-bye, Ustadz Salamat Hashim," *Philippine Daily Inquirer,* online version, August 10, 2003. For a comparison of the religious nature of the two movements and how that factor shapes their respective policies, see Eric Gutierrez, "Religion and Politics in Muslim Mindanao," in *Rebels, Warlords, and Ulama: A Reader on Muslim Separatism and the War in Southern Philippines,* ed.

Kristina Gaerlan and Mara Stankovitch (Quezon City: Institute for Popular Democracy, 2000), pp. 152–58.

19. Che Man, *Muslim Separatism,* p. 89.

20. See the *Philippine Daily Inquirer* online stories, T.J. Burgonio and Edwin O. Fernandez, "Indonesians, Moro Rebs Join Hunt for Escaped Terrorists," July 18, 2003; "Al-Ghozi Neither Killed Nor Recaptured, Says Gov't," August 12, 2003; and Agence France-Presse, "MILF Commander Protecting Al-Ghozi, Says Military," August 14, 2003.

21. Carlos H. Conde, "Siocon Raid Exposed MILF's Weakness," commentary in editorial and opinion section of the *Philippine Daily Inquirer* online, June 1, 2003.

22. Abinales, "The Recluse," p. 33.

23. Gracia Burnham, *In the Presence of My Enemies* (Wheaton, IL: Tyndale House, 2003), pp. 149–50. The most damning testimony by the July 2003 coup leaders came from navy lieutenant Antonio F. Trillanes, who wrote two papers detailing navy corruption while taking a masters course at the University of the Philippines. The Trillanes papers are available at the Philippine Center for Investigative Journalism Web site (http://www.pcij.org/HotSeat/trillanes.html). See also the center's exposé by Ed Lingao, "Arming the Enemy," *Public Eye,* July–September 2003, http://www.pcij.org/PublicEye/arming.html. See the online version of the *Philippine Daily Inquirer* for Stella O. Gonzales, "Trillanes Papers: Macapagal Weak, Navy Corrupt," July 29, 2003; and Philip C. Tubeza, T.J. Burgonio, and Alcuin Papa, "Macapagal, Reyes, Corpus Accused," July 28, 2003.

24. Eric Gutierrez, "Chronology of Events," in *Rebels, Warlords, and Ulama,* pp. xviii–xxi.

25. Eric Gutierrez and Abdulwahab Guialal, "The Unfinished Jihad: The Moro Islamic Liberation Front and Peace in Mindanao," in *Rebels, Warlords, and Ulama,* pp. 281–82. See also Vitug and Gloria, *Under the Crescent Moon,* pp. 36–41.

26. An extended account of the negotiation process from 1992 through to its completion in 1996 is detailed by former president Fidel V. Ramos in his book *Break Not the Peace: The Story of the GRP-MNLF Peace Negotiations, 1992–1996* (Quezon City: Friends of Steady Eddie, 1996). See also Vitug and Gloria, *Under the Crescent Moon,* pp. 43–51.

27. Eric Gutierrez and Marites D. Vitug, "ARMM After the Peace Agreement," in *Rebels, Warlords, and Ulama,* pp. 183–221; Eric Gutierrez, "The Problems of Peace," in ibid., pp. 225–61; Vitug and Gloria, *Under the Crescent Moon,* pp. 56–58, 74–102; and R.J. May, "Muslim Mindanao: Four Years After the Peace Agreement," in *Southeast Asian Affairs 2001* (Singapore: Institute of Southeast Asian Studies, 2001), pp. 263–69.

28. Dirk J. Barreveld, *Terrorism in the Philippines: The Bloody Trail of Abu Sayyaf, Bin Laden's East Asian Connection* (San Jose, CA: Writers Club Press, 2001), chapters 5–7, pp. 138–209; and Jose Torres, Jr., *Into the Mountain: Hostaged by the Abu Sayyaf* (Quezon City: Claretian Publications, 2001).

29. Gutierrez and Guialal, "The Unfinished Jihad," pp. 265–92. See also May, "Muslim Mindanao," pp. 269–70; Vitug and Gloria, *Under the Crescent Moon,* pp. 143–48; and Jubair, *Bangsamoro,* pp. 197–208.

30. May, "Muslim Mindanao," p. 270; Jubair, *Bangsamoro,* pp. 208–42; and Vitug and Gloria, *Under the Crescent Moon,* pp. 155–61.

31. See Barreveld, *Terrorism in the Philippines,* pp. 113–32; and Vitug and Gloria, *Under the Crescent Moon,* pp. 192–204, for an account of the Ipil raid, plus pp. 204–6

and 211–13 for a description of Janjalani's travels and activities leading to the Abu Sayyaf's founding. A good overview of Janjalani's religious thought was made by Julkipli Wadi in "They Come This Far," *Newsbreak,* Special Issue, "The Faces of Mindanao," January–June 2003, pp. 16, 18–19.

32. Barreveld, *Terrorism in the Philippines,* pp. 219–21.

33. Raymond Bonner, "Southeast Asia Remains Fertile for Al Qaeda," *New York Times,* online edition, October 28, 2002; Martin Marfil, "Hunt on for Key Al-Qaeda Man's Allies in Philippines," *Philippine Daily Inquirer,* online edition, March 4, 2003; and Barreveld, *Terrorism in the Philippines,* pp. 218, 222–24. See also Fouda Yosri and Nick Fielding, *Masterminds of Terror* (New York: Arcade, 2003), pp. 97–99; and Rohan Gunaratna, *Inside Al Qaeda: Global Network of Terror* (New York: Berkley Books, 2002), pp. 233–43.

34. Gunaratna, *Inside Al Qaeda,* pp. 243–44.

35. International Crisis Group, *Jemaah Islamiyah in South East Asia: Damaged But Still Dangerous,* ICG, Jakarta/Brussels, Asia Report No. 63, August 26, 2003, pp. 16–17, 40 et passim.

36. Ibid., pp. 16–23.

37. Paddock and Jacinto, "Bomb Maker Gunned Down in Philippines."

38. Hambali was arrested in Thailand in August 2003 and is being held in U.S. custody. Meanwhile, Faiz Abu bin Bakar Bafana was arrested in Singapore in January 2002 in a sweep that netted many Jemaah Islamiya members who were plotting an extensive campaign of bombings in that city-state.

39. See the online versions of the following reports from the *Philippine Daily Inquirer,* Philip Tubeza, "Terrorist Raps Filed vs. Asia's Most Wanted Man," July 8, 2003; AFP, "Al-Ghozi Is a Key Figure in Regional Terror Network," July 15, 2003; and Kathy I. Navarro and Jhuunex Napallacan, "Al-Ghozi Explosives 'Supplier' Nabbed," August 13, 2003.

40. Paul A. Rodell, "The Philippines: Gloria in Excelsis," *Southeast Asian Affairs, 2002* (Singapore: Institute of Southeast Asian Studies, 2002), pp. 229–30; Noel M. Morada, "Philippine-American Security Relations After 11 September," in *Southeast Asian Affairs, 2003* (Singapore: Institute of Southeast Asian Studies, 2003), pp. 230–32; and Sheldon W. Simon, "Southeast Asia and the U.S. War on Terrorism," in Sheldon W. Simon, "Managing Security Challenges in Southeast Asia," *NBR Analysis* 13, no. 4 (July 2002): 32–35.

41. Rodell, "The Philippines," pp. 230–33.

42. Belinda Olivares-Cunanan, "Big Problem," *Philippine Daily Inquirer,* October 2, 2003, p. A13.

43. *Philippine Daily Inquirer,* online version, editorials, "Angie's War," and "Rampage," on March 2 and April 27, 2003, respectively. See also Edwin Fernandez, "Fate of MILF Exploratory Talks in Malaysia Uncertain," *Philippine Daily Inquirer,* online version, May 6, 2002.

44. For details of the embarrassing political wrangling, see the following online *Philippine Daily Inquirer* stories: Christian V. Esguerra, Michael L. Ubac, and Cynthia D. Balana, "PNP Chief Refuses to Resign, Suspects Foes," July 16, 2003; Christian V. Esguerra, "Entire Command of Police Intelligence Group Sacked," July 22, 2003; Inquirer News Service, "Spy vs. Spy: Military Probing Prober of Al-Ghozi Escape," July 22, 2003; Inq7.net, "Al-Ghozi Escape Linked to Destabilization Plot," July 24, 2003; and Christian V. Esguerra and Nelson F. Flores, "Police Intelligence Official Linked to Al-Ghozi Escape," July 21, 2003.

45. Juliet Labog-Javellana, "No Proof of Al-Ghozi Collusion with Jailers," *Philippine Daily Inquirer,* online version, August 28, 2003.

46. Inquirer News Service, "Police to Investigate Edris Killing to Quell Speculation," *Philippine Daily Inquirer,* online version, August 9, 2003.

47. Julie S. Alipala, "Al-Ghozi Had 'Walked Out' to Escape from Police Camp," *Philippine Daily Inquirer,* online version, October 14, 2003.

48. T.J. Burgonio and Christian V. Esguerra, "Raiders Find Bomb Residue, Not Virus, in JI Safe House," *Philippine Daily Inquirer,* online version, October 21, 2003. For a recent update, see Kimina Lyall, "JI Grows Terror in Philippines," *Weekend Australian,* December 13, 2003, p. 16.

49. Mitchell Koss, "Near Enough to View Militancy's Many Faces," *Los Angeles Times,* December 7, 2003, opinion, part M, p. 2.

III

Southeast Asia's Ideological and Physical Enabling Environment

8

Countering Radical Islam in Southeast Asia

The Need to Confront the Functional and Ideological "Enabling Environment"

Kumar Ramakrishna

Introduction

Jemaah Islamiya (JI) represents the key terrorist threat in Southeast Asia. Through its Rabitatul Mujahideen (RM) coordinating framework, JI, whose ideological and operational locus is Indonesia, has sought to build a coalition of radical Islamist groups in its quest to forcibly establish a Darulah Islamiah Nusantara, or pan–Southeast Asian Islamic state. The RM was formed by JI spiritual leader Abu Bakar Bashir in late 1999 in Kuala Lumpur.[1] The first meeting, apart from JI core members, included elements from other regional radical Islamist groups such as Kumpulan Mujahideen Malaysia (KMM); Laskar Jundullah and Darul Islam; the Free Aceh Movement (GAM) and Republik Islam Aceh from Indonesia; the Moro Islamic Liberation Front (MILF) from the southern Philippines; the Rohingya Solidarity Organization (RSO) and the Arakan Rohingya Nationalist Organization (ARNO) from Myanmar; and the Pattani United Liberation Organization (PULO) from southern Thailand.[2] It must be emphasized that not all of these groups share JI's global jihad agenda. While the RM has not been particularly active,[3] it would be an error to disregard its significance. Because of the shared experience of jihad either in Afghanistan or Ambon in the Maluku Archipelago in eastern Indonesia, a sense of "brotherhood" exists between disparate Southeast Asian radical Islamists, and the RM mechanism can, and has, crystallized this commodity for mutual assistance and support. Hence, in late December 2000, JI colluded with MILF elements to stage bombings in Manila that killed twenty-two people. This was in retaliation for a major offensive by Filipino armed forces that had earlier in the year resulted in the capture of more than forty MILF camps in the southern Philippines.[4]

The RM should thus be seen as an informal, loose, but potentially force-multiplying extension of JI. It is the latter, however, that truly represents the transnational guiding intelligence of radical Islamist terrorism in Southeast Asia. Whatever its indigenous historical origins in the Darul Islam movement in Indonesia,[5] JI's global jihad vision makes it an al-Qaeda ally in Southeast Asia.[6] Moreover, JI's ambitions and organizational capacity renders it the center of gravity of the radical Islamist terrorist threat in the theater. At this time, JI remains a threat because of the *functional* and *political* space that it has been able to exploit.

The Problem of JI's "Functional Space"

JI's functional space—defined broadly as the freedom to carry out the various activities necessary to support the terrorist agenda—is expressed in several ways. First and foremost is the fact that the network's membership is very extensive, numbering, according to one recent authoritative estimate, "probably" in the "thousands."[7] Furthermore, JI possesses considerable expertise to cause mayhem. Included in its ranks are operatives such as Dr. Azahari Husin and Dulmatin, both of whom have the skills to construct powerful explosives such as the ones used in the Bali and Marriott blasts. In addition, scores more militants have received training in weapons and explosives use in Mindanao since about 1997.[8] Additionally, JI's functional space has been expressed through the relative ease with which militants, arms, and money have circulated throughout the region. Part of the reason for this lies in geographical realities. The region is crisscrossed by waterways, and Indonesia and the Philippines especially are fragmented archipelagic entities whose maritime boundaries are notoriously difficult to police even at the best of times. Thus the maritime approaches to significant swaths of Indonesian and Filipino territory remain inadequately monitored, expediting the movement of Southeast Asian militants. In April 2003, Jakarta and Manila expressed concern about three hundred Indonesian JI militants who had entered the southern Philippines and dispersed throughout Mindanao. In fact, the Filipino police suspect that some of these Indonesian JI may have perpetrated bomb attacks in Davao City in March and April 2003.[9]

Geography aside, the weak regulatory capacities of some governments also contribute to JI's functional space. One problem lies in still-inadequate border controls. Lax immigration and visa requirements continue to allow dubious figures into some Southeast Asian states. Thus the Filipino authorities reported in late March 2003 that a four-man Middle Eastern al-Qaeda cell, armed with "substantial amounts of money," entered central Mindanao. They had apparently been able to enter *legally* either as "tourists, preachers, or as spouses of Filipinas."[10] *Illegal* entry is another problem. While on the one hand this might be due to corrupt immigration officials at the port of entry, not all immigration authorities in the region possess the expertise to detect forged travel documents and visas.[11] Key JI leader Hambali, prior to his arrest in August 2003, had managed to slip into Thailand through a northern border crossing from Laos or Myanmar, prompting Bangkok to wonder how he had managed to elude immigration checks despite possessing a Spanish passport. It was speculated that he might have secured the false document from Thailand itself.[12] In fact, elements of foreign criminal syndicates from the Middle East and South Asia have exploited Bangkok's lax immigration rules, coming in as tourists and businessmen, and producing high quality forged passports and identity papers. The latter have been used by "worldwide Islamic terrorist networks" to facilitate terrorist movement both within and without Southeast Asia.[13] It is significant that JI has cultivated actively *preman* (criminal) elements to "arrange illegal border crossings from Indonesia to Malaysia or the Philippines; to secure false identity papers; and to transport people and goods."[14] In September 2003, ASEAN chiefs of national police identified the region's porous borders as a big problem hindering regional counterterror efforts.[15]

Critically, JI's functional space has been enhanced by the inability of some Southeast Asian states to effectively track dubious electronic money transfers due to poorly regulated financial systems. This problem is especially acute in the case of Manila and Bangkok, as Middle Eastern individuals transact huge amounts of funds and deposits.[16] The problem of poor regulation extends to foreign charities, especially Saudi ones, which have operated within Southeast Asia for years. One such Saudi charity, Al Haramain, has been used by al-Qaeda to channel funds to JI.[17] Another way in which al-Qaeda money has been laundered into the region is through the setting up of front companies, especially in Malaysia. These companies have not only masked the funding of terrorist activities, but have also generated revenue to be plowed back into those activities.[18] Finally, Southeast Asia has an extensive *hawalla* network, as hundreds of thousands of Indonesians, Filipinos, and Thais work overseas, particularly in western Asia.[19] Compounding matters is the relatively low cost of medium-scale terrorist attacks like the Bali tragedy. Rather than hundreds of thousands of dollars, the operation is estimated to have cost only about US$30,000.[20] Given the combination of the huge volume of financial flows in and around the region, the variations in regulatory capacities among states, and the modest sums involved in mounting antiterrorist strikes, isolating and tracking funding intended for terrorist operations in the region is an excruciatingly difficult enterprise.

Serious regulatory weaknesses also help explain the relative accessibility of weapons and explosives. The extremely lucrative arms trade in Southeast Asia has its locus in Thailand and Cambodia. According to an estimate by Panitan Wattanyagorn, one-third of the arms flowing through the region are smuggled out from former war zones in Cambodia. Another third come from China, via Laos and Thailand. A third come from illegal arms sales by rogue Thai military elements. Some of these weapons have found their way to radical Islamist groups in the region.[21] Certainly, firearms from Thailand have reached JI militants in Indonesia.[22] Unsurprisingly, official corruption is another source of weapons and explosives. The Abu Sayyaf Group in Mindanao, for instance, flush with cash from criminal activities, has been able to buy arms from soldiers of the Armed Forces of the Philippines (AFP).[23] Similarly, weapons, ammunition, and explosives have mysteriously been siphoned off from Indonesian military depots.[24] The largesse of sympathetic military elements is yet another source. During the Maluku conflict, for instance, it was known that elements of the Indonesian military (TNI) trained and funded the militant anti-Christian Laskar Jihad.[25]

One more factor exacerbated matters: the varying levels of political commitment among Southeast Asian governments to the U.S.-led war on terror. There are two key reasons for this. First, several Southeast Asian states have significant Muslim communities whose concerns about the perceived U.S. bias against Islam needed to be accommodated in order to forestall the possibility of a domestic backlash. Second, the region has yet to fully recover from the devastating effects of the 1997/98 Asian financial crisis, and thus governments, eager to attract both foreign investors and tourists, are naturally loath to buttress the impression often created in the Western media that their territories are radical Islamist terrorist hotbeds. This second factor helps explain Jakarta's heavily criticized hands-off stance before the Bali attacks as well as Bangkok's noncommittal official posture before August 2003, when it finally introduced tougher legislation to counter terrorist activity.[26] The image factor also explains why Jakarta and Bangkok as well as other Southeast Asian governments have been very prickly about the issuance of terrorism-related travel warnings by the United States, the U.K., and other Western countries. Tourism, for instance, generates 6 percent of GDP for Thailand.[27]

Counter-*Terrorist* Strategy in Southeast Asia: Closing Down JI's Functional Space

At the time of writing it would be fair to assert that Southeast Asian governments and their Western partners have focused in the main on eliminating the immediate, operational threat emanating from JI. In other words, theirs is a counter-*terrorist* approach seeking to detain militants and close down the network's functional space. This thrust, for example, was well illustrated by the U.S.-ASEAN Joint Declaration on Combating Terrorism initialed on August 1, 2002. The declaration committed the United States and its ASEAN partners to several initiatives: continuing and improving "intelligence and terrorist financing information sharing"; developing "more effective counterterrorism policies and legal, regulatory and administrative counterterrorism regimes"; enhancing the liaison among law enforcement agencies; strengthening "capacity-building efforts" through "training and education"; initiating consultations between "officials, analysts and field operators"; mounting joint operations; and providing assistance on "transportation, border and immigration control challenges" to "stem effectively the flow of terrorist-related material, money and people."[28]

This counterterrorist thrust against the JI threat has been operationalized through a three-tier approach: first, isolating the network from extraregional financial and operational assistance; second, disrupting the intraregional financial, logistical, and manpower flows that enable JI to operate and possibly exploit its wider informal RM partnerships; and third, eliminating active JI cells physically located within national boundaries throughout the region.

Isolating Southeast Asia from Extraregional Manpower and Financial Inflows

Some Southeast Asian states have recognized the porosity of their borders to extraregional inflows of terrorist expertise, particular from al-Qaeda. Malaysia, for example, until recently did not require visas for citizens of OIC states. In addition, as far as the Philippines is concerned, foreigners can easily marry Filipino citizens and "effectively change their identity."[29] Nevertheless, visa and entry requirements have been tightened gradually. In addition, the real problem of forged travel documents has been recognized and discussed, for instance, in March 2003 at the first ASEAN Regional Forum (ARF) Inter-Sessional Meeting on Terrorism and Transnational Crime, cochaired by Malaysia and the United States. Nevertheless, there remains much to be done to overcome the real problem of inadequate computerization of immigration databases.[30] In addition, corruption among frontline immigration officials, especially those in remoter areas, also needs firmer tackling. Singapore JI leader Mas Selamat Kastari, after slipping into Indonesia to elude the December 2001 crackdown on his group, obtained an Indonesian passport in Surabaya with a five-year validity by using a false nom de guerre, Edi Hariyanto.[31]

In addition, much more can be done to "seal" the region off from external al-Qaeda financing. The ASEAN states have agreed to work toward early accession to all U.N. conventions on terrorism such as the 1999 International Convention for the Suppression of the Financing of Terrorism.[32] As of December 2002, Singapore had become a party to the latter convention while the Philippines had signed but not yet ratified it.[33] In addition, the FBI has assisted Thailand in installing sophisticated money-tracking software for its new anti–money laundering center in Bangkok.[34] Meanwhile, Kuala Lumpur hosted an anti–money laundering seminar in July 2003 for ASEAN members,[35] while Thailand, the European Union, and the United Kingdom signed a Memorandum of Understanding on a new three-year anti–money laundering project based in Bangkok. This program will provide training and technical assistance in anti–money laundering best practices.[36]

Disrupting Intraregional Militant Logistical and Manpower Flows

In addition, attempts have already been made to reduce terrorist functional space by making maritime crossings more difficult. Three principal transit points for "men, money and weapons involved in Southeast Asian terrorism" are the Riau Archipelago, the Indonesian-Malaysian border region in eastern Kalimantan, and the island of Sulawesi, which has traditional trading links with the southern Philippine island of Mindanao.[37] It is little wonder that many JI militants in Kalimantan have trained in Mindanao with the MILF, and that key JI-linked Indonesian militants based in Sulawesi, such as Syawal Yasin, have reportedly "strong ties to the southern Philippines."[38] It appears that Sebatik Island, a tear-shaped island that is part of East Kalimantan in Indonesia, is where JI has hidden thousands of weapons as well as bomb-making material. In fact, in August 2003 the Indonesian police intercepted a speedboat carrying 2.5 tons of ammonium nitrate traveling along the Tawau (Sabah)-Sebatik-Nunukan (East Kalimantan) route. Indonesian officials suspected that the shipment was to have been used by JI in future attacks.[39] Another key arms and people-smuggling zone, the northern Straits of Malacca between the North Aceh coastline and southern Thailand, has been heavily used by GAM to smuggle weapons from southern Thai territory. The Indonesian navy admits it lacks the resources to patrol the zone effectively.[40] Nevertheless, the United States, for instance, is moving to redress the capacity shortfalls of certain ASEAN navies. The Philippine navy, currently struggling to patrol the seaward approaches to Mindanao and Basilan from North Sulawesi, will receive patrol boats as well as other defense-related articles as part of the U.S. State Department's 2004 aid package.[41] In addition, in May 2003, Washington granted Manila Major Non-NATO Ally Status, giving it enhanced access to U.S. equipment and supplies, while agreeing to launch a comprehensive review of Manila's defense needs to ascertain "how the United States can best support the Philippine military."[42] Furthermore, under the ASEAN cooperation plan launched in December 2002, the United States, inter alia, will cooperate with ASEAN in coping with transnational issues and maritime elements such as piracy, terrorism, and drug and people-trafficking.[43]

Neutralizing JI Cells Within National Territories Throughout the Region

Apart from attempting to "seal" the region off from external financial and operational succor from the likes of al-Qaeda and weakening JI's freedom of movement within the region, the third tier of the counterterrorist approach designed to shut down the network's functional space involves using state-level intelligence and law enforcement measures to identify, locate, and destroy JI cells within national boundaries. In this respect Indonesia remains the key state. An Indonesian analyst working closely with the police investigation into the Bali attacks has estimated that there are about a thousand JI members in Indonesia.[44] While since the Bali attacks Jakarta has apprehended several key Indonesian JI militants, the threat has not diminished. Key JI leaders remain at large and are the subjects of a massive manhunt being undertaken by ASEAN and other police forces. Following the capture of Hambali in Thailand in August 2003, many analysts pointed out that there were still leaders with "strategic capabilities" who could conceivably replace him.[45]

Even prior to the Bali attacks, ASEAN states had been actively exchanging information with one another on terrorist movements. This has led to the capture of many JI militants. For instance, in June 2003, Thai police, acting on information provided by their Singapore counterparts, arrested three alleged Thai JI militants in Narathiwat, southern Thailand. The trio had allegedly been planning attacks on embassies as well as tourist spots in Bangkok, Pattaya, and Phuket.[46] Moreover, Jakarta in August 2003 pushed for even closer regional cooperation through the creation of a "security community." The initiative called for, inter alia, a centralized regional database on terrorists; the streamlining of legal processes in counterterror operations; the blocking of terror assets; joint training programs; and easier access to terrorist suspects detained in member states for interrogation purposes.[47] Moreover, in the spirit of the U.S.-ASEAN joint declaration mentioned earlier, regional police agencies have surmounted capacity shortfalls by actively cooperating with both the United States and other partners such as Australia. For instance, the Australian Federal Police assisted its Indonesian counterparts in investigating the bomb blast at Jakarta's international airport in late April 2003. Significantly, despite the occasional prickly relations between the two states, the Indonesians acknowledged openly that by exploiting the "sophisticated forensic equipment" of the Australians, they would hopefully "solve this case faster."[48] In addition, several ASEAN states, including Indonesia and the Philippines, have signed memoranda of understanding with the United States and Australia to forge closer cooperation among law enforcement agencies. Under these arrangements, both the Australians and the FBI have provided training in up-to-date investigative techniques to the Indonesian and Filipino police.[49]

That there is a pressing need to enhance the professionalism of some Southeast Asian police forces was brought home forcefully by the circumstances surrounding the escape of JI explosives expert Fathur Rohman al-Ghozi from detention in Camp Crame, Manila, in July 2003. One police guard was asleep and another out shopping, and apparently al-Ghozi and two Abu Sayyaf inmates simply "walked along the main hallway, down the stairs to the ground floor and left through the main gate."[50] Moreover, the jailbreak was discovered only five hours later.[51] Then in early October, at the same facility, another detained Abu Sayyaf militant, Buyungan Bungkak, grabbed an M-16 rifle from his minder and shot the latter and two other guards before being killed. It is believed that Bungkak had not been restrained while being escorted to an exercise yard. Apparently Bungkak had tried to escape previously when his guards were not watching.[52] Al-Ghozi was subsequently killed by the Philippine police in October 2003.[53]

As mentioned, corruption is another factor that erodes the capacity of regional states to eliminate JI cells within their territories. This has been caused in part by the fact that central governmental writ does not extend adequately to remote regions. Graft also occurs because many police and military commanders and their men on the ground are so poorly paid that they need to supplement their incomes by other means. While pure self-aggrandizement of course cannot be completely ruled out, poor salaries have surely been a factor prompting elements of the Thai, Indonesian, and

Philippine militaries, for instance, to sell weapons and explosives to both criminals and terrorists. A lasting solution to the problem of corruption in some Southeast Asian states requires increasing the capacity of central governments to not only expand their administrative coverage effectively but also to pay better salaries.[54] These measures can be achieved only with bigger central budgets, which in turn depend on jump-starting economies still recovering from the Asian financial crisis of 1997–98. The Bush administration, to its credit, has recognized this. Under the Enterprise for ASEAN Initiative inked in October 2002, Washington has begun exploring the potential for establishing a "network of bilateral FTAs" in order to "increase trade and investment."[55] In fact, the United States and Singapore signed an FTA in May 2003, prompting Thailand and Malaysia to commence negotiations with Washington on similar arrangements. It is possible that the Philippines and Indonesia might pursue a similar strategy with Washington after their respective presidential elections in 2004. By 2003, U.S. investments in ASEAN had risen to US$50 billion.[56]

Finally, sustained political will is needed if Southeast Asian governments are to successfully eradicate JI cells. As noted, not all Southeast Asian states have been demonstrating this commodity with equal fervor. The decision in early September 2003 by a Jakarta court to sentence alleged JI amir Abu Bakar Bashir to a mere four years instead of the fifteen demanded by prosecutors underscores this reality.[57] The essential concern is that if governments are seen to be too closely aligned with the United States, this would provoke an electoral and even militant Muslim backlash. The problem is that among Southeast Asian Muslims—both "radicals" and "moderates"—the United States is generally perceived to be against Islam.[58] In other words, there exists among pockets of Southeast Asian Muslims, to widely varying degrees, a modicum of sympathy for JI, even if the vast majority of Muslims deplore utterly the network's modus operandi. This in turn generates what might be called *political space* within which JI can sustain itself. JI's political space complements and in truth empowers the network's functional space. It is worth recognizing two facts in this regard. First, only about thirty people were involved in the Bali operation. Second, as noted, the cost of the Bali attack ran into tens of thousands of dollars rather than hundreds of thousands of dollars. The reality therefore is that only a relative handful of militants— including a couple with some knowledge of explosives and having access to a moderate amount of funding—is all that is needed to inflict catastrophic damage. In other words, JI requires relatively *minimal functional space* in order to wreak havoc. It therefore becomes utterly crucial to undermine JI's ability to *attract* adherents in the first place. In short, one should seek to shut down JI's political space, and not just its functional space.[59]

The Problem of JI's "Political Space"

Because JI elicits some sympathy from scattered Muslim communities, for example, in southern Thailand, northern Malaysia, Indonesia, and the southern Philippines, the network has been able to generate funds, secure safe houses for militants, receive tip-offs on impending police raids, and recruit additional militants.[60] For example, JI militants have sought refuge among the conservative Muslim community in Sulawesi, which the network regards as having considerable "potential for true jihad."[61] Other pockets of JI support are dispersed throughout the region. In Thailand, where Muslims make up 4 percent of the population of 62 million, analysts acknowledge that Hambali would have needed help from "wayward" Thai Muslims[62] to expedite his "prolonged presence" and his "several entries and exits to and from" the country.[63] Apart from personal networks established by school and marriage ties,[64] the key factor that underlies JI's wider political space is radical Islamist ideology. This ideology perpetuates an adversarial mind-set toward non-Muslim and moderate Muslim polities and societies, and is characterized by a strong anti-American element. This ideological framework is in turn strengthened both by U.S. foreign policy errors and failures as well as concrete localized political and socioeconomic grievances.

It has been said with good reason that Southeast Asian Islam has traditionally been tolerant and peaceful, quite capable of coexisting with other faiths. While it is true that over the past three decades there has been a discernible increase in Islamic orthodoxy in dress, diet, and social practices in regional Muslim communities,[65] the latter phenomenon is not to be equated with radical jihadi ideology. The central thrust of the Islamic fundamentalist or Salafiyyah movement that emerged in Southeast Asia most pronouncedly in the 1980s was to revive Islamic identity by reasserting the unity of God (tawhid) in all spheres of life. Rather than seeing the world in stark black-and-white terms, the emphasis was on creating a just and equitable social order through the gradual Islamization of society from the bottom up. Anwar Ibrahim's Angkata Belia Islam Malaysia (ABIM) social organization in Malaysia has been closely associated with this type of program.[66] Somewhat similarly, Partai Keadilan (Justice Party) in Indonesia is an example of an Islamic fundamentalist political party that seeks a gradual Islamization of society through the propagation of Islamic values. In fact, Partai Keadilan is the fastest-growing political party in Indonesia, largely because of its clean image. Both ABIM and Partai Keadilan have been influenced deeply by the gradualist, Islamization-from-below ideas of the Muslim Brotherhood in Egypt.[67]

While accepting that the reality is extremely complex, it would nevertheless appear that the real roots of radical Islamism lie in the emergence, in both the Middle East and in Southeast Asia, of neo-Salafism, which blends the return-to-roots fundamentalism of traditional Salafism with the additional ideational thread of an Islam under siege from Christian, Zionist, and secular forces.[68] Saudi-funded and influenced neo-Salafiyyah *pesantren* in Southeast Asia thus propagate, over and above the traditional Salafiyyah call to return to a pristine unadulterated form of Islam, the injunction to distance oneself from Sufi Muslims, Shiite Muslims, and non-Muslims. Neo-Salafiyyah *pesantren,* while by no means dominant among Indonesia's religious schools, have nevertheless, according to former Indonesian foreign minister Alwi Shihab, permitted "stricter interpretations of Islam to gain favor."[69] Shihab adds that the rise of such a "rigid interpretation" of the Islamic faith has had "consequences."[70]

One utterly crucial consequence has been the propagation of an "inflexible, scripturalist," "'us versus them,' 'good versus evil,' 'right versus wrong,' and 'permitted (*halal*) versus prohibited (*haram*)' view of life."[71] In Southeast Asia, Islamist political parties, like PAS in Malaysia as well as social organizations like Majelis Mujahideen Indonesia (MMI), Komite Pengerakan Syariat Islam (KPSI), Dewan Dakwah Islamiyah Indonesia (DDII), and Hizbut Tahrir in Indonesia, generally propagate such binary worldviews. While it is true that such political parties and social organizations appear willing to attain their Islamist agendas gradually by working peacefully within existing political systems, the problem is that the dividing line between neo-Salafism and violent radical Salafism is rather thin. Thus the intrinsic rejectionist neo-Salafiyyah impulse animates the violent activities of disparate Southeast Asian radical Salafiyyah groups such as Laskar Mujahideen, Front Pembela Islam—and JI. Thus while neo-Salafiyyah ideology may not in and of itself promote violence directly, it certainly engenders an exclusionist mind-set that may prove particularly prone to radicalization in certain circumstances. Steven Emerson offers a somewhat analogous analysis in his discussion of the tenuous ties between some seemingly nonviolent, legitimate Islamic NGOs and radical Islamist terrorists in the United States.[72]

Thus the small number of so-called "Ivy League" radical Salafiyyah *pesantren* "that constitute the JI's educational circle" in Indonesia, which the International Crisis Group argues are incubating a new breed of "*salafi* jihadists," is not the only problem.[73] The circulation of neo-Salafiyyah ideology in some Southeast Asian Muslim quarters, propagated especially by Saudi-funded *pesantren* and mosques, creates arguably a visceral openness to JI's puritanical pan–Southeast Asian Islamic state agenda and, by implication, the political space within which JI not only attracts recruits, but also sustains itself. The role of sympathizers who are not necessarily JI operatives themselves in arranging safe houses, acting as guides, and arranging travel throughout Southeast Asia for JI militants bears testimony to how a neo-Salifiyyah ideological milieu can be hospitable to the radical Salifiyyah agenda.[74] This affinity may also explain why key leaders of MMI, ostensibly a nonviolent Islamist organization, have close links with JI.[75] It is of no small significance either that senior PAS leader Hadi Awang maintained contact with Agus Dwikarna, who prior to his detention in the Philippines on terrorism related charges in March 2002 had served as both MMI secretary-general and head of Laskar Jundullah, a JI-linked Islamist militia that took part in anti-Christian fighting in Sulawesi.[76] It is even more noteworthy that Nik Adli Nik Aziz, the son of PAS spiritual leader Nik Aziz Nik Mat, was detained by Kuala Lumpur in August 2001 for his alleged leadership role in the militant KMM group that seeks to set up an Islamic state in Malaysia by force. Moreover, both Nik Adli and an unnamed official from PAS attended the 1999 meeting in Petaling Jaya, Malaysia, that set up the Rabitatul Mujahideen.[77] Radical Salafism may not be identical to, but it surely feeds upon, a puritanical neo-Salafiyyah diet.

Neo-Salafiyyah ideological currents also aid and abet JI's political space by imparting a degree of credibility to radical Islamist propaganda, such as Washington is working with Israel to attack fellow Muslims like the Palestinians, Iraqis, and Afghans. It is instructive to realize that it is not merely militant Islamists who dislike and even abhor America. Even Southeast Asian Muslims who are quite willing to practice their faith within essentially secular political frameworks believe fervently that U.S. foreign policy is biased against the realm of Islam. A June 2003 Pew survey found that an overwhelming 83 percent of Indonesian Muslims, well known for their moderate Islam, had an unfavorable impression of the United States.[78] This image of the United States as duplicitous explains why some Muslims in Southeast Asia believed that the CIA was behind both the September 11, 2001, World Trade Center attack as well as the Bali blast of October 12, 2002.[79] Similarly, following the Marriott bombing of August 2003, a number of Indonesians believed that the CIA had again perpetrated the attack, exploiting the supposedly fictitious JI organization to camouflage the real U.S. aim of discrediting Islam, destabilizing Indonesia, and taking control of the country.[80] Among Indonesian university students exposed to neo-Salafiyyah ideological currents through, for instance, DDII *dakwah* (proselytizing) activities on campus, there is "growing acceptance" of the notion that the Islamic world is under attack by Western forces such as the United States and, crucially, "must be defended—with violence if necessary."[81] No surprise then that JI's declared anti-American program and associated propaganda are therefore another factor that wins it a modicum of legitimacy, and political space, in some Muslim quarters.

Generalized Muslim antipathy toward America stems from one single issue in particular: the plight of the Palestinians and the status of Jerusalem. As the site of the Al-Aqsa Mosque, Jerusalem is, after Mecca and Medina, the third-holiest place in Islam, while the suffering of the stateless Palestinians has served as a metaphor for the suffering of Muslims as a whole in the face of a supposed Zionist-Crusader conspiracy. As Ahmad Suhelmi, an Islamic scholar at the University of Indonesia, puts it, the *"ummah* is a unity that cannot be divided" and, like a human body, "if you hurt even one little finger the whole body feels the pain."[82] In this respect it is reassuring that Washington recognizes the central importance of the Palestinian issue and that President Bush himself has now committed his energies to seeking a settlement.[83] However, the United States does not go far enough in identifying and seeking to eliminate other sources of what might be called "political oxygen" that JI might exploit to recruit more followers.

For example, the slowness of America and the West to intervene in Bosnia to prevent Serb ethnic cleansing of the Muslims only confirmed in the minds of Muslims in the region, as elsewhere, that the *ummah* could expect no favors from the United States. One former Malaysian army officer, Lieutenant Colonel Abdul Manaf Kasmuri, who served with a Malaysian armored regiment operating as part of the United Nations Protection Force (UNPROFOR) in Bosnia between 1993 and 1994, was himself radicalized as a result of what he perceived as Western unwillingness to halt the atrocities committed against Bosnian Muslims. He established contact with al-Qaeda in Bosnia and later joined JI.[84] Significantly, U.S. military operations have also tended to generate political oxygen. The U.S.-Afghan air campaign of late 2001, while operationally successful in ousting the Taliban, nonetheless generated numerous civilian casualties, which again reinforced the perception, despite disclaimers to the contrary by President Bush, that America was at war with Islam. Indeed, anger at the U.S. attack on Afghanistan in October 2001 was one critical factor that prompted Imam Samudra, a key planner of the Bali attacks, to perpetrate the latter.[85]

In fact, the suffering of Muslims anywhere, especially where the United States is directly involved—as in the instance of collateral civilian casualties in Iraq and Afghanistan—can, as liberal Muslim scholar Akbar Ahmed points out, be "used by extremists" to "reinforce this feeling that all Muslims are under attack."[86] JI leaders are certainly skilled in exploiting every egregious instance of inadvertent U.S. military strikes against Muslim civilians in order to reinforce the stock ideological narrative of an America bent on annihilating Muslims. JI leaders, like their al-Qaeda mentors, are Internet-savvy, technically proficient, and have been known to buttress their propaganda by producing videotapes and VCDs of purported violence against Muslims by

Christians, as during the Maluku conflict that erupted in 1999. Such media are then used for recruitment purposes.[87] Worryingly, Jusuf Wanandi, a leading Indonesian analyst, points out that Indonesian Muslims were "influenced by vignettes shown on television about the miseries of the Iraqi people due to war."[88] Given that satellite channels like Al Jazeera tend to emphasize American mistakes and shortcomings in Afghanistan and Iraq, JI might well exploit such footage to empower "story lines" emphasizing that Islam is under siege everywhere—and that a true Muslim would be willing to engage in global jihad to defend his oppressed brethren. U.S. errors thus generate political oxygen that JI can filter through its virulent ideological framework to sustain political space for itself within the region.[89]

It has been suggested that "terrorism is a global problem with numerous local roots."[90] Certainly, in some Southeast Asian countries, *local* "root causes" such as political and socioeconomic marginalization are the key generators of political space for JI. In this regard, the RSO and MILF, JI's informal partners in the RM coalition, are particularly important. The MILF element is utterly crucial to the war on terror in Southeast Asia as it falls within JI's *Mantiqi 3* (Region 3), designated for training of JI militants. Mindanao is thus the Southeast Asian equivalent of Afghanistan in the 1980s and early 1990s: a vast training area for would-be jihadis.[91] While the MILF's old Camp Abu Bakar complex was overrun by the Armed Forces of the Philippines in 2000, by September 2002 new MILF training areas had reemerged in Mindanao. These were training both Filipinos for the MILF as well as Indonesians and Malaysians sent by JI.[92] In Mindanao, despite Manila's efforts to improve the lot of the people, "widespread Christian prejudice, corruption and mistreatment have not won many hearts or minds."[93] In late March 2003, a MILF senior commander claimed that the organization was getting too big and difficult to control as "there are so many who wanted to join."[94]

In Myanmar, on the other hand, the continuing political, religious, and socioeconomic repression by Yangon (Rangoon) of the Rohingya Muslims in the Arakan region contiguous to Bangladesh has generated support for the Rohingya Solidarity Organization (RSO), which has a presence on Bangladeshi soil and seeks to set up an Islamic republic across the border in the Arakan area. The RSO insurgency has been regarded by Bangladeshi military intelligence as "an extremely militant model of Islamic revolution."[95] The significance of the Rohingya factor resides in the fact that the crackdown in maritime Southeast Asia on JI has compelled its leadership "to seek new havens in Bangladesh and Pakistan."[96] In this connection it is possible that the Rohingyas might act as a conduit linking jihadis in Southeast Asia and South Asia. After all, it is suspected that a senior Malaysian JI leader, Zulkifli Marzuki, is currently in Bangladesh, while prior to his arrest Hambali had planned to leave Thailand for Bangladesh.[97] It has been suggested that the Bangladeshi government ought to move more decisively against the burgeoning number of militant Islamist terrorist groups on its soil.[98] In fact, the reality of the wider contemporary South Asia–Southeast Asia jihadi axis was underscored by the arrests by Pakistani authorities, in late September 2003, of nineteen students in Karachi. They were suspected of being second-generation JI leaders.[99] Many analysts worry that "hundreds of Indonesians are studying in the religious schools that gave the world the Taliban."[100] In a nutshell, the anger of many Filipino and Rohingya Muslims at their respective governments only strengthens the MILF and RSO. The panregional JI, whose modus operandi has involved fishing in troubled regional waters seeking opportunities for exploitation and expansion, has leveraged on Moro and Rohingya grievances to promote its ideological vision, thereby gaining strategic benefits and political space.

In order to effectively neutralize the JI terrorist threat over the medium to longer term and the wider problem of exclusionist Islam in the region, it would be necessary to move beyond the necessary but by no means sufficient immediate counter-*terrorist* measures, and embrace more systematically longer-term counter-*terrorism* elements. While a counter-*terrorist* approach that renders terrorist leaders and militants "inoperative" might reduce JI's functional space,[101] a counter-*terrorism* thrust is needed to close the network's all-important political space: in short, JI's capacity to *attract* and *retain* recruits and sympathizers to its cause must be diminished.

Developing a Counter-*Terrorism* Thrust: Closing Down JI's *Political* Space

To diminish JI's political space within pockets of Southeast Asian Muslim communities, three key counter-*terrorism* thrusts are necessary: eradicating local political and socioeconomic "root causes"; assisting progressive Islamists to win the ideological battle for Islam in Southeast Asia; and reducing the "political oxygen" issuing from U.S. policy and behavior that fuel regional radical Islamist propaganda that America is attacking the worldwide *ummah*.

Eradicating Local Root Causes

With respect to the MILF issue, there is a need to move beyond simply helping the Armed Forces of the Philippines augment its military capabilities in its campaign against the thuggish Abu Sayyaf Group. Mindanao, the locus of the Moro insurgency JI is seeking to hijack, is "not amenable to a military solution. It is a domestic social and economic problem."[102] The Filipino agrarian reform secretary has asserted that the key to achieving peace in Mindanao is "land reform."[103] It is therefore necessary to more actively coordinate international efforts to assist Manila in implementing schemes aimed at improving basic education, increasing employment by creating small- to medium-scale industries, and providing university scholarships for Muslim inhabitants of Mindanao.[104] In addition, Manila should be assisted to expand its capacity to administer Mindanao effectively and marginalize those MILF elements that have JI sympathies and links[105] in favor of Moro leaders who have genuinely nationalist credentials.[106] As far as Myanmar is concerned, the international community should persuade Yangon to pursue a more accommodating policy toward the Rohingyas and work toward granting a degree of regional autonomy to the Muslims in the Arakan region. The U.N. could also help alleviate the plight of the hundreds of thousands of Rohingya refugees in Bangladesh and help finance the social and economic rehabilitation of Arakan. Reducing the sources of Moro and Rohingya discontent would help undercut JI's ideological appeal and have a significant impact on the network's ability to preserve political space in these communities.

Helping Moderate Islamists Win the Battle for the Soul of Islam

To secure victory in the so-called "battle for the soul of Islam" in Southeast Asia, one must begin with Indonesia, which is not merely the operational but also the ideological locus of JI. Two steps are essential: first, mainstream Muslim organizations such as Nahdlatul Ulama (NU) and Muhammadiyah must promote the teachings of progressive Muslim *ulamas* and intellectuals through the print media, on television, radio, cyberspace, and in the mosques, universities, and *pesantren*. Of particular importance, a strong effort must be made to propagate among Indonesian and other Southeast Asian Islamic fundamentalist communities what the well-known Tunisian scholar Rachid Ghannoushi calls a "realistic fundamentalism." This approach involves not only reviving Islamic values in all aspects of life, but also taking full cognizance of current social, economic, and political realities as well as acknowledging the value of religious pluralism.[107]

The Swiss-born scholar Tariq Ramadan similarly calls for the elimination of a "binary vision" that sees "everything as either *halal* or *haram*" as well the "they (non-Muslims) don't like us" adversarial attitude.[108] It is noteworthy in this regard that some U.S. funding in 2003 was channeled to NU and Muhammadiyah to "promote tolerance among adherents of different faiths" as well as to "fight terrorism."[109] In this respect, Washington's plans to invest US$250 million into improving Indonesia's 178,000 state schools and

10,000 "West-tolerant" Muslim-run schools may help encourage a less binary worldview among Indonesia's young Muslims.[110] Apart from Islamic scholars from outside Southeast Asia, it must not be forgotten that Indonesia is an especially rich source of moderate, progressive, Arabic-speaking scholars who are well drilled in Islamic jurisprudence and thus able to engage in ideological combat with radicals.[111] They, however, may need to be assisted in putting their message across in ways that ordinary Indonesians and other Southeast Asians understand.[112] Public relations specialists may thus have a role to play in rendering the progressive Islamist voice more attractive than that of the radicals.[113] In addition, copying JI publicity methods might be salutary. Thus VCDs and videotapes should be mass-produced and distributed, in rural areas especially, where JI tends to recruit its foot-soldiers.[114]

Second, it should also be recognized that if thousands of Southeast Asian Muslim youth were gainfully employed, there would be less opportunities for them to be exposed to radical interpretations of Islam. One unfortunate by-product of the post-Bali disbandment of Laskar Jihad and Front Pembela Islam (FPI) was that "thousands of young, poorly educated and violence-hardened Muslim militants" had nothing else to do but to listen to militant preachers "preach suspicion of and confrontation with followers of other religions."[115] This in itself is good reason for the international community to assist Indonesia and other Southeast Asian governments to generate greater economic expansion through increased trade and investment. This is why the Enterprise for ASEAN Initiative discussed earlier is one idea that should be vigorously pursued.

In the key state of Indonesia, over time counter-*terrorism* elements such as extensive, sustained ideological counterpropaganda, increasing economic opportunities, and the emergence of a stable democratic milieu capable of accommodating all varieties of political expression would diminish the appeal of the radical Salafiyyah groups ranging from the transnational terrorist JI to indigenous violent groupings such as FPI and Laskar Jundullah, to non-violent but exclusionist, neo-Salafiyyah movements such as MMI, KPSI, and Hizbut Tahrir. The traditionally eclectic, tolerant form of Indonesian Islam would be strengthened and would have important "knock-on" effects throughout the region. At the same time, a JI delegitimized ideologically would see its political space in Southeast Asia much reduced.

Reducing the "Political Oxygen" that Fuels Anti-Americanism

To counter the JI campaign to portray an America seeking to subjugate and annihilate the worldwide *ummah*, three steps are vital: first, Washington must ensure that its public diplomacy highlights in great detail how America has genuinely helped alleviate the plight of Muslims in Kuwait, Bosnia, Kosovo, Afghanistan, and now Iraq. However, care should be taken in crafting messages. A recent $15 million public relations campaign sponsored by the State Department and produced by the advertising firm McCann-Erickson showcased the lives of Muslims in America, but featured no Southeast Asian Muslims. Indonesian Muslims watching the advertisements were upset that the State Department appeared to believe that "Muslims only lived in Arab countries and only those Muslims migrated to the United States."[116] A better approach would be for material to be fed to sympathetic Southeast Asian print and broadcast media as well as NGOs and allow them to create authentically local news Web sites, newspapers, television programs, documentaries, videotapes, and VCDs about how America has tried to be a friend of Islam.[117] In addition, there should be much more open discussion of topics such as various understandings of jihad; ways to reconcile the obligations of dual citizenship in both a national state as well as a transnational Islamic community or *ummah*; and the challenges and rewards of practicing one's faith within a modern, secular, multireligious society. What seems particularly important is more discussion on the various interpretations of the Darul Islam or realm of Islam. As well-known Egyptian-born, European-based Islamic scholar Tariq Ramadan suggests, Muslims "should not consider Europe and other 'non-Muslim' countries as lands of darkness, the *dar al-harb*, and therefore unsafe for Muslims."[118] Ramadan suggests that *ulama* and moderate Muslim professionals should form national, regional, or international committees to discuss openly these and other questions.[119]

Second, America must not undercut its own public diplomacy by inadvertently generating political oxygen that can be exploited by JI for propaganda purposes. Any air strike or military/law enforcement operation that accidentally kills, injures, or brutalizes Afghan or Iraqi civilians would only generate political oxygen that JI can exploit to fuel anti-Americanism. Importantly, Washington must in the short term take care to ensure that U.S. forces in both Afghanistan and Iraq are better trained to cope with looting and rioting. Any resort to disproportionate force as demonstrated in the unfortunate Falluja incident in late April 2003, in which fifteen Iraqis were killed by U.S. troops during an anti-American rally, would only strengthen the anti-U.S., global jihad propaganda of JI recruiters.[120] Over the longer term, it is vital that Washington and London expend sufficient resources in both Iraq and Afghanistan to ensure that both states emerge as modern, progressive Muslim members of the international community.[121] If the United States and the United Kingdom do not stay the course in both Iraq and Afghanistan, this would further reinforce the JI ideological narrative of a "crusader" America and its allies at war with Islam, and in Southeast Asia, help sustain political space for JI. The new Office of Global Communications, created by executive order of the president in January 2003, might take the lead in ensuring that Washington's words and deeds project the same positive message to a skeptical Muslim world.[122] Finally, the United States and the international community must persist in seeking the creation of an independent, viable Palestinian state side by side with Israel, and that the status of Jerusalem is justly resolved.[123] By consciously and deliberately identifying and eliminating the sources of the political oxygen that feeds anti-American sentiment among Muslims, Washington, over time, will gradually deprive the radical and neo-Salafiyyah ideological appeal in Southeast Asia of their potency and in so doing close JI's political space as well.

Conclusion

It is fair to say that thus far, Southeast Asian governments and their Western partners have been engaged mainly in what we have called a counter-*terrorist* campaign aimed at reducing the functional space of JI to operate. While such a campaign might eliminate and constrain the activities of individual terrorist cells, it would be less effective in countering the ideology that underpins the wider network and, importantly, its scattered pockets of support. This would be strategically inefficient, as a surviving ideology would sustain a steady stream of replacements for JI leaders and foot soldiers captured or eliminated as well as the political space within which militants may elude detection and secure moral and material support. The terror threat would thus be self-sustaining. Moreover, as a devastating terror attack on the scale of Bali would require only a relatively modest number of individuals and amount of funds to perpetrate, implying that relatively little functional space is all that would be needed, it becomes obvious that the underlying ideology must not be allowed to persist; it must be attacked and discredited. In other words, not only must JI's functional space be closed, its ideologically sustained political space must be reduced or eliminated as well.

Hence the dominant, short-term counter-*terrorist* thrust of regional and Western governments must be balanced by a much greater and systematic emphasis on longer-term counter-*terrorism* considerations. Short-term counter-*terrorist* elements, such as a steadily increasing regional state capacity to interdict the circulation of militants, funds, and weapons, are necessary but not enough. They must be judiciously meshed with longer-term counter-*terrorism* measures aimed at weakening JI's ideological potency. Undermining the network's underpinning ideology requires eradicating gradually the political and socioeconomic sources of regional Muslim discontent, promoting moderate Islam or a "realistic fundamentalism," and cutting off the political oxygen that fuels anti-American sentiment. In sum, only a strategy that combines both counter-*terrorist* and counter-*terrorism* elements promises to neutralize effectively the threat of radical Islamist terrorism in Southeast Asia.

Notes

Some portions of this essay were published as "US Strategy in Southeast Asia: Counter-*terrorist* or Counter-*terrorism?*" in *After Bali: The Threat of Terrorism in Southeast Asia*, ed. Kumar Ramakrishna and See Seng Tan (Singapore: World Scientific, 2003). The views expressed in this essay are solely the author's and do not represent any official position of Institute of Defence and Strategic Studies (IDSS).

1. *Cmd. 2 of 2003, White Paper on the Jemaah Islamiyah Arrests and the Threat of Terrorism* (Singapore: Ministry of Home Affairs, January 7, 2003), p. 7.

2. International Crisis Group, *How the Jemaah Islamiyah Terrorist Network Operates*, Jakarta/Brussels, December 11, 2002, pp. 8–9, n. 36.

3. Ibid., p. 36.

4. "JI Plotted Manila Bombings, Says Captured MILF Rebel," *Straits Times,* June 10, 2003.

5. Blontank Poer, "Tracking the Roots of Jamaah Islamiyah," *Jakarta Post,* March 8, 2003.

6. Singapore, *JI White Paper*, p. 6.

7. *Jemaah Islamiyah in Southeast Asia: Damaged But Still Dangerous*, Jakarta/Brussels, International Crisis Group, August 26, 2003, p. ii.

8. Ibid., p. 17.

9. Barbara Mae Dacanay, "Jakarta Offers to Help Trace 300 JI Militants," *Gulf News,* April 12, 2003.

10. "Police Monitoring Al Qaida in South," *Gulf News,* March 24, 2003.

11. "US and Asean Sign Crucial Antiterrorist Agreement," *Business Day,* August 2, 2002.

12. Nirmal Ghosh, "Money Row Led to Capture of Hambali, Says News Report," *Straits Times,* August 18, 2003.

13. "Thailand 'Source of Fake Passports,'" *Bangkok Post,* June 21, 2002.

14. *Jemaah Islamiyah in Southeast Asia*, p. 24.

15. Friena P. Guerrero, "ASEAN Chief Cops Forge Concerted Fight Vs Terror," *BusinessWorld* (Philippines), September 12, 2003.

16. Kazi Mahmood, "Indonesia, Philippines to Fight Terror, Set Up Anti-Laundering Force," *IslamOnline*, October 1, 2002.

17. Jane Perlez, "Saudi Money—and Strict Brand of Islam—Flows into Indonesia," *Straits Times,* July 7, 2003.

18. Zachary Abuza, *Militant Islam in Southeast Asia: Crucible of Terror* (Boulder, CO: Lynne Rienner, 2003).

19. Ibid.

20. Darren Goodsir, "Terrorism on the Cheap Left Island in a $3.5 bn Hole," *Sydney Morning Herald,* December 23, 2002.

21. Majeswary Ramakrishnan, "Guns and Money," *TIMEasia.com,* February 11, 2002.

22. Wassayos Ngamkham, "In the Market for a Firearm?" *Bangkok Post,* October 7, 2003.

23. Barry Desker and Kumar Ramakrishna, "Forging an Indirect Strategy in Southeast Asia," *Washington Quarterly* 25, no. 2 (spring 2002): 171.

24. ICG, *How the Jemaah Islamiyah Terrorist Network Operates*, December 11, 2002.

25. Dana Priest, *The Mission: Waging War and Keeping Peace with America's Military* (New York and London: W.W. Norton, 2003), p. 242.

26. "Thaksin's Conversion," *Straits Times*, August 15, 2003.

27. Dan Eaton, "Tourists Flock to Thailand Despite Terror Warnings," Reuters, November 14, 2002.

28. U.S.-ASEAN Joint Declaration on Combating Terrorism, August 1, 2002, available at http://www.state.gov/p/eap/rls/ot/12428.htm.

29. Frank Frost, Ann Rann, and Andrew Chin, "Terrorism in Southeast Asia," Parliament of Australia, Department of the Parliamentary Library, January 7, 2003, available at http://www.aph.gov.au/library/intguide/FAD/sea.htm.

30. Dan Murphy, "Cooperation Nets Terrorist Suspect," *Christian Science Monitor*, February 5, 2003.

31. "Singapore JI Leader Can Be Detained for Up to 40 days on Bintan," *Channel News Asia* (Singapore), February 5, 2003, available at http://asia.news.yahoo.com/030205/5/singapore31493.html.

32. U.S.-ASEAN Joint Declaration on Combating Terrorism.

33. *Patterns of Global Terrorism 2002*, U.S. Department of State, April 30, 2003, available at http://www.usis.usemb.se/terror/rpt2002.

34. Shawn W. Crispin, "Thais Clash with the FBI," *Far Eastern Economic Review* (February 13, 2003).

35. "BNM to Join Hands with Others to Fight Money Laundering," *Bernama* (Malaysia), March 26, 2003.

36. Ioan Voicu, "Solidarity Is Key in War on Terrorism," *Bangkok Post*, February 16, 2003.

37. Murphy, "Cooperation Nets Terrorist Suspect."

38. *How the Jemaah Islamiyah Terrorist Network Operates*, p. 36.

39. Derwin Pereira, "The JI's Island of Terror," *Sunday Times* (Singapore), September 28, 2003.

40. Marianne Kearney, "Indonesia: Arms Trade Thrives on Corruption and Lax Patrols," *Straits Times*, July 18, 2002.

41. Jennie L. Ilustre, "'Active Support' Nets RP More US Aid," *Philippine Daily Inquirer*, February 7, 2003.

42. "US to Provide Anti-Terrorism Aid to Philippines," Office of International Information Programs, U.S. Department of State, May 19, 2003, available at http://usinfo.state.gov/regional/ea/easec/arroyofact.htm.

43. "ASEAN Cooperation Plan," U.S. Department of State, December 4, 2002, available at: http://www.state.gov/p/eap/regional/asean/fs/2002/16599pf.htm.

44. Sian Powell, "Road to the Bali Trials," *The Australian*, April 10, 2003.

45. Shefali Rekhi, "Azahari May Not Be Next JI Chief," *Straits Times*, August 27, 2003.

46. Nirmal Ghosh, "Just a Madrasah or Hotbed of Militancy?" *Straits Times*, June 25, 2003.

47. Derwin Pereira, "Indonesia's Anti-Terror About-Face," *Straits Times*, August 9, 2003.

48. "Australian Police to Help Probe Bombing at Indonesia's Main Airport," Agence France-Presse, April 29, 2003.

49. Patrick Walters, "Linked Force to Reckon With," *Weekend Australian,* May 17, 2003, p. 24.

50. "Four Filipino Guards Charged over Escaped Terror Suspects," *BBC Monitoring International Reports,* July 17, 2003.

51. Ibid.

52. "Philippine Police End Detention Center Drama," *Taipei Times,* October 8, 2003.

53. Liz Baguioro, "JI Man's Death a 'Mere Setback,'" *Straits Times* (Singapore), October 14, 2003.

54. Desker and Ramakrishna, "Forging an Indirect Strategy," pp. 170–71.

55. "Enterprise for ASEAN Initative (EAI)," U.S. Department of State Fact Sheet, October 26, 2002, available at http://www.state.gov/p/eap/regional/asean/fs/2002/16605.htm.

56. P. Parameswaran, "US President Bush to Push Free Trade Initiative in Southeast Asia," Agence France-Presse, August 6, 2003.

57. Derwin Pereira, "Sentence Delivers Wrong Message," *Straits Times,* September 3, 2003.

58. For instance, see Ahmad Osman, "Singapore Opinion Less Strong," *Straits Times,* June 5, 2003.

59. Kumar Ramakrishna, "Squeeze Out JI by Denying Political Space," *Straits Times,* August 11, 2003.

60. Ibid.

61. *Jemaah Islamiyah in Southeast Asia,* p. 23.

62. Uamdao Noikorn, "Thailand a Prime Hide-Out for Islamic Terrorists Thanks to Fake Passports, Porous Borders," Associated Press, September 25, 2003.

63. Thitinan Pongsudhirak, "Thailand a Bystander No Longer," *Bangkok Post,* September 19, 2003.

64. *Jemaah Islamiyah in Southeast Asia,* pp. 26–29.

65. Desker and Ramakrishna, "Forging an Indirect Strategy," pp. 171–72.

66. See the chapter on Anwar Ibrahim in John L. Esposito and John O. Voll, *Makers of Contemporary Islam* (New York: Oxford University Press, 2001), p. 187.

67. Elizabeth Fuller Collins, "Dakwah and Democracy: The Significance of Partai Keadilan and Hizbut Tahrir," paper presented at the International Seminar on Islamic Militant Movements in Southeast Asia, July 22–23, 2003, Jakarta.

68. Ibid.

69. Perlez, "Saudi Money."

70. Ibid.

71. Lily Zubaidah Rahim, "The Road Less Traveled: Islamic Militancy in Southeast Asia," *Critical Asian Studies* 35, no. 2 (2003): 216–17.

72. Steven Emerson, *American Jihad: The Terrorists Living Among Us* (New York: Free Press, 2003), pp. 39–40.

73. *Jemaah Islamiyah in Southeast Asia,* pp. 26, 31.

74. For a description of how JI's informal support network of sympathizers and helpers expedites JI's functional space, see *Jemaah Islamiyah in Southeast Asia,* pp. 18–22.

75. Dan Murphy, "How Al Qaeda Lit the Bali Fuse, Part One," *Christian Science Monitor,* June 17, 2003.

76. Ibid.

77. Wong Chun Wai and Charles Lourdes, "Nik Aziz's Son Named in Report,"

Star Online, January 2, 2003, available at http://thestar.com.my/news/list.asp?file =2003/1/2/nation/hnik.

78. Perlez, "Saudi Money."

79. For instance, see the report on the views of Indonesian university students on the Bali blast investigations in Phil Zabriskie, "Did You Hear . . . ?" *Time Asia*, March 10, 2003, available at www.time.com/time/asia/covers/501030310/en_yog yakarta.html.

80. Derwin Pereira, "Indonesian Terrorist Bombings: Fact and Fiction," *Straits Times*, August 15, 2003.

81. Collins, "Dakwah and Democracy."

82. Cited in Simon Elegant, "Bullies for Islam," *Time Asia*, March 10, 2003, available at http://www.time.com/time/asia/covers/501030310/en_poso.html.

83. "I Mean It on Palestinian State: Bush," *Straits Times*, June 3, 2003.

84. "Atrocities in Bosnia Changed Military Man's View of Life," *Malay Mail* (Malaysia), March 20, 2003.

85. Dan Murphy, "How Al Qaeda Lit the Bali Fuse: Part Three," *Christian Science Monitor*, June 19, 2003.

86. Andrew Perrin, "Weakness in Numbers," *Time Asia*, March 10, 2003, available at http://www.time.com/time/asia/covers/501030310/persecution.html.

87. *How the Jemaah Islamiyah Terrorist Network Operates*, pp. 21–22.

88. Jusuf Wanandi, "The Post-Iraq War and Indonesia's Response," *Jakarta Post*, May 2, 2003.

89. Kumar Ramakrishna, "Cut Off Political Oxygen in War on Terror," *Straits Times*, June 6, 2003.

90. Janadas Devan, "To Tackle Global Terrorism, Target the Local Roots," *Straits Times*, August 27, 2003.

91. JI training shifted from Afghanistan to Mindanao in 1996. *Jemaah Islamiyah in Southeast Asia*, pp. 9–10.

92. "Mindanao Is JI's Regional Training Center," *Straits Times Interactive*, June 1, 2003, available at http://straitstimes.asia1.com.sg/asia/story/0,4386,192217,00.html.

93. Cavan Hogue, "Go Gently into the Philippines," *The Australian*, July 15, 2003.

94. "Murad Says He's Not Aware of Al Qaeda Cells in MILF," *BusinessWorld* (Philippines), March 26, 2003.

95. Suman K. Chakrabarti and Sumit Mitra, "Bangladesh: Terror's New Home," *India Today*, December 9, 2002.

96. Martin Chulov, and Kimina Lyall, "JI Recruited and Trained Here During Olympics," *Weekend Australian*, September 27, 2003.

97. Ibid.

98. Bertil Lintner, "Bangladesh: Breeding Ground for Muslim Terror," *Asia Times Online*, September 21, 2002, available at http://www.atimes.com/atimes/South_Asia/Dl21Df06.html.

99. Chulov and Lyall, "JI Recruited and Trained Here During Olympics."

100. Shawn Donnan, "Growing Piety, Anti-Americanism and Political Opportunists Put Indonesia's Brand of Islam to the Test," *Financial Times* (UK), October 14, 2003.

101. B. Raman, "Jihadi Hydra: Futile to Just Cut Off Its Heads," *Straits Times*, August 7, 2003.

102. Hogue, "Go Gently into the Philippines."

103. "DAR Chief Says Poverty, Not MILF, Is Enemy," *Philippine Daily Inquirer*, March 25, 2003.

104. "US Pledges $100 Million Assistance for Mindanao," *BusinessWorld,* March 28, 2003.

105. In June 2003 Manila captured the alleged JI-linked head of the MILF special operations group, Saifulla Yunos, alias Mukhlis. "JI Plotted Manila Bombings," *Straits Times,* June 10, 2003.

106. For a discussion of how a federal arrangement might accommodate Moro nationalist aspirations, see Romulo T. Luib, "How to Fight a Battle. And Lose," *BusinessWorld,* March 21, 2003.

107. Esposito and Voll, *Makers of Contemporary Islam,* pp. 91–117.

108. Mafoot Simon, "A New Voice in Muslim Europe," *Straits Times,* August 6, 2003.

109. "US Aid to RI Expected to Increase in 2003," *Antara* (Indonesia), December 16, 2002.

110. John Kerin, "US Aims at Terror Schools," *Weekend Australian,* October 4, 2003.

111. Karim Raslan, "The Moderate Majority," *Time Asia,* October 28, 2002, available at http://www.time.com/time/asia/magazine/article/0,13673,501021028-366388,00.html.

112. Peter Ford, "Listening for Islam's Silent Majority," *Christian Science Monitor,* November 5, 2001.

113. Ramakrishna, "Cut Off Political Oxygen."

114. Dan Murphy provides an account of how Indonesian radical Islamist groups used films of the Christian-Muslim conflict in Maluku to recruit members. Dan Murphy, "How Al Qaeda Lit the Bali Fuse, Part 2."

115. Timothy Mapes, "Militia Breakups May Spur Unrest," *Asian Wall Street Journal,* December 4, 2002.

116. Jane Perlez, "Muslim-as-Apple-Pie Videos Greeted with Skepticism," *New York Times,* October 30, 2002.

117. "Three Malaysians Among 17 Arrested in Indonesian Anti-Terror Raid," *BBC Monitoring International Reports,* April 24, 2003.

118. Simon, "A New Voice in Muslim Europe."

119. Ibid.

120. "7 Soldiers Hurt in Falluja Grenade Attack," *Straits Times,* May 2, 2003.

121. "Giving Peace a Real Chance," *The Bulletin* (Australia), available at http://bulletin.ninemsn.com.au/bulletin/eddesk.nsf/All/1190B744C1300636CA256D320008E39B.

122. Ramakrishna, "Cut Off Political Oxygen."

123. Wanandi, "The Post-Iraq War."

9

Terrorism and Transnational Organized Crime

Tracing the Crime-Terror Nexus in Southeast Asia

Tamara Makarenko

The end of the Cold War and subsequent demise of the Soviet Union ushered in a new international security environment that can no longer be explained by the dominant security paradigms utilized by most Western governments and analysts since World War II. Our understanding of security, falling under the rubric of high politics and focused on maintaining the territorial sovereignty of state actors, has been questioned by several ongoing international dynamics. For example, interstate conflicts have been replaced by rising occurrences of intrastate violence; the state as the central focus of international affairs has given way to a host of nonstate actors; and, it has become increasingly evident that the greatest threat to security emanates from the rapidly evolving phenomena of terrorism and transnational organized crime (TOC). In actuality, national, regional, and international experience with insecurity over the past decade has confirmed that terrorism and TOC deserve paramount attention precisely because they both span national boundaries and thus are necessarily multidimensional and organized; and, because they directly threaten the stability of states by targeting economic, political, and social systems.

As a result of this shift in the international security environment, once unthinkable scenarios have become common occurrences. Criminal and terrorist groups regularly engage in strategic alliances to provide goods or services—for example, Pakistani-based Indian organized criminal Dawood Ibrahim[1] has cooperated with terrorist groups including Lashkar-e-Tayyiba (LeT), the Liberation Tigers of Tamil Eelam (LTTE), and allegedly with al-Qaeda; terrorist and criminal groups converge in territory inadequately controlled by state forces—such as Afghanistan and the Western Frontier Province in Pakistan—to advance mutual interests and areas of potential cooperation; criminal groups in Southeast Asia (i.e., Phillippines and Thailand) have taken advantage of widespread instability to increase their criminal operations and secure political aspirations; and terrorist groups—such as Abu Sayyaf and the Islamic Movement of Uzbekistan—have used the veneer of Islam to secure lucrative criminal operations.

These developments in the operations of terrorism and TOC highlight the dynamic character of these phenomena. Both terrorism and TOC have evolved significantly as a result of a combination of factors, many of which are associated with the intensification of the globalization process and the end of the Cold War. Unfortunately, the shifting operational and organizational dynamics of both phenomena since 1991 have received little attention and thus are scantly understood. The relative inability of government analysts and policymakers to respond to the changing nature of post–Cold War security has thus left the world unprepared in its ability to respond to major transnational challenges. Thus, as transnational phenomena continue to evolve and terrorism and TOC continue to adapt to each other's strengths and weaknesses, the international community is left to deal with a host of culminating threats—as exemplified in the unprecedented terrorist attacks perpetrated by al-Qaeda on September 11, 2001.

In the current international environment, security must be understood as a cauldron of traditional and emerging threats that interact with one another and at times converge. The purpose of this chapter therefore is to propose a new model capable of tracing the evolution of the contemporary security threats of terrorism and TOC. Referred to as the *crime-terror continuum* (CTC), this model identifies seven major relationships that exist between the terrorist and criminal worlds, from strategic cooperation and alliance formations to the complete convergence of motivations.

Background Dynamics

The existence of links between TOC and terrorism is not a completely new phenomenon. Aspects of relations have existed since the 1970s in the Middle East (Lebanon) and Asia (the Golden Triangle), and the 1980s in South America, where drug cartels and terrorist groups have engaged in de facto strategic alliances for operational purposes.[2] Despite these previously recorded relations between organized crime and terrorist groups, it was not until after 1991—as a result of the end of the Cold War, an intensified period of globalization and developments in global illicit operations—that the relationship between these two entities grew in importance.

Among the most important consequences emanating from the end of the Cold War and subsequent fall of the Soviet Union was the erosion of communism as a motivating international ideology and a source of significant external support for several countries in the world. From this environment emerged other factors that had an impact on the international security environment, such as: the subsequent decline in state sponsorship for terrorist groups; the opening of territorial borders; the creation of a surplus of arms; and the expansion of the global marketplace. In addition to creating conditions conducive to the spread of democratization and market economization, the end of the Cold War equally created a global environment attractive for the spread of criminality by a vast array of actors.

The historical impact of the fall of the Soviet Union was exacerbated by rising evidence of the negative impact of globalization. Although most evaluations of globalization are positive, stressing values of integration for national and regional economies, expanding productive capacity, emerging markets, the subsequent prospects of eliminating poverty and spreading democracy and ending war,[3] globalization has also complicated the security environment. Among the most important negative results of globalization that have affected the nature of security is that globalization has undermined the legitimacy of states through the expansion of information, technology, finance, and manufacturing, thus giving rise to "warlords, mafias and mercenary groups, many of which have an interest in the perpetuation of conflicts."[4] Especially in the context of weak states, such as those that encompass parts of South Asia, the dynamics caused by globalization have helped create "a situation where the structure, authority (legitimate power), law and political order [of a state] have fallen apart,"[5] thus creating conditions where the hold on power is increasingly divided between "what is left of the formal institutions of the state (which are invariably corrupt), local warlords and gang or mafia leaders."[6]

Two additional consequences of globalization also need to be considered in the context of the emerging security environment. First, the inherent dichotomy of globalization (creating integration and fragmentation, homogenization and diversification, globalization and localization) has increasingly mobilized nonstate actors to react to what is commonly viewed as the "growing incompetence and declining legitimacy of established political classes."[7] In many cases this mobilization is executed in various forms of public demonstrations; however, weak states run the risk that this mobilization will evolve into the overt use of violence. Second, the contemporary wave of globalization has also expanded the operations of parallel economies in regions where "new forms of legal and illegal ways of making a living have sprung up among the excluded parts of society," and have legitimized new forms of criminal activity.[8] Mary Kaldor writes that these parallel economies are produced from the neoliberal economic policies pursued by international organizations, forcing developing and transitional states to undertake macroeconomic stabilization, deregulation, and privatization. These forced economic programs have also increased unemployment, depleted natural resources, and brought greater income disparities—creating conditions conducive to conflict and criminality. In this context it is thus imperative to recognize that the victory for capitalism and free markets in the 1990s has not necessarily created peaceful conditions, as "free enterprise can easily dovetail into economic violence, and self-help into helping oneself."[9]

Equally important to these historical events in altering the international security environment have been associated developments in TOC. Placed in environments experiencing economic and trade liberalization, technological advancements, migration flows, and border porosity—coupled with growing numbers of weak states in the world—criminal organizations have incorporated a host of new characteristics. These include the rising ability to cross national borders unhindered, the ability to cross between licit and illicit operations, the ability to recognize new opportunities in their operational environment, and the growing capability to manage risks by employing counterintelligence techniques (facilitated by access to sophisticated technology), and by engaging in strategic alliances. In fact, it is the ability to manage group and operational risks that has changed how nonstate actors organize their movements and conduct their operations in the twenty-first century.

In seeking alliances and cooperation, criminal and terrorist groups have learned to emulate one another's successful activities (i.e., smuggling and money laundering) and/or organizational dynamics (i.e., networks, cell-based structures). As a result, both TOC and terrorist groups operating in the world today often exhibit similar structures and appear to be increasingly engaged in similar criminal and political activities. For example, Barbara Harriss-White has concluded that organized criminal activities in weak states have responded to the evolving post-1991 international environment by incorporating the structure of traditional terrorist groups into their own. Referring specifically to criminal organizations involved in the drug trade in Peru, Bolivia, Colombia, Mexico, and Afghanistan, she notes that these groups "consist of specialized cells separately managing production, transport, distribution, money-laundering, communications, physical protection and recruitment. The most advanced telecommunications, weapons, means of transport and counter-intelligence technologies are used to enforce property rights."[10]

This environment, combining the decline of ideology as a motivating organizational force and the pressures of globalization placed predominantly on weak states, has laid the foundations of the crime-terror continuum. In attempting to secure their own survival by taking advantage of a state of widespread confusion, TOC and terrorism now epitomize the threats posed to security in the twenty-first century.

Defining the Crime-Terror Continuum

The CTC[11] is referred to as a *continuum* precisely because it seeks to trace past, current, and the potential future evolution of security threats. The most unstable and threatening point along the CTC is the fulcrum point, where criminal and political motivations simultaneously converge and are exemplified within one group. What the CTC primarily demonstrates is that the differences commonly identified between organized crime and terrorism are currently defunct. When assessing contemporary security threats, the reality is that it has become increasingly difficult to distinguish between political and criminal motivations. As summarized by Glenn Schweitzer,

> Such distinctions that had existed [between organized crime and terrorism] are fading fast. A few terrorist and criminal organizations already rely on the same global infrastructures for their illegal ploys, take advantage of the same breakdowns in authority and enforcement in states under siege, and seek increasing shares of the fortunes generated from narco-trafficking and other crimes. Whether mercenaries are hired to do the bidding of drug lords or of terrorist kingpins, the hit teams share a single motive in employing violence—earning their financial keep.[12]

Taking this as a starting point, the CTC at its most basic can be illustrated in Figure 9.1. Depicted in this simple diagram is the suggestion that organized crime and terrorism exist on the same plane and thus are theoretically capable of converging at a central point. Traditional organized crime is situated on the far left, with traditional terrorism shown on the far right—each holding distinct and separate positions. At the fulcrum of the continuum lies the "convergence," the point where a single entity simultaneously exhibits criminal and terrorist characteristics. The relationship between organized crime and terrorism, however, is significantly more complex than Figure 9.1 suggests. In assessing the relationship that has developed between criminal

Figure 9.1 **The Crime-Terror Continuum (A)**

Transnational Organized Crime   "Convergence"   Terrorism

and terrorist groups, seven points along the continuum are discernible. These points, however, can be divided into four general groups: alliances (1), operational motivations (2), convergence (3), and the "black hole" syndrome (4).

Point 1: Alliance Formation

The first level of relationship that exists between organized crime and terrorism is the alliance. As illustrated in Figure 9.2, alliances exist on both ends of the CTC spectrum: criminal groups forming alliances with terrorist organizations, and terrorist groups seeking alliances with criminal organizations. The nature of alliances varies and can include onetime, short-term, and long-term relationships. Furthermore, alliances include ties established for a variety of reasons such as seeking expert knowledge (i.e., money laundering, counterfeiting, or bomb-making) or operational support (i.e., access to smuggling routes). In most cases alliances are entertained in order for a group to maximize time and cost effectiveness while seeking to fulfill a specific operation or aim. In some instances, however, more sophisticated relationships between TOC and terrorist groups have emerged—this is best exemplified in international smuggling operations that move various commodities, including illicit narcotics, weapons, and human cargo, between countries and continents. As Louise Shelley succinctly notes with specific reference to organized crime, "cooperation with terrorists may have significant benefits for organized criminals by destabilizing the political structure, undermining law enforcement and limiting the possibilities for international cooperation."[13]

Despite the evident existence of alliances between organized crime and terrorist groups—and the operational purpose they have proven to serve in the past—groups will forgo creating alliances if they can. Thus as the 1990s progressed, it became increasingly apparent that criminal and terrorist groups were seeking to "*mutate* their own structure and organization to take on a non-traditional, financial, or political role, rather than cooperate with groups

Figure 9.2 **The Crime-Terror Continuum (B)**

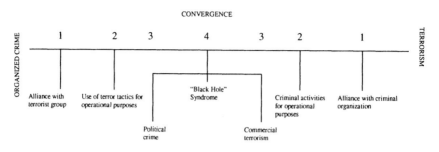

Source: *Jane's Intelligence Review* 15, no. 8 (August 2003): 6.

who are already effective in those activities."[14] The primary reason for acquiring in-house capabilities is to ensure organizational security and to secure organizational operations. In doing so, criminal and terrorist groups could avoid the inherent problems present in all alliances, including differences over priorities and strategies, distrust, the danger of defections, and the threat that an alliance could create competitors.[15] As a result, it is apparent that groups engaged in alliances will eventually incorporate the capabilities required to effectively, efficiently, and simultaneously engage in criminal and terrorist activities.

Point 2: TOC and Terrorism as Operational Tools

Criminal groups using terrorism as an operational tool, and terrorist groups taking part in criminal activities as an operational tool constitute the second component of the CTC. Although the use of terror tactics can be traced back into the history of organized crime,[16] terrorist engagement in organized crime to secure profits for future operations did not seriously emerge until the early 1990s. In both cases, however, the post–Cold War era exacerbated conditions and drove many criminal and terrorist groups to shift their operational focus. As a result, criminal groups have increasingly engaged in political activity in an effort to manipulate operational conditions present in the rising numbers of weak states; whereas terrorist groups have increasingly focused on criminal activities to replace lost financial support from state sponsors.

Traditional criminal organizations and several transnational criminal groups have regularly used terror tactics in order to fulfill specific operational aims. Although these groups have at times attempted to engage the political, it is essential to clarify that their intention is not to change the status quo, but merely to secure their operational environment. Criminal organizations use "selective and calibrated violence to destroy competitors or threaten counter-narcotic authorities. As such, a violent attack directed by a transnational criminal organization (TCO) is intended for a specific 'anti-constituency' rather than a national or international audience, and it is not laced with political rhetoric."[17] Despite utilizing terror tactics such as bombings and assassinations, the primary motivation of TCOs that use terror tactics as an operational tool remains illicit profit maximization.

Similar to criminal groups engaging in terrorism, many terrorist groups have become well versed in the conduct of criminal operations. In response to the virtual elimination of state support after the end of the Cold War, criminality was the most pragmatic avenue to secure finances for future terrorist operations. Equally important to note is that the terrorists who engage in criminal activities "ostensibly retain paramount political objectives, and as such, ill-gotten monies serve only as a means to effectively reach their political ends."[18]

As terrorist and TOC groups attain a proven economic and political capability, they run the risk of losing sight of their original motivations and aims. In the current international environment, numerous entities therefore equally display characteristics of organized crime and terrorism. Furthermore, in assessing the development of these hybrid organizations, it is evident that the motivations, organization, and operations of the two groups have also converged—thus making it analytically difficult to distinguish between the two phenomena.

Points 3 to 5: The Convergence Thesis

The "convergence thesis" refers explicitly to the idea that criminal and terrorist organizations could converge into a single group simultaneously exhibiting characteristics of both—but has the potential to transform itself into an entity situated at the opposite end of the CTC from which it began. Transformation thus occurs to such a degree "that the ultimate aims and motivations of the organization have actually changed. In these cases, the groups no longer retain the defining points that had hitherto made them a political or criminal group."[19] In an article written on "gray area" threats, Xavier Raufer's explanation of the new world disorder that emerged following the end of the Cold War reinforces this point. Using Karl Marx's analogy of "revolution as water on the stove," Raufer writes:

> Until it reaches the boiling point, the water changes only in terms of degree. Once it hits 212° and becomes steam, it changes its nature. Compared to a revolt, or a riot, a revolution represents a change in the nature, not the degree, of a country's sociopolitical reality. The same is true of

the new threats. In scientific parlance, the end of the bipolar order has caused the mutation of a host of organisms that used to be purely terrorist groups or purely criminal groups. In other words, they have abruptly and unexpectedly shifted from machines to lifeforms.[20]

According to Raufer, "machines" represent strategic-level violence perpetrated by nonstate actors that were funded and thus ultimately controlled by state actors. Thus most terrorist groups that operated during the Cold War could be classified as "machines," for their dependency on state support was almost complete. "Lifeforms," on the other hand, refer to "complex entities that are very hard to identify, understand and define within inadequately explored territories and movements."[21] It is these entities that encompass the notion of "converging threats."

In its most basic form, the convergence thesis includes two independent yet related components. First are criminal groups that display political motivations (political crime), and second, terrorist groups, which are equally interested in criminal profits, but ultimately begin to use their political rhetoric as a façade solely for perpetrating criminal activities (commercial terrorism). The first category can further be subdivided into two parts. First, it includes groups that have used terror tactics to gain political leverage beyond the disruption of judicial processes or attempts to block anticrime legislation (which is a common tactic utilized by organized crime in order to secure their operations). Instead, these groups are interested in attaining political control via direct involvement in the political processes and institutions of a state. Second, it includes criminal organizations that initially use terrorism to establish a monopoly over lucrative economic sectors of a state. In controlling economic sectors—including strategic natural resources—and financial institutions, these entities proceed to achieve political control over the state itself. This is based on the premise that in a contemporary world dominated by the dynamics of the free market economy, economic strength is the obvious prerequisite for political power; and political power subsequently sustains both the life of the organization and its activities—be they criminal and/or political. As Raufer further notes, "Grabbing control of financial institutions can both bring home the cash and advance political ambitions. Many groups, of course, will retain narrow portfolios of objectives, targets, and methods; others are becoming conglomerates of causes."[22] In this situation it becomes absolutely integral to be able to determine "if an ostensibly criminal gang is engaged in crime for personal gain or whether this criminal activity is an adjunct to political violence."[23]

The second component of the convergence thesis addresses terrorist groups that become so engaged with their involvement in criminal activities (as discussed in the previous section) that they merely maintain their political rhetoric as a façade for perpetrating criminal activities on a wider scale. There is growing evidence to indicate that, despite increasingly focusing on criminal activities, terrorist groups "maintain a public façade, supported by rhetoric and statements, but underneath, they have transformed into a different type of group with a different end game."[24] No longer driven by a political agenda but by the proceeds of crime, these formerly traditional terrorist groups continue to engage in the use of terror tactics for two primary reasons. First, they keep the government and law enforcement authorities focused on political issues and problems as opposed to initiating criminal investigations. Second, terror tactics continue to be used as a tool for these groups to assert themselves among rival criminal groups. Added to this, by continuing to portray their political component to the public domain, these terrorist groups are able to manipulate the terrorist support network that had previously been put in place. For example, they continue to focus on political grievances (combined with financial rewards) to attract recruits—giving justification to what would normally be regarded as purely criminal acts. Thus by simultaneously focusing on criminal and political goals, these groups are able to use two sets of networks that allow them to "shift focus from one application of terrorism to another, or to pursue multiple applications simultaneously."[25]

The greatest single threat to international security emerging from the CTC, however, is exhibited at the fulcrum point of the continuum. Identified as the "Black Hole," it is at this point where the convergence between criminal and political motivations within a single group allows that group to subsequently gain economic and political control over a state. Should this situation occur, there are two prevailing environments that may emerge: first, the "black hole" can help produce a failed state—such as Afghanistan—that lacks central authority, and thus displays the characteristics of anarchy; second, the "black hole" can produce a criminal state such as North Korea or Myanmar. Using terror tactics to retain their power and control over the state, government elites of these countries arguably use their official positions to engage in lucrative illicit activities for personal enrichment, or they use their official positions to create a territorial safe haven for other TCOs and/or terrorist groups.

The CTC in Southeast Asia

Although every point along the crime-terror continuum is exemplified in Southeast Asia, there exists ample evidence and indicators to illustrate several dynamics of the relationship between TOC and terrorism as defined in the CTC. As a region, Southeast Asia is increasingly comparable to South America, where the interplay between organized crime and terrorism has

Figure 9.3 **Converging Threats**

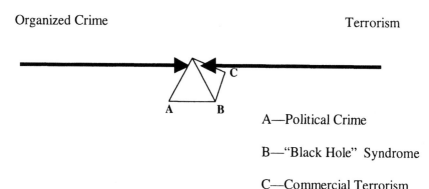

A—Political Crime

B—"Black Hole" Syndrome

C—Commercial Terrorism

evolved significantly since the 1980s. Facilitated by the weak states in which they operate—characterized by inefficient security services and law enforcement, partial government control over state territory, state inability to provide adequate social services, human rights abuses, and rampant or perceived corruption—and an environment infiltrated by terrorist groups and illicit smuggling operations, the CTC offers a way to navigate through the labyrinth of threats endemic to Southeast Asia.

In addition to the evident existence of traditional organized crime and terrorist groups in Southeast Asia, alliances between groups first appeared in the 1980s when terrorist groups entertained arms-for-drugs trades with regional criminal organizations.[26] A specific relationship that developed from these early ties was that between renowned Indian crime boss Dawood Ibrahim and the LTTE. This relationship generally centered on the drug trade. Given the role of Pakistan as a major transit route for heroin produced locally and in Afghanistan, Ibrahim and his group (D-Company) have been well placed to facilitate this alliance. Since 2000 there have also been allegations emerging in Central Asia suggesting that the LTTE has entered into alliances with local groups engaged in the drug trade and other cross-border smuggling operations.

LTTE operations, dependent on a consistent supply of weapons, have also revealed a degree of dependence on regional criminal groups that have established control over the regional arms trade. Although the LTTE is believed to operate weapons procurement cells in Pakistan and Thailand—countries with rampant arms bazaars—large consignments require indigenous criminal alliances that are adept at smuggling weapons through these states (i.e., that have established collusive or corrupt relations with the necessary state officials). Dawood Ibrahim[27] has also been implicated in cooperating with other regional terrorist groups, including those operating in Jammu and

Kashmir[28] and in Pakistan. It is also believed that criminal networks in southern Thailand have established ties to terrorist groups in Indonesia, supplying weapons to Aceh, Sulawesi, and Maluku,[29] and to Jemaah Islamiya cells.[30]

Based on the examples cited above, it is evident that the crime-terror alliances developed in Southeast Asia emerge from the most unstable regions and are invariably connected to illicit smuggling operations. Although this does not directly imply any foregone conclusion, it does indicate that it is in the interest of criminal and terrorist groups operating in unstable areas to form alliances to secure an environment conducive to both their needs. Instability is in the interest of terrorists because it diminishes the legitimacy of government in the eyes of the public—the very people terrorists seek to gain support from; and it is in the interest of criminal groups seeking to maximize criminal operations.

In the current international environment, new alliance formations between criminal and terrorist groups in Southeast Asia are increasingly unlikely because of the inherent vulnerabilities that they bring. Thus, apart from select cases that may necessitate alliances (i.e., arms acquisition), groups in the region most often seek to secure their own capability to use terror tactics and criminal activity when operationally required. Most examples that illustrate this second point of the CTC are restricted to terrorist groups; however, organized crime in the region has exhibited a willingness to use terror tactics when needed. For example, Dawood Ibrahim's group has been accused of regularly inciting riots and conducting acts of terror with the aim of destabilizing the government of India. He is currently being held responsible by India for his alleged role in the March 12, 1993, Bombay Exchange bombings that killed 257 people.[31]

As already indicated, however, the majority of "point two" cases in Southeast Asia include the operational use of organized crime by terrorist groups as a source of group financing. The groups that appear to utilize criminal activities to varying degrees are: al-Qaeda, Jemaah Islamiya (JI), and the LTTE. Although terrorist groups engaging in criminal activities in other regions of the world have a tendency to focus on highly sophisticated and thus lucrative smuggling operations, many Southeast Asian groups tend to focus on crimes that are generally classified as low to medium in sophistication. For example, JI has been implicated in bank and jewelry shop robberies, and al-Qaeda cells are known to rely on check and credit card fraud and identity theft. However, allegations also link al-Qaeda cells to trafficking in counterfeit consumer goods,[32] smuggling gold[33] and diamonds, and running relatively large-scale money laundering operations.

In terms of institutionalizing criminal activity as a significant source of funding while maintaining their ideological component as the predominant motivational factor, the LTTE may be regarded as the most successful terrorist group in Southeast Asia. Apart from allegations that the LTTE is independently involved in the illicit narcotics trade, trafficking heroin from the Golden Crescent through India and Sri Lanka to the West,[34] the group has also made significant inroads in securing its involvement in smuggling human cargo. In fact, it is strongly believed that human smuggling has become the mainstay of LTTE financial procurement.[35] The Tigers knowingly traffic people to the West via their networks in Canada, Australia, and the United Kingdom, and they allegedly use Thailand as a major transshipment point and center for obtaining forged identification.[36] The extent of LTTE involvement in human smuggling is illustrated in a single example cited by Byman et al.: "In June 2000, the Sri Lankan Criminal Investigation Department uncovered one major LTTE smuggling ring, involving an estimated 600 to 700 people who had been trafficked to the European Union on forged visas."[37] Given that the LTTE charges between US$18,000 and $32,000 per transaction, the profits of such operations are substantial.[38]

In addition to the criminal operations conducted by these groups, the environment in Southeast Asia has lent itself to criminal manipulation by other regional terrorist and insurgent groups. Kumpulan Mujahideen Malaysia was known to engage in robberies as a source of revenue; the New People's Army regularly engages in extortion, kidnap-and-ransom, robbery, and smuggling operations; and the Pattani United Liberation Organization and the United Front for the Independence of Pattani or Bersatu are involved in extortion and smuggling in contraband, narcotics, weapons, and people.[39] As a result, despite ongoing international and regional counterterrorist efforts, without placing equally focused attention and resources on the use of organized crime as a growing source of funding, terrorist groups will continue to have access to an important lifeline.

The final point along the CTC that is exemplified in the context of Southeast Asia is the point of convergence. More specifically, several groups operating in the region may be identified as commercial terrorist groups, and a couple of countries may be classified as de facto "black hole" states. Of the four groups considered to be commercial terrorist groups, one—Thailand's Gerakan Mujahideen Islam Pattani (GMIP)—appears to be truly hybrid in nature; the others—Abu Sayyaf, the Alex Boncayao Brigade, and the Pentagon Gang—seem to be losing their political aims and motivations in exchange for a predominant interest in securing their criminal operations.

GMIP was founded in 1986 as a radical Sunni group with ties to the Middle East. Its primary aim is to establish an Islamic state in southern Thailand. Influenced by conflict in southern Thailand, the war in Afghanistan—in which leader Nasori "Sori" Saesaeng fought in the early 1990s[40]—and the Taliban, there are indications that members of GMIP are increasingly influenced by the international ideology of al-Qaeda. Given a relatively modest armed following of thirty people, the GMIP has primarily focused its attention on conducting criminal activities (extortion and kidnap-for-ransom). In fact, it is apparent that most GMIP members remain committed to criminal ventures in light of the knowledge that their alleged political agenda receives scant local support, and the profits they obtain from crime have arguably been the primary factor for continued involvement in GMIP given the predominant socioeconomic conditions in the area. However, despite this penchant toward criminal activity, the leadership of GMIP is interested in promoting its political agenda. This is not only evident in the fact that Saesaeng fought in Afghanistan, but in the fact that Saesaeng has maintained ties to Kumpulan Muhajideen Malaysia and has directly supported the cause of al-Qaeda. Combined with conducting coordinated attacks against state targets,[41] this suggests that GMIP may be simultaneously entertaining an honest—as opposed to rhetorical—political goal.

Examples that highlight the transformation of a political group into a predominantly criminal one, as opposed to merely reflecting a hybrid nature, are Abu Sayyaf Group (ASG), the Alex Boncayao Brigade, and the Pentagon Gang. Regarded as one of the most violent separatist groups operating in the southern Philippines, Abu Sayyaf emerged around 1990–91 to establish an independent Islamic republic in Mindanao and the surrounding islands. This aim motivated the organization and operations of the Abu Sayyaf Group almost unquestionably until the death of the group's founder and ideological leader Ustadz Abdurajak Abubakar Janjalani in 1998. It was through Janjalani that Abu Sayyaf was tied to other militant Islamic groups, including al-Qaeda. Through ties to the international militant Islamic network (specifically al-Qaeda), Janjalani secured funds for ASG. These avenues of funding deteriorated by the mid-1990s, thus forcing ASG to secure its own profits—leading the group to focus on conducting kidnapping operations.

The death of Janjalani, however, deepened ASG involvement in kidnapping and ransom operations while reducing much of the group's interest in ascribing to ideology or seeking to fulfill the group's original political goals. Although the first kidnapping organized by the group was in 1993, it was not until 2000 that the group collapsed into various "kidnap gangs," conducting three noteworthy kidnapping operations in succession. First, in March 2000 the group kidnapped fifty-three people in Basilan; in April it kidnapped twenty-one people on the island of Sipadan;[42] and in May 2001 it kidnapped twenty tourists from Palawan. Most ASG kidnappings are accompanied by an average ransom demand of US$1 million per person, leading some analysts to conclude that the group has received annual profits of up to US$20 million.[43] In this context the argument that equally "propelling terrorists is the power of their most recent prop—money."[44] is very compelling.

Comparable to the transformation of ASG to a predominantly criminal group is the trajectory of the Pentagon Gang. Having emerged in 1998, allegedly as a splinter group from either the ASG or the Moro Islamic Liberation Front, the Pentagon Gang officially aims to establish an Islamic state in the Philippines. Despite its political rhetoric, group operations since 2000 have almost exclusively focused on kidnap-and-ransom operations in Mindanao. The group is believed to have also received average ransom payments of US$1 million per hostage. A similar predicament surrounds a faction of the New People's Army, the Alex Boncayao Brigade, which operates in the islands of the Philippines. Espousing little political rhetoric, the group is organized into small criminal gangs that conduct kidnap-and-ransom operations, extortion, and deal in counterfeit products.

Finally, in some circumstances the interplay between organized crime and terrorism in Southeast Asia has been epitomized in "black hole" states or territories. The black hole syndrome, as previously described, covers two situations: first, when the primary motivations of groups engaged in civil wars evolve from a focus on ideological goals to criminal aims; second, it encompasses the emergence of a black hole state—a state successfully taken over by a hybrid criminal-terrorist group. What these two scenarios have in common, and the reason they encompass the CTC, is that they reveal the ultimate danger of this security threat—creating or sustaining conditions of civil war to secure economic and political power. Regional states that fall into this category to varying degrees include Burma/Myanmar and North Korea. This condition, however, also has the potential to emerge in parts of Indonesia and southern Thailand.

The example of Burma/Myanmar is especially interesting because it simultaneously illustrates all aspects of the black hole syndrome. Not only has the revolutionary political ideology of Khun Sa declined since the end of the Cold War, but it has "gravitated from a strong ideological agenda to one dominated by economic aims."[45] Comparable to terrorist groups that have lost sight of their political ideology as a result of having to depend on criminal activity for their survival, these groups also appear to have betrayed their political ideals in order to hold on to power at whatever cost. Furthermore, an argument may be made that the United Wa State Army (UWSA) was primarily engaged in sustaining conflict to secure its involvement in the illicit drugs trade. As a result of its commitment to use violence against the state to remain a dominant actor in the drug trade, the UWSA has subsequently gained de facto control over parts of the country. Actively engaged in the cultivation, production, and trafficking of opiates and methamphetamines, the UWSA has expanded its territorial control from northeastern Shan State to regions of eastern Shan state to the border regions with China, Laos, and Thailand.

Also exhibiting characteristics of a weak state, the Democratic People's Republic of Korea (DPRK) is likely most illustrative of a criminal state. Officials of the DPRK have been directly engaging in criminal activities since the 1970s. For example, in 1976 the Norwegian government expelled all the staff of the North Korean embassy, alleging that they were involved in the smuggling of narcotics and unlicensed goods.[46] The DPRK has intensified its criminal activities in recent years—arguably because the leadership in North Korea has been replaced "by a younger group, less committed to the dogma of socialism and seemingly more eager to experience the good life."[47] An indication of this development is the government's establishment of Bureau 39, an official government body tasked with generating hard currency by any means, including drug trafficking, counterfeiting, money laundering, and piracy.[48]

Implications of the CTC

The CTC seeks to provide an explanation of the changing dynamics of nonstate security in the post–Cold War security environment. In doing so, its primary purpose is to highlight that neither terrorism nor TOC are static phenomena but are continually in a state of flux. It is therefore evident that these contemporary security threats are dictated by the continuously evolving environments in which they are found and by the relationships in which they are engaged. Thus, depending on the prevailing operational and international environment, groups can—and evidently do—slide across the continuum. Furthermore, the CTC illustrates that security is no longer solely about military objectives, but has been joined by "economically driven interests in continued fighting and the institutionalization of violence at what is for some clearly a profitable level of intensity."[49] The combination of political and economic motivations combined with a group prepared to attain them through the use of terror tactics and/or sustained violence reveals the inherent dangers exemplified within the CTC.

Considering the various aspects of the CTC, one consistent and relatively easily identifiable component is criminal activities. Most points along the continuum necessitate some degree of involvement with crime. As a result, the CTC inherently implies that focusing on the criminal as opposed to the political in formulating security policy has been underutilized. It is important to understand the political motivations of terrorist groups; however, on a practical level counterterrorist policy and initiatives would likely meet with greater initial success in breaking a group if they focused on suppressing access to illicit avenues of funding. Thus it is essential that greater attention and resources be given to cutting off funds acquired through crime (i.e., credit card and insurance fraud, money laundering, smuggling) and on eliminating criminal services that terrorist groups are dependent on (i.e., document and identity fraud). Eliminating the funding not only reduces the operational capability of terrorist groups, but it also threatens to reduce the membership base of groups whose recruitment is dependent on financial incentives. Furthermore, given indications that criminal and terrorist groups often use the same smuggling routes, creating obstacles for smuggling operations not only acts as a counterterrorist success in some regions, but simultaneously acts as an anticrime victory.

In the context of Southeast Asia—where smuggling routes are rife, criminal intent is expanding, and terrorist operations are evidently increasing in volume and destruction—the CTC provides a tool that can be used to identify adversary vulnerabilities. Gauging the movement and evolution of terrorist and criminal groups along the continuum not only tells us something about the nature of the group itself but also reveals an inherent weakness that can be taken advantage of. Recognition of trends pointing to a group's propensity to entertain operational or organizational changes has the potential to act as a strategic bonus for the security services engaged in finding ways to diminish the threat posed to society from transnational organized crime and terrorism in the short and long term. Failure to recognize the benefits of tracing the relationship between crime and terrorism, especially in vulnerable regions such as Southeast Asia, may contribute to the rising complexity of the regional security environment. It is the failure to seek alternative ways to understand the various dimensions of threats that contributes to the age-old dilemma of the state constantly being "one step behind."

Notes

1. In October 2003, Dawood Ibrahim was designated by the U.S. State Department as a terrorist supporter. http://www.treas.gov/press/releases/reports/fact_sheet.pdf (October 20, 2003).

2. The specific alliance created between drug traffickers and terrorist groups in Latin America was specifically referred to as "narcoterrorism," and generated some academic attention. Key to the study of narcoterrorism was the seminal book *Narcoterrorism* written by Rachel Ehrenfeld in 1990 (New York: Basic Books).

3. Barbara Harriss-White, "Globalization, Insecurities, and Responses: An Introductory Essay," in *Globalisation and Insecurity: Political, Economic, and Physical Challenges,* ed. Barbara Harriss-White (Hampshire and New York: Palgrave, 2002), pp. 1–3.

4. Harriss-White summarizing an argument initially presented by Susan Willett, ibid., p. 11.

5. Ibid.

6. Susan Willett, "Globalisation and the Means of Destruction: Physical Insecurity and the Weapons Industry at the Turn of the Millennium," in Harriss-White, *Globalisation and Insecurity,* pp. 190–91.

7. Mary Kaldor, *New and Old Wars: Organized Violence in a Global Era* (Cambridge: Policy Press, 1999), p. 78.

8. Ibid., pp. 78–79.

9. David Keen, *The Economic Functions of Violence in Civil Wars,* International Institute for Strategic Studies Adelphi Paper, No. 320 (1998), p. 44.

10. Harriss-White, "Globalization, Insecurities, and Responses," p. 31. This dynamic is also illustrated in Tamara Makarenko, "Bumper Afghan Narcotics Crop Indicates Resilience of Networks," *Jane's Intelligence Review* 14, no. 5 (May 2002), and Tamara Makarenko, "Colombia's New Crime Structures Take Shape," *Jane's Intelligence Review* 14, no. 4 (April 2002).

11. For a comprehensive analysis of the crime-terror nexus, see Tamara Makarenko, *The Crime Terror Nexus* (London: Hurst, forthcoming 2004). This section is based on an earlier article, "The Crime-Terror Continuum: Tracing the Interplay Between Transnational Crime and Terrorism," *Global Crime* 1, no. 1 (forthcoming 2004).

12. Glenn E. Schweitzer, *A Faceless Enemy: The Origins of Modern Terrorism* (Cambridge, MA: Perseus, 2002), p. 288.

13. Louise Shelley, "Identifying, Counting, and Categorizing Transnational Organized Crime," *Transnational Organized Crime* 5, no. 1 (spring 1999): 12–13.

14. Chris Dishman, "Terrorism, Crime, and Transformation," *Studies in Conflict and Terrorism* 24 (2001): 48.

15. Phil Williams, "Criminal Cooperation: Trends and Patterns," Jane's Conference on Transnational Organized Crime, September 20–21, 2000.

16. For example, the Sicilian mafia, as it emerged in the nineteenth century, existed primarily as a political movement seeking various political changes in support of the livelihood of the local populations.

17. Dishman, "Terrorism, Crime, and Transformation," p. 45.

18. Ibid, p. 47.

19. Ibid, p. 48.

20. Xavier Raufer, "New World Disorder, New Terrorisms: New Threats for Europe and the Western World," *Terrorism and Political Violence* 11, no. 4 (winter 1999): 35. Raufer first introduced his thoughts about gray area threats in Xavier Raufer, "Grey Areas: A New Security Threat," *Political Warfare* (spring 1992).

21. Ibid., p. 36.

22. Ibid., p. 289.

23. Ian O. Lesser, "Countering the New Terrorism: Implications for Strategy," in *Countering the New Terrorism,* ed. Ian Lesser and Bruce Hoffman et al. (Washington, DC: RAND, 1999), p. 85.

24. Dishman, "Terrorism, Crime, and Transformation," p. 48.

25. Lesser, "Countering the New Terrorism," p. 98.

26. This alliance is discussed in K. Prabha, "Narco-Terrorism and India's Security," *Strategic Analysis* 24, no. 10 (January 2001), and confirmed in a confidential discussion held with a member of the Sri Lankan intelligence community (2001).

27. It is worth noting that other criminal groups emanating from India have established alliances to terrorist groups. For example, Aftab Ansari—arrested in Dubai in 2002—is believed to have forged ties to several terrorist groups, including al-Qaeda, while serving a sentence in a New Delhi jail. For details, see Paul Watson, "Gangster with Terror Links Is Jailed in India," *Los Angeles Times,* February 10, 2002, p. 11.

28. B. Raman, "Islamic Terrorism in India: The Hydra-Headed Monster," *South*

Asia Analysis Group, http://www.saag.org (June 4, 2003).

29. Anthony Davis, "The Complexities of Unrest in Southern Thailand," *Jane's Intelligence Review* 14, no. 9 (September 2002).

30. "Components for Six SAMs Smuggled into Thailand in Advance of APEC Summit," *White House Bulletin* (October 6, 2003).

31. U.S. Treasury Fact Sheet, "Dawood Ibrahim," http://www.treas.gov/press/releases/reports/fact_sheet.pdf (October 20, 2003).

32. David Johnston, "Threats and Responses: The Money Trail," *New York Times,* July 16, 2003, p. 11.

33. Nick Ridley, "Al-Qaeda and Trends in Terrorist Fundraising," *Jane's Terrorism and Intelligence Centre Briefing,* August 8, 2003.

34. Daniel Byman et al., *Trends in Outside Support for Insurgent Movements* (Santa Monica, CA: RAND, 2001); Stefan Leader and David Wiencek, "Drug Money: The Fuel for Global Terrorism," *Jane's Intelligence Review* 12, no. 2 (February 2000).

35. Byman et al., *Trends in Outside Support for Insurgent Movements.*

36. Ibid.

37. Ibid.

38. Ibid.

39. This information is compiled from the relevant group profiles provided by the Jane's Terrorism and Insurgency Centre online database, and from the terrorism database at the Centre for the Study of Terrorism and Political Violence, St. Andrews University.

40. Anthony Davis, "Thailand Faces Up to Southern Extremist Threat," *Jane's Intelligence Review* 16, no. 10 (October 2003).

41. Ibid.

42. Yael Shahar, "Libya and the Jolo Hostages: Seeking a New Image or Polishing the Old One?" International Policy Institute for Counter-Terrorism, http://www.ict.org.il (April 9, 2003).

43. Brian Joyce, "Terrorist Financing in Southeast Asia," *Jane's Intelligence Review* 15, no. 11 (November 2002). Joyce specifically notes that the ASG is believed to have profited by US$20 million in 2000 alone just in the collection of ransoms.

44. Schweitzer, *A Faceless Enemy,* p. 33.

45. Keen, *The Economic Functions of Violence in Civil Wars,* p. 11.

46. Mark Galeotti, "Criminalisation of the DPRK," *Jane's Intelligence Review* 13, no. 3 (March 2001): 10.

47. Ibid.

48. Douglas Farah and Thomas Lippman, "North Korea 'Cashes in on Drugs,'" *Washington Post,* reprinted in *Guardian Weekly,* April 4, 1999, p. 16.

49. Mats Berdal and David M. Malone, eds., *Greed and Grievance: Economic Agendas in Civil Wars* (Boulder, CO, and London: Lynne Rienner, 2000), p. 2.

10

Trading the Tools of Terror

Armed Groups and Light Weapons Proliferation in Southeast Asia

David Capie

Since the terrorist attacks of September 2001, much of the international community's counterterrorism efforts have focused on weapons of mass destruction (WMD). The fear that terrorists might use a radiological, chemical, or biological weapon to attack a heavily populated target such as a major Western city has provoked a concerted international effort to control access to these technologies.[1] Indeed, the U.S. and U.K. invasion of Iraq in March 2003 was justified in large part as a means of preventing terrorists from gaining access to "the world's most dangerous weapons."[2] But while efforts to control WMD have seized media attention, Anthony Cordesman notes that "one of the problems with asymmetric or terrorist warfare is you don't need highly sophisticated weapons to do a lot of damage."[3] Rather, the weapons most commonly employed by terrorist groups around the globe continue to be small arms and light weapons—"weapons of individual destruction" as one writer has dubbed them.[4] Controlling access to these arms, along with ammunition and explosives, is a challenging but critically important part of any effective counterterrorism strategy.[5]

This chapter examines linkages between nonstate armed groups and the proliferation of illicit small arms and light weapons in Southeast Asia. It considers the extent to which the widespread availability of these weapons constitutes an enabling factor making it possible for groups to commit acts of terrorism. Rather than focus on the inventory of any one terrorist group, this chapter examines the multitude of pathways through which weapons pass to terrorist and insurgent groups. It describes four principal channels of proliferation and critically examines regional efforts to address Southeast Asia's small-arms problem.

This chapter argues that while there has been impressive rhetorical commitment to cooperate against transnational crime, insufficient attention has been paid to the domestic sourcing of weapons by terrorists, in particular from corrupt security forces and poorly safeguarded state armories. Completely eliminating the illicit arms trade in Southeast Asia is a nearly impossible challenge, but there are ways to make it more difficult for groups to obtain weapons and ammunition. However, doing so will require regional states to adopt a comprehensive and collaborative strategy that targets transnational smuggling but also acknowledges the links between licit and illicit trade and addresses the fundamental problem of weak governance structures across Southeast Asia.

Small-Arms Proliferation and Nonstate Actors in Southeast Asia

As has been described in detail in previous chapters, Southeast Asia is home to a host of nonstate and substate armed groups, many of which have been denounced as "terrorists." These groups vary enormously in terms of their size, resources, goals, tactics, and organizational structures. Some resemble traditional armies, fighting for control of specific territory and the right to build their own homeland or state. Others exemplify the shadowy networks of small, autonomous cells of fighters that have become synonymous with international terrorism since 9/11. Still others are motivated more by profit rather than any political grievance or religious cause.[6] Whether these groups should be called "terrorists," "rebels," "criminals," or "freedom fighters" is highly subjective. Usually the label says more about the observer than it does about any particular group's goals, methods, or ideology. However, while these groups vary in many respects, they all have one thing in common: a fundamental need for weapons and ammunition.[7]

Small arms and light weapons along with explosives constitute weapons of choice for Southeast Asian insurgents and terrorist groups. They are generally inexpensive, easily concealed and transported, durable, and simple to maintain. They are also well suited to the tactics employed by irregular armed forces: attacks on soft targets, ambushes, and guerrilla operations. While it is difficult to generalize, the inventory of a Southeast Asian armed group typically includes sidearms, automatic rifles, light machine guns, and rocket-propelled grenades (RPGs). Better-equipped groups with either a state sponsor or access to significant resources have heavy machine guns, light mortars, and even artillery and rockets. There is also evidence that a number of organizations are seeking more sophisticated armaments, in particular standoff weapons such as antiarmor rockets and portable surface-to-air missiles.[8]

There are four channels through which regional armed groups gain access to the basic tools of terror. They can make purchases on the regional or international black market, acquire them via so-called "gray market" transfers from sympathetic states, or obtain them from a diverse range of domestic sources including theft from civilian stocks and illicit transfers from security forces. In addition, some groups have demonstrated a nascent capacity to produce their own arms. Understanding these multiple and overlapping proliferation pathways is critical to developing and implementing an effective regional counterterrorism strategy.

Black Market Transfers

Southeast Asia's transnational black market in small arms is large and sophisticated, involving weapons imported from outside the region as well as arms sourced in several Southeast Asia states. While there are obvious limits to what we can know about any illicit enterprise, evidence indicates that the majority of weapons that pass through black market channels are not new. Although some groups have reportedly been able to buy weapons directly from factories in China, seizures suggest that the overwhelming majority of the weapons involved are "recycled," originating from postconflict states or surplus stocks sold by militaries.[9] A shadowy network of brokers, arms dealers, and financiers plays a crucial intermediary role in organizing the purchase, financing, and shipment of these arms, frequently using bogus end user certificates (EUCs) and other false documentation.[10]

Within Southeast Asia the most important source for illicit military small arms has historically been Indochina, particularly Cambodia. Millions of weapons poured into the kingdom during its long and bloody civil war, with the Soviet Union and Vietnam supplying the government in Phnom Penh while the West and China shipped weapons to the Khmer Rouge and the noncommunist opposition. With the signing of the Paris Peace Accords and the end of the civil war in 1991, Cambodia has gone from being a major importer to being perhaps the single largest source of arms for insurgent and terrorist forces in Southeast Asia.

Today, illegal exports of Cambodian weapons and ammunition come from two sources: Royal Cambodian Armed Forces (RCAF) stocks, and surplus weapons that have been collected and stored as part of the country's peace process. Hundreds of thousands of surplus weapons have been collected under various demobilization and disarmament programs, and until the recent introduction of a weapons security program, many were simply piled up in unlocked and poorly guarded depots, police stations, and warehouses.[11] Not surprisingly, many were removed and sold by military personnel seeking to supplement their meager wages. While small-scale theft is endemic, of far greater concern is the well-organized diversion of large numbers of military weapons to arms dealers and brokers. These transactions require the complicity of senior Cambodian government officials and military officers, and in some cases brokers have even been able to deal directly with government ministries.[12] One British arms dealer interviewed by an NGO working to address small-arms problems claimed to have purchased illicit arms directly from the Cambodian Ministry of Defense. The ministry even agreed to supply the arms in containers, ready for shipment, at the southern port of Kompong Som.[13]

Cambodia's reputation as a veritable supermarket for black market military arms has led a number of regional terrorist groups to establish a presence there. Regular buyers include the Liberation Tigers of Tamil Eelam (LTTE), Burmese ethnic militias, and armed groups operating in India's northeastern states.[14] The LTTE has used restaurants and vehicle repair shops in Phnom Penh as fronts for their arms acquisition efforts and at one time was believed to have as many as sixty agents working in Cambodia. Its chief procurement officer, Tharmalingham Shunmugham (alias Kumaran Pathmanathan, or KP), was seen frequently in Phnom Penh after 1996, allegedly seeking to open a direct route to Cambodian arms suppliers rather than operating through Thai middlemen. Indian intelligence has reported that Naga militant groups base themselves just across the border in Thailand. Thai arms dealers also buy weapons from Cambodian sources for shipment to Aceh and Burma.[15]

Black Market Trafficking Routes

Weapons exported from Indochina typically pass through Thailand en route to their final destinations. According to Thai military sources, as much as 80 percent of arms shipments out of Cambodia are moved by sea, shipped from southern ports along the coastline to Rayong and Pattaya in the Gulf of Thailand.[16] Islands in the Andaman Sea off Phuket as well as the southern provinces of Ranong and Satun have all been identified as important points for organizing consignments of weapons for shipment.[17] With large sums of money to be made, a wide range of actors play a role in the movement of these arms. They include corrupt military, police, and government officials, an assortment of unscrupulous arms brokers and dealers, and terrorist operatives as well as criminal gangs.

In sourcing and shipping arms out of Southeast Asia, few groups can match the reach and experience of the LTTE. Indeed, the LTTE is so well established it has even reportedly shipped arms for other groups on a contractual basis.[18] According to intelligence reports, the group operates out of bases near the southern Thai town of Trang.[19] From there, it is able to dispatch weapons across the Bay of Bengal, where they are transferred to speedboats off the coast of Sri Lanka.[20] Tamil Tiger operatives maintained a boatbuilding yard in Phuket, where they produced high-speed craft for use in smuggling operations. When Thai police raided the yard in 2000, they also discovered a half-built miniature submarine.[21]

The sheer number of vessels working these waters complicates the task of intercepting arms traffickers moving between Thailand and Bangladesh, Burma, India, and Sri Lanka. More than 100 fishing trawlers cross between Ranong and Burma every day, and some 10,000 vessels are known to operate in Thai waters.[22] The numerous tiny islands are also ideal for caching weapons and arranging transshipment. The complicity of elements in the Thai and Burmese militaries in smuggling operations also undermines anti-smuggling operations.[23] For all these problems, however, there is some evidence that closer cooperation between regional governments and improved naval surveillance has at least made it more difficult for the LTTE to land smuggled weapons in Sri Lanka.[24]

A second major arms trafficking pipeline passes through southern Thailand and across the Straits of Malacca to Aceh. While the Aceh Merdeka movement (GAM) sources many of its weapons locally, it has in the past received supplies of arms from China, Cambodia, and directly from Thai 4th Army stocks.[25] Weapons smuggled from outside Indonesia move through southern Thailand, often with the assistance of Thai criminal syndicates or sympathetic groups like the Gerakan Mujahideen Islam Pattani (GMIP).[26] Hat Yai is considered one important transit point, as is the Malaysian city of Penang, with its large Acehnese population.[27] Smugglers use fishing trawlers and small craft to ferry arms across the Straits of Malacca to final destinations in Sumatra like Lhokseumawe, Padang, Tanjungbalai, and Peureulak.[28] Former or serving Thai naval and army officers reportedly own some of the vessels used in these operations.[29]

A third and increasingly important trafficking route runs through the southern Philippines and into Indonesia. According to Philippines police sources, gunrunners are known to be especially active in Agusan, Misamis, Surigao, Sulu, Basilan, Tawi-tawi, and Zamboanga Provinces. Weapons from the Philippines were being freely traded in Maluku during the intercommunal violence there in 2000, leading one Indonesian navy commander to complain that "anyone with a certain amount of money can purchase guns [in Mindanao]."[30] Although there are occasional rumors of aircraft flying in loads of weapons, the shipping of weapons on small craft and passenger boats seems to be more prevalent.[31] In July 2000, three ships loaded with unspecified weapons were stopped en route to Halmahera and Ternate in North Maluku. In early 2001 the Indonesian navy intercepted what it called a "traditional vessel" destined for the Malukus carrying a small number of rifles and ammunition.[32]

More recently, the southern Philippines has been identified as an important route for the movement of weapons between Mindanao and Jemaah Islamiya (JI) operatives in Indonesia, particularly those in the strife-torn provinces of Sulawesi and Maluku. Interrogation of arrested JI members has revealed that in the late 1990s, regular trips were made between General Santos City and other parts of Mindanao and northern Indonesia.[33] New recruits for JI were dispatched from Java to train at the MILF's Camp Abu Bakar while weapons were being smuggled south through the Sangihe and Talaud Islands off the coast of North Sulawesi, and from there to Manado. Once recruits had completed their training, they would return to Indonesia, often bringing more weapons with them. The Indonesian police have claimed that arms used in the recent intercommunal violence in Poso, allegedly instigated by JI members, also came from the Philippines.[34]

Gray Market Transfers

In addition to the thriving regional black market, "gray market" transfers of arms and ammunition represent an important source of military hardware for some groups. These transactions involve the covert supply of weapons from a state to a nonstate actor in another country. They are "gray" rather than "black" because the deals take place with the knowledge of the supplier state's government. They are typically politically rather than commercially motivated and frequently involve military or intelligence agencies.[35]

There is a long history of ties between Southeast Asian armed groups and foreign state suppliers. During the Cold War, gray market transfers were largely motivated by geopolitics or ideology, with both superpowers using a number of irregular forces in the region as proxy armies. In the 1980s, Vietnam provided tons of abandoned U.S. weapons and ammunition to the communist New People's Army (NPA) in the Philippines and to communist fighters in Central America.[36] Similarly, the Reagan administration used donations from POW-MIA groups to secretly arm and supply anticommunist rebels in Laos.[37] In South Asia, the Indian external security service, the Research and Analysis Wing (RAW), was a major provider of arms and assistance to the LTTE prior to 1987 and continued to supply some arms until the assassination of Prime Minister Rajiv Gandhi in 1991.[38]

Geopolitical incentives for arming nonstate groups declined with the end of the Cold War, but the practice has not ended altogether. Until recently some regional states continued to actively support terrorist organizations fighting in other countries. One remarkable case provides a rare glimpse into the murky world of gray market arms transfers. In early 1998 a series of successful Indian navy antismuggling operations inadvertently exposed a covert RAW plan to ship weapons to rebel groups fighting in Burma.[39] According to a subsequent investigation carried out by the Indian Central Bureau of Intelligence (CBI), RAW purchased the arms in Cambodia and arranged for their shipment to groups fighting in Burma's Arakan and Chin Provinces.[40] Various rationales for the deal were offered. One was that it was somehow intended to counter growing Chinese influence on the military regime in Rangoon.[41] Indian intelligence officials also claimed that the weapons were intended to go to groups whose help they needed in combating insurgents like the National Socialist Council of Nagaland (NSCN), the United Liberation Front of Asom (ULFA), and the People's Liberation Army of Manipur (PLA). Whatever the intent, news of the transfers infuriated the Indian army, which argued that a large proportion of the arms was finding its way back across the border to the separatist groups they were fighting.[42]

There have also been persistent reports about gray market arms transfers from Middle Eastern governments to Islamic armed groups in the Philippines. Iran, Lebanon, Pakistan, Sudan, and Libya have all been linked to Islamic rebels in the southern Philippines.[43] President Muammar al-Khadafi once publicly declared that he had sent arms and funds to Muslim forces in Mindanao, and Libyan agents are believed to have been active in the Philippines for decades.[44] Members of the Abu Sayyaf Group (ASG) and GAM were trained in Libya, and Tripoli reportedly facilitated the transfer of large numbers of Pakistani-made RPG-7s, HK-33s, and MP-5s to the Moro National Liberation Front (MNLF), using financing from the Bank of Credit and Commerce International (BCCI).[45] Indeed, according to former Filipino national security adviser Jose Almonte, Libyan support for the MNLF was so generous that there was a time during the early 1970s when "the secessionists were better armed than the forces of the Philippine state."[46]

Apart from the Islamic connection, North Korea, China, and Vietnam have also been mentioned as past suppliers of illicit arms to groups in the Philippines.[47] According to Philippine intelligence reports, representatives from the MILF reportedly met with North Korean agents in May 2000 to discuss the purchase of antitank and antiaircraft missiles, using $3 million received from groups associated with Osama bin Laden. A Malaysian arms dealer named Samuan Bin Akmad allegedly brokered the deal.[48] As Anthony Davis has noted, however, there is no evidence that any arms were ever delivered, and the reports have the strong smell of disinformation.[49] China has been accused of supplying arms to the Revolutionary Proletarian Army–Alex Boncayao Brigade (RPA-ABB) urban terrorist cell, a charge the Chinese government denies. The group itself claims it relies on domestic supporters.[50]

The aftermath of 9/11 seems to have had an ambiguous impact on the practice of supplying arms to nonstate actors. On the one hand, the U.S. government now views with great concern the transfer of any weapons or matériel to groups it considers foreign terrorist organizations. However, at the same time, Washington has itself relied on the transfer of arms to nonstate actors as part of its global counterterrorism strategy. The provision of aid and weapons to the Northern Alliance in Afghanistan in late 2001 is perhaps the best known, but not the only example.[51] Perhaps because of this ambivalence, some gray market transfers continue in Southeast Asia. The Thai government has adopted a quiet policy of providing arms, intelligence, and logistical support to some of the ethnic militias fighting along the Thai-Burma border as part of its policy to defeat drug trafficking cartels such as the United Wa State Army (UWSA).[52]

Domestic Sourcing of Arms

While reports of clandestine transnational arms smuggling operations and nefarious arms dealers seize the imagination, many terrorist groups and rebel factions acquire their weapons in a rather more mundane fashion from a range of local sources. These include thefts and leakage from state arsenals, from defecting members of the security forces, and weapons stolen from civilian owners.

Leakage from police and military armories is a serious problem in many parts of Southeast Asia and one of the most significant sources of illicit military weapons. In the Philippines, the gross mismanagement of the security forces' arms over several decades has provided countless opportunities for weapons to be diverted onto the local black market and ultimately into the hands of terrorists. In October 2000 the police director for the Western Visayas Region ordered the return of more than 600 weapons that had been issued to police who were no longer assigned to the area.[53] Around the same time, police officers in Negros Occidental were sued for failing to return hundreds of more weapons, including Armalite military rifles.[54] In August 2003 a senior AFP officer admitted to *Jane's Intelligence Review* that more than 8,000 army weapons had gone missing in Sulu Province alone over a fourteen-year period.[55] Many of these had been given or sold to groups like Abu Sayyaf and the Moro Islamic Liberation Front (MILF).

Similar problems afflict the police and armed forces in Indonesia. Hundreds of military weapons were stolen from overrun police stations and military armories during violence in Maluku in 2000. In just one incident at Tantui, more than 800 military-style rifles were looted along with thousands of rounds of ammunition.[56] There have also been allegations that weapons and ammunition have gone missing directly from the country's national arms producer, PT Pindad.[57] In January 2000 a large consignment of arms bearing Pindad markings was intercepted en route to GAM.[58] These disappearances led Indonesian NGOs to call for a complete audit of TNI and police weapons.[59] More recently, Jakarta has admitted it has difficulties controlling the production of explosives, in part because of the large numbers of licensed producers.[60] In September 2003, a senior defense official told the Indonesian House of Representatives that a spate of bombings may have been the result of a lack of control over the commercial production and distribution of explosive materials.[61]

The most dramatic recent examples of leakage, however, have come in southern Thailand and Malaysia. In January 2004, more than thirty gunmen attacked a Thai army depot in the southern town of Narathiwat, killing four soldiers and making off with more than 100 military weapons.[62] In April 2004, dozens of poorly-armed militants launched simultaneous raids on fifteen police bases, village defense posts and district offices in Yala, Pattani, and Songkhla provinces in an attempt to seize weapons. Police and military forces had been tipped off, however, and in the resulting firefight, more than 112 people were killed.[63]

In Malaysia, a large cache of weapons was stolen from a Malaysian army camp in Perak state in July 2000. A group of men posing as military officers made off with more than a hundred M-16 and Steyr AUG rifles, machine guns, grenade launchers, mortar shells, and thousands of rounds of ammunition.[64] The Malaysian government blamed the raid on an Islamic radical group known as al-Maunah but an investigation also implicated several soldiers sympathetic to the group.[65] The theft was not unprecedented. Steyr rifles were stolen from another army camp in Kamaunting in July 1999.[66]

In addition to leakage through theft and negligence, security forces are also complicit in the transfer of weapons to domestic paramilitaries and militant groups, either for political purposes or for profit. One of the most notorious examples of this was the supply of arms to Timorese militias by the Indonesian military (TNI) in the lead-up to the September 1999 independence referendum.[67] Despite the arrest and trial of some of the officers involved, the practice continues in Indonesia's many conflict zones. The TNI has provided weapons and ammunition to combatants in Maluku and Ambon, both directly and through radical groups like Laskar Jihad. In Aceh there have been numerous cases where TNI soldiers have been caught selling weapons to the GAM rebels they are supposed to be fighting.[68] Most of the military arms and ammunition used in recent fighting in Poso in Sulawesi are believed to come from TNI stocks.[69]

In the Philippines, insurgent groups have long admitted that their most important sources of weapons are the Armed Forces of the Philippines (AFP), the Philippines National Police (PNP), and the various well-armed citizen militias.[70] In just one case, a police raid in September 2000 led to the arrest of ten men in Bulacan and Nueva Ecija provinces and the seizure of a shipment of high-powered military firearms and crew-served weapons. The weapons included various assault rifles (M-16s and Belgian FN-FALs), grenade-launchers, machine guns, mortars, explosives, and ammunition, and were believed to be destined for Mindanao.[71] According to the government's Anti–Organized Crime Task Force, a military connection to the smugglers was certain, as "most of the weapons [could] only be found in the government's armory."[72] The fact that the MILF and Abu Sayyaf have fought "overwhelmingly" with American-made weapons such as M-16s, M-203 grenade-launchers, and M-60 machine guns also lends support to the view that most of their arms are acquired from AFP stocks and are not smuggled imports.[73] The issue of security forces' complicity was thrown into the international spotlight in July 2003, when more than three hundred junior AFP officers took over a shopping mall in central Manila to protest the involvement of senior officers in selling arms and ammunition to terrorist groups.[74]

Another important domestic channel involves the theft and unlawful transfer of privately owned civilian weapons. Of the millions of firearms in Southeast Asia, by far the majority are in private hands. In the Philippines, official records show that 824,328 weapons were registered with the police in early 2003. Estimates as to the number of unregistered guns vary from 270,000 to 600,000.[75] One 2003 press report claimed there were 439,119 firearms "loose" within the country and another source claims the total number of private weapons may be as high as 5.3 million.[76] The Thai government has reported the country as having 1,080,394 licensed private firearms, but news accounts place the number of licensed weapons at about 3.7 million, and there could be as many as 10 million illicit arms in circulation.[77] The combination of vast stocks of privately owned weapons with weak and corrupt law enforcement and poor regulation provides many opportunities for theft and diversion.

The role of private gun shops in supplying arms to criminals and terrorists has also come under scrutiny recently. In April 2001, Thai air force officers were implicated in a scam to resell imported duty-free 9mm Glock pistols onto the local black market.[78] A subsequent investigation revealed that as many as 30,000 weapons had been diverted in this way, with an unknown number sold to terrorist organizations and criminals.[79] In May 2003, three Sri Lankans linked to the LTTE and several Thai police and air force soldiers were arrested for trying to perpetrate a similar scam.[80] Bangkok gun shops were buying police firearms permits from officers for about twenty-five dollars. They were then selling them to a Thai air force officer who procured weapons and ammunitions for the LTTE. The arrests led the Police Crime Suppression Division to conclude that legal gun shops "formed the core of the illegal arms trade" in Thailand.[81] Similar scams have been identified in the Philippines. One popular technique is for arms dealers to acquire import permits on behalf of a government agency, but to order more weapons than can actually be paid for by the agency's budget. The excess weapons can then be surreptitiously sold on the local black market.[82]

Illicit Production

Finally, some groups in Southeast Asia have developed the means to manufacture their own arms and ammunition. In 1999, reports emerged claiming the MILF had built an arms factory in central Mindanao.[83] A spokesman, Ustadz Shariff Mohsin Julabbi, told the *Philippine Daily Inquirer* that the factory had nearly one hundred employees and produced high-caliber weapons and ammunition, including replicas of the Russian RPG-2, 60mm mortars, and unspecified "bullets and bombs."[84] He claimed the factory could produce almost 200 RPG-2s a month and said that the MILF had about 1,500 of the weapons in its inventory.[85] A more senior MILF figure, Ghadzali Jaafar, confirmed the existence of the factory and said that as well as producing RPGs, .45-caliber pistols, and 60mm mortars, it also converted M-1 rifles into fully automatic M-14s.[86] More recent accounts, however, raise questions about the quantity and quality of the arms being produced.[87] Furthermore, the loss of Camp Abu Bakar and other bases during fighting in 2000 has apparently "severely disrupted" MILF weapons production.[88]

While few regional armed groups have the facilities and know-how available to the MILF, some others have produced their own weapons, albeit with varying levels of success. In February 2001 there were unconfirmed reports that GAM may have developed a basic arms production capability. According to a wire service report, four GAM members were killed when TNI forces raided a warehouse in the village of Batee in Bireun District. The building had apparently been used for making weapons, and a number of unspecified pistols and rifles were seized, although the quality of the weapons remains unclear.[89] A number of other groups fighting in Indonesia have also produced their own homemade weapons. Many of these were seen fighting in

Ambon in 2000. Recent reports from Sulawesi allege that JI members have set up camps near Poso, training local men to make weapons and explosives.[90] Groups in the Philippines and Burma are also known to have produced their own blast and fragmentation mines and victim-activated improvised explosive devices (IEDs).[91]

Regional Responses to Small-Arms Proliferation

As the above analysis shows, contemporary Southeast Asia faces an alarming convergence between a large number of insurgent and terrorist groups and a ready supply of small arms and light weapons. How then have regional states attempted to shut down these four proliferation pathways?

Efforts to tackle arms trafficking in Southeast Asia predate the terrorist attacks of 2001 and the launch of the "global war on terrorism." At the regional level, ASEAN adopted a Declaration on Transnational Crime at a meeting in December 1997, with its members pledging to cooperate and coordinate efforts against a range of criminal threats, including arms smuggling.[92] Further meetings took place in March 1998 and June 1999 with a May 2000 regional seminar in Jakarta, marking the first time a meeting was specifically devoted to illicit small-arms issues.[93] It concluded with an informal agreement to improve law enforcement coordination and intelligence sharing.

Antitrafficking efforts have significantly increased since the 9/11 terrorist attacks and the October 2002 bombings in Bali. Pressure from Washington has forced several countries to make more concerted efforts to counter the activities of terrorist groups operating within their borders. Thailand in particular has increased its pressure on the LTTE, which had operated with relative impunity in the country for a number of years.[94] U.S.-AFP exercises in the southern Philippines have severely disrupted the activities of the ASG and to a lesser extent the MILF.

U.S. pressure has also been an important catalyst for improved cooperation between regional states. At the working level there has been an expansion of ties between law enforcement, customs, and intelligence agencies, although much of it remains informal. In early 2002, ASEAN heads of military intelligence held an unprecedented meeting in Kuala Lumpur to discuss cooperation against Islamic militants.[95] In May 2002 their counterparts in the ASEAN Chiefs of Police also adopted a work program on combating arms-trafficking. The plan encourages regional states to exchange information about illicit arms flows, build law enforcement capacity, destroy surplus weapons, and harmonize the marking of their arms and ammunition. A May 2002 Agreement on Information Exchange between six ASEAN members also explicitly identified the importance of sharing intelligence to combat weapons smuggling.

Regional leaders and senior officials have addressed the issue of arms-trafficking through trans-Pacific institutions such as the ASEAN Regional Forum (ARF) and Asia Pacific Economic Cooperation (APEC). The 2003 APEC Leaders Meeting in Bangkok produced one of the more notable initiatives, identifying the particular threat posed to commercial aircraft by terrorist acquisition of man-portable air defense systems (MANPADS). Large numbers of these are believed to have leaked from Cambodian military stocks, and some have been seized from groups fighting on the Thai-Burma border.[96] APEC nations agreed to adopt strict export controls on these systems, to secure their existing stockpiles and to regulate the production, transfer, and brokering of portable surface-to-air missiles. They also agreed to outlaw the transfer of MANPADS to nonstate actors.[97]

The extent to which these regional agreements will be matched with practical action remains to be seen. To date, bilateral and national measures appear to be more important than multilateral initiatives.[98] Bilateral border surveillance arrangements between Malaysia and Thailand have been strengthened.[99] Bangkok and Jakarta agreed to work to prevent the flow of arms to Aceh, following a visit by President Megawati Sukarnoputri to Thailand in mid-2003. Burma and India have made their own counterterrorism agreement, pledging to curb, "control and contain cross-border militancy in their respective territory." The agreement stands alongside a similar four-party arrangement among Thailand, India, Bangladesh, and Sri Lanka, signed in April 1999. Regional militaries have also begun to improve their coordination in patrolling well-known smuggling routes like the Straits of Malacca.[100] In October 2003 the Japanese government announced it would provide a vessel and personnel to help Indonesian law enforcement improve its ability to patrol in national waters.

At the national level, some of the most impressive action against arms-trafficking has been preventive, in particular working to reduce the vast stockpiles of surplus arms that present a tempting target for unscrupulous brokers or terrorist operatives. Several countries have enacted illegal gun amnesties and collection and destruction programs to reduce this point of vulnerability. The largest program is in Cambodia, where the National Commission for Weapons Management and Reform (NCWMR) has collected some 120,000 surplus weapons and destroyed 111,161 through burning and crushing.[101] Cambodia has also introduced a badly needed program to improve the security of military and police weapons stockpiles. In the Philippines, 45,000 weapons had been collected, confiscated, or surrendered to police by December 2002. Another 6,500 confiscated weapons were destroyed in July

2001, and a smaller number were destroyed in 2002.[102] In late 2003, Thai authorities collected more than 100,000 pistols, rifles, and machine guns, and more than 250,000 mines and rocket-propelled grenades during a two-month-long amnesty on illegal weapons.[103]

There have also been some ad hoc efforts to tighten gun control legislation in regional states. In May 2003, Thailand's Ministry of the Interior ordered gun dealers to suspend sales of rifles to the public and introduced limits on the number of weapons any individual could own.[104] The initiative was part of Prime Minister Thaksin Shinawatra's ambitious plan to make Thailand a "gun-free society" within six years. Gun bans have been introduced in areas that rely heavily on tourism, including Phuket, Chiang Rai, and Pattaya.[105] Along with restrictions on the issuing of new licenses, the Thaksin government also launched a brutal crackdown on so-called "dark influences," including drug dealers and arms-traffickers.

More modest law reform measures have been introduced in the Philippines. The government has imposed restrictions on the carrying of weapons in public places and continues to ban gun sales in the lead-up to elections.[106] These ad hoc responses have not, however, been accompanied by wider legislative reform, and they have been strongly opposed by the country's influential gun lobby.[107] In several regional states, loopholes and anachronistic firearms legislation continue to make it easy for weapons to fall into the wrong hands.[108] Only Cambodia has reviewed and comprehensively overhauled its gun laws. In 2002 it introduced new legislation on small arms, extending restrictions on the right to bear arms and imposing higher penalties for violations.

Despite some progress, significant gaps remain in regional efforts to reduce illicit arms-trafficking. First, there is a marked reluctance on the part of regional states to acknowledge the links between the licit and illicit trade in small arms and ammunition. Although problems with leakage, the diversion of arms shipments, and the flawed end user certification system are well-known, regional governments have been unwilling to consider any kind of regional arms register or mechanism to promote greater transparency. A modest United Nations proposal for states to name a national "point of contact" on small-arms issues in order to strengthen export controls and improve cooperation has been adopted by only five of ASEAN's ten members.

Second, there has been no effort to better control the activities of the region's numerous arms dealers and brokers. While many dealers and brokers engage in a lawful business, an unscrupulous minority plays a critical role in the movement of weapons to nonstate actors. Brokers are crucial facilitators in many arms deals, and they are frequently involved in "gray market" transfers, where the supplier state wants to disguise its involvement. Requiring the regulation of brokers and ensuring that national laws apply to them even in cases where the arms do not physically enter the broker's home country would be an important step toward countering one significant part of the illicit arms trade.

Third, because ASEAN has to date largely framed the small-arms problem as a transnational crime issue, it has underplayed the importance of domestic supply routes. This is in part because it is easier to prescribe solutions for intercepting international smugglers than face up to endemic corruption in police forces, militaries, and government bureaucracies. To be sure, improving the professionalism of military and police forces is a challenging and time-consuming task, not helped by the fact that international donors are often reluctant to invest funds in security sector reform. However, while it takes time to build effective, transparent, and honest security institutions, a crucial first step is acknowledging the scale of the problem. In Thailand and Indonesia in particular, senior government officials continue to deny that security forces are involved in illicit arms-trafficking.[109]

Finally, the above analysis suggests that some aspects of the war against terrorism in Southeast Asia could in fact be counterproductive. For example, Washington's decision to provide the Armed Forces of the Philippines (AFP) with more than 30,000 M-16 rifles under its Excess Defense Articles (EDA) program risks simply increasing the stocks of weapons available for theft and diversion.[110] Indeed, according to testimony before the Philippines Senate in mid-2003, M-16 rifles provided to the AFP by Washington have already been recovered in camps belonging to the Abu Sayyaf Group.[111]

Conclusion

This chapter has provided an overview of four principal paths through which armed groups in Southeast Asia acquire illicit weapons. While it is impossible to know with any certainty the proportion of arms that move through these various channels, there is clear evidence that although transnational trafficking receives most of the attention, domestic suppliers are an extremely important source of arms for many groups. Weapons stolen or lost from military arsenals and the illicit transfer of lawfully purchased "civilian" firearms are vitally important sources for groups in Burma, the Philippines, and Indonesia. Unfortunately, while there has been some useful action to reduce vulnerable stockpiles of surplus weapons, not enough has been done to close loopholes in firearms legislation or address the involvement of security forces in the illicit transfer and trafficking of weapons. Unless these fundamental issues are confronted, other measures will have only a limited impact, and deadly "weapons of individual destruction" will continue to flow to Southeast Asia's many insurgent and terrorist groups.

Notes

I am very grateful for comments on earlier drafts of this paper from Paul Smith, Sally Hill, and Pablo Policzer. Funding for research was generously provided by the Rockefeller Foundation's Global Inclusion Program and the New Zealand Peace and Disarmament Education Trust (PADET).

1. In December 2003, U.S. Deputy Secretary of Defense Paul Wolfowitz said the need to interdict the global trade in materials required for weapons of mass destruction "has never been greater." As one sign of its determination to counter this threat, the United States created the sixteen-nation Proliferation Security Initiative (PSI) to prevent the spread of weapons of mass destruction to state and nonstate actors. See "Deputy Defense Secretary Paul Wolfowitz's Remarks to Proliferation Security Initiative," Washington File—East Asia and the Pacific Edition, December 17, 2003, available at http://www.usinfo.state.gov.

2. George W. Bush, State of the Union Address 2002, available online at http://www.whitehouse.gov/news/releases/2003/01/20030128-19.html.

3. Cited in *Small Arms Survey 2003: Development Denied* (Oxford: Oxford University Press, 2003), p. 60.

4. Raenette Taljard, "The Bigger Problem: Weapons of Individual Destruction," *YaleGlobal,* October 15, 2003, http://yaleglobal.yale.edu/display.article?id=2632.

5. There is no single consensus definition for small arms and light weapons. This chapter adopts the terminology used in the 1997 United Nations *Report of the Panel of Governmental Experts on Small Arms,* which defined small arms as "revolvers and self-loading pistols, rifles and carbines, sub-machine guns, assault rifles and light machine guns" as well as the ammunition they require. Light weapons include "heavy machine guns, hand-held under-barrel and mounted grenade launchers, portable anti-tank and antiaircraft guns, recoilless rifles, portable launchers of antitank and anti-aircraft missile systems, and mortars of less than 100mm calibre." United Nations Document A/52/1998, August 27, 1997.

6. For an insightful conceptual analysis of the nexus between crime and terrorism, see Tamara Makarenko, "A Model of Terrorist-Criminal Relations," *Jane's Intelligence Review* (August 2003): 6–11.

7. This chapter interprets the term "terrorists" broadly, as including a wide range of armed groups in Southeast Asia, only some of which are designated formally as foreign terrorist organizations. An inclusive approach is justified by the fact that these otherwise very different groups often use many of the same sources and arms-trafficking routes and also by evidence of links between territorially based armed groups like the MILF and networks including Jemaah Islamiya.

8. Rohan Gunaratna, "Terrorism and Small Arms and Light Weapons," paper presented to the United Nations Symposium on Terrorism and Disarmament, October 25, 2001. Prior to the Asia Pacific Economic Cooperation (APEC) leaders' meeting in Bangkok in October 2003, the Thai military expressed concerns that terrorist groups might seek to import SA-7 surface-to-air missiles from Cambodia. See Wassana Nanuam, "End to Arms Smuggling Urged Ahead of Summit," *Bangkok Post,* September 22, 2003; Kimina Lyall, "Thai Police Confess They Can't Find SAM Missiles,"

The Australian, October 2, 2003; Agence France-Presse, "Thailand Hunting for Smuggled Portable Missiles Ahead of APEC Summit," October 1, 2003. In March 2003 there were also reports alleging that the LTTE had attempted to buy SA-16 Igla missiles from a Russian arms dealer based in Vientiane, Laos. According to diplomatic sources, LTTE cadres contacted an agent for the Russian arms producer Rosboronoexport. The dealer reported the contact to the Russian embassy in Vientiane, who informed the Sri Lankan government. See Agence France-Presse, "Sri Lanka to Probe Rebel Attempt to Seek Russian Missiles in Laos," March 16, 2003; also Anthony Davis, "Sri Lanka Intercepts New Arms Purchases," *Jane's Intelligence Review* (April 1, 2003).

9. There are persistent but unconfirmed rumors that the United Wa State Army has purchased arms directly from Norinco. According to sources in Bangkok, the Wa buys from Norinco to meet its own needs and also sells weapons to other insurgent factions for profit. See David Capie, *Small Arms Production and Transfers in Southeast Asia,* Canberra, Paper no. 146, Strategic and Defence Studies Centre, Australian National University, 2002, p. 65. *Small Arms Survey* has also reported that the Aceh Merdeka Movement (GAM) has been able to obtain new Chinese-produced arms through brokers in Thailand.

10. For more on the role of brokers and arms dealers, see *Small Arms Survey 2001: Profiling the Problem* (Oxford: Oxford University Press, 2001), chapter 3.

11. There has been progress in securing weapons stocks in Cambodia. By the end of 2002, two of the six military regions in Cambodia had had their weapons stocks audited, registered, and stored securely. Eight arms depots in Phnom Penh were also made secure. The country is aiming to implement the program nationwide by 2006.

12. Raymond Bonner, "A Tamil Tiger Primer on International Arms Bazaar," *International Herald Tribune,* March 10, 1998.

13. *Curbing the Demand for Small Arms: Focus on Southeast Asia* (Geneva: Center for Humanitarian Dialogue, 2003), p. 22.

14. "Thai Military, Police Officers Arrested for Selling Guns to Sri Lanka Rebels," *Star,* September 23, 2003; "Arms Seized by Thai Navy Destined for Indian Rebels," *Thailand Times,* March 18, 1997; Anthony Davis, "Thailand Tenders Anti-Trafficking Plan to Others," *Jane's Defence Weekly* (April 21, 1999).

15. John McBeth, Nate Thayer, and Bertil Lintner, "Worse to Come," *Far Eastern Economic Review* (July 29, 1999): 18; Robert Karniol, "Sri Lanka Says Tigers Are Trading Arms in Cambodia," *Jane's Defence Weekly* (October 2, 1996). According to one account, the restaurant concerned was the Ranni, owned and operated by Tamil rebels. See Bertil Lintner, "LTTE Purchases, a Link with Cambodia," *Jane's Intelligence Review* (December 1, 1996). The Indian military has identified several extremist groups that have agents on the Thai side of the border. See the comments of one Indian army officer based in Assam, quoted in Armed Forces of the Philippines, "India on Alert for Rebel Arms Shipment," December 12, 2000.

16. Senior Thai military officer quoted in Craig Skehan, "Thais Run Huge Arms Trade," *Sydney Morning Herald,* August 14, 1999.

17. Davis, "Thailand Tenders Anti-Trafficking Plan."

18. Pakistan's military intelligence service, the ISI, reportedly "introduced" the ULFA to LTTE transporters who, for a fee, undertook to transport arms from Southeast Asia into Myanmar. In April 1996, Bangladesh seized more than 500 AK-47 rifles, 80 machine guns, 50 rocket launchers, and 2,000 grenades from two ships off Cox's Bazaar. Four Tamils were among those arrested. See the entry on the ULFA in

the South Asian Terrorism Portal, available online http://www.satp.org/satporgtp/countries/india/states/assam/terrorist_outfits/ULFA.HTM.

19. Prior to 1996 the LTTE also had a base on Twante Island in a delta south of Rangoon, which it established with the connivance of some members of the Burmese military.

20. The LTTE also uses its own fleet of vessels, known as "sea pigeons," to transfer larger internationally sourced consignments. "Chuan Pledges Watch on Tamil Arms Link," *The Nation,* May 29, 1999; Robert Karniol, "Sri Lanka Says Tigers Are Trading Arms in Cambodia," *Jane's Defence Weekly* (October 2, 1996); Lintner, "LTTE Purchases, a Link with Cambodia."

21. Marwaan Macan-Markar, "Thailand Turns on Tamil Tigers," Inter Press Service, November 9, 2003.

22. Simon Montlake, "Myanmar's Drug Trade Switches to Sea Routes," *South China Morning Post,* November 25, 2003.

23. "Thai Military, Police Officers Arrested for Selling Guns to Sri Lanka Rebels," *The Star* (Malaysia), September 23, 2003; "Leader of Captured Weapons Linked to Pirates," *Thailand Times,* March 13, 1997; "Navy Seizes Weapons Reportedly Destined for Tamil Tigers," *Thailand Times,* March 12, 1997; "Army Chief Insists Rebels Have Local Base," *The Nation,* March 29, 2000; and "Tamil Tigers 'Extend Net in Thailand'" *The Nation,* August 4, 2000.

24. P.K. Balachanddran, "Naval Surveillance Is the Millstone Around LTTE's Neck," *Hindustan Times,* October 14, 2003.

25. In May 2001, two Royal Thai Army (RTA) noncommissioned officers, in two pickup trucks loaded with mines and ammunition destined for Aceh, were arrested by police. More senior officers were implicated in a subsequent investigation. See Davis, "Thailand Moves to Curb Arms Trafficking." Some reports claimed the weapons were destined for the LTTE. See Edward Tang, "Military Rogues," *Straits Times,* May 16, 2001.

26. Tamara Makarenko, "Tracing the Dynamics of the Illicit Arms Trade," *Jane's Intelligence Review* (September 1, 2003). On the involvement of the MIP, see "Dead Separatist Was a Gun Runner: Thaksin," *The Nation,* August 30, 2003; Muhamad Ayub Pathan, "Arms Trio Linked to Separatists," *Bangkok Post,* July 6, 2003.

27. "FOKUS: Cara GAM Mengail Dana," *Forum Keadilan* 31 (November 5, 2000): 80–86; Pathan, "Arms Trio Linked to Separatists"; "Dead Separatist Was a Gun Runner."

28. John McBeth, Nate Thayer, and Bertil Lintner, "Worse to Come," *Far Eastern Economic Review* (July 29, 1999).

29. Skehan, "Thais Run Huge Arms Trade."

30. Commodore Djoko Sumarsono, quoted in "National Rights Body Team Visits Devastated Maluku," *Jakarta Post,* July 28, 2000.

31. BBC Summary of World Broadcasts, January 11, 2000, FE/D3734/S1.

32. "RP Ship Captured for Running Guns," *Jakarta Post,* January 16, 2000; "National Rights Body Team Visits Devastated Maluku."

33. *Jemaah Islamiyah in Southeast Asia: Damaged But Still Dangerous,* International Crisis Group, Brussels, August 2003.

34. Interviews, Jakarta, November 2003; "Guns in Poso Came from the Philippines," *Jakarta Post,* November 3, 2003; "Mystery Warmongers," *Tempo,* October 27, 2003.

35. For a description of the different kinds of illicit transfers, see *Small Arms Survey, 2001,* p. 166.

36. The United States abandoned between 1.5 and 1.8 million small arms and 150,000 tons of ammunition in South Vietnam when it withdrew in 1975. Edward C. Ezell, Carlos G. Davila, and P. Labbett, *Small Arms Today: Latest Reports on the World's Weapons and Ammunition* (Harrisburg, PA: Stackpole Books—Arms and Armour Press, 1984), p. 229. According to a regional diplomat who served in the Philippines at the time, the United States has satellite imagery of the transfer to the NPA.

37. Richard Cole, "Senate Report Shows NSC Used POW Groups to Fund Laotian Rebels," Associated Press, January 13, 1993.

38. Daniel Byman, Peter Chalk, Bruce Hoffman, William Rosenau, and David Brennan, *Trends in Outside Support for Insurgent Movements* (Washington, DC: RAND, 2001), appendix B, p. 117; Chris Smith, "In the Shadow of a Ceasefire: The Impacts of Small Arms Availability and Misuse in Sri Lanka," Occasional Paper no. 11, Small Arms Survey, Geneva, October 2003, p. 10.

39. Rahul Bedi, "Turf Wars Muddy the Waters of Indian Intel," *Jane's Intelligence Review* (March 1, 1999): 38.

40. Ibid.

41. At the same time, the Indian government was also offering assault rifles, electronic warfare equipment, radar, and communications technology to the Burmese government.

42. The debacle prompted reforms within Indian intelligence. For more, see Rahul Bedi, "'Failures' Prompt India to Reform Intelligence Service'" *Jane's Intelligence Review* (June 2001): 2–22.

43. "Abu Sayyaf Weapons Capabilities, Foreign Supporters Listed," *Philippines Daily Inquirer,* July 31, 1994, pp. 1, 12.

44. Merliza M. Makinano and Alfredo Lubang, "Disarmament, Demobilisation, and Reintegration: The Mindanao Experience," in *South Asia at Gun Point: Small Arms and Light Weapons Proliferation,* ed. Dipankar Banerjee (Colombo: Regional Centre for Strategic Studies, 2000), p. 148.

45. "Libya-Trained Rebels Blamed for Current Aceh Violence," *Jakarta Post,* July 30, 1999; Cathy Rose A. Garcia and Manolette C. Payumo, "MILF Tells Gov't to Choose: Talk Peace or Resume War," *BusinessWorld,* February 22, 2000.

46. Jose T. Almonte, "Intra-State Conflict and Arms Proliferation in East Asia," paper presented to the International Conference on Small Arms Proliferation and Trade in the Asia-Pacific, Hotel Sofitel Cambodiana, Phnom Penh, Cambodia, February 19–20, 2001.

47. "Breakaway Group Vows More Manila Terror Attacks," *Manila Times,* March 4, 2000.

48. Carlito Pablo, "MILF Buying Weapons from N. Korea, Says AFP," *Philippine Daily Inquirer,* June 21, 2000; Dona Pazzibugan, Christine Avenda, and Cynthia Balana, "Government Urged to Postpone Ties with North Korea," *Philippine Daily Inquirer,* June 22, 2000; Deutsche Presse-Agentur, "North Korea Assures It Has Sent No Arms to Filipino Moslem Rebels," July 14, 2000.

49. Anthony Davis, "Philippine Security Threatened by Small-Arms Proliferation," *Jane's Intelligence Review* (August 2003): 32–37.

50. *Small Arms Survey, 2001,* p. 183.

51. Foreign occupation forces in Iraq, Sierra Leone, and Kosovo have also had to fashion pragmatic working arrangements with armed groups that previously lacked any international legitimacy. In some cases this has included the provision of arms

and other military assistance. For a detailed examination of the consequences of this changing attitude toward sovereigns and nonstate actors, see William Reno, "Sovereign Predators and Non-State Armed Group Protectors?" Paper presented to the Curbing Human Rights by Armed Groups Conference, Centre of International Relations, University of British Columbia, Vancouver, November 14–15, 2003. The paper is available at http://www.armedgroups.org.

52. In April 2000, Deputy Prime Minister Sukhumnhand Paribatra admitted that Thailand was supporting what were described as "clandestine sabotage operations" against the UWSA inside Burma. See Rodney Tasker and Shaun Crispin, "Frustration over Burma's Illegal Drugs," *Far Eastern Economic Review* (June 1, 2000). In May 2002, Burmese officials summoned the Thai military attaché in Rangoon to the Ministry of Defense to protest transfers of Thai military weapons to fighters of the Karen National Union. BBC Worldwide Monitoring, "Burmese Officials Formally Protest to Thai Military Attaché," May 25, 2002. The Burmese military regime has itself provided arms and ammunition to both the UWSA and the Democratic Karen Buddhist Army (DKBA).

53. Carla Gomez, "Policemen Sued for Failing to Return Pistols, Rifles," *Philippine Daily Inquirer,* October 4, 2000.

54. Ibid.

55. Davis, "Philippine Security Threatened by Small-Arms Proliferation," pp. 32–37.

56. "Calls for Int'l Troops in Maluku Brushed Aside," *Jakarta Post,* August 7, 2000.

57. "Pindad, Police Give Conflicting Account on AG Office Bomb," *Jakarta Post,* July 8, 2000.

58. Rohan Gunaratna, "The Structure and Nature of GAM," *Jane's Intelligence Review* (April 1, 2001).

59. See the comments of Adnan Pandupradja, secretary-general of the NGO Police Watch, quoted in Devi Asmarani, "Jakarta Groups Call for Audit of Military and Police Weapons," *Straits Times,* July 25, 2002.

60. BBC Monitoring International Reports, "Indonesia Admits Difficulty Controlling Explosives Production," September 19, 2003.

61. Ibid.

62. BBC News, "Armed Raids in Southern Thailand," January 4, 2004.

63. "Southern Carnage: Kingdom Shaken," *The Nation,* April 29, 2004; BBC News, "Scores Killed in Thai Gun Battles," April 28, 2004. See also, Muhamad Ayub Pathan, "Arms Trio Linked to Separatists," *Bangkok Post,* July 6, 2003.

64. "Military Combs Malaysian Jungle for Missing Weapons," *Straits Times,* July 5, 2000; Thomas Fuller, "Malaysia Armory Thieves Surrounded," *International Herald Tribune,* July 5, 2000.

65. Jestyn Cooper, "Rebel Group Threatens Malaysian Security," *Jane's Intelligence Review* (September 1, 2000); Wan Hamidi Hamid, "Mahathir: Arms Heist Gang Out to Topple Government," *Straits Times,* July 11, 2000; "Nine More Soldiers Involved in Arms Heist Questioned," *Straits Times,* July 13, 2000.

66. See "Two Cases of Theft at Army Camps in Last Five Years," *Bernama* (November 22, 2000).

67. "Indonesia Admits Arming Militias," BBC, February 6, 1999; David Jenkins, Mark Dodd, Bernard Lagan, and Simon Mann, "Blood on Their Hands," *Sydney Morning Herald,* October 2, 1999.

68. "Indonesian Solider Arrested for Aceh Weapons Sales," Australian Broadcast-

ing Corporation, January 6, 2000; BBC Worldwide Monitoring, "Indonesia: Military Policeman Dies in Custody Following Lynching," January 7, 2000.

69. "Poso's Pain," *Straits Times,* November 24, 2003.

70. "Senator Confirms Military Supplied Arms to Abu Sayyaf," *Manila Standard,* October 1, 1994, p. 2.

71. Dave M. Veridiano, "Government Men Eyed in Big Arms Haul," *Philippine Daily Inquirer,* September 2, 2000.

72. Ibid.

73. Peter Chalk, "Light Arms Trading in Southeast Asia," *Jane's Intelligence Review* (March 2001).

74. Friena P. Guerrero, "Mutiny Leaders Blame 'Corruption' in Military," *BusinessWorld,* August 14, 2003.

75. According to a Philippines government report to the United Nations, there are 284,100 loose firearms, of which 189,766 were not reregistered, 45 were "lost" firearms, and a total of 94,313 arms were in the hands of various armed groups and criminals. *National Report on the Implementation of the Programme of Action (POA) to Prevent, Combat and Eradicate the Illicit Trade in Small Arms and Light Weapons in All Its Aspects,* Government of the Republic of the Philippines, July 3, 2003.

76. *Manila Times,* February 10, 2003; the 5.3 million figure is cited in *Small Arms Survey, 2002,* p. 99.

77. Wassayos Ngamkham, "Guns the 'Weapons of Choice' in Murders," *Bangkok Post,* September 15, 2003; "Ban on Sales Won't Work," *Bangkok Post,* September 10, 2003.

78. "Airforce Firearms Theft: Informants Hand in 25 of the Stolen Glock Pistols, Only Five Still Not Accounted For," *Bangkok Post,* April 16, 2001; "Officer Who Ordered Pistols Claims He Was Duped," *The Nation,* April 19, 2001.

79. "Firearms Imports," *Bangkok Post,* April 28, 2001.

80. Wassayos Ngamkham, "In the Market for a Firearm?" *Bangkok Post,* October 7, 2003.

81. Ibid.

82. Davis, "Philippine Security Threatened by Small-Arms Proliferation," p. 35.

83. Julie Alipala-Inot and Carolyn O. Arguillas, "Muslim Rebels Admit Having Firearms Factory," *Philippine Daily Inquirer,* January 11, 1999.

84. Ibid.

85. Ibid.

86. Ibid.

87. Davis, "Philippine Security Threatened by Small-Arms Proliferation," p. 35.

88. Ibid.

89. "Aceh Rebels, Jakarta Agree to Peace Deal," *Bangkok Post,* February 26, 2001, p. 7.

90. "Poso's pain."

91. *Landmine Monitor, 2003* (International Campaign to Ban Landmines, Washington, DC, 2003).

92. *ASEAN Declaration on Transnational Crime,* December 20, 1997, text available at the Web site of the ASEAN Secretariat, http://www.aseansec.org.

93. *Manila Declaration on the Prevention and Control of Transnational Crime,* March 25, 1998, Manila; *Joint Communique of the Second ASEAN Ministerial Meeting on Transnational Crime,* June 23, 1999. The text of these agreements is available

at the Web site of the ASEAN Secretariat, http://www.aseansec.org.

94. Macan-Markar, "Thailand Turns on Tamil Tigers."

95. Leslie Lau, "Asean Believes Terror Network Dealt Severe Blow," *Straits Times,* January 30, 2002.

96. Edward Tang, "Golden Triangle Now a Haven for Terror Arms," *Straits Times,* September 4, 2002. In 1995, Thai police seized three Soviet SA-7 Strela SAMs being shipped out of Cambodia for Khun Sa's Mong Thai Army (MTA). There were also vague reports in September 2003 of plans to shoot down an El Al aircraft in Bangkok using MANPADS. No actual missiles were seized, however, and the report was dismissed by Thai authorities. See "Bangkok Police Thwart Plot on El Al," *Jerusalem Post,* September 24, 2003.

97. See the text of the Bangkok Declaration on Partnership for the Future, APEC Leaders Meeting, Bangkok, October 21, 2003.

98. A plethora of bilateral intelligence and information-sharing agreements have been signed since 9/11, all of which have at least indirect relevance to preventing the illicit movement of weapons. In addition to the measures discussed here, others include a Counter-Terrorism Agreement between Indonesia and Australia (February 2002); a Counter-Terrorism Agreement between the United States and the Philippines (May 2002); an MOU on Counter-Terrorism between Australia and Thailand (October 2002); a Counter-Terrorism Agreement between Brunei and the Philippines (January 27, 2003); an Anti-Terrorism Pact between Australia and Malaysia (August 2003); an Anti-Terrorism Pact between Australia and Cambodia (June 2003); and an Anti-Terrorism Pact between Australia and the Philippines (March 4, 2003). Australia, Indonesia, and East Timor also signed a tripartite Counter-Terrorism Agreement in August 2003.

99. Sujatani Poosparajah, "Malaysia, Thailand to Step Up Cooperation on Border Security," *New Straits Times,* November 8, 2002.

100. "Three Straits in Indonesia Prone to Weapons Smuggling—Navy," Antara, August 12, 2003; "Sea Exercise Planned to Curb Arms Flow," *Bangkok Post,* May 27, 2003.

101. *Working to Build Peace, Security, and Prosperity: Curbing Small Arms and Light Weapons in Cambodia* (National Commission for Weapons Management and Reform: Phnom Penh, July 2003). According to NCWMR, 36,505 weapons were crushed and 74,656 were burned.

102. *Philippines National Report on the Implementation of the UN Programme of Action,* p. 13. Available online at the *Small Arms Survey*'s database, http://www.smallarmssurvey.org.

103. Kylie Morris, "Thai PM Ups War on Illegal Guns," BBC News, December 16, 2003.

104. *National Report of the Kingdom of Thailand on the Implementation of the 2001 United Nations Programme of Action (POA) to Prevent, Combat, and Eradicate the Illicit Trade in Small Arms and Light Weapons in All Its Aspects,* July 2003, p. 5. Available online at the *Small Arms Survey*'s database, http://www.smallarmssurvey.org.

105. "Take a Break and Park Your Gun," *Phuket Gazette,* November 12, 2003.

106. Mylene Corpuz, "Arroyo Takes on Armed Society," *Bangkok Post,* February 5, 2003.

107. Joel R. San Juan, "Gun Ban 'Unconstitutional,'" *Manila Times,* October 6, 2003.

108. Katherine Kramer, *Legal Controls on Small Arms and Light Weapons in Southeast Asia* (*Small Arms Survey*, Occasional Paper No. 3, July 2001).

109. Responding to a report in *Time* magazine, Thai defense minister Chavalit Yongchaiyudh told *The Nation* in 2002 that, "It is not true that our army personnel are involved in the smuggling of illegal weapons, or that our country is a base for the supply of illicit weapons." He also said it was impossible that weapons were being smuggled between Thailand and Malaysia. See BBC Monitoring International Reports, "Thailand: Defence Minister Rejects Time Report on Arms Trafficking," February 6, 2002; Foreign Minister Surakiyart Sathirathai made a similar denial about trafficking into Aceh during a visit to Indonesia in May 2003. Xinhua, "Thailand Denies Arms Smuggling into Aceh," May 23, 2003; for comparable Indonesian denials, see Devi Asmarani, "Jakarta Groups Call for Audit of Military and Police Weapons," *Straits Times,* July 25, 2002.

110. The EDA program is managed by the Department of Defense's Defense Security Cooperation Agency. For more information, see http://www.dsca.osd.mil.

111. Brett M. Decker, "A Fair Fight in the Philippines," *New York Times,* October 18, 2003.

11

Border Security and Transnational Violence in Southeast Asia

Paul J. Smith

On August 11, 2003, officers from the Thai Special Branch Police, with the assistance of the American Central Intelligence Agency, arrested Riduan Isamuddin, commonly known as Hambali, a man for whom they had been searching for several years and who was considered the top operational director of the Jemaah Islamiya (JI) terrorist group based in Southeast Asia. Authorities viewed Hambali's capture as a major victory not only because he was an instrumental leader in the Jemaah Islamiya terrorist organization, but also because he was a critical link between that organization and the larger al-Qaeda network.[1] In addition, Hambali had been linked, directly or indirectly, to virtually every major terrorist act in Southeast Asia within the past three years, including the attack in Bali, Indonesia, in October 2002. Furthermore, U.S. officials believe that he may have played a significant role in facilitating the September 11, 2001 attacks in New York and Washington, D.C.

One of the major factors leading to Hambali's arrest was his possession of a forged Spanish passport that enabled him to travel undetected in and out of Thailand. Authorities learned about this passport following interrogation of various al-Qaeda and Jemaah Islamiya operatives, including Mohamad Farik bin Amin (Zubair).[2] U.S. and Thai authorities had determined that the passport would soon expire, and this would require Hambali to seek out a passport forger to "renew" his passport. Subsequently, a prominent passport forger based in Chiang Mai was tracked down and, based on photographs he possessed in his office, authorities were able to make a connection with Hambali. Police later determined Hambali's whereabouts after interrogating two of his agents who had arrived to pick up the new forged passport.[3]

At first glance, Hambali's possession of a forged travel document might be considered merely an interesting collateral matter to this important arrest. But further inquiry indicates that this case, and cases like it around the world, reveals a much greater challenge in the global war on terrorism—the problem of porous borders, lax immigration controls, and forged travel documents. Transnational terrorism is almost invariably intertwined with clandestine international mobility. Like their transnational crime counterparts, terrorists must be able to move seamlessly through multiple countries to recruit new members, raise money, or conduct operations—including attacks—and, moreover, to evade subsequent state responses. Consequently, terrorists will utilize virtually any kind of identity fraud method to achieve this end. In Southeast Asia, porous borders, passport fraud, and lax immigration procedures are contributing significantly to the region's enabling environment that is fostering the growth of terrorism and other forms of transnational violence.

From a historical perspective, borders in Southeast Asia have never been permanent—they are largely artificial constructs inherited from colonial powers, reinforced by the formalities of maps, and solidified by modern state identity. As one scholar noted, ". . . the modern territorial conception of borders was alien to this part of the world and was introduced only forcibly by Europeans. . . ."[4] In daily life, moreover, borders often matter very little, particularly in maritime Southeast Asia. In many parts of the region, informal border crossing is routine, and often considered a normal way of life. But this relaxed attitude toward border security has a downside: it allows transnational criminals and terrorists to slip into and out of countries beyond the purview of national authorities.

Indeed, Southeast Asian authorities are increasingly recognizing that the region's attraction, from the transnational terrorists' point of view, may be its long, unmonitored borders. Transnational terrorists need territory to train, hide, and operate. Thus they must seek out weak states where border security is lax. Southeast Asia's vulnerability to such activities is also evident in multiple other aspects of illegal migration—passport fraud, human smuggling, and large pools of illegal migrant labor. Consequently, reports that certain exogenous groups—such as al-Qaeda—wish to transfer operations to the region should come as no surprise. This chapter will examine the challenge of border security in Southeast Asia as well as provide global context to trends being witnessed in the region.

Porous Borders, Fake Passports, and Real Terrorists

In January 2002, Philippine authorities arrested Fathur Rohman al-Ghozi, an Indonesian national considered to be a key bomb-maker for the terrorist group Jemaah Islamiya, which remains active in Southeast Asia. Al-Ghozi was found to be carrying at least four fake or forged passports issued by the governments of Indonesia and the Philippines, among other countries.[5] He acquired at least one Indonesian passport by engaging in breeder document fraud, a technique in which a passport applicant presents fraudulent primary documents—such as a birth certificate, a driver's license, or a school-issued identification card—and thus receives a legitimate passport from an official passport-issuing authority. Al-Ghozi's possession of multiple fraudulent passports is not particularly surprising in light of his need for clandestine international mobility.

Al-Ghozi's portfolio of fraudulent passports reflects the fact that clandestine international migration remains a critical part of any successful terrorist operation. In fact, authorities investigating document forgery in the context of terrorism have discovered that "theft and forgery of travel documents [have] become a huge logistical sub-business for terrorist groups around the world."[6] Due to the networked structure of contemporary terrorist organizations, terrorists must overcome border controls in order to remain viable. They must constantly seek innovative means to enter and transit countries, in an undetected manner, as part of their recruitment, fundraising, or operational activities.

The importance of passport fraud in transnational terrorism was demonstrated on September 9, 2001, by the assassination, just days before the attacks in New York and Washington, D.C., of Northern Alliance leader Ahmed Shah Massoud by al-Qaeda operatives. Sometime in early 2001, senior al-Qaeda leaders based in Afghanistan activated a Belgian-based suicide cell for an operation to assassinate Massoud. The cell tasked for the mission was based in Belgium and was comprised of ethnic Tunisians and Algerians. Relying on forged Belgian passports, the assassins traveled from Belgium to the United Kingdom, then onward to Pakistan and Afghanistan.[7] Eventually the men reached Afghanistan in August 2001 and, posing as European-based journalists, arranged an interview with Massoud. In the interview room, the assassins positioned the video camera to be level with the victim's chest. As the interview began, one of the assassins posed a question to Massoud. As the question was being translated, the camera, which had been packed with powerful explosives, detonated. One of the assassins died immediately in the explosion while the other was shot by a nearby guard. Commander Massoud, who endured extensive wounds, died several days later.[8]

Investigators would later discover that a key element in the success of this suicide strike involved the assassins' possession of forged Belgian passports. European officials determined that the forged passports had been part of a collection of passports stolen during break-ins at the Belgian embassy in the Netherlands and the Belgian consulate in Strasbourg, France, in 1999. The choice of Belgian passports revealed that the assassins had chosen their operational base wisely. In recent years, Belgium has quietly emerged as the "global capital of identity fraud."[9] Since 1990 an estimated 19,050 blank Belgian passports have been stolen from town halls, embassies, consulates, and honorary consulates.[10] Blank passports are considered ideal for document fraud because they contain no biographical data and thus can be easily manipulated without creating the appearance of tampering or alteration.

Apart from Belgium, a vast and lucrative black market in forged passports thrives in various corners throughout the world, and in many cases these forged passports fall into the hands of transnational terrorists. For instance, Abu Zubaydah, one of the top leaders of al-Qaeda prior to his capture in March 2002, was known to travel the world "with virtual impunity using a variety of false identities, forged passports and other documents."[11] Ayman al-Zawahiri, al-Qaeda's second-in-command, reputedly possesses "a bewildering variety of passports" that has allowed him to enter numerous countries—such as the United States—for fund-raising purposes.[12] In Europe, al-Zawahiri reportedly possessed French and Swiss passports bearing the name of Amin Othman while his Dutch passport bore the name of Sami Mahmoud el-Hifnawi.[13]

Canadian authorities arrested a Yemeni national, Nageed Abdul Jabar Mohamed al-Hadi, suspected of having al-Qaeda links and who possessed three Yemeni passports, all of which had al-Hadi's photograph but each with different names. Yemen is suspected of freely distributing its passports "to former mujahideen from many different nations."[14] The perpetrators of the U.S. embassy attacks in Kenya and Tanzania, for example, relied on Yemeni passports.[15] In 1999, three Kurdish Workers' Party (PKK) members—including the former leader Abdullah Ocalan—relied on various forged passports to enter Kenya as part of a ploy to avoid arrest by Turkish officials (despite his efforts, Ocalan was ultimately arrested). Mr. Ocalan possessed a forged Cypriot passport while two of his female collaborators possessed forged passports from an undisclosed country.[16]

Passport fraud comes in various shapes and sizes, ranging from the less sophisticated photo-substitution fraud to more sophisticated manipulation of previously blank passports and even complete fabrication. Certain regions of the world—Belgium and Thailand, for instance—are known as international centers of passport and identity card forgery. Transnational criminal and terrorist groups will often have key individuals predesignated as passport forgers. But passport fraud, if it is to be successful, requires a high level of sophistication and specific knowledge. As noted above, it is often much easier for terrorists or criminals to acquire forged "breeder documents"—such as fake driver's licenses, birth certificates, and school identification cards—that can be used to establish the necessary identification to subsequently acquire a passport. It is virtually an ideal criminal act in that the terrorist, or other actor seeking the forged passport, actually acquires a legitimate document issued by a government based on false pretenses. The breeder document fraud problem remains a key vulnerability within the international passport system today.

In late December 1999, U.S. authorities working near the U.S.-Canada border discovered a passport acquired through breeder-document fraud. Ahmed Ressam, acting on the behest of—or at least inspired by—al-Qaeda, entered the United States at Port Angeles, Washington, in December 1999. One of his objectives was to blow up the Los Angeles airport. Ressam had successfully used fraudulent breeder documents (particularly a forged Quebec baptismal certificate) to acquire a legitimate Canadian passport with the alias Benni Antoine Noris.[17] With his passport and a bomb in the trunk of his car, he set off on a ferry from Victoria, B.C., Canada, to Port Angeles, Washington, and managed to evade U.S. immigration authorities in the process. Ressam was later captured as he attempted to flee from a U.S. customs agent who had become suspicious following a more comprehensive interview. As one immigration expert has noted, legitimate passports acquired through fraud are virtually impossible to detect unless the host country—where the fraud occurred—becomes aware of the fraud and alerts authorities in other countries.[18]

In Southeast Asia, passport forgery is a major criminal enterprise that thrives in a milieu of government corruption and sophisticated forging syndicates from around the world. Thailand is considered one of the key locations where passports are forged or fabricated. Law enforcement officials regularly describe Thailand as one of the global centers for passport forgery.[19] Much of the illicit industry is allegedly controlled by ethnic Chinese, Pakistani, and African gangs.[20] Moreover, the regionwide problem appears to be getting worse. In October 2003, Japanese authorities disclosed that they had detected a 42 percent increase (compared to the year before) in illegal passports, fake visas, and other fraudulent travel documents, half of which involved Chinese nationals.[21]

Southeast Asia's Porous Borders: Implications for Terrorism

On April 23, 2000, operatives from the Abu Sayyaf Group (ASG) terrorist organization kidnapped a group of international tourists from the Malaysian diving resort of Sipadan and then whisked the hostages back into the Philippines. Once established in their bases, the ASG began to negotiate with the Philippine government to arrange an exchange for the hostages. Eventually, the ASG demanded a million U.S. dollars for each hostage, some of which was eventually paid. Later the ASG would kidnap additional hostages (including journalists who had arrived to report on the crisis) and periodically release others.

The ability of Abu Sayyaf operatives to brazenly conduct this transnational operation—without any concern or respect for international borders—demonstrates the attractiveness of Southeast Asia for transnational terrorist groups. Although Malaysia and the Philippines regularly cooperate on law enforcement and other security matters, the simple reality is that police and military officials from both countries are constrained by jurisdictional barriers. For terrorists and transnational criminals such as the ASG, borders (and hence legal jurisdictions) exist only on paper, not within their particular field of operations.

Porous borders are an acknowledged reality in Southeast Asia. Such fluid borders can be attributed to two major factors: geography and policy. On the geographic front, Southeast Asia has thousands of miles of unpatrolled and unmonitored borders. The region's archipelagic marine geography, featuring thousands of miles of unmonitored maritime and land borders, provides a potentially ideal environment for terrorist or criminal groups seeking to hide out or secretly train operatives. Indonesia, for example, is composed of more than thirteen thousand islands, with maritime borders considered among the world's most porous.[22] The border between Thailand and Malaysia has been described as a "meandering ribbon of dun-colored water" where "border guards are few" that, among other things, facilitated the clandestine passage of Hambali from Malaysia into Thailand in January 2002.[23]

Equally important are the policy and cultural realities that have contributed to border porosity in Southeast Asia. Borders exist on maps in Southeast Asia and are enforced in some places more vigorously than others, but the day-to-day reality of cross-border flows remains a constant. Historically, clandestine cross-border trade and migration have been common features throughout Southeast Asia. Moreover, the various flows of goods and contraband across borders "have become major issues now in Southeast Asia's geopolitics."[24]

In some cases, governments are lax about immigration enforcement because of a desire to encourage tourism and other perceived positive features of cross-border human flows. Cultural practices of turning a blind eye to illegal migration and passport fraud also play a role. The porous border along Thailand's Golok River has been described as a major sieve for Thailand. Moreover, the general welcoming attitude of the Thai people toward strangers "makes the country a perfect terrorist haven."[25] On a more sinister note, government corruption also plays a major role in undermining border security. Bribes and secret arrangements between criminals, terrorists, and government officials allow borders to be crossed with minimal risk. According to a recent survey, corruption is rampant throughout Southeast Asia, with Indonesia, Thailand, the Philippines, and Vietnam receiving special recognition as being among the most corrupt nations in the region.[26]

Whatever the primary causes, the negative consequences of loose border controls have become apparent in recent months. For example, in Cambodia, officials have recently linked their country's porous borders and lax immigration procedures to an influx of Jemaah Islamiya (JI) operatives entering from neighboring countries.[27] Similarly, in late 2003, Philippine officials were reportedly shocked to discover infiltration by JI operatives as well. Philippine authorities revealed that since the mid-1990s, Indonesian JI terrorists began to infiltrate the Philippines to train in camps there. It is for this reason that some have speculated that the Philippines could emerge as a "kind of Afghanistan east."[28] In Thailand, officials have reported that up to 220 terrorists—including operatives from al-Qaeda and Jemaah Islamiya— have passed through that country in 2001 and 2002. Many more may have passed through the kingdom while using forged passports or circumventing immigration controls altogether.[29]

Another troubling factor in Southeast Asia's border security is the existence of large illegal migrant populations throughout the region. These migrant communities reflect economic disparities among countries in the region and the degree to which cross-border migration has become structurally established in the region. Malaysia, for instance, hosts hundreds of thousands of migrant workers from neighboring Indonesia—many of them illegal. One scholar has noted that "the long-term, undocumented migration flow of Indonesians into Malaysia is arguably the second largest flow of illegal immigrants after the movements across the U.S.-Mexico border."[30] This migration phenomenon has generated social and political tensions between the two countries. Most recently, concerns about terrorism in Indonesia have prompted Malaysian officials to scrutinize and restrict migration from Indonesia even further.[31]

Other Southeast Asian countries have experienced chronic illegal migration challenges. In Singapore, illegal immigrants can face up to six months in jail and substantial fines, but such strict laws often fail to act as a deterrent. In the first eight months of 2002, Singapore officials reported that they had arrested more than 9,400 illegal immigrants, and the year before more than 16,000 illegal immigrants were detected.[32] Thailand also hosts illegal migrants from other Southeast Asian countries as well as South Asia. In October 2003, Thai officials repatriated over a thousand Burmese back to their homeland and in another operation forcibly repatriated 921 Cambodian beggars.[33] Illegal migration in Southeast Asia does not necessarily correlate with terrorism, but it does demonstrate the extent of border porosity and loose immigration rules and procedures in the region. It is within this enabling environment that loose networks of terrorists could potentially thrive.

In summary, the tradition of loose border controls and relaxed monitoring has had a long and established history in Southeast Asia, and in many cases this tradition has been viewed as relatively benign (and in some cases economically and culturally beneficial). But in an age of transnational terrorism and crime, many experts and officials in the region now view border security as one of the region's key vulnerabilities. The risk that many Southeast Asian countries face is that porous borders and lax immigration policies may transform the region into fertile grounds for both homegrown and exogenous terrorist groups.

Human Smuggling and Terrorism: An Emerging Nexus?

In August 2001, a migrant smuggling vessel with more than 430 migrants aboard traveling from Indonesia to Australia encountered distress and began to signal an SOS, which was picked up by an Australian Coastwatch flight.[34] The Australians issued a mayday, which was answered by a nearby Norwegian freighter, the *Tampa*. The *Tampa* subsequently came to the ship's rescue and took on the more than 430 migrants. Australia subsequently refused to accept the migrants and insisted that the Norwegian freighter leave Australian waters. The incident generated intense international scrutiny and media coverage; however, it was indicative of a much larger migration—much of it facilitated by migrant smugglers—originating from Central Asia and the Middle East, transiting Southeast Asia, and moving toward Australia.

The *Tampa* incident occurred during a period when Western governments, particularly the United States, were concerned about potential terrorist threats in Southeast Asia. In the summer of 2001, the United States had intelligence suggesting that terrorists were seeking to bomb U.S. embassies and other American targets in Japan, Indonesia, and elsewhere. Consequently, a new worry emerged that the human smuggling crisis involving Australia and Southeast Asia might be linked to increased terrorist threats in the region. In early

September 2001, prior to the attacks in New York and Washington, D.C., a senior U.S. official, Assistant Secretary of State James Kelly, commented that the flow of asylum seekers through Southeast Asia into Australia could potentially open a gateway for terrorists seeking to infiltrate the region.[35]

A few days following Kelly's comments, the September 11 attacks took place in the United States. In the aftermath of these attacks, several Australian politicians began to publicly echo Kelly's concerns. For instance, one Australian legislator stated that "there is a connection between illegals and terrorists and we ought to consider that many of the people that claim to be refugees are people who come from Afghanistan."[36] Later, Australia's prime minister, John Howard, who was facing a tough election battle in November 2001, expressed his concerns that terrorists might be hiding among asylum-seekers.[37] Howard added that Australia's tough stance against refugees was justified in the wake of the September 11 attacks in the United States.[38]

However, Australian officials subsequently admitted that there was little if any evidence linking asylum-seekers to terrorism. Addressing the transfer of more than six hundred asylum-seekers to Nauru, Australian Deputy Prime Minister John Anderson admitted there was no connection between these asylum-seekers and terrorism.[39] Nevertheless, the worry has persisted, not only in Australia, but also in other countries where migrant trafficking syndicates operate. Human smuggling is a growing trade, with profits exceeding $10 billion per year. Moreover, human smugglers have mastered the art of evading immigration controls and providing forged passports—skills ideal for international terrorists.

This of course raises an important and fundamental question: in light of the burgeoning trade in human beings, will terrorist organizations seek to use these pathways to achieve clandestine migration to a target country? Overall, the evidence worldwide is limited, although certain examples do exist. One of these cases occurred in North America in the mid-1990s and involved an official with the Mexican government.

On November 30, 2001, Angel Salvador Molina-Paramo, a former Mexican immigration official, was sentenced by a U.S. federal judge to thirty months in federal prison for his role in a global human smuggling ring spanning several continents. Molina-Paramo's partner and the chief of the smuggling operation was George Tajirian, an Iraqi-born human smuggler accused of trafficking hundreds of illegal immigrants from the Middle East across the U.S.-Mexican border throughout the 1990s. U.S. authorities had arrested Tajirian in 1998 and, following a plea agreement, he was sentenced to thirteen years in U.S. federal prison. Prosecutors alleged that the ring smuggled Palestinian, Jordanian, Syrian, Iraqi, Yemeni, and other illegal immigrants through Mexico to the United States.[40] The smuggling operation "included smuggling stations in Jordan, Syria, Palestine, and Greece; and staging areas in Greece, Thailand, Cuba, Ecuador, and Mexico."[41]

Molina-Paramo was sentenced just weeks after the September 11 terrorist attacks in the United States. As a result, the obvious question that surrounded this case was whether any of the migrants—most of whom were smuggled in between 1996 and 1998—were possibly terrorists. Mr. Tajirian did not appear to be intentionally operating a terrorist-smuggling operation. However, the investigation also revealed that Mr. Tajirian was not particularly fussy about any criminal or terrorist background of his migrant clients. During Tajirian's prosecution, authorities introduced evidence that Tajirian had smuggled into the United States "persons with known ties to subversive or terrorist organizations as well as individuals with known criminal histories."[42] If a migrant had a known criminal background, Mr. Tajirian simply raised the smuggling fees.[43] Overall, U.S. officials believe that Mr. Tajirian and his cohorts smuggled more than one thousand Middle Eastern residents illegally into the United States.[44]

Whether a case similar to the Tajirian case has occurred—or would likely occur—in Southeast Asia remains an open question. Current evidence suggests that transnational terrorists prefer more convenient and direct forms of clandestine international migration, such as relying on a forged passport with an alias. Turning to a smuggling syndicate to achieve clandestine entry into a country might compromise the terrorist organization's secrecy or pose other risks. Terrorists tend to be conservative by nature and prefer tested methods to achieve certain goals.

Nevertheless, the possibility of a convergence between human smuggling and terrorism will remain, particularly if governments crack down hard on alternative methods—such as, for example, eliminating current passport technology in favor of biometric techniques to ascertain a traveler's true identity.[45] If this transition occurs, Southeast Asia will be particularly vulnerable due to the fact that the region is a critical crossroads in the human smuggling trade emanating from multiple sources, including China, South Asia, and the Middle East.

In the Chinese context, criminal gangs often use Thailand and Cambodia as transit points to obtain forged passports and visas.[46] Migrants are often kept in "safe houses" in various cities in Southeast Asia, such as Bangkok, prior to onward travel to Europe or North America. In addition to human smuggling of Chinese, Southeast Asia is also a transit region for migrants from the Middle East, many of whom have been smuggled to Australia since the late 1990s. According to one law enforcement assessment, the smuggling "organization appears like a chain, with the first links in Iraq and Syria, the next links in Pakistan and Bangkok, and the final link in Jakarta."[47]

The active human smuggling trade in Southeast Asia once again demonstrates the region's persistent problem of porous borders and its vulnerability to illegal migrants—including criminals and terrorists. Human smuggling syndicates have found an enabling environment in Southeast Asia—lax immigration procedures, corrupt government officials, and a robust forged passport industry—that has allowed the trafficking of people to persist. Similarly, transnational terrorists benefit from that same environment, which suggests that Southeast Asia will most likely provide a hospitable environment for terrorism for many years to come.

International "Watch Lists" and Intelligence-Sharing: An Alternative Line of Defense?

As Southeast Asian countries have acknowledged the threat posed by terrorism, many have called for greater reliance on intelligence-sharing and more dependable "watch lists," which are often used at border stations (including international airports) to screen names against lists of known or suspected criminals and terrorists. A 2002 meeting of regional defense ministers held in Singapore urged that a shared intelligence database between neighboring countries be created to deter terrorism. At the same meeting, the Philippine defense minister called for a shared intelligence database to be used throughout Southeast Asia to help track terrorists.[48] Recent initiatives, such as beefing up the ASEANPOL database, suggest that intelligence-sharing has increased in the region to confront terrorism and other transnational threats.

But the most sophisticated computerized databases and watch lists are not necessarily magical solutions. For example, terrorists have been known to evade such lists by slightly changing the spelling of their names. Mir Aimal Kansi, a Pakistani-born man who murdered two CIA employees in 1993, was able evade a terrorism watch list by entering the United States with a name that had one letter's difference in spelling.[49] But the greater challenge is not the database itself, but rather the culture of information compartmentalization, interagency rivalry within governments, or intergovernmental suspicions that thwart effective information-sharing.

Few would deny that prior to September 11, 2001, the United States maintained one of the most sophisticated criminal and terrorist databases in the world. Yet this sophisticated database could not thwart the terrorist attacks that eventually occurred. In January 2000, for example, Khalid al-Mihdhar and Nawaf al-Hazmi, two of the nineteen men who participated in the September 11 plot, attended a meeting in Malaysia held in a condominium owned by Yazid Sufaat. Agents of the U.S. CIA were aware of this meeting and subsequently learned significant details about the immigration status—vis-à-vis the

United States—of the two men. Another U.S. intelligence office, the National Security Agency, knew that at least one of the men, al-Hazmi, was associated with the al-Qaeda network. Several days after the meeting, Nawaf al-Hazmi entered the United States via Los Angeles International Airport. He was able to enter the United States unhindered because the CIA had not entered key information into the U.S. State Department's electronic watch list.[50]

On October 12, 2000, two men conducted a suicide strike on the USS *Cole*, a U.S. Navy destroyer that was refueling in Aden, Yemen. As a result of the investigation into that incident, the Federal Bureau of Investigation learned that an individual linked to the *Cole* bombing was also present at the January 2000 meeting in Malaysia. This prompted CIA investigators to reexamine the Malaysia meeting and determine its significance. By January 2001 the CIA had information linking Khalid al-Mihdhar and Nawaf al-Hazmi to al-Qaeda and other individuals responsible for the USS *Cole* bombing. Yet, even with that information, the CIA still did not enter the information into the State Department's watch list database. One of the individuals, al-Mihdhar, was able to make additional overseas trips and apply for a new visa to the United States using a different passport than the one he had used to enter the United States on January 15, 2000.

On August 23, 2001—only weeks away from September 11—the Central Intelligence Agency sent an urgent cable to the U.S. State Department requesting that Khalid al-Mihdhar and Nawaf al-Hazmi, along with several other individuals, be placed on the watch-list immediately "due to their confirmed links to Egyptian Islamic Jihad operatives and suspicious activities while traveling in East Asia."[51] However the two individuals were already in the United States. This prompted an urgent search at major hotels in New York and Los Angeles. But it was too late. On September 11, Khalid al-Mihdhar and Nawaf al-Hazmi hijacked American Airlines Flight 77, which later crashed into the Pentagon.

The case of Khalid al-Mihdhar and Nawaf al-Hazmi illustrates the strengths and weaknesses of electronic databases used by governments around the world. In this case, the watch list is known in the U.S. government as CLASS, or Consular Lookout and Support System, which was created in 1994 to prevent visas from being issued to inadmissible foreign nationals. CLASS contains a subdatabase known as TIPOFF, which is an "intelligence database that receives information on suspected terrorists from law enforcement, intelligence, and other agencies."[52] TIPOFF contains 48,000 records of known or suspected terrorists.[53] Prior to September 11, 2001, CLASS contained sensitive information on more than 6.1 million individuals. Information that might trigger a CLASS alert included (1) previous visa refusal; (2) previous immigration violation; (3) lost or stolen passport or visa information; and (4) evidence of terrorism or terrorist affiliation. Apart from TIPOFF sources, information from CLASS is derived from a variety of U.S. intelligence and law enforcement agencies.

In the case of the two American Airlines Flight 77 hijackers, the CLASS database may have prevented the subsequent terrorist attacks. For various unknown policy or bureaucratic reasons, however, CIA officials did not take advantage of its potential. In other instances, though, reliance on electronic databases may result in a false sense of security. For instance, the CLASS database and other similar databases used by governments around the world are subject to technical limitations and failings. U.S. officials admit that the CLASS database suffers because of "system idiosyncrasies, inaccurate applicant information on travel documents, and Arabic naming customs and patterns."[54] Incomplete or inaccurate entries into the database would thus allow nondeserving applicants to obtain a visa. In the case of Arabic names, the report noted that "citizens of Arab countries have the common practice of using four or five official names, with some names being extremely common."[55]

In some cases, incomplete intelligence reports result in inaccurate name entries, a problem that could result in innocent applicants being erroneously flagged as having potential terrorist ties. In Cairo, for instance, U.S. consular officials have reported receiving "hits" (possible name matches) for up to 75 percent of all visa applicants.[56] During the 2003–4 Christmas–New Year holiday period in the United States, American officials halted several international flights to the United States because of false "hits" on its database. One of the suspected names that drew U.S. scrutiny turned out to be a five-year-old boy who had a name similar to that of a suspected Tunisian terrorist; another name belonged to an elderly Chinese woman, and a third suspect turned out to be a Welsh insurance agent.[57] Clearly, these examples demonstrate that technical databases can be no substitute for the more arduous process of visa interviews and other background inquiries.

In Southeast Asia, reliance on databases tends to be inconsistent throughout the region. The more developed countries, such as Singapore, regularly rely on such systems. But other countries have been slower to adopt modern technologies for economic or political reasons. In a recent case, Thai officials ran old records through a new database, which contained new intelligence, and discovered that numerous terrorists had arrived in the country. One suspects that if Thailand had earlier had access to a reliable database system, the country might have become less hospitable to terrorists than has been the case during the past five years. But this again raises another issue. While databases potentially are useful, they are most likely going to be used in wealthier Southeast Asian countries. To evade this screening, terrorists may gravitate to poorer countries, or travel to less common international gateway cities where databases or computer technology are less available. Yet despite these limitations, implementation of reliable database systems—which would ideally include intelligence gained from regionwide intelligence-sharing—would assist Southeast Asian countries in detecting and deterring potential terrorists. At the very least, it would constrain terrorists' mobility and limit their geographic range of operations.

Conclusion

Southeast Asia's border security challenge is potentially a major barrier in the combat against transnational terrorism. Porous borders, lax immigration procedures, and a vibrant forged passport industry are creating an enabling environment for transnational terrorism and crime. Southeast Asian governments have immense challenges ahead in addressing these vulnerabilities. They must balance the interests of "positive" globalization—international travel, commerce, and tourism—with the need to prevent "negative" globalization in the form of terrorism or crime.

One way that governments will seek to meet this challenge is to rely increasingly on technology, including databases and possible biometric solutions. Nevertheless, the human element will remain critical if countries are going to be successful. It was the human element—specifically a customs inspector named Diana Dean—that led to the interception of would-be terrorist Ahmed Ressam in December 1999. In Southeast Asia, the question remains whether countries are willing to seriously confront the border security challenge. Until that time, terrorists will find Southeast Asia a fertile region for cultivating their ideologies, conducting their training, and, ultimately, launching their attacks.

Notes

The views in this chapter are the author's own and do not reflect the opinions or positions of the U.S. government or U.S. Department of Defense.

1. Rohan Gunaratna, "Al-Qaeda's Operational Ties with Allied Groups," *Jane's Intelligence Review* (February 1, 2003).

2. Anthony Davis, "Southeast Asia Fears New Terrorist Attacks," *Jane's Intelligence Review,* November 1, 2003 (Internet Edition).

3. "Hambali was Targeting Embassies, Planes, and Tourist Spots: Thai Source," Agence France-Presse, September 21, 2003.

4. Eric Tagliacozzo, "Border Permeability and the State in Southeast Asia: Contraband and Regional Security," *Contemporary Southeast Asia* 23, no. 2 (August 1, 2001): 254.

5. Yogita Tahil Ramani, "Govt Acts to Cope with Terrorism," *Jakarta Post,* January 23, 2002.

6. Philip Shishkin, "Attack on America: Forging Travel Papers Is Growing Industry—Investigators Try to Trace Fake Passports," *Wall Street Journal,* October 8, 2001.

7. Paul J. Smith, "Transnational Terrorism and the al Qaeda Model: Confronting New Realities," *Parameters* (U.S. Army War College Quarterly) 32, no. 2 (Summer 2002): 38–39.

8. Ed Blanche, "Ahmad Massood's Assassination Remains a Mystery," *Middle East,* October 2002.

9. Jeff Goodell, "How to Fake a Passport," *New York Times,* February 10, 2002, p. 44.

10. Ibid.

11. Ed Blanche, "Top al-Qaeda Official Detained in Pakistan," *Jane's Intelligence Review* (May 1, 2002).

12. Ed Blanche, "The Egyptians Around Bin Laden," *Jane's Intelligence Review* (December 1, 2001).

13. Ed Blanche, "Ayman al-Zawahiri: Attention Turns to the Other Prime Suspect," *Jane's Intelligence Review* (November 1, 2001).

14. Eric Watkins, "Fitting the Bill: The Yemeni Connection," *Wall Street Journal,* September 24, 2001.

15. Ibid.

16. Takis Michas, "How the PKK Took an Embassy," *Wall Street Journal,* March 10, 1999.

17. Stewart Bell, "Passport Office Takes Blame in Ressam Case," *National Post* (Canada), December 4, 2003, p. A1.

18. Author's interview in 2001 with official of the U.S. Immigration and Naturalization Service.

19. "Thai Police Arrest 29 Chinese in Smuggling Ring," Associated Press Worldstream, May 27, 1999.

20. "Tackling Transnational Crime," *Bangkok Post,* August 13, 2000.

21. "Over 1,700 Fake Passports, Documents Found in Jan.-June Period," Japan Economic Newswire, October 8, 2003.

22. Rajiv Chandrasekaran, "Al Qaeda Feared to Be Lurking in Indonesia," *Washington Post,* January 11, 2002, p. A01.

23. Ellen Nakashima, "Frontier Exploited by Terrorists," *Gazette* (Montreal, Quebec), January 28, 2003, p. A18.

24. Eric Tagliacozzo, "Border Permeability and the State in Southeast Asia: Contraband and Regional Security," *Contemporary Southeast Asia* 23, no. 2 (August 1, 2001): 254.

25. Uamdao Noikorn, "River Gives Terrorist Access to Thailand," Associated Press Online, September 24, 2003.

26. Tobias Nischalke, "US Businesses Call for Anti-Corruption Measures by ASEAN," *World Markets Analysis,* November 10, 2002; "China: Corruption—What's It Worth?" *EIU Business China,* May 27, 2002; "Vietnam Risk: Government Effectiveness Risk," *EIU RiskWire,* August 7, 2003.

27. Rafael D. Frankel, "Arrests Anger Cambodian Muslims," *Boston Globe,* July 13, 2003, p. A13.

28. Alan Sipress and Ellen Nakashima, "Al Qaeda Affiliate Training Indonesians on Philippine Island," *Washington Post,* November 17, 2003, p. A18.

29. "Key Terrorists Passing Through Kingdom," *The Nation* (Thailand), November 26, 2003.

30. Joseph Liow, "Malaysia's Illegal Indonesian Migrant Labor Problem: In Search of Solutions," *Contemporary Southeast Asia* 25, no. 1 (April 1, 2003): 44.

31. Ibid.

32. "SIR Foils 2 Attempts by Illegal Immigrants to Enter Singapore," *Channel NewsAsia,* December 18, 2002.

33. "Thailand Expels 1,000 Illegal Migrants, Sending Them Back to Myanmar," Agence France-Presse, October 5, 2003.

34. Robert Garran and Vanda Carson, "Refugees Trapped at Sea . . ." *The Australian,* August 28, 2001, p. 1.

35. Daniel Cooney, "Senior US Official Warns of Terrorist Threat Due to Increased Flow of Refugees," Associated Press Worldstream, September 1, 2001.

36. "NSW: Terrorists Could Be Coming to Australia—MP," AAP Newsfeed, September 19, 2001.

37. Richard C. Paddock, "Australia Reelected Premier Who Kept Refugees at Bay," *Los Angeles Times,* November 11, 2001, p. A1.

38. "Australia: Boat People Could Be Terrorists, PM says," *Ottawa Citizen,* November 7, 2001, p. A14.

39. "Fed: No Evidence Terrorists Among Boatpeople: Anderson," AAP Newsfeed, September 23, 2001.

40. Smith, "Transnational Terrorism and the al Qaeda Model," p. 40.

41. *Former Mexican Immigration Official Sentenced to Federal Prison for Role in Alien Smuggling Organization,* U.S. Attorney's Office—Western District of Texas— Press Release. Accessed from the Internet on January 14, 2002, at http:// www.usdoj.gov/usao/txw/Molina.htm.

42. Ibid.

43. Sam Dillon, "Iraqi Accused of Smuggling Hundreds in Mideast to U.S.," *New York Times,* October 26, 2001, p. A18.

44. Ibid.

45. Biometrics refers to the use of immutable characteristics of a human being— such as fingerprints, DNA, or retina patterns—to establish true identity.

46. Hamish McCardle, "Human Trafficking Routes Through the Asia-Pacific Region," prepared for the CSCAP Working Group on Maritime Cooperation and Transnational Crime, Sydney, Australia, November 1999, p. 10.

47. Ibid., p. 22.

48. Alexa Olesen, "Southeast Asia Defense Ministers Call for Cooperation and Aid in Fight Against Terror," Associated Press, June 1, 2002.

49. Donna Howell, "New Technology Streamlines Name Game," *Investor's Business Daily,* December 4, 2003, p. A04.

50. Eleanor Hill, Staff Director, Joint Inquiry Staff, *The Intelligence Community's Knowledge of the September 11 Hijackers Prior to September 11, 2001,* September 20, 2002, available at http://www.fas.org/irp/congress/2002_hr/092002hill.html.

51. Ibid.

52. Ibid.

53. *Border Security: Visa Process Should Be Strengthened as an Antiterrorism Tool,* General Accounting Office, Washington DC, Report GAO-03-132NI, p. 11.

54. Ibid., p. 26.

55. Ibid., p. 27.

56. Ibid., p. 34.

57. Dana Priest and Sara Kehaulani Goo, "Three Air Routes Focus of Scrutiny; Al Qaeda Suspects Sought," *Washington Post,* January 4, 2004, p. A01.

12

Media, Information Revolution, and Terrorism in Southeast Asia

Shyam Tekwani

Introduction

Throughout the ages, terrorists have relied on various forms of media as a means of pursuing their particular political or military goals. In the current era, modern media technology, communications satellites, and the rapid spread of television have had a marked effect in increasing the publicity potential of terrorism.[1] The globalization of mass media and the emergence of new media and communication technologies (NMCTs) such as the Internet and cellular phones have intensified and extended the use of contemporary tools of communication by terrorists.

The Internet in particular has emerged as a tool, a weapon, and even a potential target. While the Assassin sect of Shia Islam—one of the precursors to modern terrorism—which was active in the Muslim world in the Middle Ages, relied upon word of mouth in the mosques and marketplaces to relay news of their attacks, today's terrorists turn to advanced computer technologies to achieve the same goal.[2] For instance, a contemporary Palestinian-Islamic terrorist group, the Popular Front for the Liberation of Palestine (PFLP), posted a note on its Web site claiming responsibility for the assassination of Israeli tourism minister Rehavam Zeevi in October 2001.

Across the globe, extremists of all kinds are merging onto the "information highway" to communicate, raise funds, recruit, and spread propaganda. Middle Eastern groups such as Hamas, the Liberation Tigers of Tamil Eelam (LTTE) in South Asia, and the globally networked al-Qaeda are consummate masters of media technology, both new and old, using it not only to communicate, but also to plan and carry out attacks on potential targets. While the use of these technologies varies according to the sociopolitical, cultural, and ideological contexts within which the group emerges and operates, there is ample evidence to support the growing belief that cyberspace is emerging as a new theater of war.[3]

Reliance on information technologies is also occurring among terrorist groups operating in Southeast Asia. In addition to creating their own Web sites, groups such as the Moro Islamic Liberation Front (MILF), Moro National Liberation Front (MNLF), and Abu Sayyaf Group (ASG) are using technologies such as electronic mail, mobile phones, SMS (short messaging service), and radio and video technology to communicate with each other and to disseminate their message to the general public.

This chapter will first examine the role of media technologies in the spread of terrorism and provide a global perspective on the changes brought about in the tactics and strategies of terrorist organizations by the information revolution. It will also examine whether and how the new media technologies, especially the Internet, are enabling terrorists to form transnational networks of terror, and how these technologies are impacting the pursuit of their ideological and strategic objectives.

Finally, the chapter will closely examine four terrorist or militant groups in Southeast Asia—Jemaah Islamiya (JI), the Moro Islamic Liberation Front, al Qaeda and the Abu Sayyaf Group—and examine their use of communication technologies and situate them in the global context.

The Media and Terrorism

Previous research examining the relationship between media and terrorism has often been colored by trite and somewhat superficial observations such as "publicity is the oxygen of terrorism."[4] Walter Laqueur said famously that the "terrorist act by itself is nothing, publicity is all," and referred to the media as the "terrorists' best friends."[5] However one views the role of the mass media in the propagation of terrorist acts, it is an established fact that publicity is a central goal of terrorists. Bruce Hoffman describes terrorism as "a violent act that is conceived specifically to attract attention and then, through the publicity it generates, to communicate a message."[6]

Throughout history, terrorists have progressed in their use of communication techniques, from relying in earlier times on very basic word-of-mouth accounts to more recently turning to print media, radio, and television to propagate their particular political messages. The advent of television has particularly enhanced the propaganda potential of terrorist acts. In earlier days, terrorists used press interviews, press releases, and printed statements and photographs to communicate with the media and through them to a wider audience. With the rise of television, terrorist groups have been able to use video recorders to report on the condition of hostages; alternatively, they sometimes have used hostages as spokespersons to directly address live television audiences.[7]

In recent years, new media technologies such as satellite phones, mobile phones, and the Internet have emerged as new and more potent communication tools. The biggest difference between these and any previous advances in technology is that, for the first time, terrorists do not have to depend solely on others to carry their messages across the world. Using the Internet, they can put their own "spin"—or interpretation—on events and use their own videos and audiotapes to augment their version of events. Their Web sites on the Internet are a permanent archive for their ideologies and propaganda, and form a virtual library that can be accessed by supporters, dispersed members, journalists, and the general public.

Apart from generating publicity, terrorists often have numerous short- and long-term tactical and military goals. For example, they may seek to free prisoners or exact revenge against enemies or simply create chaos and generate fear.[8] While such short-term goals may be realized with a single act of terror, long-term goals—such as creating an independent state for a particular ethnic or religious group—require a more sustained campaign on several fronts. Paul Wilkinson notes that while terrorists have rarely succeeded in their long-term goals to capture political power or bring about the fall of governments they oppose, they have been far more successful in generating publicity for a particular cause and relaying the terrorist threat to an ever-widening audience.[9]

Wilkinson argues that when one says *terrorism* in a democratic society, one is typically referring to *media*. He further argues that "terrorism by its very nature is a psychological weapon which depends upon communicating a threat to the wider society."[10] This is why terrorism and the media are enveloped within a symbiotic relationship, and it is also why the media and new media technologies are a critical part of terrorist strategy.[11] According to Wilkinson, terrorists use mass media (such as television and radio) to accomplish four key objectives.

First, these technologies allow terrorists to convey the fact that the terrorist deed occurred and thus, in turn, this allows fear to be spread among target groups (and the larger surrounding population). Second, mass media allow terrorists to publicize their cause and emphasize the righteousness of their cause. Third, the media allow terrorists to frustrate and disrupt government responses, for example, by displaying the government's weakness and by suggesting that government responses against terrorism are excessive, inherently tyrannical, and counterproductive. Fourth, the mass media allow terrorists to mobilize, incite, and boost their constituency of actual and potential supporters and in so doing to increase recruitment, raise more funds, and inspire further attacks.[12]

In addition to traditional mass media, terrorists are also relying on new media and communication technologies such as the Internet and satellite telephones to achieve these objectives as well. Specifically, such technologies facilitate terrorism by allowing dispersed groups and nodes of large networked groups to stay in touch cheaply and consistently. Militant groups in the Philippines are known for their extensive use of texting.[13] Osama bin Laden is known to have invested huge sums in computers and satellite communications in his Afghanistan hideouts.[14] In this era of transnational terrorist networks, groups such as al-Qaeda and Hamas rely on these technologies to communicate with each other.

New media technologies also play a role in nonoperational international networking. Diaspora groups settled outside their homelands are often involved in the political events of their home country.[15] They are also known to be extensive users of the Internet, logging on to keep abreast of news from home, and they are increasingly becoming involved in political and social movements online.[16] A recent study found that Asian-Americans are more likely to use the Internet on a daily basis than white, black, or Hispanic Americans.[17] Asians living overseas use the Internet to keep abreast of news from home and to network with others from their community. Diaspora groups may also use the Internet to support terrorist movements by providing political support in the form of propaganda and by seeking to influence international public opinion. They also help raise funds and offer logistical support to militants.[18]

A third role for new media technologies involves agenda-setting for terrorist groups. The Internet allows terrorists to frame their actions and their ideologies any way they wish, without the intervention of government or media censors. This last point is perhaps the single most important advantage of the Internet over other media technologies, new and old. Through their Web sites, terrorist groups can now portray their ideologies and their actions to suit their needs and the political and social environment they function in. The world after 9/11 has seen a tremendous hardening of international attitudes toward terrorists. Governments now have the political and economic support to go after and disrupt terrorists and their operations. Despite the immense publicity that terrorism and its perpetrators receive from the media, it is debatable whether such coverage encourages a more favorable opinion of terrorists or terrorism in the public mind. A RAND study that examined how public opinion is affected by terrorist acts and public perceptions of terrorists and their deeds found that public approval for terrorists was almost nil.[19]

The Internet allows terrorists to tailor messages to specific audiences. The Islamic Jihad Web site, for instance, is available in English and in Arabic. The English site makes no mention of Islamic Jihad's latest bloody exploits. But the Arabic site reproduces posters that praise martyrs, or *shahids,* who died while conducting attacks on Israelis. It lists the names of about sixty martyrs who have died for the Islamic Jihad since the early 1990s and provides their histories.[20] Many terrorist Web sites are established by supporters or often as a front or a "political wing" of the rebel movement as distinct from a military wing, keeping alive the rhetoric of the "purity of the cause."

New Media and Communication Technology: Implications for Terrorism

Increasingly, new media and communication technologies (NMCTs) are enabling terrorists to sustain longer campaigns on several fronts by acting as publicity force multipliers, thereby bringing greater force to bear upon the governments they oppose in the form of international media attention and the resulting pressure generated by international and domestic public opinion. These technologies are also strengthening terrorist organizations by speeding up their internal communication networks and facilitating covert planning operations. The Internet in particular, unlike previous developments in communication technology, is unrestricted by geographical, cultural, and economic boundaries, thus magnifying its potential reach. The difficulty in imposing controls on Internet communications is compounded by the easy access—anyone with a computer or access to an Internet service provider has a forum that transcends borders. And due to the way in which information searching is conducted—through the use of keywords, population targeting, and newsgroups—the message can be focused to reach particular elements of the population.

A search using the keywords Moro Liberation, for instance, will uncover not only the Moro Islamic Liberation Front (MILF) and Moro National Liberation Front (MNLF) Web sites, but will also highlight links to a variety of Islamic online journals and sites that carry interviews with MILF or MNLF leaders or reports on the Moro fight for independence. Such search results would also provide links to information on the history of Moro culture as well as endless archives and news stories on the two groups' militant activities. Such a search will also show links to other "liberation struggles" and other Islamic radical movements, from al-Maunah, a radical cult in Malaysia, to the Hizbollah in Lebanon. This *newsgrouping* in the media offers a new capability to terrorists, allowing them to target their message to different demographic sectors across a global scale in a manner similar to commercial advertisers.

Convergence, the new buzzword in the field of communications technology, further compounds the potential of NMCTs. The linking of telephone, videophone, and TV and radio to the Internet is creating a technologically driven information and communication environment that is bound to affect the way almost every group in society functions. Terrorists are no exception. NMCTs bring a number of advantages for terrorist groups. First, they are inexpensive and easy to use. And they are freely available, even in the developing world. They facilitate immediate point-to-point communication. They enable groups functioning in isolated or inaccessible bases (Osama bin Laden in Afghanistan, Prabhakaran in the jungles of Vanni, for instance) to keep in touch with their cells, members, and supporters in distant locations, enabling increased interconnectivity and networking. Hamas uses the Internet to share operational information[21] and e-mails to coordinate activities across Gaza, the West Bank, and Lebanon.[22]

NMCTs act as a force multiplier by enhancing power and enabling extremists to "punch above their weight."[23] The audio- and videotapes released to TV and radio channels by Osama bin Laden and Saddam Hussein—prior to his capture—are broadcast around the world by global TV networks. These tapes, according to the *New York Times,* then "assume some of the power of the media they use, creating the appearance of a potent force that can counter American military might."[24] In the current media-saturated environment, this impression of force is further amplified through all the media channels it travels through, from TV and radio to print and the Internet.

NMCTs also allow terrorist groups to operate more effectively and more covertly. Short messaging service (SMS), for instance, helps terrorist groups communicate with media or with government agencies, as in the case of Abu Sayyaf, and with each other, as Islamic groups operating in Kashmir have demonstrated.[25] Moreover, this communication can take place without the terrorists being forced to disclose their particular location. Authorities have found that SMS messages pose a greater potential danger because, unlike e-mails or cell and satellite phones, they are untraceable and leave no record. Cell phones and satellite phones can be tapped and voices recorded and identified, but SMS messages—and their originators—are much more difficult to track down.[26]

NMCTs also empower terrorists by allowing them to reach their target audience when other media outlets are denied to them because of censorship or other reasons. The Internet and new communication technologies have helped level the playing field between small groups of terrorists and the monolithic states they oppose. At the height of the civil war in Sri Lanka, when all media including the foreign press were kept out of the conflict zone by the Sri Lankan army, the LTTE used its Web presence to broadcast graphic images of Tamil victims of the army campaign. LTTE supporters overseas updated the Web sites daily with news reports from the front.

Information Communication Technologies (ICTs) and the Enabling of Networks

Like the large numbers of private corporations that have embraced information technology (IT) to operate more efficiently and with greater flexibility, terrorists are harnessing the power of IT to enable new operational doctrines and forms of organization. And just as companies in the private sector are forming alliance networks to provide complex services to customers, so too are terrorist groups "disaggregating" from hierarchical bureaucracies and moving to flatter, more decentralized, and often changing webs of groups united by a common goal.[27]

As terrorism, like the Internet, becomes increasingly transnational, terrorist groups are adopting a more networked form of organization. With terrorism increasingly becoming the fiefdom of smaller substate groups, networking and interconnectivity become necessary to find allies, recruits, and funds as well as to "effect command and control."[28] The transition to the transnational in the practice of terrorism coincides with the deepening impact of the information revolution. Many experts now concede that the "rise of networks means that power is migrating to nonstate actors who are able to master the network form" more easily than their hierarchical opponents.[29]

The literature on networks and netwars frequently cites the example of Hamas to illustrate the point that the new, networked nature of terrorism is exemplified by groups organized in loosely interconnected cells that have no central command hierarchy. Hamas is also networked to other terrorist groups and nonstate organizations as well as state sponsors such as Iran and Syria.[30] Such networked forms of organization are increasingly seen in Southeast Asian groups such as the Abu Sayyaf, the MILF, and Jemaah Islamiya, which have extensive transnational networks with support groups stretching from the Middle East to South and Southeast Asia (particularly Malaysia, Thailand, and Singapore). These groups are also known to have linkages with each other and to al-Qaeda.

As evidence to the rising importance of networking technology in terrorist operations, authorities in Southeast Asia routinely find computers and diskettes on raids on terrorist hideouts across Asia, from Ramzi Yousef's Manila lair to LTTE hideouts and JI cells in Singapore. The same is true outside of Asia. When the Peruvian group Tupac Amaru seized the Japanese embassy in Lima, a Web site in Canada was claiming victory for the revolutionaries only fifteen minutes after the attack. This "synchronization" and use of the Internet to put their own version of the event and its significance across to an international audience—even as events are still unfolding at the scene of the attack—reflects a high level of sophistication in computer use and is an indicator that NMCTs are an important component in terrorist attacks.[31]

The information revolution, in combination with other factors such as economic globalization, cheaper international travel, and increased migration, has clearly contributed to the ability of terrorist groups in the region to network with others of their ilk to form transnational networks that cooperate in disseminating propaganda and fund-raising and recruitment. It has also greatly enhanced the ability of terrorists to plan and execute operations across international borders with greater ease. Terrorism in fact is one of the paradoxes of globalization.[32] Even as militant groups decry globalization and what they perceive as the "Americanization" of the world, they are adapting the very symbols and tools of globalization to facilitate their resistance to it.

Ramzi Ahmed Yousef, the 1993 WTC bombing mastermind who subsequently planned the aborted Operation Bojinka plot to bomb eleven U.S. airliners in Asia, exemplifies the "globalized terrorist."[33] Born in Kuwait of Pakistani and Palestinian parents, educated in computer technology in the United Kingdom, and trained in terrorism in Afghanistan, Yousef came to the United States to organize the 1993 bombing of the World Trade Center. He then emerged in Manila, where he was discovered by authorities while attempting to organize and execute Operation Bojinka. Finally the authorities arrested him in Pakistan, where he was planning more terrorist attacks in Asia. An international traveler trained in computers and engineering, Yousef used a laptop computer for his work. He had utilized sophisticated encryption algorithms to protect the data on his computer from being deciphered by law enforcement in the event of capture. When his Toshiba laptop was seized in a raid in the Philippines, the FBI called in a forensics expert from Microsoft to crack his codes.[34] As more educated and technologically savvy youth like Yousef are drawn to the ranks of religious fundamentalist groups, it is inevitable that they will bring to their practice the latest in technological advances.[35]

Terrorism in Southeast Asia and New Media and Communication Technologies

Recent events in international terrorism such as the Bali bombing, the foiled JI plot in Singapore, and revelations about the networked presence of al-Qaeda in the region and its emerging links to regional terrorist groups have shifted the focus of international attention to Southeast Asia. Terrorism in the region is not a new phenomenon, although there has been a significant spurt in terrorist activity in the region in recent times. What is new is the global networking of terrorist groups, aided by modern communications and transportation technologies, that enables Southeast Asian Islamic terrorism to connect local grievances with the globally networked al-Qaeda.[36]

Southeast Asia is a region with one of the largest concentrations of Muslims in the world, with 200 million Muslims in Indonesia alone. Muslims are also a majority in Malaysia and form important minority groups in Thailand and the Philippines. This is important because many of the terrorists and militant groups in the region, including the three selected for this paper, are associated with radical Islamic ideologies. The deterioration of economic and social conditions after the economic crisis in Southeast Asia and the political crises in Indonesia since the downfall of former President Suharto have contributed to an environment favorable to radical groups. These radical groups are believed to have linkages with each other and with like-minded groups in Afghanistan and the Middle East.

Although globalization has intensified the linkages between these various groups (described extensively in previous chapters), other factors have also played a major role. These include the lax intelligence and enforcement environment in some Southeast Asian countries, the easy availability of weapons that are traded freely and cheaply, and the social, religious, and economic linkages with the Middle East. Radical Islam moved in quickly to take advantage of the genuine and perceived grievances of minority Muslims, with cash inflows from philanthropic Gulf institutions flowing inward to fund fundamentalist schools and organizations.

Perhaps one of the most important enabling factors, however, has been the increased reliance on communication technologies among these groups. The Internet and other new media technologies have played an active role in the politics of the region for some time now. The Internet gave students and other dissidents in Indonesia unprecedented freedom of speech, enabling them to foment an upsurge in prodemocratic activity that led to the overthrow of Indonesian President Suharto during the uprising of May 1998. East Timor's National Council for Maubere Resistance, the main body of resistance to Indonesian rule, has used for many years a Web site (http://www.uc.pt/Timor/TimorNet.html) hosted on a server at Portugal's University of Coimbra to disseminate information on the movement. The OPM or the Free West Papua Movement (Organizasi Papua Merdeka), agitating for the separation of the west half of the island of Papua from Indonesia, uses its Web site (http://www.converge.org.nz/wpapua) hosted from New Zealand for its propaganda purposes. The BFM or the Bougainville Freedom Movement, of the Bougainville Revolutionary Army has been fighting the Papua New Guinea government for a separate homeland. The Republic of Bougainville's Web site http://www.magna.com.au/~sashab/BFM.htm hosted from Sydney mobilizes support from sympathizers all over the world. The Free Burma campaign by overseas opponents of the military junta in Burma is frequently cited in the literature on new media use by NGOs and grassroots activists.[37] More recently, SMS texting in the Philippines is believed to have played a significant role in mobilizing the mass demonstrations that brought down the government of former President Estrada.

In a parallel development, regional terrorist groups are also taking up the new tools available to them. Although Southeast Asian Islamic terrorist groups, unlike their counterparts in South Asia and the Middle East, have been relatively slower to adapt to the new technologies, most of the groups already have Web sites and are known to be equipped with the latest in communication technologies from satellite technology to mobiles (cellular telephones) and laptops, using them to network with al-Qaeda and other smaller regional groups. Of the groups examined for this paper, the Philippine groups have the most prominent Web presence. MILF Web sites in particular (there are more than one, and many are interlinked to other general sites on the Bangsamoro people and their culture) have extensive video and audio links as well photographs and maps of the Moro homeland that they hope to transform into an independent state. The use of NMCTs in the Southeast Asian region is more apparent in intragroup communication, as seen in the extensive use of SMS by the Abu Sayyaf. Observers in the Philippines will often quip that it is a matter of time before the Abu Sayyaf begins sending its ransom notes via SMS.[38]

The next section looks at four groups in the region within the context of their reliance on NMCTs.

Abu Sayyaf Group

Abu Sayyaf is the smaller of the Islamist groups fighting to establish an Iranian-style Islamic state in Mindanao, an island in the southern Philippines. The Abu Sayyaf Group, whose name means "Bearer of the Sword," split from the Moro National Liberation Front (MNLF) in 1991. Unlike some other groups in the Philippines, Abu Sayyaf does not maintain a Web site currently, but it is known for its use of relatively older technologies such as the videotape and newer ones such as the mobile phone. In the past Abu Sayyaf has released videos of its training footage to the media as propaganda and as an indicator of its potential and intent. More recently in the Philippines, authorities released to the media videotapes made by Abu Sayyaf showing its members beheading kidnap victims. The government's stated intent was to depict the militants as brutal and merciless. The graphic videos were broadcast by more than one local network, and reports of the video and responses to the government's decision to make them public played in the media for weeks and were even reported on international networks such as the BBC, ABC, and CNN, and broadcast on several online sites as well. The resultant publicity bought the group more airtime and column width than many of its recent acts of violence.

In the country where SMS texting made headlines as an instrument of the People Power movement that ousted former President Joseph Estrada in 1999, it is to be expected that even terrorists in that country would communicate via SMS.[39] Abu Sayyaf operatives have been quick to appropriate the technology for their less-than-democratic purposes. According to the Philippine news media, Abu Sayyaf is extremely savvy about communications technology, making lucrative use of mobile phones and the Internet for text messaging and e-mail. Aside from utilizing mobile phones to contact relatives and negotiators, Abu Sayyaf is also reportedly SMS texting the relatives of their kidnap victims in Manila.[40]

MILF/MNLF

The Moro insurgency dates back to the sixteenth century, when the Moros led the opposition to Spanish rule in the Philippines. The movement strengthened during the American occupation and continues to the present day. The MILF was founded in 1984 with the stated goal of independence for Filipino Muslims and the creation of an Islamic state implementing traditional Sharia (Islamic) law. The MILF represents a significant military force estimated at around 8,000 soldiers by the Philippine government (although the figures vary wildly; with the MILF claiming a strength of 120,000 and the U.S. government putting the figure at 40,000).[41] MILF is a splinter faction of the Moro National Liberation Front (MNLF), which had led a struggle for autonomy for Muslim areas of the southern Philippines from 1972.

The MILF is the most prominent among the Southeast Asian groups on the Internet. It has several Web sites disseminating propaganda and espousing the Moro cause. The sites include the official Web site morojihad.com (http://morojihad.stcom.net/tell.html) that by its very title clearly espouses its religious and separatist agenda. This site has all the features of an active

Web community, with several online forums, an e-mail account facility, and a chat room, all of which have the potential to be used to target sympathizers and potential recruits as well as to communicate with each other and with other groups. The morojihad site is clearly designed to cater to different levels of awareness, both of the Moro cause as well as Islam in general, and it features information that ranges from basic facts about Islam and the Moro struggle to informed discussions on related topics. The site also caters very specifically to the media and the wider world outside Mindanao and the Philippines. This is evident from the fact that the site is in English, as opposed to Bahasa or Tagalog, and thus is able to reach foreign media as well as members of the Moro diaspora.

Another MILF site is www.luwaran.com, also a professionally designed site that offers MILF video and audiotapes, press releases, photographs, and maps. This site is more focused on the MILF's political and military campaign and is an expansive data source with sections dedicated to news, interviews, articles, archives, and encounters with MILF leaders. There is also a section called *Jihad*, which is currently not accessible. MILF is also present at www.bangsamoro.com, a very aesthetically produced pan-Moro site that focuses on the cultural and historical aspects of Moro civilization. While the site itself aims to be more of a sociocultural meeting point online for Moros, its home page has a prominently displayed section on the Moro struggle that includes a historical account of Moro resistance and separate links to the Web sites of the MILF and MNLF. The site carries news and features of and by Moros. It also links to and features reports on Muslims in other parts of the world from Iran and Iraq to Palestine, Afghanistan, and Malaysia. Pertinent topics on the discussion board range from the "War in Minadanao" to "Ethnic Issues."

Although the MILF is a breakaway faction of the MNLF, and the MNLF itself is not a significant actor on the political scene, it continues to maintain a comprehensive Web site at www.mnlf.net. This site offers a detailed history of the Bangsamoro movement and the cultural traditions of its people. It leads with current news about the group and features links to articles in the media about its activities. The site also has extensive links to online Islamic activity and offers links to other militant groups, such as the PLO's home page. This is a professionally designed page that even offers a link to the "MNLF Foreign Office," which features archived articles and press releases, as well as links to all the political negotiations and agreements signed by the MNLF with Islamic organizations and other Islamic groups in the region. The site features news articles not just from the Philippines' media, but also from the entire Southeast Asian region as well as from the Middle East, including newspapers such as the *Gulf Times*.

Jemaah Islamiya

The words Jemaah Islamiya simply translate as "Islamic community." Jemaah Islamiya (JI) was founded in the mid-1990s with the goal of establishing an independent Islamic state encompassing Indonesia, Malaysia, and the southern islands of the Philippines. JI, set up in Malaysia by Indonesian nationals, is largely believed to have been co-opted by al-Qaeda and has a network of supporters across Southeast Asia extending in recent times as far south as Thailand and Burma.[42]

Arrests in Singapore and later Malaysia and the Philippines since late 2001 suggest that Jemaah Islamiya has had an extensive and shadowy network of secret operatives. In keeping with its status as a franchisee of al-Qaeda, JI appears to have adopted many of its mentors' tools to drive its tactical operations. Singapore intelligence officials who foiled the JI plot to bomb the American, British, and Australian embassies in Singapore in 2001 found encrypted diskettes and top-of-the-line digital photographs among JI possessions.[43] Such technology indicates a significant familiarity with computers and computer-aided media technologies. It also implies a significant investment in the software and hardware as well as some expertise in its handling. JI members also used digitized video cameras to tape their potential targets and used such cameras for surveillance and operations planning. The tape was similar to one found in the rubble of an al-Qaeda house in Afghanistan and handed to Singapore authorities. Both tapes showed a Singapore subway station that may have provided potential American targets for a terrorist attack. Investigators into the Bali bombing in Indonesia also found a propaganda videotape showing military-style training at a camp they believed to be in central Sulawesi.

JI also relied on audio- and videotapes to spread their propaganda. Abu Bakar Bashir, spiritual leader of the JI, who was recently sentenced to a four-year prison term, made extensive use of audio- and videotapes to spread his radical message. Hundreds of video- and audiotapes of his speeches are in circulation in Indonesia and Malaysia.

Al-Qaeda in Southeast Asia

The Arabic word al-Qaeda means "the base." An ironic choice of name for a group that is known for its shadowy networked nature consisting of dispersed cells of operatives, linked ideologically to, but operating independently of, a mobile central command. Emerging from the shadows following the 1990–91 Persian Gulf War and the deployment of U.S. troops in Saudi Arabia, the group operates as a deeply intertwined network spanning cells in over forty countries, organized in self-contained nodes that function autonomously with limited communication and support from the center. Al-Qaeda's dispersed cells are known to communicate through the Internet using encryption software. Its funds are transferred through local exchanges with global connections, and its members move freely across the borders of diverse multicultural societies.[44]

Al-Qaeda is a critical element of any analysis of terrorism in the region because of the increasingly networked nature of transnational terrorism and the well-known covert reach of its tentacles. Just as al-Qaeda transfers funds and training to other groups in the region, it also enables the percolation of its technological know-how and communications strategies to its allies and franchisees. Computer logs from within the United States and data from computers seized in Afghanistan indicate that the group has reconnoitered critical infrastructure systems within the United States, thus lending credence to the belief that cyberattacks were a part of the group's evolving agenda.[45]

Information Technology and Implications for Terrorism in Southeast Asia

When analyzing the impact of information technology on terrorism, it is useful to delineate the effects of certain criteria. One useful model has been proposed by scholars in the context of information terrorism, defined as using computer mediated methods to attack computer systems and dependent infrastructure. Although information terrorism is not yet a widespread problem in Southeast Asia, this model is still potentially useful in examining ways in which information technology shapes or facilitates terrorism in Southeast Asia.

Jerrold Post et al. have proposed that factors that predispose terrorists to rely on computer technology can be summarized as follows: (1) ideology of the group; (2) the group members' technological capabilities; (3) the degree to which the environment is information-rich; (4) the extent of provocation (use of computers against the group); (5) the extent of a rival group's use of information terrorism; (6) The degree to which the specific adversary is perceived to be dependent on information terrorism; (7) the degree to which a group already uses information terrorism, and; (8) the leader's computer literacy.

While ideology of the group, the extent of provocation/use of computers against the group, and the degree to which the adversary is dependent on information technology are contexts that apply more specifically to the use of information terrorism, the other factors are relevant as contextual factors that tend to support the adoption of new media and communication technologies by terrorist groups.[46]

The Leader's Computer Literacy

Experts believe that al-Qaeda's technology-driven strategies are an outcome of Osama bin Laden's personal knowledge and interest. Bin Laden, who has a degree in economics and public administration, is described as a "terrorist CEO: essentially having applied business administration and modern management techniques to the running of a transnational terrorist organization."[47]

The Group Members' Capabilities

A look at the JI members arrested in Singapore reveals that almost all of them had some form of technical education, ranging from qualifications in metal machining or maintenance fitting to degrees in computer information technology and electrical engineering. Ramzi Yousef, with his technical education from the United Kingdom and his aptitude for computers, is another case in point. Elsewhere, of the twenty-seven suspects arrested in India following the 2002 Mumbai bombings, many were professional degree holders including chemical engineers, an MD in forensics, master's degree holders in computer science and computer management, and engineering graduates with degrees in instrumentation and chemical engineering.[48] Several of the radical Muslims arrested in Malaysia subsequently were discovered to be educated professionals from technical and engineering backgrounds.

The Degree to Which the Environment Is Information-Rich

The current political and economic environment in Asia and Southeast Asia is poised for rapid technology-driven development, including the e-government initiatives in Singapore, the multimedia corridor (MMC) in Malaysia, the spread of Internet cafés in Indonesia, and the rapid expansion of mobile/cellular phones and Internet connectivity all across the region. Although this environment may not be as technologically developed as those in some Western countries, it nevertheless is developed enough to facilitate the use of NMCTs as a valuable tool.

The Extent of a Rival Group's Use of Information Technology

From Web sites and e-mail to sophisticated audio and video enhancements of online multimedia presentations, terrorist groups both in the region and their counterparts elsewhere are investing considerable expertise and effort on their new media dimension. Hamas, MILF, LTTE, Islamic Jihad, Aleph, and Lashkar-e-Tayyiba (LeT) are just some Middle Eastern and Asian groups making extensive use of NMCTs. As the networking between regional and transnational groups deepens, one can expect that these technologies will only continue to proliferate.

The Degree to Which a Group Already Uses Information Technology

Most of the groups in Southeast Asia, from Abu Sayyaf to Jemaah Islamiya, use new media and communication technologies in some form or other—from the Internet and mobile phones to audio and video technology. Even obscure radical cults such as the al-Maunah group in Malaysia have developed and currently maintain a Web presence. While the degree of NMCT use varies, most of the groups are using these technologies to communicate, to recruit, to raise funds, and to spread propaganda.

The Communications Enabling Environment

In the context of new media technologies and terrorist groups in Southeast Asia, it is necessary to look at two types of environments that enable terrorism to proliferate in the region. One is the current environment of heightened terrorist activity in the region brought about by the increased regional and transnational networking among terrorist groups, the Islamic groups in particular. The other is the prevailing technological environment, such as the proliferation of networked computers, Internet cafés, mobile phone services, and other communication technology–related developments. This environment reflects a growing conviction of regional governments in the role of information technologies (IT) in development and thus explains their rush to develop IT and IT-related infrastructure. The convergence of these two environments, which are developing along parallel lines, creates the perfect enabling environment in Southeast Asia for the spread of terrorism.

The links between Southeast Asian groups as well as their external links to groups in the Middle East and South Asia are well documented. These exchanges of propaganda, technology, training, and funds are serving to fuel terrorist activity in the region. Given the heightened tensions in the Middle East as well as the ongoing war in Iraq and growing anger against the United States and its allies among Muslim nations and Muslim people in the region, one can expect that the anger that fuels such rage, which is in turn harnessed by radical Islamists, is not going to abate anytime soon. This is in fact a time of almost frenzied activity among Islamic radicals in particular and terrorist groups in general.

Southeast Asia is also surrounded by pockets of networked terrorist activity. Besides the Middle Eastern and Afghan groups, whose activities in the region have been discussed in previous sections, there are the South Asian groups such as the pro-Pakistan Kashmiri groups operating out of Pakistan and the LTTE in Sri Lanka who also have a regional presence. The LTTE, one of the pioneers among terrorist groups on the Internet, has well-documented linkages with criminal organizations in Southeast Asia. The group is known to use Thailand as a shipping base and a training base as well as a market for arms. The LTTE has also at various times been active in parts of the Philippines, Singapore, Burma, Hong Kong, and Malaysia, procuring arms and smuggling narcotics.[49]

All these regional groups are also extensive users of media technology, new and old. From Web sites and e-mail to sophisticated audio and video enhancements of online presentations, these groups are investing considerable expertise and effort on their new media dimension. In the current environment where transnational organizations transfer knowledge and technology—much like their multinational business counterparts transfer media technology—such technology transfers may well become routine between terrorist organizations in the region. The networks are in place, the support system is ready, and the political atmosphere is ripe.

On the technology front, the environment could not be more ideal for terrorist groups in the region. Connectivity is multiplying at a rapid rate. The general technological environment in Southeast Asia is one of aggressive growth. According to the United Nations World Development Report (UNWDR), in 1990 there were only 6 telephone lines per 1,000 people in Indonesia, 10 in the Philippines, 24 in Thailand, 89 in Malaysia, and 385 in Singapore. By 2001 the statistics had changed dramatically, with the number of lines per 1,000 people rising to 35 in Indonesia, 42 in the Philippines, 99 in Thailand, 198 in Malaysia, and 562 in Singapore.[50] Cellular phone users in the Philippines jumped from 0 in 1990 to 150-per-thousand users in 2001.[51] Japan, the home of Aum Shinrikyo (now known as Aleph), has 60 million Internet users and is one of the most wired countries in the world. In addition, Asia accounts for 36 percent of the world's telecommunications market, a figure that is expected to go up to 50 percent in 2007. Asia also has the world's largest regional user base for cell phones, 33 percent of the world's Internet user base, and seven of the world's top ten most profitable telecom operators.[52] Although most of these statistics are dominated by countries such as South Korea, Singapore, and Japan, the Philippines, Indonesia, and Malaysia are high on the list of countries that have a rapidly growing user base for computers, Internet services, and mobile phones. As the technology percolates in the region, it becomes more available to terrorists.

It is also pertinent to remember that the creator of the "I Love You" computer virus, which caused at least $2.6 billion in economic damage in 1999,[53] was a young Filipino working out of Manila—an indicator of the nascent technological climate in this region. The Sari Club bomb in Bali (October 2002) as well as the Marriott Hotel bomb in Jakarta (August 2003) are believed to have been set off by cell phones. Among the perpetrators of these two bombings were Imam Samudra, a thirty-three-year-old computer expert whose laptop yielded crucial evidence to earn him the death sentence, and Dr. Azahari Husin, a Malaysian university professor and an electronics expert whose Internet surfing habits reveal an intensive search for ways to improve the design of his bombs. Further, nearly 40 percent of all cyber attacks globally involve computers located in Asian nations,[54] with Malaysia leading the pack in the number of attacks.

Conclusion

French sociologist and criminologist Gabriel Tarde noted that "Epidemics of crime follow the telegraph."[55] The copycat syndrome in criminal psychology is a commonly known fact. In exploring the link between media coverage and the emulation of terrorist acts, Weimann and Winn (1994) describe what they call the "contagion effect."[56] A similar effect is described in terrorist literature as "tactical contagion," when a particular tactic or strategy used successfully by one group is picked up by others. As Post et al. point out:

> Tactical and technical contagion is a fact of terrorist tactics. From hostage-taking, to hijacking to car-bombs, new methods have been quickly absorbed and copied among terrorist groups. A move to IT by one group can be expected to be followed quickly by others. Combined, these processes could theoretically produce a rapid outbreak of information terrorism tactics among traditional groups.[57]

As newer and more technology-oriented tactics evolve and are adopted into practice, they will not only be copied by other groups, they will also be distributed through electronic mail, mailing lists, and newsgroups, which act as a repository of collective information, keeping all parties informed of all new developments in tactics and technology.[58] Given the extent and nature of networking between Southeast Asian groups and the already documented use of new media and communication technologies by regional and transnational groups with links in the region so far, it is highly probable that new communications technology use among Southeast Asian groups will escalate and further intensify terrorist activity in Southeast Asia.

Notes

1. Paul Wilkinson, "Media and Terrorism—A Reassessment," *Terrorism and Political Violence* 19, no. 2 (summer 1997): 51–64.

2. The Assassins, a Shia sect (A.D. 1090–1275), committed their acts of terror on holidays and in crowded locations such as busy marketplaces to ensure that news of their deed would spread quickly to the largest possible audience.

3. Jerrold M. Post, Keven G. Ruby, and Eric D. Shaw, "From Car Bombs to Logic Bombs: The Growing Threat of Information Terrorism," *Terrorism and Political Violence* 12, no. 2 (summer 2000): 97–122.

4. Attributed to former British prime minister Margaret Thatcher.

5. Walter Laqueur, "The Futility of Terrorism," *Harpers* (March 1976), cited in Gabriel Weimann and Conrad Winn, *The Theater of Terror: Mass Media and International Terrorism* (New York: Longman, 1994), p. 52.

6. Bruce Hoffman, *Inside Terrorism* (London: Victor Gollancz, 1998), p. 131.

7. Russell P. Farnen, "Terrorism and the Mass Media: A Systematic Analysis of a Symbiotic Process," *Terrorism* 13, no. 2. (March–April 1990): 99–143.

8. B.L. Nacos, "Accomplice or Witness? The Media's Role in Terrorism," *Current History*, April 2000, pp. 174–78.

9. Wilkinson, "Media and Terrorism."

10. Ibid., p. 4.

11. Ibid.

12. Ibid., pp. 6–7.

13. Alexander M. Young, "Abu Sayyaf Goes Hitech" *Zamboanga Times,* available at: http://www.lazamboangatimes.com/abu_sayyaf.html; accessed September 17, 2003.

14. Bin Laden's satellite telephone records emerged during the trial of four al-Qaeda terrorists for the bombing of the two American embassies in Kenya and Tanzania. See report in (London) *Sunday Times,* March 24, 2002, "Al-Qaeda's Satellite Phone Records Revealed," available at http://www.sunday-times.co.uk/article/0,,178-245683,00.html.

15. Shyam Tekwani, "The Tamil Diaspora, Tamil Militancy, and the Internet," in *Asia.com: Asia Encounters the Internet,* ed. K.C. Ho, Randolph Kluver, and Kenneth C.C. Yang, (London and New York: Routledge Curzon, 2003), pp. 175–92.

16. Shanthi Kalathil and Taylor C. Boas, *Open Networks, Closed Regimes: The Impact of the Internet on Closed Regimes* (Washington, DC: Carnegie Endowment for International Peace, 2003).

17. The use of the Internet by Asians living in the United States is insightful. See the Pew Internet Project, "Asian Americans and the Internet: The Young and the Connected," available at http://www.pewinternet.org/reports/toc.asp?Report=52.

18. Tekwani, "The Tamil Diaspora, Tamil Militancy, and the Internet."

19. T. Downes-LeGuin and Bruce Hoffman, "The Impact of Terrorism on Public Opinion, 1988 to 1989" (RAND Corporation, MR-225-FF/RC, 1993), p. 16. See also discussion in Hoffman, *Inside Terrorism,* pp. 143–44.

20. T. Lightly and S. Franklin, "Activist Targets Jihad's Web Site," January 5, 2003, available at http://www.chicagotribune.com/technology/chi0301050233-jan05,1,6016350.story?coll=chi%2Dtechtopheds%2Dhed; accessed September 24, 2003.

21. Michele Zanini, "Middle Eastern Terrorism and Netwar," *Studies in Conflict and Terrorism* 22, no. 3 (July–September 1999): 247–56.

22. Ibid.

23. For a detailed account of the advantages of ICTs for extremist groups, see Michael Whine, "Cyberspace: A New Medium for Communication, Command, and Control by Extremists," *Studies in Conflict and Terrorism* 22, no. 3 (July–September 1999): 231–45.

24. Alexander Stille, "Cameras Shoot Where Uzis Can't," *New York Times*, September 29, 2003, p. B9.

25. Siddharth Srivastava, "Terrorists Turn to SMS Now," *Times of India*, March 16, 2002, available at http://ww1.timesofindia.indiatimes.com/cms.dll/articleshow?art_id=3901639; last accessed on January 27, 2004.

26. Ibid.

27. Michele Zanini and Sean E. Edwards, "The Networking of Terror in the Information Age," in *Networks and Netwars*, ed. John Arquilla and David R. Ronfeldt (Santa Monica, CA, RAND, 2001), p. 30.

28. Whine, "Cyberspace."

29. Arquilla and Ronfeldt, *Networks and Net Wars*, p. 193.

30. John Arquilla, David Ronfeldt, and Michel Zanini, "Networks, Netwar, and Information Age Terrorism," in *Countering the New Terrorism* (Santa Monica, CA, RAND, 1999), pp. 39–46.

31. Post, Ruby, and Shaw, "From Car Bombs to Logic Bombs."

32. Christopher Coker, "Security, Independence, and Liberty after September 11: Balancing Competing Claims," 21st Century Trust (January 2002). Available at http://www.21stcenturytrust.org/post911.htm.

33. Paul R. Pillar, "Terrorism Goes Global; Extremist Groups Extend Their Reach Worldwide," *Brookings Review* 19, no. 4 (fall 2001): 34–37. Also available at http://www.brookingsinstitution.org/press/review/fall2001/pillar.htm.

34. Simon Reeve, *The New Jackals: Ramzi Yousef, Osama bin Laden, and the Future of Terrorism* (London: Andre Deutsch, 1999).

35. Post, Ruby, and Shaw, "From Car Bombs to Logic Bombs."

36. Ronald D. Palmer, "Terrorism in Southeast Asia: Local Origins, Global Consequences" (2003). http://www.unc.edu/depts/diplomat/archives_roll/2003_07-09/palmer_seaterr/palmer_seaterr.html.

37. See Tiffany Danitz and Warren P. Strobel, "Networking Dissent: Cyber Activists Use the Internet to Promote Democracy in Burma," in *Networks and Netwars*, ed. Arquilla and Ronfeldt, pp. 129–69.

38. Young, "Abu Sayyaf Goes Hitech."

39. http://itmatters.com.ph/news/news_01142002b.html; accessed September 17, 2003.

40. Young, "Abu Sayyaf Goes Hitech."

41. L. Cline, "Islamic Insurgency in the Philippines," *Small Wars and Insurgencies* 11, no. 3 (winter 2000): 115–38.

42. "Indonesia Backgrounder: How the Jemaah Islamiyah Terrorist Network Operates," International Crisis Group, Asia Report No. 43, 11 (December 2002).

43. Singapore Intelligence document, "On ISA Arrests 11 January 2002," available at www.4law.co.il/Lea54.pdf.

44. Ronald J. Deibert and Janice Gross Stein, "Hacking Networks of Terror," *Dialog-IO* (spring 2002): 1–14, available at http://mitpress.mit.edu/journals/INOR/Dialogue_IO/diebert.pdf.

45. Al-Qaeda, Council on Foreign Relations, available at http://cfrterrorism.org/groups/alqaeda.html; accessed October 20, 2003.

46. Given that the same set of questions is used to seek answers to a different use of technology, some liberties have been taken in the interpretation of the questions, which may differ from that of Post et al.

47. Bruce Hoffman, "Rethinking Terrorism and Counter-Terrorism Since 9/11," *Studies in Conflict & Terrorism* (2002): 308.

48. "MD, MA, MBA: The New Degrees of Terror," *Express News Service: The Indian Express,* September 3, 2003; available at: http://www.indianexpress.com/full story.php?content-id=30833.

49. Peter Chalk, "LTTE's International Organization and Operations: Preliminary Analysis," *A Canadian Security Intelligence Service Publication* (March 17, 2000), commentary no. 77.

50. UNDP Report 2003, available at: http://www.undp.org/hdr2003/pdf/hdr03_HDI.pdf.

51. Ibid.

52. ITU 2002, Asia-Pacific Telecommunications Indicators, International Telecommunications Union; available at http://www.itu.int/ITU-D/ict/statistics/International Telecommunications Union.

53. "The GDP and Stuff," Fortune.com, October 15, 2003; available at http://www.fortune.com/fortune/thisjustin/0,15704,518593,00.html; accessed October 20, 2003.

54. "More Cyber Attacks Coming from Malaysia," *Star Online,* September 4, 2002; available at http://asia.cnet.com/newstech/security/0,39001150,39078835,00.htm; accessed October 12, 2003.

55. Gabriel Tarde, *Penal Philosophy* (Monclair, NJ: Patterson Smith, 1912), as cited in Gabriel Weimann and Conrad Winn, *The Theater of Terror: Mass Media and International Terrorism* (New York: Longman, 1994).

56. Weimann and Winn, *The Theater of Terror,* pp. 211–34.

57. Post, Ruby, and Shaw, "From Car Bombs to Logic Bombs," p. 118. Derived from G. Wardlaw, *Political Terrorism: Theory, Tactics and Countermeasures,* 2d ed. (New York: Cambridge University Press, 1989), pp. 77–78.

58. Michael Wilson, "Terrorism in a New World: Evolution in Revolution," available at http://www.emergency.com/evo-revo.htm.

About the Editor
and Contributors

Zachary Abuza is Associate Professor of Political Science and International Relations, Simmons College, and the author of *Militant Islam in Southeast Asia: Crucible of Terror* (2003). He specializes in security issues in Southeast Asia.

David Capie is an Assistant Professor in Political Science at Victoria University of Wellington, New Zealand. His research focuses on conflict and security in the Asia-Pacific, with a particular interest in small arms and light weapons and nonstate armed groups. He is the author of numerous books and articles, including *The Asia-Pacific Security Lexicon* (with Paul Evans, 2002), *Small Arms Production and Transfers in Southeast Asia* (2002), and *Under the Gun: The Small Arms Challenge in the Pacific* (2003).

Peter Chalk is a policy analyst working in the Project Airforce and National Security divisions of the RAND Corporation, Santa Monica, California. He is author of *Non-Military Security and Global Disorder: The Impact of Extremism, Violence and Chaos on National and International Security* (2000), and *West European Terrorism and Counter-Terrorism: The Evolving Dynamic* (1996), in addition to numerous journal articles and other scholarly publications. He is currently a member of the Standing Committee of the Washington-based International Research Group on Political Violence (IRGPV) and serves as Associate Editor of *Studies in Conflict and Terrorism*.

Alan Dupont is a Senior Fellow at the Lowy Institute for International Policy in Sydney, Australia. He has worked on Asian security issues for thirty years as a strategic analyst, diplomat, and academic, and is a regular contributor to the Australian and international press. He is the author of over sixty academic publications on defense and security, including *East Asia Imperilled: Transnational Challenges to Security* (2001). Dr. Dupont is a graduate of the Royal Military College, Duntroon, and holds a PhD in international relations from the Australian National University.

Rohan Gunaratna is Head, International Centre for Political Violence and Terrorism Research at the Institute of Defence and Strategic Studies in Singapore; Fellow, U.S. Military Academy at West Point; and Honorary Fellow, International Policy Institute for Counter Terrorism, Israel. He has eighteen years of policy, operational, and academic experience in counterterrorism. He is the author of eight books including the international bestseller *Inside Al Qaeda: Global Network of Terror* (2002). He has a master's in international peace studies from Notre Dame, U.S., and a doctorate in international relations from St. Andrews, U.K.

Tamara Makarenko is a research fellow with the Centre for the Study of Terrorism and Political Violence, University of St. Andrews (U.K.). Having researched the crime-terror nexus for over a decade, she regularly serves as a consultant to governments on this issue. She is an adviser and regular contributor to *Jane's Intelligence Review* and has written extensively for various academic and professional publications. Her first book, *The Crime-Terror Nexus,* is due to be published in 2004.

Kumar Ramakrishna is Assistant Professor and Head (Studies) at the Institute of Defence and Strategic Studies (IDSS), Nanyang Technological University, Singapore. A specialist on counterterrorism and propaganda, he is the author of *Emergency Propaganda: The Winning of Malayan Hearts and Minds, 1948–1958* (2002) as well as coeditor of *The New Terrorism: Anatomy, Trends and Counter-Strategies* (2002) and *After Bali: The Threat of Terrorism in Southeast Asia* (2003).

Paul A. Rodell is Associate Professor of History at Georgia Southern University. After serving with the U.S. Peace Corps, he studied at the Asian Center, University of the Philippines, where one of his instructors was Nur Misuari, founder of the Moro National Liberation Front. A frequent visitor to Manila and Southeast Asia, he has contributed to *Southeast Asian Affairs, Pilipinas,* and *Peace & Change* among other journals and serials, and has chapters in five books. He edited a special issue on Southeast Asia for the *Journal of Commonwealth and Postcolonial Studies* (2000) and authored *Culture and Customs of the Philippines* (2002). From 1996–2002 he was executive director of the Association of Third World Studies.

Anthony L. Smith is a Senior Research Fellow at the Asia-Pacific Center for Security Studies in Hawaii. His main research interests are in democratization in Indonesia, Indonesian foreign policy, and modern conflict in Indonesia and East Timor. He has contributed to such journals as *Contemporary Southeast Asia, Asian Journal of Political Science, Journal of Democracy,* and the *New Zealand Journal of Asian Studies.* Dr. Smith has a PhD from the University of Auckland.

Paul J. Smith is Assistant Professor at the Asia-Pacific Center for Security Studies in Hawaii, where he specializes in transnational security issues in the Asia-Pacific region, with particular reference to China and Southeast Asia. He has published in *Contemporary Southeast Asia, Fletcher Forum of World Affairs, Harvard Asia-Pacific Review, Jane's Intelligence Review, Parameters,* and *Survival.* He is editor of *Human Smuggling: Chinese Migrant Trafficking and the Challenge to America's Immigration Tradition* (1997). He holds a BA from Washington and Lee University, an MA from the University of London, and a JD from the University of Hawaii.

Shyam Tekwani is Assistant Professor in the School of Communication and Information at Nanyang Technological University in Singapore. A photojournalist for nearly fifteen years, Tekwani has produced an exclusive portfolio of work covering the ethnic conflict in Sri Lanka. Tekwani's current research focuses on new media technologies and terrorism, with particular emphasis on how contemporary terrorist groups use new media, particularly the Internet, in their operations. His recent publications include a chapter on "The Tamil Diaspora, Tamil Militancy and the Internet" in *Asia.com: Asia Encounters the Internet,* published by Routledge, 2003.

Carlyle A. Thayer is Professor and Director of the UNSW Defence Studies Program at the Australian Defence Force Academy. He is concurrently Deakin University's Academic Coordinator at the Centre for Defence and Strategic Studies at the Australian Defence College. Professor Thayer worked previously at the Asia-Pacific Center for Security Studies in Hawaii (1999–2001). He was educated at Brown, Yale, and the Australian National University. Thayer has been studying Southeast Asia regional security issues for over thirty years and is the author of over three hundred publications including *Multilateral Institutions in Asia: The ASEAN Regional Forum* (2000).

Index